EUROPEAN RACISM

THE **BROADVIEW SOURCES** SERIES

European Racism

A HISTORY IN DOCUMENTS

edited by LISA M. TODD AND GARY K. WAITE

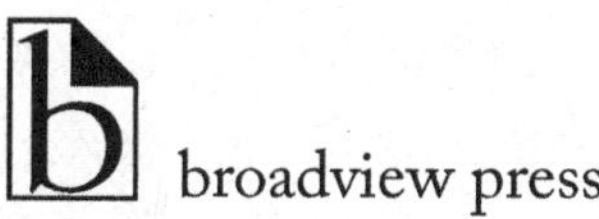

BROADVIEW PRESS
Peterborough, Ontario, Canada

Founded in 1985, Broadview Press is a fully independent academic publishing house owned by approximately twenty-five shareholders—almost all of whom are either Broadview employees or Broadview authors. Broadview is supported by a collaboration with Trent University, a liberal arts university located in Peterborough, Ontario—the city where Broadview was founded and continues to operate. Broadview is committed to environmentally responsible publishing and fair business practices.

Library and Archives Canada Cataloguing in Publication

Title: European racism : a history in documents / edited by Lisa M. Todd and Gary K. Waite.
Names: Todd, Lisa Marie, editor. | Waite, Gary K., 1955- editor.
Series: Broadview sources series.
Description: Series statement: The Broadview sources series | Includes bibliographical references.
Identifiers: Canadiana (print) 20240324846 | Canadiana (ebook) 20240324854 | ISBN 9781554814855 (softcover) | ISBN 9781460408223 (EPUB) | ISBN 9781770488908 (PDF)
Subjects: LCSH: Racism—Europe—History—Sources. | LCSH: Europe—Race relations—Sources.
Classification: LCC D1056 .E97 2024 | DDC 305.80094—dc23

Broadview Press handles its own distribution in Canada and the United States:
PO Box 1243, Peterborough, Ontario K9J 7H5, Canada
555 Riverwalk Parkway, Tonawanda, NY 14150, USA
Tel: (705) 482–5915
email: customerservice@broadviewpress.com

For all territories outside of Canada and the United States, distribution is handled by Eurospan Group.

Broadview Press acknowledges the financial support of the Government of Canada for our publishing activities.

Copy-edited by Juliet Sutcliffe
Book design by Em Dash Design

Broadview Press® is the registered trademark of Broadview Press Inc.

PRINTED IN CANADA

CONTENTS

CHRONOLOGICAL TABLE OF CONTENTS

1. ANCIENT AND MEDIEVAL

2. SIXTEENTH CENTURY

4. EIGHTEENTH CENTURY

5. NINETEENTH CENTURY

6. TWENTIETH CENTURY, TO 1945

7. TWENTIETH AND TWENTY-FIRST CENTURIES, FROM 1945

ACKNOWLEDGEMENTS

This project began when Broadview Press representative Brett McLenithan approached both of us separately to discuss the possibility of writing Sources books. We soon decided it would be more fun and productive to write a book together. In the weeks that followed, this project went in many different directions; throughout we were adamant we would take advantage of our joint interests in the histories of racism and that we wanted to write a textbook that broke down traditional temporal boundaries between the early modern and modern histories of prejudice. We are very grateful to Brett for supporting us for several years, including through the COVID-19 pandemic. We have had nothing but great experiences working with the folks at Broadview, including Jacqueline Kwan, Juliet Sutcliffe, and Tara Lowes, and thank them especially for their patience as we navigated the complicated world of permissions and copyright. We also thank our graduate student research assistants, Jordyn Bailey, Kate McGregor, Emily McPherson, and Jarrett Weston, for helping us identify documents and images and to the many students in undergraduate and graduate classes at the University of New Brunswick who gave us intelligent and perceptive feedback on this volume. We are also grateful to the two anonymous reviewers who provided fulsome and helpful critiques of this project and to our colleague Sean Kennedy for his insights and good humor. We thank the Social Sciences and Humanities Research Council of Canada for their financial support. Writing a book on this difficult subject has been challenging but made possible through our friendship, which has remained intact, despite having to navigate definitional, editorial, and copyright conundrums. Gary would like to thank his wife, Kate, for her encouragement, support, and many insightful conversations on the subject of this book. Lisa thanks her family—Jacob, Ben, and Anna—for being fantastic travel companions and for always making her laugh at the end of a long day.

INTRODUCTION

In 2009, the Swedish government, in a bid to crack down on "illegal" immigration, instructed police officers to conduct "spot" identification checks. This policy caused fear and frustration for the many racialized citizens being stopped simply because of the color of their skin. In response to public criticism, the Minister of Justice Beatrice Ask replied that accusations of racial profiling were "just a matter of personal experience," and refused to change the policy. The writer **Jonas Hassen Khemiri** composed a March 2013 open letter to the minister that became a massive internet sensation. He noted that while both he and the minister were full citizens of Sweden and thus equal before the Law, her comment about personal feeling led him to ask: "When does a personal experience become a structure of racism? When does it become discrimination, oppression, violence? And how can looking at 'the big picture' rule out so many personal experiences of citizens?" He then challenged her to exchange "our skins and our experiences" for a day, so that he could better "understand what it's like to be a woman in the patriarchal world of politics." In turn, she could

Jonas Hassen Khemiri: Award-winning Swedish author of novels, short stories, plays, and essays.

> borrow my skin to understand that when you go out into the street, down into the subway, into the shopping center, and see the policeman standing there, with the Law on his side, with the right to approach you and ask you to prove your innocence, it brings back memories. Other abuses, other uniforms, other looks. And no, we don't need to go as far back as World War II Germany or South Africa in the eighties. Our recent Swedish history is enough, a series of random experiences that our mutual body suddenly recalls.

Khemiri then recounted vivid memories of the many times he, as a person of color, experienced racial profiling in Sweden:

> Suddenly someone came up on our right side, a broad man with an earpiece. "How's it going?" He asked for ID and then he pushed our arms up in a police grip and transported us toward the police van, where we were apparently supposed to sit while waiting for him to receive confirmation that we were who we said we were. Apparently we matched a description. Apparently we looked like someone else. We sat in the police van for twenty minutes. Alone. But not really alone. Because a hundred people were walking by. And they looked in at us with a look that whispered, "There. One more. Yet another one who is acting in complete accordance with our prejudices."

In continuing his request to the justice minister, Khemiri wrote,

> And I wish you had been with me in the police van, Beatrice Ask. But you weren't. I sat there alone. And I met all the eyes walking by and tried to show them that I wasn't guilty, that I had just been standing in a place and looking a particular way. But it's hard to argue your innocence in the back seat of a police van.
>
> And it's impossible to be part of a community when Power continually assumes that you are an Other.[1]

Khemiri's experiences remain all too common in societies built on histories of systemic racism. Despite global invocations of "never again" after the horrors of World War II (1939–1945), racism and prejudice continue in the twenty-first century to provoke hatred and violence against many groups of people. Modern scientists now clarify that in genetic terms, there is no such thing as race, that we are all *homo sapiens*, and that differences in place of origin, skin color, tribe, or nation are minuscule compared to the commonalities in our DNA.[2] Scientifically speaking, "race" is therefore an identity imposed on groups of people within a society or in other regions.[3] But this does not mean that race is inconsequential. The concept of race remains a powerful tool for those seeking scapegoats, gathering support for a cause, or justifying exclusion from majority-held rights. Racism has led to ostracization, mob action, judicial prosecution, mass murder, and genocide. Global Islamophobia—the hatred of Muslim peoples—has escalated since 9/11. Recent attacks on Black citizens, persons of color, and Indigenous peoples, often by police, have sparked massive protests and the rise of the Black Lives Matter movement. Far-right and white supremacist groups and political parties are gaining support across Europe, often in conjunction with anti-immigrant sentiment and frustration over COVID-19 measures. These events occur even as we write this Introduction.

The subject of racism, especially that of European racism, requires an historical perspective, for it was over the last several centuries that various church leaders, intellectuals, writers, and scientists turned populist hostility toward minority groups into a concept of hierarchical and distinct "races." The documents in this Reader show how the evolution of the social construct

---

1 Jonas Hassen Khemiri, "An Open Letter to Beatrice Ask," *Dagens Nyheter, 13 March 2013; reprinted by Asymptote, https://www.asymptotejournal.com/nonfiction/jonas-hassen-khemiri-an-open-letter-to-beatrice-ask/.*

2 Constance F. Citro, Marilyn Dabady, and Rebecca M. Blank, *Measuring Racial Discrimination* (Washington, DC: National Academies Press, 2004), 26.

3 John Barnshaw, "Race," in *Encyclopedia of Race, Ethnicity, and Society*, vol. 1, ed. Richard T. Schaefer (Thousand Oaks, CA: SAGE, 2008), 1091–93.

of "race" was neither natural nor necessary. In the Classical period (roughly 500 BCE to roughly 400 CE), Greek writers and philosophers did see themselves as ethnically superior to the peoples outside of Greece. The Romans, in contrast, developed a multicultural society wherein foreigners, whom they called "Barbarians" for their incomprehensible languages, could become citizens and generals. Roman writers believed that differences in skin color were a result of the variations in the strength of the sun's rays based on latitude; the closer to the equator, the darker the skin. Their slavery, moreover, was based on military conquest, not skin color, and slaves could buy their freedom.

Medieval residents had no concept they were living in a region that would later be called Europe. Most people prior to the nineteenth century did not see themselves as belonging to a community beyond their village or town. Their first allegiance was to the local landlord or town council, and only over time, beginning in the later Middle Ages, to a royal overlord. Even so, writers distinguished groups based on language and social customs, laying the groundwork for the biological forms of racial distinctions that would come in subsequent centuries.[4] Before national identities fully emerged, most saw themselves as members of the "body of Christ," or Christendom, with the Roman Catholic pope as the theoretical head binding the various principalities together. To the East was the Byzantine Empire, a Greek Christian realm that was the remnant of the Eastern Roman Empire, and Muslim lands. These called the Europeans "Latins" in reference to the official language of the Catholic Church. Even though the sixteenth-century Reformation destroyed Christian unity, national identities emerged in the early modern era (c. 1450–1800), and military conflicts convulsed Europe from the sixteenth to the twentieth centuries, the idea of "Latin" Europe as a region distinct from the rest of the world remained. In short, Europeans continued to identify themselves as a collective against other parts of the globe.

The concept of race was therefore the product of numerous events and decisions, and often arose out of competition among the religions of Christianity, Judaism, and Islam. With each new crisis, this competition intensified and morphed into an antipathy that crossed the line of religious difference into ethnic hatred. Jewish peoples were long perceived as "outsiders" within Europe. By the fifteenth century antisemitism—the hatred of Jews—had formed a physiological framework in which Christians believed that Jewish blood was distinct from Christian. Added to this were earlier myths devised by Christians that Jews committed acts of **ritual murder** and conspired against Christendom. The result was a powerful racialized myth

ritual murder: The belief that Jews kidnapped and killed a Christian child as a ritualistic act of murdering Christ again. See Documents 2, 3, 9, 11, 12, and 19 below.

4 See Geraldine Heng, *The Invention of Race in the European Middle Ages* (Cambridge: Cambridge University Press, 2018).

with frightening long-term consequences. Over time, Christian Europeans adapted these antisemitic ideas to Muslims, Africans, Asians, the Romani, and Indigenous peoples. In the process they focused less on religious and ethnic difference and more on skin color and alleged physical distinctions among groups of people.

This emphasis on physical distinctions such as skin color and hair texture as markers of racial difference was also largely constructed. Outside the Mediterranean region, medieval Europeans had little broad experience with persons of color (except for those who lived in their communities), and their explanations of skin color tended to follow the ancient Romans in emphasizing climate and geography. However, in the fifteenth century, the Portuguese began their travels down the western coast of Africa and interacted with African rulers, especially in the Congo. They soon discovered that they could replace Indigenous workers in their expanding plantations in the Canary Islands and the West and East Indies with African slaves. Soon European sailors were not only participating in African slavery but began developing it into the extremely lucrative and brutal Atlantic slave trade. In the process, Europeans racialized slavery as something tightly linked to skin color. To do so, as seen in Document 56 by Edward Long, they adapted the purity of blood laws of Spain (Document 5 below) to apply to skin color. These laws were developed originally against Jewish and Muslim converts as a means of maintaining the purity of the Old Christian population against what **Spanish Inquisitors** identified as the infection of "**Judaizing**," that the Conversos or New Christians—the descendants of Jews who had converted to Christianity generations before—were secretly practicing Judaism. The Inquisition was in fact part of the Spanish Reconquista when Christian princes conducted a crusade to recapture Iberia from Muslim control and then to purify it of non-Christian blood. As they expanded this crusade overseas in the late fifteenth and sixteenth centuries, they gradually applied the blood purity laws to skin color, so that slavery and Blackness became synonymous, and Black peoples were perceived by many Europeans who profited from enslavement to be sub-human. At the same time, white Europeans began to speak about themselves in terms of color, increasingly using lighter skin as a marker of status and power. A recent essay collection suggests not only that this new concept of whiteness was a growing concept by 1600, reflected in the influential plays of Shakespeare, but that the playwright's works "actively engage in white-people-making."[5] It was, therefore, in the early modern period when the concept of "whiteness" entered discourse in many levels of society, merging with the concept of "Christian" as a pan-European identity.

Spanish Inquisitors: Judges in religious tribunals set up by the Spanish crown in 1478 to determine if descendants of Jews who had converted to Christianity were still practicing Judaism in secret.

Judaizing/Judaizers: Descendants of Jewish converts to Christianity who were suspected of still practicing their old faith.

---

5 Arthur L. Little, Jr., ed., *White People in Shakespeare: Essays on Race, Culture and the Elite* (London: Bloomsbury, 2023), 1.

The tendency to use racial categories to denote physical traits intensified through the eighteenth and nineteenth centuries. In 1758, the Swedish botanist Carl Linnaeus, who previously had built his career around classifying species of flowers, now laid out his four categories of humans—those whom he denoted as red, white, yellow, and black.[6] This categorization of global humanity into four colors continued largely unchanged, even as the eras of the **Enlightenment** and the French Revolution marked a transformation in conversations around human rights, political representation, and national belonging. Documents such as *The Declaration of the Rights of Man and the Citizen* promised increased toleration for some minority groups; at the same time, the nineteenth-century expansion of nation states promoted notions of belonging, exclusion, and otherness. New social sciences like anthropology, sociology, psychology, and criminology saw human life as an object of planning and administration, and promised objectivity when solving society's ills. The accompanying rise of experts challenged longstanding moral and religious beliefs. For instance, in debating the origins of human life, proponents of **monogenism** supported a common origin theory, as had been taught to Christians and Jews in the Book of Genesis. **Polygenists**, in contrast, posited that different races of humans had developed over time. Racial anthropologists theorized that some races were more evolved than others and carried out research projects to gather supposed proof of human difference. As they measured skulls, catalogued skin, eye, and hair colors, and linked moral characteristics with physical appearance, they further legitimized categories that separated "us" from "them." European imperialists then used these "scientific" findings to legitimize their exploitation of global territories. Missionaries, entrepreneurs, schoolteachers, and doctors often proclaimed membership in a civilizing mission that sought to raise up peoples considered less civilized than themselves. As Angela Saini writes, "the more powerful we humans become, the more our power begins to be framed as natural as well as cultural."[7] We see examples of the blatant intertwining of racial science and imperial greed throughout this volume. And while white supremacy was further marginalizing racialized peoples, Europeans were simultaneously intrigued and titillated by physical and cultural differences they deemed exotic. In 1978, cultural theorist Edward Said coined the term Orientalism to explain the process by which European portrayals of "exotic," or "exciting" or "mysterious" parts of the world served to create and reinforce racist beliefs. You will see many examples of Orientalism in this Reader.

Enlightenment: Period in the late seventeenth through the late eighteenth centuries that saw new approaches to philosophy, society, economics, and politics that were based on human reason rather than divine revelation.

monogenism: Supports a common origin for all humans, usually assumed by Christians and Jews to be the coupling of Adam and Eve in the Book of Genesis. In contrast, **polygenists** argued that God placed different peoples around the world, meaning they all had distinct origin stories.

That scientific racism emerged on a parallel track to campaigns for human equality was no accident. Scholars like George M. Fredrickson

6 Angela Saini, *Superior: The Return of Racial Science* (Boston: Beacon Press, 2019), 27.

7 Saini, *Superior*, xiii.

have suggested this very dichotomy differentiated Western racism. He writes "First came the doctrine that the Crucifixion offered grace to all willing to receive it and made all Christian believers equal before God. Later came the more revolutionary concept that all 'men' are born free and equal and entitled to equal rights in society and government." Fredrickson maintains that in cultures premised on inequality (such as the Indian caste system) there exists no incentive to create a racist hierarchy. Where the promise of equality exists, but there are groups who do not fit societal norms, the "upholders" of these norms invent some "extraordinary deficiency that makes them less than fully human," and thus deny their equality. Frederickson concludes, "it is uniquely in the West that we find the dialectical interaction between a premise of equality and an intense prejudice toward certain groups that would seem to be a precondition for the full flowering of racism as an ideology or worldview."[8] While readers are free to disagree with this argument, we encourage you to consider the examples in this Reader where the languages of human equality and racial inequality have either been symbiotic or used against each other.

These practices continued past 1900; indeed, many scholars argue that racism reached its zenith during the twentieth century, especially in racist regimes created in the American South, in Nazi Germany, and in apartheid-era South Africa. While these societies were unique in several ways, they all shared common structures and practices, including, but not limited to, bans on intermarriage and an insistence on the "racial purity" of the dominate group, separate rules, laws, and legal systems based on racial distinctions, segregationist community structures including housing, schooling, and medical facilities, and unequal access to political, economic, and social decision-making. Importantly, in each instance, governments, bureaucrats, and ruling elites passed laws that dictated their societies operate on racist principles. This Reader well illustrates such longstanding and ongoing exclusionary and violent practices across the European continent. While we chose documents to illustrate the intertwined histories of white supremacy and European racism, we also seek to highlight moments in the long history of anti-racist activism by people of color and their allies. Even racial categories themselves can become powerful counter-narratives when used as tools for equity-seeking groups—witness the reappropriation of derogatory identifying terms within communities and also witness Black feminist movements such as "Black Is Beautiful." These examples reveal the constant evolution of this long history of racism.

---

8 George M. Fredrickson, *Racism: A Short History* (Princeton: Princeton University Press, 2002), 11–12.

ORGANIZATION

This Reader uses primary documents to introduce you to the long history of European persecution against several groups: Jews, Muslims, Black peoples, the Romani, Asians, and Indigenous communities, each from the medieval period to the present. This is by no means a comprehensive collection, which would have to be enormously large and unwieldy, nor is it wholly representative. Instead, we provide some snapshots or moments that illustrate white European attitudes toward other peoples in particular times and places. We provide a brief introduction to each document or image, which gives information on the author, the type of source, or the society in which it was created. We also include marginal definitions and explanations for certain terms, names, and places. We have modernized the spelling of most of the earlier documents to provide clarity and ease of reading. At the beginning of the collection, you will find a timeline to help you compare parallel histories of marginalized communities, a list of discussion questions, and at the end of the collection, a list of recommended readings and resources.

By organizing our parts according to the categories of race developed by mostly white Europeans, we run the risk of seeming to support the very persecutory processes we seek to critique. Parts organized around specific groups also threaten to present those groups as monolithic, as opposed to wonderfully diverse collections of individuals, each with distinct **intersectional** identities rooted in gender, sexuality, religion, age, ability, and language. After many long discussions as editors, we made the choice to present these thematic parts for three main reasons: first, we invite you to look for examples of continuity and change among themes, stereotypes, accusations, and uses of language between past and present. In this way we hope you can see more clearly how European attitudes toward one religious, ethnic, or geographical group compared to that towards others during the same period, and how they may have been transposed from one group to the other or reshaped over time. Second, we want you to consider the similar and different experiences of several groups in European history, and to compare the lived experiences of these communities. Third, while we do present each part in chronological terms, we also consciously seek to challenge progress narratives that insist our societies are continually becoming more tolerant and inclusive. Not only does this assumption underestimate the sophistication of past societies, but it also downplays the prejudice and racism people face today. The scholar Ibram X. Kendi writes of a "dual and duelling history of racial progress and the simultaneous progression of racism"; indeed, he says,

Intersectional: In 1989 law scholar and civil-rights advocate Kimberlé Crenshaw coined the term intersectionality to describe an analytical framework that explains how multiple factors combine to create layers of privilege and discrimination.

"racist progress has consistently followed racial progress."[9] For those readers who wish to study the documents chronologically rather than thematically, we include an alternative table of contents.

We edit this volume as white scholars who have benefited from our positions in society as descendants of European immigrants and as settlers in Turtle Island/Canada. We see this textbook as part of a multi-faceted and crucial project to mitigate the ongoing effects of systemic racism and respectfully acknowledge the prior and ongoing work of anti-racist activists who work to identify the many causes of bigotry and hatred, and to combat the everyday effects of racialized discrimination. In doing so, they seek precision in language, while acknowledging the complicated and often contested status of terminology. As you use this Reader, you may wish to consult online resources for terminology and definitions.[10] We also acknowledge that, as readers, you will all experience these primary sources differently. We encourage you to approach the material with an open mind, and to treat yourselves with care.

HOW TO READ PRIMARY SOURCES AND IMAGES

Historical research and understanding depends on locating and reading primary sources. There are several strategies for evaluating and understanding documents and materials produced in the past, including:

1. Determine the **type of source**: there are many kinds of written historical sources, including letters, government and legal documents, diaries and memoirs, religious tracts, pamphlets and newspaper articles, and scientific reports. Historians also use material culture artefacts and images and visual culture, including paintings and drawings, photographs, cartoons and caricatures, illustrated journals and magazines, and advertisements. Each type of source can tell us something distinct about the society in which it was created and how people communicated and shared ideas.
2. Determine the **historical context**, the place and time, of the source. Is this a source written at the time of the events described? What was going on in that place at that time that might help you, the reader, to understand it better?

---

9 Ibram X. Kendi, *Stamped from the Beginning: The Definitive History of Racist Ideas in America* (New York: Nation Books, 2016), x–xi.

10 You may wish to search the Anti-Oppression Network, Terminologies of Oppression; Canadian Race Relations Foundation Glossary of Terms; and the TriCollege Libraries Research Guide on Allyship and Anti-Oppression.

3. Note the **author or creator of the source**, and any information you can readily obtain on their gender, age, religion, social status, ethnicity, profession, or place of residence.
4. Seek to discover the **extent of the author's perspective or knowledge**. Are they writing on events they witnessed, people they met, or places they have personally visited? Or, do they rely on rumor, hearsay, superstition, or "common knowledge"? In this text, we have sought to include sources produced by persecuting parties, persecuted peoples, and bystanders. What difference do those distinctions make in your reading of the documents?
5. Make note of the **intent of the arguments**, the content of the descriptions, and the author's choice of examples and use of language. Does the author have a particular axe to grind?
6. Determine the **intended audience** for the source. For instance, who did the author or creator think would be reading the article, viewing the cartoon, or debating the parliamentary statute? Was the source intended to be private, like a personal diary, or public, like a published document? Was it a piece of fiction, or a news report? What difference does that make for its interpretation?
7. How does the source **compare** with other historical documents on this subject? In this book, we have often intentionally paired sources that either speak to similar aspects of a topic or provide contrasting views on subjects. As you read the parts, consider **common themes** such as skin color and appearance, religious belief and practice, power and influence, culture and ethnicity, gender norms and sexual practices, economic and social standing, scientific and medical theories, and authorities and emotions such as fear.
8. Finally, consider the **impact, meaning, and significance** of the historical source. Did it change peoples' views at the time? Has it had a long-term impact on the development of beliefs and practices? For example, it has been suggested that Martin Luther's treatise against Jews did not have an immediate impact, but later readers such as Adolf Hitler used it as an inspiration for laws and policies. On the other hand, was the source largely ignored or forgotten?

CHRONOLOGY

c. 33 CE Crucifixion of Jesus of Nazareth.

632 The Prophet Muhammad's death.

711 Muslims conquer Spain and establish a Muslim state in Western Europe.

1096 Crusades to the Middle East begin against Muslim control; attacks on Jewish communities in Europe follow.

1099 Christian Crusaders conquer Jerusalem, slaughter most of the Muslim, Jewish, and local Christian inhabitants, and establish the Crusader States.

1150 First story of Jewish ritual murder in England.

1240 Mongols conquer Russia; establishment of the Golden Horde, the name for the region under Mongol rule outside of Mongolia.

1290 Jews expelled from England.

1291 Fall of the last Crusader State (Acre).

1295 Italian merchant and explorer Marco Polo returns from China.

1347–48 Black Death—Bubonic Plague wipes out a quarter of Europe's population; numerous **pogroms** against Jewish communities in response.

pogroms: Mob attacks on Jews or other ethnic groups.

1391 Antisemitic sermons lead to attacks on Jewish communities of Spain. Half of Spain's Jews convert to Catholicism, and they are termed Conversos (converts).

c. 1430 First mention of the presence of Romani people (the Roma) in Western Europe.

1453 Capture of Constantinople by the Ottoman Sultan Mehmet II, opening Europe to Ottoman invasion.

1460 Death of Prince Henry the Navigator of Portugal, whose ships reached Western Africa and negotiated with the African rulers.

1463 Sarajevo founded as a Muslim city on the edge of Christian Europe.

1471 Anti-Roma law passed in Switzerland.

1475 The famous ritual murder trial of Jews accused of killing the Catholic child Simon of Trent.

1478 Spanish Inquisition established against Judaizers.

1482 Anti-Roma laws passed in the German lands.

1492 Expulsion of Jews from Spain by King Ferdinand and Queen Isabella.

1492 Conquest of Muslim Granada by the Spanish crown, ending Muslim rule in Iberia.

1492 Christopher Columbus, sponsored by King Ferdinand and Queen Isabella, lands in the West Indies; Indigenous population decimated.

1494 Portuguese merchants begin participating in the African slave trade.

1498 First of Italian navigator John Cabot's voyages to coastal North America.

1498 Portuguese explorer Vasco da Gama lands at Calicut on the Malabar Coast; by 1510 the Portuguese have established control over parts of Western India.

1498 Anti-Roma laws passed in Spain; Romani become subjects of Inquisition as heretics.

1500 Holy Roman Emperor Maximilian I orders **Gypsies** to leave Germany.

Gypsies: An arcane, derogatory term for the Roma.

1502 Louis XII expels Romani from France.

1517 German theologian Martin Luther's *95 Theses* criticizing some aspects of papal authority is published, sparking the Reformation.

1521 Conquistador Hernán Cortés defeats Moctezuma II to conquer the Aztec Empire of Mexico.

1526 First transatlantic slave voyage from Africa to Brazil.

1529 Ottoman Sultan Suleiman the Magnificent lays siege to Vienna.

1530 Egyptian Act passed in England.

1536–89 Anti-Roma laws passed in various European states.

c. 1540	Purity of Blood Statutes have become standard in Spain, allowing Inquisitors to determine Judaizing by a suspect's degree of Jewish ancestry. Jewishness is now in the blood.
1543	Luther publishes his antisemitic *Of the Jews and Their Lies*.
1563	Romani denied entrance into priesthood by Council of Trent.
1603	Some of the Portuguese Nation (Conversos) revert to Judaism in Amsterdam, and are quickly tolerated.
1604	French explorer Samuel de Champlain's first voyage to New France, beginning French colonization.
1609–14	Expulsion of Moriscos (Muslims who had converted to Catholicism) from Spain.
1619	Anti-Roma law decreed by Philip III of Spain.
1648–57	Mass slaughter of Jews in Ukraine during the Khmelnytsky Uprising.
1650	Last known hanging in England for the crime of being a gypsy.
c. 1650	Beginnings of the Society of Friends (Quakers).
1655	Amsterdam rabbi Menasseh ben Israel visits London to persuade Oliver Cromwell, Lord Protector of England, to readmit the Jews.
1700s	"Gypsy hunts" across parts of Germany, the Netherlands, and France.
1772	French philosopher Denis Diderot critiques European treatment of Indigenous peoples.
1789	French Revolution begins; the Declaration of the Rights of Man and of the Citizen promotes select human rights; some begin calling for the end of slavery.
1791–1804	Haitian Revolution.
1795	Anthropologist Johann Friedrich Blumenbach describes the "five races of man."
1807	Abolition of the Slave Trade Act (Britain).
1820	Founding of Liberia by formerly enslaved African Americans.
1822	Exhibition of Laplander peoples in Piccadilly, London, one of many examples of human zoos.

1830 French invasion of Algeria, a country France would occupy until 1962.

1833 British Slavery Abolition Act.

1839–42 First Opium War.

1844 Scottish publisher and writer Robert Chambers, in *Vestiges of the Natural History of Mankind*, argues that each race represents a different stage of human evolution.

1844 Beginning of the Irish Potato Famine, which ultimately results in the deaths of at least one million people.

1840s The Romantic art movement Orientalism creates fantastical portrayals of the East for European audiences.

1851 English author Charles Dickens publishes the essay "The Noble Savage" in his weekly magazine *Household Words*.

1853 French author Arthur Comte de Gobineau publishes *An Essay on the Inequality of the Human Race*.

1856–60 Second Opium War.

1860 Russian Empire annexes parts of Sakhalin Island, resulting in a loss of autonomy for the Nivkh peoples.

1863 American Emancipation Proclamation.

1864 English philosopher Herbert Spencer coins the term "survival of the fittest" in response to Charles Darwin's *On the Origin of the Species* of 1859.

1865 French anthropologist Paul Broco develops a system for classifying skin color.

1870 Wilhelm Marr coins the term "antisemitism."

1880 Numerous violent pogroms in the Russian Empire force large numbers of Jewish refugees out of Eastern Europe.

1880 Abraham Ulrikab and his family travel with German recruiters from Labrador to Germany where they are put on display at the Hamburg Zoo.

1883 British polymath Francis Galton coins the term "eugenics."

1884	Berlin Conference formalizes the European "Scramble for Africa," the process by which all African territories except Liberia and Ethiopia came under the control of European powers.
1889	English Muslim convert Abdullah Quilliam opens London's first mosque.
1891	French painter Paul Gauguin travels to Tahiti for inspiration for his artistic works.
1894	The Dreyfus Affair during which a French Jewish army captain was accused of selling military secrets to the Germans, lead to public debates over antisemitism in French.
1900	Ritual murder investigation in the town of Könitz, Germany.
1902	British historian and politician James Bryce delivers lecture, "The Relations of the Advanced and Backward Races of Mankind" at Oxford University.
1904	Genocide of the Herero and Nama peoples in German Southwest Africa.
1905	Founding of the German Society for Racial Hygiene.
1912	First International Conference of Eugenics in London.
1912	First issue published of the *African Times and Orient Review—A Monthly Journal devoted to the interests of the coloured races of the world.*
1913	John Richard Archer elected as first Black mayor of a London borough (Battersea).
1914–19	Britain recruits 1.5 million Indian men into the British army and more than 50,000 Chinese to work in the World War I Labour Corps.
1916	American lawyer and writer Madison Grant's *The Passing of the Great Race* splits Europe into three races: Nordics, Alpines, and Mediterraneans.
1919	Race riots across Great Britain.
1921	Second International Congress of Eugenics at the American Museum of Natural History.
1929	Germany creates fenced-in camps for Romani.

1930	Islamic scholar Muhammad Marmaduke Pickthall publishes the first English translation of the Qur'an by a believer.
1933	First Romani prisoners in Nazi concentration camps.
1933–39	More than 400 separate segregationist decrees restrict German Jews from participating in civil, political, and economic society.
1934	First forced sterilization of Roma and Black women and men in Nazi Germany.
1935	Nazi Party passes the Nuremberg Laws, legally defining membership in the so-called Aryan race.
1935	First European Muslim Congress held in Geneva.
1936	80,000 Moroccan soldiers fight during the Spanish Civil War.
1938	Nazis establish a central office to manage the "final solution to the Gypsy problem."
1938	Nazi party officials orchestrate a nation-wide pogrom against the Jewish population.
1938	British army restricts entry to those of "pure European descent."
1938	At the Evian Conference, 32 nations debate the "problem" of Jewish immigration. Only the Dominican Republic agreed to increase their quotas.
1938	Eugenicist Reginald Ruggles Gates uses blood samples from children at a residential school to study the existence of "pure blood Micmac Indians."
1941	First mass shootings of Jews and Romani in Nazi-occupied Eastern Europe.
1945	End of World War II and of the Nazi regime
1946	Ritual murder pogrom in Kielce, Poland.
1948	Apartheid, legally sanctioned racial segregation, established in South Africa.
1948	Founding of the Jewish state of Israel.
1948	The ship *Empire Windrush* arrives in Britain from Jamaica, beginning a process of increased Black immigration to the United Kingdom.

1948 United Nations ratifies the Convention on the Prevention and Punishment of the Crime of Genocide.

1950s Mau Mau uprising against British colonial rule in Kenya.

1954 Notting Hill race riots, as West Indians fight back against Teddy Boy gangs.

1954–62 Algerian War.

1955 Bandung Conference, when several leaders of African and Asian countries meet in Indonesia to help each other economically and in opposition to colonialism.

1959 Kelso Cochrane, a Black man, is murdered by a gang of white youths in West London. No charges are laid.

1959 Swastika epidemic begins with the defacing of a Cologne synagogue, and leads to antisemitic graffiti in public spaces around the world.

1962 Commonwealth Immigrants Act restricts immigration to Britain from the former empire.

1963 Report of the Commission on Itinerancy attempts to force Roma into "brick and mortar" housing in Ireland.

1965 United Nations ratifies the International Convention on the Elimination of All Forms of Racial Discrimination.

1967 Founding of the National Front, a far-right anti-immigrant organization with ties to the British fascist movement.

1968 British politician Enoch Powell's "Rivers of Blood" speech, denouncing immigration.

1968 Britain's Race Relations Act makes it illegal to refuse housing, employment, or public services based on ethnicity.

1968 Founding of the International Work Group for Indigenous Affairs, a global human rights organization.

1971 Grenadian politician Bernard Coard publishes the pamphlet, *How the West Indian Child Is Made Educationally Subnormal in the British School System*.

1978 Scholar Edward Said publishes *Orientalism*.

1981 Brixton race riots.

1982 Germany formally recognizes Roma as victims of the Holocaust.

1982 A group of academics publish their "Heidelberg Manifesto" as a call against immigration to Germany, claiming foreigners would "taint the German blood."

1982 German Turkish poet Semra Ertan, author of "My Name Is Foreigner," takes her own life in a public act of self-immolation.

1987 Black History Month established in Britain.

1994 French ban on symbols of faith, including Muslim hijabs and burqas, Christian crucifixes, Jewish skullcaps, and Sikh turbans.

1995 Bosnian Serbs murder thousands of Muslim Bosniak boys and men at Srebrenica, in the first act of European genocide since 1945.

1995 French president Jacques Chirac acknowledges his nation's role in deporting Jews during World War II.

2001 9/11 attacks in the United States.

2004 Terrorists explode 10 bombs on four trains in Madrid, resulting in 193 deaths and 2,000 people injured.

2005 Protests in France in response to the police killing of two young men of North African origin.

2005 Suicide bomb attacks on July 7 kill 52 London commuters, injure 700 others, and lead to increased persecution of Muslim peoples in Britain.

2007 The United Nations adopts the Declaration on the Rights of Indigenous Peoples.

2010 French President Nicholas Sarkozy begins systemic deportation campaign against Romanian and Bulgarian Roma communities. This act is condemned by UN as evidence of growing racist attitudes.

2011 Protests in Britain, in response to the police killing of Black British man Mark Duggan.

2012 German government creates memorial to the Sinti and Roma victims of Nazis.

2013 Britain agrees to pay compensation to those tortured during the Mau Mau uprising.

2015 During the 2015 European migrant crisis, 1.3 million people request asylum in the European Union, prompting debates on refugee policies and practices across the continent.

2015 Several French municipalities ban the burkini worn by Muslim women.

2017 French President Emmanuel Macron admits his nation's colonial activities in Algeria amounted to a "crime against humanity."

2020 The COVID-19 pandemic prompts anti-Asian sentiment across Europe.

2022 A Berlin court declares that the wearing of the yellow Star of David by anti-COVID-19 vaccine protesters is a form of "secondary antisemitism."

QUESTIONS TO CONSIDER

1. One of the obvious themes in this Reader is the incredible persistence of racist beliefs across a thousand years of European history. Why? What are the roots of racism; are they somehow inherent in social organization? In religious attitudes? In economic competition?

2. Several of the documents included in this collection are laws regulating the treatment of minority groups, or legislating their expulsion or in some cases, their toleration. Why would governments pass these laws? Were legislators motivated by racist attitudes, concerns over mob action, or economic factors? What were the likely results of these laws?

3. In what ways did religious beliefs and prejudices seen in the parts on Jews and Muslims contribute to racist attitudes toward other peoples, such as Africans, Romani, Asians, or Indigenous? For example, how did ideas about blood and purity that Europeans first developed about Jews contribute to shifting attitudes about skin color?

4. According to historian Gavin Langmuir, it was in the twelfth and thirteenth centuries when anti-Judaism—the antipathy toward Jews by Christians arising from religious competition—became antisemitism. This he identifies as the irrational hatred of the Jews as a people, seeing this in the ritual murder and host desecration myths. Other scholars see the turn to antisemitism only later in the fifteenth-century Spanish purity of blood laws. Other historians of modern Europe see the shift only in the nineteenth century. Based on the excerpts included here, how would you conclude?

5. To what extent was the Catholic religion of most of the Irish a factor in the prejudicial views held by British Protestant writers? To what extent do those beliefs continue to shape attitudes and relations with respect to the Irish in the modern era?

6. Women as well as men suffered from the effects of racist action, yet most of the sources here were written by men. Can you discern gendered distinctions in racist writings? Did women experience racism differently from men? How and why?

7. One of the major features of antisemitism was the fear that Jewish males sought sexual relations with Christian women, and this kind of anxiety runs through the sources in all the other parts. What explains the breadth and persistence of this fear? More broadly, how have fears of miscegenation (sexual "race-mixing") influenced lawmakers, medical professionals, and commentators over the past several centuries? Why do you think sexual behaviors have been so tightly controlled at so many different times and in so many different places?

8. Is it possible to draw conclusions about the operation of racist practices in certain regions of Europe? Or, has there been too much similarity and overlap to make national or regional distinctions irrelevant? What might be the historical conditions that make one region more or less likely to promote racist attitudes toward minorities at a particular time? For example, the seventeenth-century Dutch Republic was famed for its promotion of religious diversity and toleration, yet it was also engaged in the transatlantic slave trade and in the enslavement and maltreatment of Indigenous peoples in the West and East Indies. How do we explain this apparent contradiction?

9. As seen in a number of these documents, there were efforts to oppose racist beliefs throughout the early modern and modern eras, yet racist attitudes and actions continue to arise, and at times, to predominate. Why?

10. The law scholar Kimberlé Crenshaw coined the term intersectionality in 1989 to denote the complicated ways various identities (gender, sex, ethnicity, religion, age, etc.) intersect to influence how people experience the world. Where can you find examples of intersectionality in these documents?

11. What types of documents, perspectives and voices are missing from this Reader? What might these "silences" tell us about the history of racism? How does the type of document (letter, law, newspaper article, painting, etc.) influence what we may learn from it about the history of racism? What types of historical sources could we use to fill in these blanks?

12. Language matters when considering the long history of prejudice. For example, the term "Gypsy" comes from the mistaken belief that the peoples emigrated from Egypt; Columbus declared North American peoples to be "Indians" because he thought he was in India. What are some other examples of how groups have self-identified but then been labeled differently by others? And how have some groups appropriated these terms to survive at different times and in different places?

13. As Europeans used non-white skin color to racialize others, they also developed an identity as "white." In the nineteenth and twentieth centuries, this sense of whiteness merged with growing national identities with horrific results. Why is skin color such a powerful tool in identity formation?

14. In 1978, scholar Edward Said wrote the book *Orientalism*, in which he argued that European portrayals of "exotic," or "exciting" or "mysterious" parts of the world served to create and reinforce racist beliefs. What examples can you find of "exoticizing the Other" in the sources?

15. How might we use these sources to examine the historical roots of the Holocaust? What might the Nazi persecution and murder of Jews, Roma, Black Germans, and other racialized peoples tell us about the radicalization of longstanding hatreds? For example, the historian Doris Bergen writes about the preconditions of genocide by using the literary allusion of a house fire. She writes that for a house to burn you need flammable materials, the right weather conditions, and a spark to ignite it; in Nazi Germany, she argues, the dry wood was centuries of prejudice, the conditions were World War II, and the spark was the Nazi regime. Do you agree with this analogy? If so, how might it be used to explain other historical events?

16. What were some of the professions of the authors in this volume, and what might this tell us about the "experts" involved in debates over race and racism? And, how did the development of so-called race science, racial anthropology, and criminology impact the categorization of peoples?

17. The *Merriam Webster Dictionary* defines a white supremacist as "a person who believes that the white race is inherently superior to other races and that white people should have control over people of other races." How do these readings support, or refute, that view?

18. How has the creation of racialized hierarchies worked to justify European expansionism and imperialism around the globe? How did those same power structures then operate to ensure the maintenance of imperial power?

19. How have contemporary debates around history and memory (statues, building names, school curricula, etc.) been influenced by the history of racism?

PART 1

Racism against Jewish Peoples

INTRODUCTION

The roots of modern antisemitism are found in the ancient and medieval world. In the ancient Roman Empire, antipathy toward Jews for their separateness and refusal to participate in the **imperial religious cults** was balanced by Rome's respect for the antiquity of Jewish culture. Relations between Rome and the Jewish kingdom of Judea became strained in the first century as groups of Jews fought for independence from Roman rule. This was the backdrop to the origin story of Christianity, as Jesus was a wandering Jewish **rabbi** whom some followers identified as the deliverer, or messiah, who would restore Israel to its place as God's chosen kingdom. In the early 30s CE Jesus was crucified by the Roman governor, Pontius Pilate. This act, however, did not end the movement, as his disciples, and especially Saul of Tarsus, or **St. Paul**, took their message of Jesus' sacrificial death on behalf of humanity and resurrection from the dead to the non-Jewish or gentile population of the Roman Empire. When, however, the Jews of Judea rose in rebellion against the Roman emperor, the result was an army of conquest under the new emperor Vespasian, which in 70 CE demolished the city of Jerusalem. Now the followers of Jesus feared that Rome would regard them as implicated in the Jewish rebellion. Since all four of the New Testament gospels were written after 70 CE, the authors sought to show to Rome that Christianity was distinct from Judaism, and that Jews were in fact of the Devil, not God.[1]

imperial religious cults: Religious activity formally approved by the Roman state.

rabbi: A teacher of Scripture in the Jewish tradition.

St. Paul: Saul of Tarsus, a first-century Jew of Palestine who converted to Christianity, becoming its most important missionary. He was executed in Rome c. 64/65 CE.

Despite the loss of Judea, **diaspora** Jews were spread across the cities of the Roman Empire, acting as merchants and traders. With the decline of Roman authority in the West in the fifth century and the rise of Islam in the East in the sixth, Jewish traders became valued intermediaries for princes who came to regard them as their personal property. Even so, antipathy toward Jews for rejecting Jesus as messiah and for allegedly orchestrating his execution remained a powerful force, combined with Christian resentment towards their economic success when they were supposed to have been rejected by God. Such hostility rose to the surface during the

diaspora: The scattering of a people from their traditional geographical locale.

---

1 Elaine Pagels, *The Origin of Satan: How Christians Demonized Jews, Pagans, and Heretics* (New York: Vintage, 1995).

crusades: A series of holy wars called by Catholic popes against non-Christians like Muslims, beginning in the late eleventh century.

deicide: The act of killing God, in this case in the person of Jesus Christ, whom most Christians believed was divine, as well as human.

Eucharistic wafers: The bread used in the Lord's Supper, one of the Christian church's sacraments providing divine grace or assistance to participants.

Mass: The Catholic Church Eucharist included the miracle of the transformation of bread and wine into the true body and blood of Christ.

Black Death: The outbreak of bubonic plague that ravaged Europe and the rest of the Eurasian world from 1346 to 1351, killing about a quarter of the population.

mendicant friars: Orders of itinerant monks established in the early thirteenth century to preach against heresy; they relied on begging for their subsistence.

Spanish Inquisition: A tribunal to determine guilt in matters of heresy, specifically of secret Judaism, established by the Spanish crown c. 1478.

crusades starting in 1096, which saw attacks on Jewish communities as crusaders marched across Europe. The documents below reveal how medieval Europeans developed increasingly strange beliefs about the Jews, including the **deicide** myth, and in the twelfth century, accusations of ritual murder, followed by accusations of host desecration wherein Jews were alleged to take consecrated **Eucharistic wafers**, which Christians believed became the body of Christ during the **Mass**, and stab them in their desire to kill Christ.[2] Such unreasonable stories—in that Christians should have known that Jews would not believe that a consecrated wafer was anything but bread—became a sad commonplace of accusation, torture, confession, and execution through to the twentieth century.[3] These prejudicial beliefs about Jews meant, as the historian Gavin Langmuir has suggested, that "antisemitism in all but name was widespread in Northern Europe by 1350, when many believed that Jews were beings incapable of fully rational thought who conspired to overthrow Christendom, who committed ritual crucifixions, ritual cannibalism, and host profanation, and who caused the **Black Death** by poisoning wells—even though no one had observed Jews committing any of those crimes."[4] The elaboration and dissemination of these myths transformed anti-Judaism—the traditional enmity felt by Christians toward the religion of the Jews—into antisemitism, the hatred of Jews as a people.

Such illogical accusations were compounded in the development of purity of blood laws of fifteenth- and sixteenth-century Spain. In 1390–91 ritual murder stories were spread by **mendicant friars** in Southern Spain where there lived a large Jewish community, members of which had played important mediatory roles for Christian princes governing a large Muslim populace. Mob violence ensued, and in 1391 masses of Jews accepted baptism into the Christian faith rather than suffer death. This resulted in a new group, Conversos or New Christians, which the Old Christians suspected were still secretly Jewish. In 1478 the Spanish rulers established the **Spanish Inquisition** to weed out secret Jews from among the Conversos, believing that many Conversos had maintained some elements of their former faith, and were thus Judaizing. By the sixteenth century Inquisitors were determining guilt for Judaizing heresy not from confessions, but through investigations into the family lineage of the accused to determine the level of Jewish blood in their veins.

---

2 See also Miri Rubin, *Gentile Tales: The Narrative Assault on Late Medieval Jews* (Philadelphia: University of Pennsylvania Press, 2004).

3 For more on the myth of ritual murder, see R. Po-chia Hsia, *The Myth of Ritual Murder: Jews and Magic in Reformation Germany* (New Haven: Yale University Press, 1988); and Magda Teter, *Blood Libel: On the Trail of an Antisemitic Myth* (Cambridge, MA: Harvard University Press, 2020).

4 Gavin I. Langmuir, *Toward a Definition of Antisemitism* (Berkeley: University of California Press, 1990), 302.

Even though these purity of blood laws did not immediately infiltrate into Northern Europe, antisemitic hostility continued to hound the Jews. When **Martin Luther** and others began the **Protestant Reformation** around 1520, he believed that Jews would convert to his new version of Christianity if shown kindness. By the late 1530s, however, he became angry at their unwillingness to convert, and wrote Document 7 below, one of the most virulent tracts against the Jews published in the early modern era, and one that Adolf Hitler eventually read.

Martin Luther: German monk and professor (1483–1546) who became the leader of the Lutheran Church that split from the Catholic Church during the Protestant Reformation.

Protestant Reformation: Led by Reformers such as Luther, this was a movement of dissent and separation from the Catholic papacy.

Suspicion and hatred of Jews remained a prominent feature of European culture into the modern era. This antisemitism formed the core for other forms of European racism, that differences among peoples existed in the blood and defined the "Other" as a conspiratorial enemy. The stories told by Christian Europeans about the Jews were, of course, all false. Such myths, however, proved powerful in the hands of those seeking to blame a ready-made minority for whatever problems they were facing. On the other hand, some of the documents below, such as those relating to the efforts of the Amsterdam rabbi Menasseh ben Israel to persuade England's parliament in 1655 to readmit the Jews (Documents 8 and 10) and Jan Jacob Mauricius's successful defense of Jews accused of a ritual murder in Nijmegen, The Netherlands in 1715 (Document 11), show attitudinal shifts in some regions. Yet other sources (Documents 9, 12, etc.) reveal that the Enlightenment was not an entirely positive philosophical movement on the subject of racism, most especially the documents in Part 3, as the Enlightenment era was also the period of the Atlantic Slave Trade.

By the late eighteenth century, Jewish leaders increasingly used the language of human rights to advocate for equal rights in their societies. At times, they were successful, as illustrated in the process of emancipation that began in Revolutionary France and spread across the continent during the nineteenth century. However, that language of emancipation was not applied equally to all groups of people. The Revolutionary government continued to exploit enslaved Black Africans in their colonies until the Haitian Revolution (1791–1804) and declaration of independence. Why were the French able to conceive of Jews as citizens but not Black Africans? The reader of these documents will be able to observe many such examples of inconsistent European attitudes toward those they regarded as "Other."

Emancipation brought increased political and civic rights; in short it allowed Jews to become citizens of their own countries, but it also opened debates around assimilation, and frequently led to calls to solve the so-called Jewish Problem. Antisemites adopted new racist tropes, ones that centered around ideas of foreignness, subversion, and economic dominance, while continuing to rely on those that were centuries old. In an age of expanding electoral politics, they formed political parties that proudly boasted antisemitism as the central focus of their platforms. Racial scientists sought additional "proof" that Jews constituted a separate race. They proclaimed connections between physical appearance and social behaviors, citing darker-toned skin and hair and "hook-shaped" noses as evidence that Jews were not only culturally, but also biologically, different from their neighbors (see Documents 14, 16, and 18).

These newer forms of prejudice existed alongside older forms of persecution. Even as Jewish women and men took on greater roles in European civil, economic, academic, and social society, they could still be targeted in violent pogroms, and by **blood libel** accusations. In 1900, the town of Könitz, Germany became embroiled in a murder case where dubious sleuthing by local police officers gave credence to the falsehood that local Jews had murdered a nineteen-year-old student and used his body for religious rites.[5] As we see in Document 17, a mob in Kishinev, Russia, yelled "Kill the Jews" as they slaughtered 120 of their neighbors.

blood libel: The accusation that Jews were responsible for the death of Jesus Christ, that his blood remained on their heads.

Through World War I and into the 1920s, some European Jews sought to assimilate into secular society, while others remained strictly **Orthodox**. At the same time, the rise of far-right political movements, especially those associated with forms of **fascism**, increasingly singled out Jewish communities as scapegoats for societal problems. "Inner enemies" led to military defeat, economic crises resulted from Jewish-controlled banks, immorality was the result of corrupting Jewish influences. Adolf Hitler and the National Socialist German Worker's Party (NSDAP) capitalized on such fears and worries to gain electoral support. The Nazis singled out Jews as the cause of Germany's decline, eventually promising a "Jew-free" society as the solution to national problems (see Documents 19 and 20). A radicalization of government policies during the twelve years of the **Third Reich** effectively removed Jews from social, cultural, and political society, while creating a hierarchical community based on race. Hundreds of thousands of European Jews fled the continent in response. During World War II, persecution turned genocidal. Across Occupied Europe, Nazi officials planned and facilitated the deportation of Jewish families into ghettos, the imprisonment and murder of Jews in camps, and mass shootings of men, women, and children. You will read an account by a survivor of Auschwitz-Birkenau in Document 21. What we now refer to as the Holocaust, or the Shoah, the Nazis called the Final Solution to the Jewish Problem, in reference to the idea that expulsion and mass death were needed to finally rid Europe of its Jews.

Orthodox: The theologically conservative branch of Judaism which considers the Torah to have been revealed by God to Moses and advocates strict observance of Jewish law.

fascism: A far-right political ideology that values dictatorship, militarism, nationalism, and conformity and opposes democracy, liberalism, Marxism, feminism, and multiculturalism.

Third Reich: The Nazis believed they were reviving the two earlier German empires (Reichs)—the medieval and early-modern Holy Roman Empire (800–1896) and the modern German Empire (1871–1918). They said it would last 1,000 years, but it lasted 12.

Persecution and prejudice continued in some forms after 1945, even as Holocaust survivors struggled to rebuild their lives. In 1946, the people

5 See Helmut Smith, *The Butchers Tale: Murder and Anti-Semitism in a German Town* (New York: W.W. Norton, 2002).

of Kielce waged a pogrom against their neighbors, in response to a blood libel accusation. British officials tried to stop emigration into Palestine. Soviet Bloc officials sometimes targeted Jews as enemies of communism. At the same time, women and men married, started families, and rebuilt communities. For many, the new state of Israel provided a refuge from centuries of European prejudice. However, this Jewish homeland, founded on lands already occupied by Palestinians, amplified existing hatreds and fears in the Middle East. These violent animosities between Jews and Muslims have at times led to physical attacks on European soil (see Document 22) and have revitalized antisemitic attitudes around the globe. A 2019 article proclaimed, "Anti-semitism is back in Europe," and reported that France had recently seen a 74 percent increase (and Germany a 60 percent increase) in violent attacks against Jewish citizens. A survey of 16,000 Jewish Europeans found 90 percent of respondents believed antisemitism to be increasing, 30 percent said they had been harassed, and many stated they feared for their physical safety when visiting Jewish events or sites.[6] As has been the case throughout history, a rise in antisemitism often signals wider societal fears and frustrations and is encouraged by extremist politicians. Different now is the likelihood that non-Jews will stand up in defense of their Jewish neighbors.

6 William Echikson, "What's Behind Europe's Surge in Anti-Semitism? Violent Attacks against Jews Are Multiplying as Fringe Politics Become the Norm," *Politico*, 4 March 2019.

DOCUMENT 1

From John 8:31–34, 42–52, 58–59, 18:33–40, 19:1–7, 12, 14–16 (Revised Standard Version)

In this passage from the gospel of John (the last of the four gospels to be written), the writer has Jesus arguing with the Pharisees, a leading group of rabbis whose teaching, despite what is said here, deeply shaped the approach of Jesus himself.

John 8: 31–34, 42–52,58–59 (Revised Standard Version)

31 Jesus then said to the Jews who had believed in him, "If you continue in my word, you are truly my disciples, 32 and you will know the truth, and the truth will make you free." 33 They answered him, "We are descendants of **Abraham**, and have never been in bondage to any one. How is it that you say, 'You will be made free'?" 34 Jesus answered them, "Truly, truly, I say to you, every one who commits sin is a slave to sin."

Abraham: An ancient figure claimed by Jews, Christians, and Muslims to have been the father of their faiths.

42 Jesus said to them, "If God were your Father, you would love me, for I proceeded and came forth from God; I came not of my own accord, but he sent me. 43 Why do you not understand what I say? It is because you cannot bear to hear my word. 44 You are of your father the devil, and your will is to do your father's desires. He was a murderer from the beginning, and has nothing to do with the truth, because there is no truth in him. When he lies, he speaks according to his own nature, for he is a liar and the father of lies. 45 But, because I tell the truth, you do not believe me. 46 Which of you convicts me of sin? If I tell the truth, why do you not believe me? 47 He who is of God hears the words of God; the reason why you do not hear them is that you are not of God."

48 The Jews answered him, "Are we not right in saying that you are a **Samaritan** and have a demon?" 49 Jesus answered, "I have not a demon; but I honor my Father, and you dishonor me. 50 Yet I do not seek my own glory; there is One who seeks it and he will be the judge. 51 Truly, truly, I say to you, if any one keeps my word, he will never see death." 52 The Jews said to him, "Now we know that you have a demon. Abraham died, as did the prophets; and you say, 'If any one keeps my word, he will never taste death' ...." 58 Jesus said to them, "Truly, truly, I say to you, before Abraham was, I am." 59 So they took up stones to throw at him; but Jesus hid himself, and went out of the temple.

Samaritan: A sub-group of the ancient Israelites who formed their own ethnic identity in the Holy Land and who often clashed with other Jewish groups in the centuries leading up to Christ.

[The writer of this gospel diverts responsibility for the crucifixion of Jesus from Pontius Pilate, the Roman governor (who alone possessed the authority to sentence someone to death by crucifixion), to the Jews as a people, hence the deicide or blood libel accusations.]

John 18: 33 Pilate entered the **praetorium** again and called Jesus, and said to him, "Are you the King of the Jews?" 34 Jesus answered, "Do you say this of your own accord, or did others say it to you about me?" 35 Pilate answered, "Am I a Jew? Your own nation and the chief priests have handed you over to me; what have you done?" 36 Jesus answered, "My kingship is not of this world; if my kingship were of this world, my servants would fight, that I might not be handed over to the Jews; but my kingship is not from the world." 37 Pilate said to him, "So you are a king?" Jesus answered, "You say that I am a king. For this I was born, and for this I have come into the world, to bear witness to the truth. Every one who is of the truth hears my voice." 38 Pilate said to him, "What is truth?" After he had said this, he went out to the Jews again, and told them, "I find no crime in him. 39 But you have a custom that I should release one man for you at the Passover; will you have me release for you the King of the Jews?" 40 They cried out again, "Not this man, but **Barab'bas**!" Now Barab'bas was a robber.

praetorium: The officers' quarters.

[Chapter 19:1] Then Pilate took Jesus and **scourged** him. 2 And the soldiers plaited a crown of thorns, and put it on his head, and arrayed him in a purple robe; 3 they came up to him, saying, "Hail, King of the Jews!" and struck him with their hands. 4 Pilate went out again, and said to them, "See, I am bringing him out to you, that you may know that I find no crime in him." 5 So Jesus came out, wearing the crown of thorns and the purple robe. Pilate said to them, "Behold the man!" 6 When the chief priests and the officers saw him, they cried out, "Crucify him, crucify him!" Pilate said to them, "Take him yourselves and crucify him, for I find no crime in him." 7 The Jews answered him, "We have a law, and by that law he ought to die, because he has made himself the Son of God...." 12 Upon this Pilate sought to release him, but the Jews cried out, "If you release this man, you are not **Caesar's** friend; every one who makes himself a king sets himself against Caesar...." 14 Now it was the day of Preparation of the Passover; it was about the sixth hour. He said to the Jews, "Behold your King!" 15 They cried out, "Away with him, away with him, crucify him!" Pilate said to them, "Shall I crucify your King?" The chief priests answered, "We have no king but Caesar." 16 Then he handed him over to them to be crucified.

Barab'bas: An alleged prisoner whom Pilate offered as a choice to the crowd to release during Passover.

scourged: Whipping with a multiple-strap lash, often with metal or bone at the ends to increase the severity of the wounds.

Caesar: The Roman Emperor.

DOCUMENT 2

From Thomas of Monmouth, "The Life and Miracles of St. William of Norwich" (c. 1173)[7]

Every Easter season, when Christians were told in vivid terms how the Jews had killed Jesus (the act of deicide), resentment against the small Jewish communities intensified. In the twelfth century this accusation took on new form with the ritual murder accusation. The story told here is the first known such story, told by the monk Thomas of Monmouth, who arrived in Norwich, England, several years after the discovery of the corpse of the boy William around 1144. He wrote his account in Latin around 1173, but word spread quickly thanks to the monastic communication networks. In this case the Jews were not arrested. In all subsequent ones, however, they were, as ritual murder accusations spread across England and continental Europe.

I have learnt from certain Jews, who were afterwards converted to the Christian faith, how that at that time they had planned to do this very thing [i.e., martyr a Christian boy] with some Christian, and in order to carry out their malignant purpose, at the beginning of **Lent** they had made choice of the boy William, being twelve years of age and a boy of unusual innocence....

Lent: 40-day period of fasting and penance leading up to Easter in the Christian calendar.

Palm Sunday: The Sunday before Easter celebrating the entry of Jesus into Jerusalem.

Passover: Jewish festival (Pesach) celebrating the Israelites' escape from Egypt.

At the dawn of day, on the Monday [March 20, 1144] after **Palm Sunday** ... the boy, like an innocent lamb, was led to the slaughter.... [O]n the next day [Tuesday March 21], which in that year was the **Passover** for them, after the singing of the hymns appointed for the day in the synagogue, the chiefs of the Jews ... suddenly seized hold of the boy William as he was having his dinner and in no fear of any treachery, and ill-treated him in various horrible ways. For while some of them held him behind, others opened his mouth and introduced an instrument of torture which is called a teazle [a wooden gag] and, fixing it by straps through both jaws to the back of his neck, they fastened it with a knot as tightly as it could be drawn....

But not even yet could the cruelty of the torturers be satisfied without adding even more severe pains. Having shaved his head, they stabbed it with countless **thornpoints**, and made the blood come horribly from the wounds they made....

thornpoints: Marks presumably from a crown of thorns like that placed on Christ's head; John 19:5.

And thus, while these enemies of the Christian name were rioting in the spirit of malignity around the boy, some of those present adjudged him to be fixed to a cross in mockery of the Lord's Passion, as though they would say:

7 Jacob R. Marcus, ed., *The Jew in the Medieval World: A Source Book: 315–1791* (New York: Atheneum, 1978), 121–26.

"Even as we condemned the Christ to a shameful death, so let us also condemn the Christian, so that, uniting the lord and his servant in a like punishment, we may retort upon themselves the pain of that reproach which they impute to us."

Conspiring, therefore, to accomplish the crime of this great and detestable malice, they next laid their bloodstained hands upon the innocent victim, and having lifted him from the ground and fastened him upon the cross, they vied with one another in their efforts to make an end of him.

And we ... did both find the house, and discovered some most certain marks in it of what had been done there.... For report goes that there was there instead of a cross a post set up between two other posts, and a beam stretched across the midmost post and attached to the other on either side. And as we afterwards discovered, from the marks of the wounds and of the bands, the right hand and foot had been tightly bound and fastened with cords, but the left hand and foot were pierced with two **nails**. Now the deed was done in this way, lest it should be discovered, from the presence of nailmarks in both hands and both feet, that the murderers were Jews and not Christians, if eventually the body were found....

nails: Christ was nailed to a cross.

Thus then the glorious boy and martyr of Christ, William, dying the death of time in reproach of the Lord's death, but crowned with the blood of a glorious martyrdom, entered into the kingdom of glory on high to live forever. Whose soul rejoiceth blissfully in heaven among the bright hosts of the saints, and whose body by the Omnipotence of the divine mercy worketh miracles upon earth....

As a proof of the truth and credibility of the matter we now adduce something which we have heard from the lips of **Theobald**, who was once a Jew, and afterwards a monk. He verily told us that in the ancient writings of his fathers it was written that the Jews, without the shedding of human blood, could neither obtain their freedom, nor could they ever return to their fatherland.... Hence it was laid down by them in ancient times that every year they must sacrifice a Christian in some part of the world to the Most High God in scorn and contempt of Christ, that so they might avenge their sufferings on Him; inasmuch as it was because of Christ's death that they had been shut out from their own country, and were in exile as slaves in a foreign land....

Theobald: Presumably a fellow monk of Thomas.

Wherefore the chief men and Rabbis of the Jews who dwell in Spain assemble together at Narbonne, where the **Royal seed** [resides], and where they are held in the highest estimation, and they cast lots for all the countries which the Jews inhabit; and whatever country the lot falls upon, its metropolis has to carry out the same method with the other towns and cities, and the place whose lot is drawn has to fulfill the duty imposed by authority.... These words—observe, the words of a converted Jew—we reckon to be all the truer, in that we received them as uttered by one who was a converted enemy, and also had been privy to the secrets of our enemies.

Royal seed: The seat of Spanish royalty.

DOCUMENT 3

Image: Crucifixion of William of Norwich, from a Church in Loddon, UK (15th Century)[8]

This image dates to the fifteenth century; nothing is known about the artist, but it is part of a series of panels depicting the life of the Blessed Virgin Mary. William (see Document 2 above) was declared a saint of Norwich, and miracles were ascribed to his relics. Several churches have images of St. William, typically of him holding nails. The one below, from a church in Loddon, Norfolk, depicts the alleged crucifixion scene painted upon a **rood screen**. These were richly decorated dividers between the nave of the church—the space for laypeople to observe the mass—and the chancel—the area around the altar—that were popular from the fourteenth to the sixteenth centuries. See also the images in Documents 6, 12, and 19, revealing how such depictions helped propagate the myth of ritual murder into the twentieth century.

rood screen: A screen separating the nave, where worshippers gathered, from the altar space where the Mass or Eucharist was celebrated. The screen was intended to heighten the mystery of what transpired behind the screen.

8 Image courtesy of Nick Stone.

DOCUMENT 4

From the Bull of Pope Gregory X (7 October 1272)[9]

Various popes sought to suppress the rising tide of antisemitic sentiment and violence spreading across Europe. They encouraged tolerating Jews as proof of the verity of the Christian story about Jesus and his death, resurrection, and return for judgment, before which Jews were expected to convert to Christianity. Such tolerance was always tempered by Christian belief that they had supplanted Jews as God's chosen people, hence Jews could not be allowed to prosper above Christians, who passed various laws restricting the activity of Jews. They also forbade Jews from having sexual relations with Christian women. Here Pope Gregory X (r. 1271–76) has issued a **bull** on October 7, 1272, built on earlier decrees by Pope Innocent IV in 1247 and 1253 condemning ritual murder accusations.

bull: A formal decree of the Catholic pope.

Even as it is not allowed to the Jews in their assemblies presumptuously to undertake for themselves more than that which is permitted them by law, even so they ought not to suffer any disadvantage in those [privileges] which have been granted them. Although they prefer to persist in their stubbornness rather than to recognize the words of their prophets and the mysteries of the Scriptures, and thus to arrive at a knowledge of Christian faith and salvation; nevertheless, inasmuch as they have made an appeal for our protection and help, we therefore admit their petition and offer them the shield of our protection through the clemency of Christian piety [here the pope condemns forced baptisms and violence against Jews].

... Since it happens occasionally that some Christians lose their Christian children, the Jews are accused by their enemies of secretly carrying off and killing these same Christian children and of making sacrifices of the heart and blood of these very children. It happens, too, that the parents of these children or some other Christian enemies of these Jews, secretly hide these very children in order that they may be able to injure these Jews, and in order that they may be able to extort from them a certain amount of money by redeeming them from their straits.

... Jewish law in this matter precisely and expressly forbids Jews to sacrifice, eat, or drink the blood, or to eat the flesh of animals having claws. This has been demonstrated many times at our court by Jews converted to the Christian faith: nevertheless very many Jews are often seized and detained unjustly because of this. We decree, therefore, that Christians need not be

9 Excerpted from Marcus, *The Jew in the Medieval World*, 151–54.

obeyed against Jews in a case or situation of this type, and we order that Jews seized under such a silly pretext be freed from imprisonment, and that they shall not be arrested henceforth on such a miserable pretext, unless—which we do not believe—they be caught in the commission of the crime. We decree that no Christian shall stir up anything new against them, but that they should be maintained in that status and position in which they were in the time of our predecessors, from antiquity till now.

DOCUMENT 5

Example of a Purity of Blood Law: Anonymous, Sentencia-Estatuto de Toledo (1449)[10]

Purity of Blood laws were created by Spanish Old Christians to distinguish themselves from the Conversos or New Christians. Fearing that New Christians were still secretly practicing Judaism, in 1478 Queen Isabella and King Ferdinand of Spain created the Spanish Inquisition to eradicate such heresy. At first Inquisitors tortured the accused into confessing their heresy, but in the sixteenth century they came to determine the level of Jewish heresy by the measure of Jewish blood an accused possessed; if this was more than 1/16 of their lineage, they were Judaizers. This practice was a theological heresy, for it implied that the Catholic sacrament of baptism did not work on Jewish blood. No one with Jewish blood could hold governmental or church offices, or own land, or marry into the nobility. The pure blood laws established the idea that Jewish identity was fixed, a precursor to the biological notions of race developed in the nineteenth century; they would also be applied to Muslim converts, the **Moriscos**. This is one of the first such laws from Toledo, 1449.

Moriscos: Descendants of Spanish Muslims who had converted to Christianity.

We, Pedro Sarmiento, head ***repostero*** of our lord the **king** ... and head mayor of the very noble and loyal city of Toledo, along with the mayors, constables, knights, squires, citizens and common people of the said city of Toledo, proclaim and declare that, in as much as it is well known through civil and canon law that *conversos* of Jewish lineage, being suspect in the faith of our Lord and Savior Jesus Christ, frequently belittle it by judaizing, they shall not be allowed to hold office or benefices public or private through which they might cause harm, aggravation, or bad treatment to good old Christians (*Christianos viejos lindos*), nor shall they be able to act as witnesses against them....

***repostero*:** In any noble household, the *repostero* was traditionally the one responsible for the dining implements. Here we can assume that it was a largely honorific title.

king: Juan II (1406–54).

In as much as it has been shown that a large portion of the city's *conversos* descending from the Jewish line are persons very suspect in the holy Catholic faith; that they hold and believe great errors against the articles of the holy Catholic faith; that they keep the rites and ceremonies of the **old law**; that they say and affirm that our Savior and Redeemer Jesus Christ was man of

old law: The Hebrew law and scripture.

10 This excerpt was translated by Kenneth Baxter Wolf and is included here with Dr. Wolf's references, and with his kind permission. A good introduction to the subject, and to the following excerpt by Martin Luther, is Jerome Friedman, "Jewish Conversion, the Spanish Pure Blood Laws and Reformation: A Revisionist View of Racial and Religious Antisemitism," *Sixteenth Century Journal* 18 (1987): 3–30.

their lineage who was killed and whom the Christians worship as God; that they say that there is both a god and a goddess[11] in heaven; and in as much as, on **holy Thursday**—while the holy oil and **chrism** is being consecrated in the church of Toledo and the body of our Redeemer is being placed on the altar—the said *conversos* slaughter lambs and eat them and make other kinds of holocausts and sacrifices, thus Judaizing....

holy Thursday: The Thursday before Easter, a day of fasting for Christians.

chrism: Oil consecrated by a bishop used in the sacraments and other church rituals.

And in as much as the said *conversos* live and act without fear of God and have shown and still show themselves to be enemies of the said city and of the old Christians living in it....

And because the said *conversos* descended from Jews have through great deceit taken and robbed great and innumerable quantities of ***maravedis*** and silver from our lord the king and from his rents and rights and taxes, and have destroyed and ruined many noble ladies, knights and ***hidalgos***; and because they have oppressed, destroyed and robbed all the most ancient houses of the "Old Christians" of this city and of all the realms of Castile, as is well known; and in as much as during the time that they held public offices in this city and its environs, the greater part of the city was depopulated and destroyed and the land and places of the city lost and alienated, since they took all the *maravedis* in the form of rent and interest, to such an extent that all the goods and honors of the countryside were consumed and destroyed, becoming lords to destroy the holy Catholic faith and the Old believing Christians in it; and in confirmation of this it is known that the said *conversos* of this city a short time ago rose up and armed themselves and set out to destroy all the "Old Christians" and me, the said Pedro Sarmiento, throwing us out of the city and handing it over to our enemies....[12]

***maravedis*:** Iberian coins of various denominations, depending on metal used (gold, silver, copper).

***hidalgos*:** Members of the landowning nobility.

Therefore we find that we ought to declare and do declare that all the said conversos descended from the perverse line of the Jews, in whatever situation they may be ... be held as incapable and unworthy to hold public or private office in the said city of Toledo and in its lands, by means of which they would be able to hold lordship over Old Christians believing in the holy Catholic faith of Our Lord Jesus Christ and cause damage, injury, and to be incapable and unworthy of giving testimony and faith as public notaries or as witnesses....

11 A concept connected to the cabalist movement within medieval Iberian Judaism. The idea of a female counterpart to God—known as Shekhina—may have been influenced by Latin Christian devotion of Mary, which intensified in the twelfth century.

12 A reference to the struggles within Toledo between the "Old Christians" and the conversos.

DOCUMENT 6

Image: Woodcut Portraying the 1475 Death of Simon of Trent (1493)[13]

As ritual murder accusations spread, many of the alleged victims were declared saints, most famously Simon of Trent, whose death in 1475 in Trent, Northern Italy, led to the trial, torture, forced confession, and execution of several Jews. His image became a major iconographic device in antisemitism. Here the artists Michel Wolgemut and Wilhelm Pleydenwurff also portray the false accusation that Jews forcibly **circumcised** Christians. Simon's sainthood was repealed only in 1965.

circumcised: Circumcision was the ritual cutting off of the foreskin of the penis required to be done to all male infants as a sign of their membership in the Jewish community.

13 From *Weltchronik* (*World Chronicle*), Hartmann Schedel (1493).

DOCUMENT 7

From Martin Luther, *On the Jews and Their Lies* (1543)[14]

Martin Luther (1483–1546) was a former monk who began the Protestant Reformation from Wittenberg, Northern Germany. By 1520 Luther had rejected the authority of popes in favor of scripture alone and believed that his reform of the church would be attractive to Jews. In 1523 he published *That Jesus Christ Was Born a Jew* condemning Catholic anti-Judaism. In 1543, however, fearing that Jews were converting Christians to a quasi-Judaism called Sabbatarianism, he wrote *Of the Jews and Their Lies*, which embarrassed many of Luther's closest supporters.

I had made up my mind to write no more either about the Jews or against them. But since I learned that those miserable and accursed people do not cease to lure to themselves even us, that is, the Christians, I have published this little book, so that I might be found among those who opposed such poisonous activities of the Jews and who warned the Christians to be on their guard against them.

... It is not my purpose to quarrel with the Jews, nor to learn from them how they interpret or understand Scripture; I know all of that very well already. Much less do I propose to convert the Jews, for that is impossible.... They have failed to learn any lesson from the terrible distress that has been theirs for over fourteen hundred years in exile.

wrath of God: The anger of God over sin, which elicited fear over the punishments he would send, such as plagues and storms.

... For such ruthless **wrath of God** is sufficient evidence that they assuredly have erred and gone astray. Even a child can comprehend this. For one dare not regard God as so cruel that he would punish his own people so long, so terribly, so unmercifully, and in addition keep silent, comforting them neither with words nor with deeds, and fixing no time limit and no end to it. Who would have faith, hope, or love toward such a God? Therefore this work of wrath is proof that the Jews, surely rejected by God, are no longer his people, and neither is he any longer their God.

vipers: Poisonous snakes.

... Our Lord also calls them a "brood of **vipers**"; furthermore, in John 3:39 he states: "If you were Abraham's children you would do what Abraham did.... You are of your father the devil." It was intolerable to them to hear

14 Excerpted by permission from Franklin Sherman, ed., Martin H. Bertram, trans., *Luther's Works*, vol. 47, *The Christian in Society* IV (Philadelphia: Fortress Press, 1971), 268–78. It is important to note that the views expressed by Luther in this work do not reflect the views of either the Evangelical Lutheran Church in America or the Lutheran Church Missouri Synod, the co-publishers of Luther's works. For more on Luther's turn to antisemitism, see Mark U. Edwards, Jr., *Luther's Last Battles: Politics and Polemics 1531–46* (Ithaca, NY: Cornell University Press, 1983).

that they were not Abraham's but the devil's children, nor can they bear to hear this today. If they should surrender this boast and argument, their whole system which is built on it would topple and change.

... What shall we Christians do with this rejected and condemned people, the Jews? Since they live among us, we dare not tolerate their conduct, now that we are aware of their lying and reviling and blaspheming. If we do, we become sharers in their lies, cursing and blasphemy. Thus we cannot extinguish the unquenchable fire of divine wrath, of which the prophets speak, nor can we convert the Jews. With prayer and the fear of God we must practice a sharp mercy to see whether we might save at least a few from the glowing flames.... I shall give you my sincere advice:

First, to set fire to their **synagogues** or schools and to bury and cover with dirt whatever will not burn, so that no man will ever again see a stone or cinder of them. This is to be done in honor of our Lord and of Christendom, so that God might see that we are Christians, and do not condone or knowingly tolerate such public lying, cursing, and blaspheming of his Son and of his Christians.

... Second, I advise that their houses also be razed and destroyed. For they pursue in them the same aims as in their synagogues. Instead they might be lodged under a roof or in a barn, like the **gypsies**. This will bring home to them the fact that they are not masters in our country, as they boast, but that they are living in exile and in captivity, as they incessantly wail and lament about us before God.

Third, I advise that all their prayer books and **Talmudic writings**, in which such **idolatry**, lies, cursing, and **blasphemy** are taught, be taken from them.

Fourth, I advise that their rabbis be forbidden to teach henceforth on pain of loss of life and limb.

... Fifth, I advise that **safe-conduct** on the highways be abolished completely for the Jews. For they have no business in the countryside, since they are not lords, officials, tradesmen, or the like. Let them stay at home....

Sixth, I advise that **usury** be prohibited to them, and that all cash and treasure of silver and gold be taken from them and put aside for safekeeping. The reason for such a measure is that, as said above, they have no other means of earning a livelihood than usury, and by it they have stolen and robbed from us all they possess. Such money should now be used in no other way than the following: Whenever a Jew is sincerely converted, he should be handed one hundred, two hundred, or three hundred **florins**, as personal circumstances may suggest. With this he could set himself up in some occupation for the support of his poor wife and children, and the maintenance of the old or feeble. For such evil gains are cursed if they are not put to use with God's blessing in a good and worthy cause.

synagogues: Places of worship and instruction for Jewish communities.

gypsies: Archaic for Roma; see Part 5 below.

Talmudic writings: The Talmud is a collection of rabbinical interpretation of the Hebrew Scriptures, gathered over centuries.

idolatry: The worship of idols or images; unlike most Christians, Jews forbid religious images in their places of worship.

blasphemy: To insult the divine; Reformation European governments harshly punished incidents of blasphemy.

safe-conduct: Typically a government document granting safe passage from one territory to another.

usury: Charging interest on loans; a sin in biblical law, although medieval popes allowed charging moderate interest rates, especially by non-Christians like Jews.

florins: A gold or silver coin that by Luther's day had become the standard currency (gulden in German states).

flail: An agricultural implement used to separate wheat from its husks.

distaff: A spindle onto which wool is wound for spinning; a symbol of women.

Adam: In Genesis, the first human created by God.

Goyim: Hebrew term for gentiles or non-Jews.

… Seventh, I recommend putting a **flail**, an ax, a hoe, a spade, a **distaff**,or a spindle into the hands of young, strong Jews and Jewesses and letting them earn their bread in the sweat of their brow, as was imposed on the children of **Adam** (Gen. 3 [:19]). For it is not fitting that they should let us accursed **Goyim** toil in the sweat of our faces while they, the holy people, idle away their time behind the stove, feasting and farting, and on top of all, boasting blasphemously of their lordship over the Christians by means of our sweat. No, one should toss out these lazy rogues by the seat of their pants.

But if we are afraid that they might harm us or our wives, children, servants, cattle, etc., if they had to serve and work for us … then let us emulate the common sense of other nations such as France, Spain, Bohemia, etc., compute with them how much their usury has extorted from us, divide this amicably, but then eject them forever from the country.… Therefore, in any case, away with them!

… In brief, dear princes and lords, those of you who have Jews under your rule: if my counsel does not please you, find better advice, so that you and we all can be rid of the unbearable, devilish burden of the Jews. Lest we become guilty sharers before God in the lies, the blasphemy, the defamation, and the curses which the mad Jews indulge in so freely and wantonly against the person of our Lord Jesus Christ, his dear **mother**, all Christians, all authority, and ourselves. Do not grant them protection, safe-conduct, or communion with us. Do not aid and abet them in acquiring your money or your subjects' money and property by means of usury.

mother: The Virgin Mary; while Lutherans rejected Catholic veneration of Mary as a saint, they still respected her as the mother of Jesus Christ.

… I have read and heard many stories about the Jews which agree with this judgment of Christ, namely, how they have poisoned wells, made assassinations, **kidnaped children**, as related before. I have heard that one Jew sent another Jew, and this by means of a Christian, a pot of blood, together with a barrel of wine, in which when drunk empty, a dead Jew was found. There are many other similar stories. For their kidnaping of children they have often been burned at the stake or banished (as we already heard). I am well aware that they deny all of this. However, it all coincides with the judgment of Christ which declares that they are venomous, bitter, vindictive, tricky serpents, assassins, and children of the devil who sting and work harm stealthily wherever they cannot do it openly. For this reason I should like to see them where there are no Christians. The **Turks** and other **heathen** do not tolerate what we Christians endure from these venomous serpents and young devils. Nor do the Jews treat any others as they do us Christians. That is what I had in mind when I said earlier that, next to the devil, a Christian has no more bitter and galling foe than a Jew. There is no other to whom we accord as many benefactions and from whom we suffer as much as we do from these base children of the devil, this brood of vipers.

kidnaped children: The ritual murder accusation; see Document 2 above.

Turks: Muslim peoples who controlled Eurasia from Hungary across to modern day Iran.

heathen: Non-Christians apart from Jews and Muslims.

DOCUMENT 8

From Edward Nicholas, *An Apology for the Honorable Nation of the Jews* (1648)[15]

This pamphlet was purportedly written by an English gentleman, Edward Nicholas, but the one known lord with this name—King Charles II's secretary of state—was a **crypto-Catholic** in exile on the continent at this time and was not likely the author.[16] Instead, the author writes as an English Protestant, but the phrases used strongly suggest it was composed by the Dutch rabbi Menasseh ben Israel, who was closely affiliated with a number of **millenarian Protestants** and published other works seeking to persuade Oliver Cromwell, Lord Protector of England, to allow the Jews to return to England from whence they had been banished in 1290.[17] In *The Hope of Israel* of 1652, Ben Israel announced that since the Lost Tribes of Israel had just been discovered in the South American forests, biblical prophecy of the messiah's arrival would be fulfilled.[18] Although the **Whitehall Conference** of legal experts and clergy decided in 1655 not to admit the Jews, Cromwell allowed them to return in a piecemeal fashion.

crypto-Catholic: It was illegal still to be a Roman Catholic in England, but many practiced their faith secretly or were suspected of harboring Catholic beliefs.

millenarian Protestants: Those who expected the establishment of Christ's kingdom on earth in the very near future.

Whitehall Conference: A meeting of leading clergy and members of Parliament in 1655 at the government offices at Whitehall, London, to discuss whether to admit the Jews.

Those that are in authority in this kingdom [England], and we all, may make the application; that the crying sins of our Nation do call for vengeance, which we have just cause to expect, unless we meet God by repentance, and satisfaction of the oppressed.

... But the sin principally intended here, is, The strict and cruel Laws now in force against the most honorable Nation of the world, the Nation of the Jews, a people chosen by God, as appears by the many and large expressions of his favor to them, styling them, His Gems, his firstborn, a precious people above all peoples of the earth, a kingdom of priests, an holy people unto himself: And further says, they are his own servants, and should not be in bondage to any, being only to serve six years, and the seventh to go out free, and in the **year of Jubilee**, every man was to return to his inheritance:

year of Jubilee: The year of Jubilee, every 50th year, which was to be a year of liberty and rest (Leviticus 25). The medieval Catholic Church adopted it as a year of remission of sins.

15 Edward Nicholas, *An Apology for the Honorable Nation of the Jews* ... (London, 1648), fols. 3–6, 11–15.

16 Gary K. Waite, "Seventeenth-Century English Writers on Dutch Nonconformists: The Cases of David Joris (George) and Menasseh ben Israel," in *Anglo-Dutch Connections in the Early Modern World*, ed. Sjoerd Levelt, Esther van Raamsdonk, and Michael Rose (New York: Routledge, 2023), 225–34.

17 Fernando Díaz Esteban, "La *Apología por la Noble nación de los judíos*, de Eduardo Nicholas (1649)," *Sefarad* 59 (1999): 251–62. See also Gary K. Waite, *Jews and Muslims in Seventeenth-Century Discourse: From Religious Enemies to Allies and Friends* (Abingdon, UK: Routledge, 2019), 176–86.

18 Menasseh ben Israel, *The Hope of Israel* (London, 1652); Menasseh ben Israel, *To His Highnesse the Lord Protector of the Common-Wealth of England ... in behalf of the Jewish Nation* (n.p., n.d.).

But above all, that privilege of theirs, the benefit whereof hath an influence on all the faithful, and redounds to their happiness, That in thee and thy seed shall all nations of the earth be blessed: So strong an obligation are we bound in to them through God's mercy.

And now let all faithful servants of God take to their considerations, how great enduring that honorable Nation hath suffered, what bloody slaughters have been made of them in London, in the North country of England, and divers other parts of this kingdom, and how they have been proscribed and banished [from] this kingdom, and denied that commerce allowed to all others, even to barbarous **Infidels**; so that the transcendency of this sin is not to be paralleled, in regard they being so honorably styled and owned by God himself; in rejecting them, we highly incense the Majesty of **Jehovah**.

Infidels: Generic term for unbelievers.

Jehovah: A variation of the Hebrew name for God, Yahweh.

... 'Tis objected, the great guilt that lies on the Jews for crucifying Christ, and that therefore, and for refusing the Gospel, they are rejected of God, so unworthy of favor, assistance, and compassion herein desired. In answer, though this be imputed to the whole Nation, yet it is apparent in the Gospel, that that action was done by the **Elders, chief Priests, and Scribes**, his Doctrine reproving their Hypocrisy, and laziness and pride, that they wrought a faction against him, and not that the whole Nation were guilty; ... what God in his secret will and judgement intended in the scattering of the Jews, I presume not to understand or to guess at: my purpose is only to prove, That God yet owns them for his people, and though cast off for a time, yet their certain future reduction is promised,

Elders, chief Priests, and Scribes: The major leaders of the Jewish community in first-century Palestine, as described in the Christian gospels.

... The rage of men in all countries of the world have been very extreme against Jews, 'tis not so much wonder see the barbarous Infidels robbing them and **imbruing** their hands in their blood, as that men that profess more of God's truth (though falsely:) In Spain there were 120,000 Jews cast and banished, in the year **1493**. In Italy and other places, the like hardship they have endured.

imbruing: Archaic term for staining one's hands with another's blood.

1493: The actual year of the expulsion of the Jews from Spain was 1492.

But I hope better things of our Nation [England],

... Whereas I style them [the Jews] honorable, though it may seem ridiculous to their Enemies, and the ignorant; yet I may truly say, They are of the highest and most honorable descent of any Nobility in any Country in the world, being ennobled by God himself, and the reason is given which must be most righteous; not for any thing in them, or for their multitude, but because God set his love upon them.... The **Papists** are especially offended with them, because the Jews so much abhor the Imagery and Idolatrous Worship of theirs, for touch that [worship], and touch the corner stone of their Politique foundation: the **Jesuits** do nestle into all Kingdoms and States of Christendom, and have an influence on their Counsels....

Papists: Like popists, a term of derision used by Protestants against Catholics.

Jesuits: The Society of Jesus, a Catholic religious order founded by St. Ignatius Loyola in 1540 to defend the Catholic faith against Protestant incursions.

I humbly offer this Apology, with these considerations, to the whole Kingdom of England, from the highest to the lowest, that as God hath exceedingly blessed this Kingdom above others, ... so now that we all show ourselves compassionate and helpers of the afflicted Jews; and pray, that the same Authority that proceeded against them formerly, that now same authority and power will repeal those severe Laws made against them: That our receiving them again, and giving them all possible satisfaction, and restoring them to commerce in this kingdom may be exemplary to other Nations that have done them, and continue to do them wrong; till which time (**God putting their tears into his bottle**) God will charge their sufferings upon us; and will avenge them on their persecutors.

God putting their tears into his bottle: An allegorical reference to God remembering the suffering of his people from Psalm 56:8: "You number my Wanderings: Put my tears into Your bottle."

DOCUMENT 9

From William Prynne, *A Short Demurrer to the Jewes* (1656)[19]

Puritan: Name for English Protestants, especially those who opposed Catholic elements in the Church of England.

William Prynne (1600–69) was a **Puritan** lawyer who wrote numerous works against Catholicism and new religious groups that had sprung up in England during the Civil War and Interregnum period (1642–60). The work excerpted here, *A Short Demurrer*, was a particularly nasty response to Menasseh ben Israel. Prynne presents his own interpretation of the Whitehall Conference of 1655 and recycles the old ritual murder and host desecration myths, something which a good Protestant should have relegated to the "superstitions" of Catholicism.

Mr. Nye: Philip Nye (1595–1672), a leading independent (i.e., separate from the Church of England) preacher and Oliver Cromwell's advisor on religious matters. He supported the readmission of the Jews to England.

Moveables: Moveable property, including cash.

Apostasy: The act of renouncing the true faith.

Clippers: The act of clipping a piece out of a coin, thus reducing its weight and value.

Lincoln's-Inn Fields: A large public square in London near the city's law offices and court.

In my return homewards that day by the Garden-wall at White-Hall, **Mr. Nye** the Minister, going very fast, there overtook, and saluting me by name, presently demanded this unexpected Question of me; Whether there were any Law of England against bringing in the Jews amongst us? For the lawyers had newly delivered their Opinions, there was no laws against it. To which I answered, That the Jews were in the year 1290 all out of England, by Judgement and Edict of the King and Parliament, as a great Grievance, never to return again: for which the Commons gave the King the fifteenth part of their **Moveables**: and therefore, being thus banished by Parliament, they could not by the Laws of England, be brought in again, without a Special Act of Parliament.... That it was now a very ill time to bring in the Jews, when people were so dangerously and generally bent to **Apostasy**, and all sorts of Novelties and Errors in Religion; and would sooner turn Jews [i.e., convert to Judaism], than the Jews Christians.... I told him, The Jews had been formerly great **Clippers** and Forgers of Money, and had crucified three or four Children in England at least, which were principal causes of their banishment. To which he replied, That the crucifying of Children was not fully charged on them by our Historians, and would easily be wiped off. Whereon I answered, He was much mistaken: and so we parted. As I kept on my way, in **Lincoln's-Inn Fields**, passing by seven or eight maimed soldiers on Stilts, who begged of me; I heard them say aloud one to another, We must now all turn Jews, and there will be nothing left for the poor. And not far from them another company of poor people, just at Lincoln's-Inn back Gate, cried aloud to each other: They are all turned Devils already, and now we must turn all Jews. Which ... made such an

19 William Prynne, *A Short Demurrer to the Jewes long discontinued barred remitter into England* (London, 1656), esp. fols. A3r–A4r, B2r-v, and pages 6–7, 26–28, 101. See Waite, *Jews and Muslims*, 187–88, and *Anti-Anabaptist Polemics: Dutch Anabaptism and the Devil in England, 1531–1660* (Thunder Bay, ON: Pandora Press, 2023), 159–67.

impression on my Spirit, that before I could take my rest that night, I perused most of the passages in our English Histories concerning the Jews' carriage in England, ... making some Collections out of them, ... for the general information, satisfaction of others, and honour of my blessed Lord and Saviour Jesus Christ the righteous, whom the Jews with malicious hearts, and wicked hands crucified in person heretofore, and their posterity by their blasphemies, despiteful actions against Christ, his Kingdom, Offices, Gospel crucify afresh, every day trampling under foot the Son of God, putting him to open shame, **offering despite** to the Spirit of Grace, & and counting the blood of the Covenant an unholy thing. And in all their public and private Devotions, praying constantly for the sudden, universal, total, final subversion, extirpation, perishing of Christ's Kingdom, Gospel, and all his Christian Members, which they plot, and continually expect, such is their implacable transcendent malice.

offering despite: Archaic for despising or disrespecting.

... [S]eeing their Proposals are, not only to be admitted and received into our Commonwealth under the protection and safeguard of our governors, AS THE NATIVES THEMSELVES: ... And to be allowed PUBLICK SYNAGOGUES, ... A clear evidence of intended design in them, only to set up their **Synagogues of Satan**, Judaism, & Jewish Ceremonies in the highest degree, amongst us, as lawful, in direct opposition and subversion of our only Lord ... and Christianity itself, without any thoughts of turning Christians themselves.

Synagogues of Satan: From Revelation 2:9, 3:9; a term often used also against religious opponents, as well as witches.

... By this History we may perceive what a prevailing Engine the Jews' money is, both to screw them into Christian Kingdoms, though the most bitter, inveterate, professed Enemies of Christ himself, Christians, and Christianity; and how their money can induce even Christian Princess to perpetrate most unchristian, and antichristian actions....

In the year of the Lord, 1145 during the reign of King Stephen, the Jews grew so presumptuous in England, that they crucified a child called William, in the city of Norwich in derision of Christian Religion.[20] ... And in the same King's reign [Henry II], Anno 1181, up on the same account, the Jews on the Feast of Easter martyred and crucified another child at St. Edmonds-bury, called Robert; who was honourably interred soon after in the Church of St. Edmunds, and grew famous by miracles there wrought;

... The introduction of the Jews into England and other Nations, never advanced the public wealth of the Natives and Republic, but much impaired it by their Usuries and Deceits, clipping and falsifying monies, engrossing all sorts of commodities into their hands, usurping the Natives' trades, and becoming such intolerable grievances to them, that they were never quiet till they were banished....

20 See Documents 2 and 3 above.

DOCUMENT 10

From D.L., *Israel's Condition and Cause Pleaded* (1656)[21]

Not all English Protestants agreed with Prynne; many wrote in support of Menasseh ben Israel and decried Prynne's tone, language, and, as in this excerpt, his retelling of the old ritual murder myths. The author was likely a member of the religious nonconformists who supported ben Israel.

Where shall we find any charitable Christian alive who intercedes and acts for this People's Conversion or Preservation?

... The long, heavy, and sad punishment inflicted on this dejected, despised, and dispersed people, has various and strong impressions upon men's spirits; some scorning any society with them, others hating their very name, and persons, and some compassionating their despicable condition: hence some Countries banish and expel them, others do miserably and cruelly oppress and injure them by base and uncivil words and actions; ... we have some in this Nation, who are so bitter against that poor people, that they have vented their unsatiable spleen and malice by their pens, and rather than their indiscreet passions should not take place, and work others against them, have raked together all the rabble of **Popish** Authors, and filled men's brains with strange stories, and their late printed books with marginal notes of Friars, and Monks, Abbots relations, to render that Ancient and Honourable Nation of the Jews, odious and detestable.[22]

Popish: Papal, but here a generic term for Catholics.

And 'tis to be wondered at that men who profess themselves such adversaries to all Popery and Popish superstitions should yet search all the withered and Moth-eaten writers of that Romish faction, and fight only with Popish weapons against the Jews....

[F]or if ever a Nation may truly take up **Job's complaint**, certainly 'tis this of the Jews, "Pity me, oh pity me, ye my friends, for the hand of the Lord hath touched me";[23] and though 'tis true all affliction is justly inflicted, where sin proceeds, provokes, and procures the Punishment, and that this people are deep in accounts, yet there is no bar in God's Word to hinder a tender compassion and Christian love to be shown towards them, much less is there any Rule to hate them, oppress them, expel them our Country, or our Commerce ... for though God in his justice did threaten to scatter them

Job's complaint: The Old Testament story of Job whose faith God, through Satan, tested by afflicting him with various disasters and diseases.

21 D.L., *Israels Condition and Cause pleaded; or some Arguments for the Jews Admission into England* (London, 1656), fols. A2v–4v, pp. 1–4. For more on this, see Waite, *Jews and Muslims*, 189–90.

22 A clear reference to Prynne's work.

23 Job 19:21.

into all Nations, yet he doth not say they shall be cast out of all Nations, and have no being amongst men; and to speak truth, they are to be scattered amongst all people, for if they should not be amongst all Nations, how should God (if he intends it) gather them out of all Nations?

DOCUMENT 11

From Jan Jacob Mauricius, *Account of a Ritual Murder Accusation in Nijmegen* (1715)[24]

In the early seventeenth century the Dutch Republic became a place of refuge for Jews, who could worship there in synagogues. Even so, antisemitic attitudes occasionally rose to the surface, as in this story from Nijmegen told by the Dutch lawyer Jan Jacob Mauricius, who had befriended the city's Jews. He became incensed when a young man, Isaak Saxel, implicated them in ritual murder. Mauricius interrogated the witnesses, investigated the reputation of the accuser, and checked the alibis of the accused. Thanks to his efforts, the accused were released from prison and Saxel punished for malicious prosecution. Mauricius would later become the governor of the Dutch colony of Suriname, South America, where he ruthlessly put down **Maroon** rebellions, while also advocating for the religious instruction of the enslaved.

Maroon: Free descendants of enslaved Africans who formed their own settlements.

Last December in the year 1715 it happened at Ludenscheid, a city in the Duchy of Cleves, that a young tramp of eighteen years, by the name of Isaak Saxel, a Jew by birth but baptized as a Christian, was apprehended, not just out of guilt for the theft of another's goods, but also for his bad behavior, and especially his mocking changeableness in religion, of which you will find abhorrent examples here. This young profligate, finding himself in a poor state, and among other things very much in debt to a certain Jew who had loaned him some money, found no other escape than to say that the Jews deserved no trust, and among other ridiculous means to make them hateful, he claimed that their bitterness toward the Christians was so great, that they ate [Christian] flesh, after cooking it and pissing on it. He said that such was witnessed by a Jewish butcher at Altona (a city two hours from Ludenscheid) with whom he had lived and he also accused him of allegedly stealing some letters and money from him.

The lord, high count of Ludenscheid, fascinated, sent him immediately to Altona, but since the accused Jew had not only expurgated himself with the **oath**, but also to the contrary, the high count cast our Saxel into an even scarier and deeper prison. On this account he was advised that there was no

oath: Expurgation, proving one's innocence by having honorable neighbors testify to one's innocence.

24 The first excerpt is from Mauricius's *Kort Bericht Wegens de Historie van zekeren Isaak Saxel, En de beschuldiging der Jooden te Nymegen, Over 't Slachten van een Kristen Kind* (Amsterdam: Hendrik van de Gaete, 1716), fols. A2r–A3v. The second is from Mauricius's *Remonstrantie Aan den Ed. En Achtb. Raad der Stad Nymegen. Overgegeeven door de aldaar woonende Jooden, Beneevens de annexe Documenten* (Amsterdam: Hendrik van de Gaete, 1716), 1–9. Translated by Gary Waite. On Mauricius and the Jews, see Waite, *Jews and Muslims*, 249–51; for his rule as governor, Anton de Kom, *Wij slaven van Suriname* (Amsterdam, 1934), 76–87.

chance of escaping justice, and finally he made an oath to reveal something that would lead to an eternal hatred of the entire Jewish Nation and was of great benefit to his Royal Majesty of Prussia. Hereupon came into the light of day nothing other than the old, oft played tune that the Jews, in their ceremonies, used Christian blood. He however mentioned specially that in 1710 (when he was just twelve years old) he was at the **Day of Atonement** ceremony at Nijmegen when the Jews there allegedly killed a Christian child. He described the circumstances thusly: "The child was brought to the Synagogue in a basket by his father, a sergeant with one arm. Present were about 30 or 40 people, both old and young. After a speech by the Cleves regional rabbi, who was also present, and the songs sung by the **Cantor**, [the child] was circumcised by the Cleves circumciser. Then the oldest Jew, named Solomon, took him up, and cut its neck, and then another, named Benedict, cut off the head. A third pulled off the navel and tapped the blood of this six-month-old infant into two large jars, one of which they stoppered well and sent to the Jews at Amersfoort. The other Jews skinned the child and threw the skin into the room of the aforementioned Solomon to be guarded there. The flesh was cut from the bones, and given to the dogs to eat, and the bones were washed clean by the women and taken to a place, which he named, to be buried."

Day of Atonement: Yom Kippur, the holiest day in the Jewish calendar.

Cantor: The singer and prayer leader in a Jewish religious service.

... [When further interrogated, Saxel] promised to take his interrogators to Nijmegen where he would show them the *corpus delicti*, pledging that if he was not telling the truth, they could burn him....

The **Gentlemen of Nijmegen** decided to send their city **bailiff** to Cleves, and then to meet with all the Jews of Nijmegen who had been imprisoned the evening before. However much [Saxel] claimed that he could show them the skin and the bones of the slain child, such proved futile, regardless of the number of times that they took him out of the prison for this purpose. They also confronted him many times with the apprehended Jews, though all in vain. [The magistrates considered all of the evidence and after three weeks released the Jews from prison. They then concluded:]

Gentlemen of Nijmegen: The city magistrates.

bailiff: The legal representative of a city or state.

... [T]hat in the present case the accuser is a proven liar, who provided false parents and birthplaces, who from his youth has been embittered towards his fellow Jews, and in his true birthplace of Prague escaped the scaffold, that he has scandalously mocked all religion, above all having been baptized many times ... now he is Protestant, now a Catholic, then again a Jew....

[Mauricius hopes that the attached **Remonstrations** will demonstrate not only the falsehood of these reports but also the impossibility of such accusations. His documents include various edicts from popes and kings against the blood libel, the testimony of Jewish converts to Protestantism,

Remonstrations: Legal documents based on testimony against a criminal charge.

and even the deposition of an Amsterdam physician affirming that no infant could produce the amount of blood that Saxel had claimed.]

So the complainants have, in order to erase this undeserved blame, as well as out of love for the justices, brought this action forward to inform your Noble and Honourable Gentlemen, as it is by no means finished. It is instead so far from true, that the killing or the shedding of Christian blood should conform to their religion; instead, they [the Jews] regard such as an abomination, and as completely contrary to their religion. For how mightily the Old Testament forbids the killing or shedding of human blood is well known to your Noble and Honourable Gentlemen....

And that the killing or shedding of Christian blood is not only contrary to their religion, but also that the accusations over facts of a similar nature, mentioned by some histories, especially among the papists, were falsely made up out of hatred toward Judaism, just as in previous and ancient times the Christians were not exempt from similar calumny....

It appears that this accuser, Isaak Saxel, has already been punished with the scaffold and imprisonment at Prague for his bad behavior. It appears that to win his release from prison, he adopted the Catholic faith, and accordingly received baptism. Then this novice again deviously, on account of his inward and mortal hatred toward the Jews of Prague, began to express these same questions, so that, were it possible, to cause undesirable effects. It went so far that this same person was forbidden to come into the **Jewish street**. He thus left the city of Prague, and in a state of desperation, the accuser approached the Count of Colverade in Bohemia, requesting to be baptized in the Christian Religion [i.e., **Reformed**], but once this was done, he ran away again....

Jewish street: Jews typically lived in particular quarters and streets of a European city; in some cities this was formalized into a ghetto.

Reformed: The variation of Protestantism that followed the theology of the Genevan Reformer John Calvin, rather than Luther, and which became the public church of the Dutch Republic.

Roman: Roman Catholic.

[Mauricius tracks Saxel's peregrinations across Germany into Cleves, where he was baptized again, then to Cranenburg where he converted to Catholicism.]

[I]n these various places he gave himself out to be a Jew, needing to be baptized, then next a **Roman**, then again into the Reformed Religion, making it clear as day, that the same person has pursued an abandoned and god-neglecting life, shamelessly reviling the Christian as well as the Jewish religion. Thus, the same person has no religion, showing not a hint of remorse of conscience....

On the contrary, one must necessarily conclude that the entire accusation has arisen purely from a bitter hatred toward Judaism....

[Mauricius then proves that much of Saxel's testimony was filled with falsehoods, for example:] the same [Saxel] claimed that the pretended slain Christian child was circumcised by a rabbi of Cleves. Now, it is, on the contrary, true and certain, that during the Day of Atonement in 1710, the circumcizer of Cleves was not at Nijmegen, but [was there] a full ten days prior and thereafter was away from Cleves, and thus it is impossible that this same person could have been present at the supposed event.

Further, it is pure madness to believe that a Christian child would be circumcised, for this is only for a Jew. So now the Jews, as this calumniator claims, had need of Christian blood, how would they be able to distinguish the blood of a circumcised child as Christian blood?

... Finally, ... this individual is nothing other than a false and godless accuser.

DOCUMENT 12

Image: *The Judensau*, from Eighteenth-Century Frankfurt[25]

witch-hunts: Across Europe thousands of women and men were accused, tried, and executed for practicing harmful magic (witchcraft) and worshipping the devil between the 1420s and 1755.

Torah: The first five books of the Hebrew Scripture, which set down the laws required of Jews.

The images of ritual murder in Documents 3 and 6 above were further developed in late-medieval and Reformation Germany, but now with diabolical elements associated with the ongoing **witch-hunts**. This particular image is based on a 1475 painting on a Frankfurt am Main bridge. In this eighteenth-century version, we see Simon of Trent at the top, and Jews suckling from a swine (an ironical association with Jews who were forbidden in the **Torah** to consume pork). Here too is an allusion to the obscene kiss, the sealing of the devil's pact by witches on the anus of the devil who took the form of an animal, as well as an implication that the Jewish woman has a goat familiar (the devil in the form of an animal). Note too the horned devil. This fusion of images from witches onto Jews had happened in reverse in the fifteenth century when fears of Jewish ritual murder and host desecration were added to the accusations against witches. Several different versions of this image are extant. It is important to note that such antisemitic images were contemporaneous with calls to consider Jews as citizens. This was debated during the French Revolution when in 1789 Abbé Jean-Siffrein Maury opposed expanding the rights of citizenship to Jews, although he conceded that they "should not be persecuted," for no "one can be disturbed for his religious opinions … Let them be protected therefore as individuals and not as Frenchmen for they cannot be citizens." He ultimately lost the debate, as France became the first country to initiate an emancipation of its Jewish population.[26]

---

25 Image of the Judensau from eighteenth-century Frankfurt. For more on this, see Lyndal Roper, *Witchcraze: Terror and Fantasy in Baroque Germany* (New Haven: Yale University Press, 2004), 76; and Gary K. Waite, *Heresy, Magic, and Witchcraft in Early Modern Europe* (Basingstoke, UK: Palgrave Macmillan, 2003), 19–33. For an alternative version, see https://www.britishmuseum.org/collection/object/P_1876-0510-518.

26 "Abbé Maury, speech of 23 December 1789," *The French Revolution and Human Rights: A Brief Documentary History*, trans. and ed. Lynn Hunt (Boston/New York: Bedford/St. Martin's, 1996), 88–89.

1475 am Grunen-Donnerstag war das kindlein Simon 2½ Iahr alt von den Iuden umbrac
Au Weyh Rabb Ansch au au mauschi au Weyh au au.

DOCUMENT 13

From Frederick Wilhelm III, King of Prussia, "Edict Concerning the Civil Status of the Jews in the Prussian State" (1812)[27]

Before the emancipation of German Jews, which accompanied national unification in 1871, each principality, kingdom, duchy, and state made its own rules about civil belonging. Here, Frederick Wilhelm III, King of the Protestant state of Prussia, distinguishes between legally protected propertied Jews, and merely tolerated Jews, many of whom were from the Polish lands.

We, Frederick Wilhelm [III], by Grace of God
King of Prussia etc. etc.,
having resolved to grant to the members of the Jewish faith in Our monarchy a new constitution suitable to the general welfare, declare all heretofore established laws and regulations for the Jews, unless confirmed in the current edict, to be abolished, and decree as follows:

§1. Jews and their dependents dwelling at present in Our States, provided with general privileges, patent letters of naturalization, letters of protection and concessions, are considered natives [Einländer] and as state citizens of Prussia.

§2. The maintenance of this designation as native and state citizen is allowed only under the following obligation:
that they bear strictly fixed surnames;
and
that they use German or another living language not only in keeping their commercial records but also in the drawing of contracts and legal declarations of intention; and they should use only German or Latin script for their signatures.

§3. Within six months of the publication date of this Edict, any individual protected or licensed Jew must declare to the authority at his place of residence the surname that he will bear permanently. He must identify

27 Gesetz-Sammlung für die Königlichen Preußischen Staaten 1812 (Berlin: Georg Decker, 1812), 17–22. Reprinted in Walter Demel and Uwe Puschner, eds., *Von der Französischen Revolution bis zum Wiener Kongreß 1789–1815* [*From the French Revolution to the Congress of Vienna, 1789–1815*], *Deutsche Geschichte in Quellen und Darstellung*, ed. Rainer A. Müller, vol. 6 (Stuttgart: P. Reclam, 1995), 211–16. Translated by Richard Levy for German Documents and Images.

himself by this name both in public proceedings and documents, as well as in ordinary life, just like any other citizen....

§7. ... Jews who qualify as natives shall enjoy the same civil rights and liberties as Christians.

§8. They may therefore hold any academic teaching and school posts, as well as municipal offices, for which they are qualified.

§9. We reserve the right, over the course of time, to determine by law the extent to which the Jews might be allowed to perform other public services and state functions.

§10. They are free to settle in cities as well as in the countryside.

§11. They may, like Christian inhabitants, acquire any sort of real estate and may also pursue any permitted trade, so long as they observe the general legal regulations.

§12. The right to freedom of trade that comes with state citizenship also pertains to commerce.

§13. Jews and their dependents living in the countryside may only pursue those branches of commerce permitted to the other [i.e., Christian] inhabitants.

§14. Native Jews, as such, will not be burdened with special taxes.

§15. They are, however, obliged to fulfill the same civil obligations and duties toward the state and their municipality as Christians and must bear the same [tax] burdens as other citizens, with the exception of payments for [Christian] ceremonial services.

§16. Native Jews are likewise subject to military conscription or to serving in the cantonal system and to all existing special legal regulations related thereto....

§17. Native Jews may marry each other without a special permit or the prior issuing of a general marriage certificate insofar as agreement or permission to marry is not required by the regulations of Others [other authorities] in the first place.

§18. This is also the case when a native Jew marries a foreign Jewess.

§19. Marrying a native Jewess does not confer upon a foreign Jew the right to settle in these states.

§20. The private legal relationships among Jews are to be adjudicated by the same laws and legal principles that pertain to other Prussian citizens....

§29. Regarding their jurisdictional status and the related matter of guardianship cases, there shall be no differences between Christians and Jews. The only exception remains Berlin, where Jews are assigned a special court of jurisdiction as ordered.

§30. In no case may rabbis or Jewish Elders arrogate to themselves either legal jurisdiction or the right to declare or administer legal guardianship.

§31. Foreign Jews are not allowed to settle in these states as long as they have not acquired Prussian citizenship....

§34. Foreign Jews may not serve as rabbis, church servants, or apprentices, nor may they be employed in workshops or as domestics. This, however, does not apply to those Jews already settled in Our states at the time of the publication of the present edict....

§36. Foreign Jews are permitted to enter the country for purposes of transit or the pursuit of sanctioned trade or commerce. Police officials will be provided with special instructions concerning the surveillance procedures to be followed with regard to this matter.

§37. On grounds of the general prohibition against peddling, police measures will also put an end [to the practice] among Jews....

Let all Our state officials and subjects observe the above rulings.

DOCUMENT 14

Image: Thomas Rowlandson, *Ladies Trading on Their Own Bottom* or *Solomon Enjoys Himself with Two Pretty Christian Girls* (1810)[28]

Thomas Rowlandson was a caricaturist who often used semi-pornographic images to provide political and social satire of Georgian England. This image works on the antisemitic stereotype that Jewish men are sexual predators, who seek Christian women for their pleasure. This prejudice conflicted with another set of falsehoods, which insisted that Jewish men were weak and effeminate, in contrast with stronger, more masculine Christian men.

LADIES TRADING ON THEIR OWN BOTTOM.

28 Thomas Rowlandson, *Ladies Trading on Their Own Bottom*, 5 October 1810, The Metropolitan Museum of Art, New York, Elisha Whittelsey Collection, Elisha Whittelsey Fund, 1959.

DOCUMENT 15

From Mary Antin, "A Little Jewish Girl in the Russian Pale" (1890)[29]

Mary Antin was born in Polotzk in the Pale of Settlement, the area of czarist Russia in which Jews were allowed to live. Even in the Pale, social, economic, and political life for Jews was very restricted, and marked with outbreaks of extreme violence. When Antin was 13, her family, like hundreds of thousands of others, left Russia and immigrated to America. Antin attended university and became a famous American author.

The Gentiles used to wonder at us because we cared so much about religious things about food and Sabbath and teaching the children Hebrew. They were angry with us for our obstinacy, as they called it, and mocked us and ridiculed the most sacred things. There were wise Gentiles who understood.... They were always respectful and openly admired some of our ways. But most of the Gentiles were ignorant. There was one thing, however, the Gentiles always understood, and that was money. They would take any kind of bribe, at any time. They expected it. Peace cost so much a year, in Polotzk. If you did not keep on good terms with your Gentile neighbors, they had a hundred ways of molesting you. If you chased their pigs when they came rooting up your garden, or objected to their children maltreating your children, they might complain against you to the police, stuffing their case with false accusations and false witnesses. If you had not made friends with the police, the case might go to court; and there you lost before the trial was called unless the judge had reason to befriend you.

The cheapest way to live in Polotzk was to pay as you went along. Even a little girl understood that. In your father's parlor hung a large colored portrait of **Alexander III**. The czar was a cruel tyrant—oh, it was whispered when doors were locked and shutters tightly barred, at night—he was a Titus, a Haman, a sworn foe of all Jews—and yet his portrait was seen in a place of honor in your father's house. You knew why. It looked well when police or government officers came on business.

Alexander III: Tsar of Russia, 1881–94, responsible for a sharp increase in antisemitic persecution and violence that resulted in organized massacres across the Russian Empire and led to emigration of millions of Jewish people out of Russia.

The czar was always sending us commands,—you shall not do this and you shall not do that,—till there was very little left that we might do, except pay tribute and die. One positive command he gave us: You shall love and honor your emperor. In every congregation a prayer must be said

29 Mary Antin, "A Little Jewish Girl in the Russian Pale," in *The World's Story: A History of the World in Story, Song and Art*, vol. 6, *Russia, Austria-Hungary, the Balkan States, and Turkey*, ed. Eva March Tappan (Boston: Houghton Mifflin, 1914), 243–47.

for the czar's health, or the chief of police would close the synagogue. On a royal birthday every house must fly a flag, or the owner would be dragged to a police station and be fined twenty-five rubles. A decrepit old woman, who lived all alone in a tumble-down shanty, supported by the charity of the neighborhood, crossed her paralyzed hands one day when flags were ordered up, and waited for her doom, because she had no flag. The vigilant policeman kicked the door open with his great boot, took the last pillow from the bed, sold it, and hoisted a flag above the rotten roof.

The czar always got his dues, no matter if it ruined a family. There was a poor locksmith who owed the czar three hundred rubles, because his brother had escaped from Russia before serving his time in the army. There was no such fine for Gentiles, only for Jews; and the whole family was liable. Now the locksmith never could have so much money, and he had no valuables to pawn. The police came and attached his household goods, everything he had, including his bride's trousseau; and the sale of the goods brought thirty-five rubles. After a year's time the police came again, looking for the balance of the czar's dues. They put their seal on everything they found....

Business really did not pay, when the price of goods was so swollen by taxes that the people could not buy. The only way to make business pay was to cheat—cheat the government of part of the duties. Playing tricks on the czar was dangerous, with so many spies watching his interests. People who sold cigarettes without the government seal got more gray hairs than banknotes out of their business. The constant risk, the worry, the dread of a police raid in the night, and the ruinous fines, in case of detection, left very little margin of profit or comfort to the dealer in contraband goods. "But what can one do?" the people said, with that shrug of the shoulders that expresses the helplessness of *the Pale*. "What can one do? One must live."

... Perhaps I should not have had so many foolish fancies if I had not been so idle. If they had let me go to school—but of course they didn't. There was one public school for boys, and one for girls, but Jewish children were admitted in limited numbers—only ten to a hundred; and even the lucky ones had their troubles. First, you had to have a tutor at home, who prepared you and talked all the time about the examination you would have to pass, till you were scared. You heard on all sides that the brightest Jewish children were turned down if the examining officers did not like the turn of their noses. You went up to be examined with the other Jewish children, your heart heavy about that matter of your nose. There was a special examination for the Jewish candidates, of course: a nine-year-old Jewish child had to answer questions that a thirteen-year-old Gentile was hardly expected to answer. But that did not matter so much; you had been prepared for the thirteen-year-old test. You found the questions quite easy. You wrote your answers triumphantly—and you received a low rating, and there was no appeal.

I used to stand in the doorway of my father's store munching an apple that did not taste good any more, and watch the pupils going home from school in twos and threes; the girls in neat brown dresses and black aprons and little stiff hats, the boys in trim uniforms with many buttons. They had ever so many books in the satchels on their backs. They would take them out at home, and read and write, and learn all sorts of interesting things. They looked to me like beings from another world than mine. But those whom I envied had their troubles, as I often heard. Their school life was one struggle against injustice from instructors, spiteful treatment from fellow students, and insults from everybody. They were rejected at the universities, where they were admitted in the ratio of three Jews to a hundred Gentiles, under the same debarring entrance conditions as at the high school: especially rigorous examinations, dishonest marking, or arbitrary rulings without disguise. No, the czar did not want us in the schools.

DOCUMENT 16

Images: Émile Courtet, *Jewish Virtues According to Gall's Method* (1893) and Photograph of Alfred Dreyfus (1894)[30]

In 1894, Captain Alfred Dreyfus, a young Alsatian French artillery officer of Jewish descent, was wrongfully accused of sharing military secrets with the German military and charged with treason. The resulting scandal (the Dreyfus Affair) divided society and illustrated the depth of antisemitism in the French Third Republic. This cartoon uses the imagery of phrenology (or Gall's method), a set of pseudo-scientific theories from the mid-nineteenth century that purported to tell a person's character by "reading" the shape of their head. Here, Courtet suggests the various unsavory aspects of Dreyfus' personality. Note the caricaturist also draws Dreyfus with a stereotypical "Jew nose," though Dreyfus looked very different in real life, as can be seen in the second image.

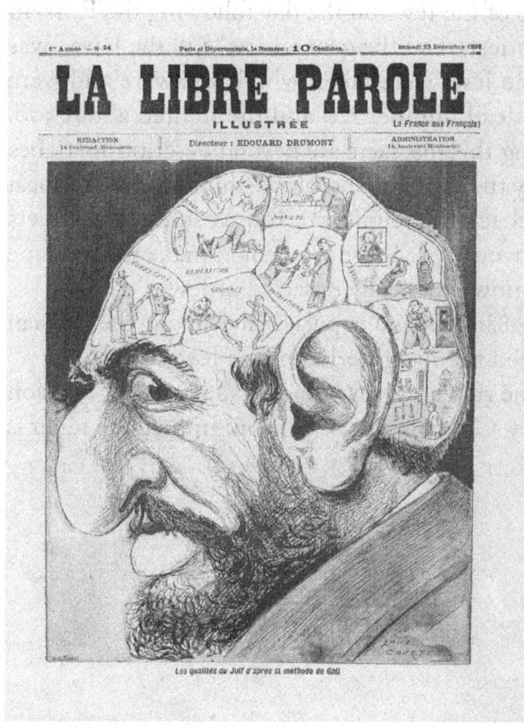

30 Photomechanical print on paper, Jewish Museum, New York, no. 1990-189; Aaron Gerschel photograph of Alfred Dreyfus, 1894.

DOCUMENT 17

"Jewish Massacre Denounced: East Side Mass Meeting Plans to Help the Victims of Russians in Kishinev" (1903)[31]

This American newspaper article describes the Kishinev pogrom of 1903. Part of a mass wave of violence that swept through the Russian Empire after the 1880s, the pogrom at Kishinev was inspired by false charges of child murder and blood libel and encouraged by local government officials, religious leaders, and newspaper editors. In retaliation, Christians beat, murdered, and raped their Jewish neighbors, while also destroying their homes, property, and businesses. This article illustrates part of the international outcry against pogrom violence in czarist Russia.

Bessarabia: A region inhabited by people for thousands of years and now situated in both Moldavia and Ukraine, Bessarabia became part of the Russian Empire following the Russo-Turkish War of 1806–12.

ST. PETERSBURG, April 25 (Taken across the border for transmission in order to escape the censor.)—The anti-Jewish riots in Kishinev, **Bessarabia**, are worse than the censor will permit to publish. There was a well-laid out plan for the general massacre of the Jews on the day following the Russian Easter. The mob was led by priests, and the general cry, "Kill the Jews," was taken up all over the city. The Jews were taken wholly unaware and were slaughtered like sheep. The dead number 120 and the injured about 500. The scenes of horror attending this massacre are beyond description. Babes were literally torn to pieces by the frenzied and blood-thirsty mob. The local police made no attempt to check the reign of terror. At sunset the streets were piled with corpses and wounded. Those who could make their escape fled in terror, and the city is now practically deserted of Jews.

Just as in the riots of 1880–1881 there is a popular belief among the Russian peasants that the Czar decreed the slaughtering of the Jews.

The immediate cause of the riot, however, is the ritual murder accusation against the Jews in Dubosary, Government of Kerson. Immediate relief is wanted....

31 "Jewish Massacre Denounced: East Side Mass Meeting Plans to Help the Victims of Russians in Kishinev," *New York Times*, 28 April 1903.

DOCUMENT 18

From Thomas Athol Joyce and Northcote W. Thomas, *Women of All Nations. A Record of Their Characteristics, Habits, Manners, Customs, and Influence* (1909)[32]

Antisemites, along with other racists, used gendered physical appearance to deride the objects of their study. Thomas Athol Joyce and Northcote W. Thomas were colleagues in the British Royal Anthropological Institute when they wrote this book comparing the appearance and behaviors of women from around the world. Using a mixture of cultural and physical anthropology, the authors suggest racial hierarchies of peoples, in which the Jews of the Ottoman Empire play an interesting role.

Judged by the same standard as the Mohammedan and Christian women, the native Jewish women have small pretension to good looks, even when young; but the national costume worn by those of the lower order in Smyrna might make even a beauty look plain. Besides the usual Turkish trousers, it consists of as many voluminous coats of different material and colour (and generally dirty) as can possibly be put on at the same time. The head-dress of the married women is a solid-looking bag of black silk or cloth, which entirely conceals what hair they have and hangs down the back and is surmounted by a ridiculous little cap that looks like a caricature of a Scotch "**Glengarry**." The old women are pitiful hags, and the custom of leaving exposed their brown and skinny bosoms adds the finishing touch to their gruesome aspect. The Jews are, in fact, the most abject and degraded race in Asia Minor and both men and women look so. At the same time, Jewish women have, among their own people, a higher status comparatively than Christian women have among theirs.

Glengarry: A man's cap, also called a Glengarry bonnet, now usually worn by people in Highland costume or as part of some military uniforms.

32 U.T. Athol Joyce and N.W. Thomas, *Women of All Nations. A Record of Their Characteristics, Habits, Manners, Customs, and Influence* (London: Cassell and Co., 1909).

DOCUMENT 19

Julius Streicher, "The Murderous People" (1934)[33]

The Nazi Party member Julius Streicher ran the publishing firm behind *Der Stürmer*, a newspaper that published vicious antisemitic propaganda during the Third Reich. In these excerpts, Streicher illustrates how the Nazi hatred of Jews was based on a combination of old and new prejudices. Below is Streicher's introduction to the special "Ritual Murder" edition, and a copy of the front page with illustration. Streicher was arrested by the US Army in May 1945 and tried by the International Military Tribunal at Nuremberg. He received the death penalty for his role in inciting hatred as part of the Final Solution.

... Anyone who knows about the monstrous accusations that have been leveled at the Jews from the beginning of time will see them in a different light and know they are not only a peculiar, strange-looking people, but also criminals, murderers, and devils in human form. Whoever knows about this will also be overcome with holy anger and hatred towards these people.

The Jews are under suspicion for murder. They are accused of luring non-Jewish children and adults, slaughtering them, and draining their blood. They are accused of baking this blood into their matzo (unleavened bread) and using it to perform superstitious magic. They are accused of terribly torturing their victims, especially the children, during which time they hurl curses, threats, and spells against Gentiles. This orchestrated murder has a name. It is called ritual murder.

The knowledge of Jewish ritual murder is already millennia old. It is as old as the Jews themselves. The Gentiles have passed it from generation to generation. It has been handed down through the Scriptures. The masses know about it, even those living in secluded rural villages. Our ancestors told their own children about ritual murder and this knowledge has been passed down through the generations to today.

Other nations also know about ritual murder. Wherever in the world a corpse is found bearing the marks of ritual murder, people immediately make this accusation, and they only make it against the Jews. Hundreds of other peoples, tribes and races inhabit this globe; however, no one accuses them of orchestrating the murder of children or thinks of calling them murderous people. This accusation is hurled only at the Jews and has been

---

33 Julius Streicher, "Das Mördervolk," *Der Stürmer: Deutsches Wochenblatt zum Kampfe um die Wahrheit* 12, no. 1 (May 1934): 1–2. Translated by Lisa Todd.

supported by many great men. Dr. Martin Luther wrote in his book, "The Jews and their Lies": "They stabbed and tore the body of Simon of Trent and murdered other children. The sun never shone on a more bloodthirsty people than the Jews, who want nothing more than to murder and strangle the heathen." And Jesus Christ, the mighty preacher of Nazareth, said to the Jews, "You are not the children of God, you are the children of the devil, he who has always been a murderer."

Preis 30 Pfennig

Ritualmord-Nummer

Der Stürmer

Deutsches Wochenblatt zum Kampfe um die Wahrheit

HERAUSGEBER: JULIUS STREICHER

Sonder-Nummer 1	Nürnberg, im Mai 1934	12. Jahr 1934

Jüdischer Mordplan

gegen die nichtjüdische Menschheit aufgedeckt

Das Mördervolk

Die Juden stehen in der ganzen Welt in einem furchtbaren Verdacht. Wer ihn nicht kennt, der kennt die Judenfrage nicht. Wer die Juden nur ansieht, wie Heinrich Heine (Chaim Bückeburg) sie beschreibt: „Ein Volk, das zu seinem Unterhalt mit Wechseln und alten Hosen handelt und dessen Uniform die langen Nasen sind," der ist auf falschem Wege. Wer aber weiß, welch eine ungeheuerliche Anklage schon seit Anbeginn gegen die Juden erhoben wird, dem erscheint dieses Volk in einem anderen Lichte. Er sieht in ihnen nicht nur ein eigenartiges, seltsam anmutendes Volk, er sieht in ihnen Verbrecher und Mörder und Teufel in Menschengestalt. Und es überkommt ihn gegen dieses Volk ein heiliger Zorn und Haß.

Der Verdacht, in dem die Juden stehen, ist der des Menschenmordes. Sie werden bezichtigt, nichtjüdische Kinder und nichtjüdische Erwachsene an sich zu locken, sie zu schlachten und ihnen das Blut abzuzapfen. Sie werden bezichtigt, dieses Blut in die Mazzen (ungesäuertes Brot) zu verbacken und auch sonstige abergläubische Zauberei damit zu treiben. Sie werden bezichtigt, ihre Opfer, besonders die Kinder, dabei furchtbar zu martern und zu foltern. Und während dieses Folterns Drohungen, Flüche und Verwünschungen gegen die Nichtjuden auszustoßen. Dieser planmäßig betriebene Menschenmord hat eine besondere Bezeichnung, er heißt

Ritualmord.

Das Wissen vom jüdischen Ritualmord ist schon Jahrtausende alt. Es ist so alt wie die Juden selbst. Die Nichtjuden haben es von Generation zu Generation übertragen. Es ist uns durch Schriften überliefert. Es ist aber auch in der breiten Volksmasse vorhanden. In den verstecktesten Bauerndörfern stößt man auf dieses Wissen. Der Ahne sprach von ihm zu seinem Enkel. Und dieser wieder trug es weiter auf Kinder und Kindeskinder. So vererbte es sich bis zum heutigen Tag.

Es ist auch in den anderen Völkern vorhanden. Wo irgendwo in der Welt eine Leiche gefunden wird, die die Anzeichen des Ritualmordes trägt, erhebt sich sofort laut und groß die Anklage. Sie richtet sich überall nur gegen die Juden. Hunderte und aberhunderte von Völkern, Stämmen und Rassen bewohnen den Erdball. Niemand denkt daran, sie des planmäßigen Kindermordes zu beschuldigen und sie als Mördervolk zu bezeichnen. Den Juden allein wird diese Anklage aus allen Völkern entgegengeschleudert. Und viele große Männer haben

Judenopfer

Durch die Jahrtausende vergoß der Jud, geheimem Ritus folgend, Menschenblut
Der Teufel sitzt uns heute noch im Nacken, es liegt an Euch die Teufelsbrut zu packen

Die Juden sind unser Unglück!

DOCUMENT 20

Images: Pages from the Children's Storybook *The Poisonous Mushroom* and the Board Game "Jews Out!" (1938)[34]

This 1938 children's storybook was published in Nazi Germany as part of a wide-ranging propaganda campaign against the Jewish population. The book contains several illustrated stories, each which uses longstanding antisemitic prejudices to teach about the "dangers" of German Jews. The final stories illustrate that only the Nazi Party had the answers to solving the Jewish Problem in Germany. The five illustrations reproduced here with their original captions give an idea of the tone and intent of the book.

Book Cover

34 Ernst Hiemer, *Der Giftpilz* (Nuremberg: Stürmerverlag, 1938); reprinted with translated captions at the German Propaganda Archive; Juden Raus! (board game) held at the Wiener Holocaust Library, London.

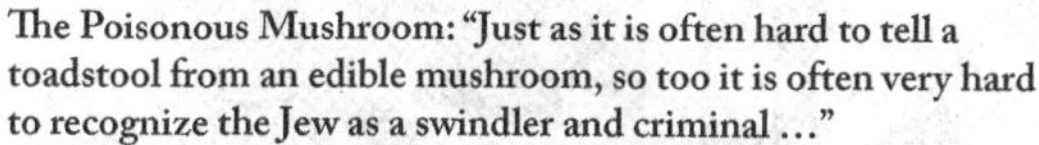

„Wie die Giftpilze oft schwer von den guten Pilzen zu unterscheiden sind, so ist es oft sehr schwer, die Juden als Gauner und Verbrecher zu erkennen ...“

The Poisonous Mushroom: “Just as it is often hard to tell a toadstool from an edible mushroom, so too it is often very hard to recognize the Jew as a swindler and criminal ...”

„Die Judennase ist an ihrer Spitze gebogen. Sie sieht aus wie ein Sechser ...“

How to Recognize a Jew: “The Jewish nose is bent. It looks like the number six ...”

„Hier, Kleiner, hast du etwas ganz Süßes! Aber dafür müßt ihr beide mit mir gehen ...“

The Experience of Hans and Else with a Strange Man: “Here, kid, I have some candy for you. But you have to come with me ...”

„Der Gott des Juden ist das Geld. Und um Geld zu verdienen, begeht er die größten Verbrechen. Er ruht nicht eher, bis er auf einem großen Geldsack sitzen kann, bis er zum König des Geldes geworden ist.“

Money is the God of the Jews: “The God of the Jews is money. To earn money, he commits the greatest crimes. He will not rest until he can sit on a huge money sack, until he has become the king of money.”

Like *The Poisonous Mushroom*, this board game in which players competed to see who could get the most Jews out of Germany and "off to Palestine," was marketed by a private company in Nazi Germany. It illustrates, in game form, the intense forced emigration program orchestrated by Hitler's government in the years before World War II. Indeed, between 1933 and 1939, nearly 300,000 of 503,000 Jewish people left Germany. The remaining men, women, and children were subjected to the murderous phase of the Nazi Final Solution. For more information on the Jewish head covering on this game piece, see Documents 3 and 6.

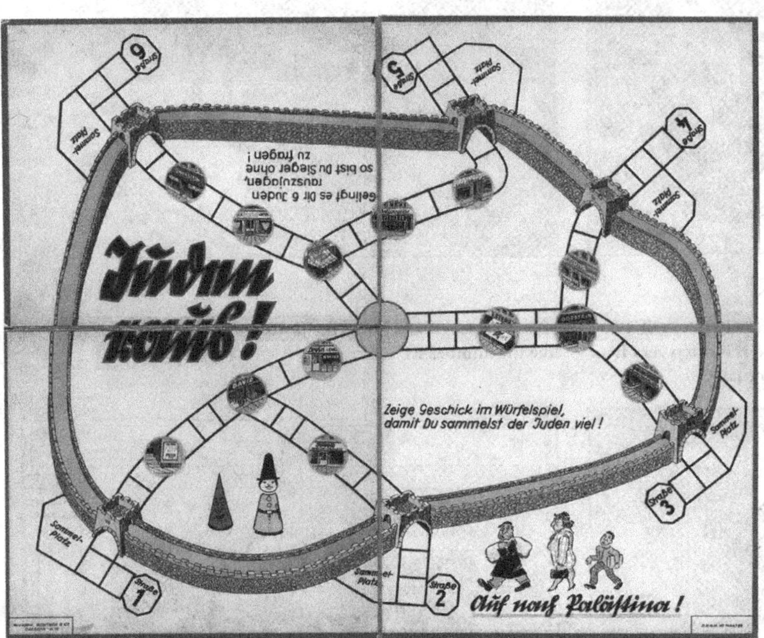

DOCUMENT 21

From Eta Fuchs Berk, *Chosen: A Holocaust Memoir* (1992)[35]

The Holocaust was a Nazi plan to murder Jewish men, women, and children across Europe. In Nazi rhetoric, they were presenting a "final solution" to the "Jewish Problem." Through legalized segregation, forced emigration, ghettoization, slave labor, starvation, physical violence, mass shootings, and gas chambers, Germans and their collaborators decimated the Jewish populations of Europe. Eta Fuchs Berk was 16 years old when Nazi forces entered her community in Hungary. This excerpt from her memoir recounts how she, her parents, her sister Liebe, and her three-year-old niece, Sossy, experienced their deportation to the death camp at Auschwitz-Birkenau. In 45 days in the summer of 1944, 434,351 Jews and thousands of Romani were deported by train to the camp. Berk was one of only a few thousand to survive. She immigrated to Canada after the war, and spent most of her life in Fredericton, New Brunswick.

Primo Levi said that most Holocaust stories begin with a train. The boxcars and cattle wagons bound for Auschwitz were places of fear and filth, causing shock and disorientation among the passengers and further reducing them to a confused and docile mass. Thus, the death trains not only transported the victims to the killing centres but provided the final conditioning for their arrival. I have seen the German photographs of the arrival at Auschwitz in late May 1944, of Jews from the Carpatho-Ruthenian region of Hungary. Their train could not have been more than a few weeks ahead of our own. The photographs show people ready for "selection" and "special handling." They appear stunned, exhausted, confused, yet relieved that their hard journey is over, and that they can at last see sunlight again and breathe the open air. No doubt we arrived in the same condition. We too thought that the worst was over. As our train passed slowly through the camp, we could see people outside, walking around, working, watching from a distance. "There is life here," one of us said. "At least everyone is still alive." This kind of wishful thinking came to an end in the "selections" at the railway camp.

Primo Levi: Italian Holocaust survivor and author of several books, including *Survival in Auschwitz* (1947/1958) and *The Drowned and the Saved* (1986).

The ritual of this "selection" process, of course, had a long history before I passed through it. After earlier experiments, the Nazis had smoothed out the procedures at the ramp, and by now the SS made their "selections"—dispatching prisoners to death or to labour—in assembly-line fashion. Thus,

35 Eta Fuchs Berk and Gilbert Allardyce, *Chosen: A Holocaust Memoir* (Fredericton, NB: Goose Lane Editions, 1992), 59–65.

in terms of the history of Auschwitz as a whole, we Hungarian Jews came at the end of the line, when the murderers were in high gear and the whole operation was simply murder incorporated. This was the Holocaust in final form, mass slaughter at the end of a history of trial and error. Jews didn't live long around here. Generally, four trains from Hungary arrived at the ramp every day, dumping out a total of some 12,000 to 14,000 Jews. Reports indicate that traffic was heavy, crematoria worked full blast, and warehouses were filled with the belongings of victims. The camp was so full of corpses that pits were dug to burn the bodies in the open. Braham estimates that, all told, almost 435,000 Hungarian Jews arrived at Auschwitz in this summer of 1944, and only about 40,000 came safely through the "selection" and escaped the gas. I was one of them. After this, in fact, I would survive "selection" after "selection" at Auschwitz, on and on, day in and day out. The SS search for the failing and "unfit" made "selections" a daily routine in the camp, and every morning I stood for hours under the eyes of doctors or nurses of some kind. But the first "selection" at the railway camp was the tragedy of my life.

There, when the doors of our boxcar were opened, the first men that we saw were dressed in striped prison clothes. These were camp workers, mostly Jews of Polish origin, whose task was to get us out of the train and form us into lines, separating men and women, along the ramp. Most worked in silence, but some of them whispered a message to us: give the babies and little children to your old people. My mother took Sossy from the arms of my sister Liebe. With this, an SS guard ordered Liebe and me to move away to another group of people lined up for "selection." But Liebe turned back to be with her child. We separated. Quickly my family was gone, lost from sight in the mass of old people and children. I imagined, of course, that they would reappear, that we would see each other again. However, I now know how things worked on the ramp. The young and healthy, those aged somewhere between their teens and up to fifty or so, passed through the "selections"; the others, children, the old, mothers with infants, the sick, these went directly to the gas chambers.

What a terrible thing. When I think of the Holocaust, of what it did to my life, I think most of these moments on the ramp. I have lived them over and over again in my mind. They were the beginning of a sadness in my life that never goes away. I keep seeing Sossy's face. I see Liebe turning back to be with her. I see my family in a crowd of bewildered people about to be murdered together. What a terrible thing was done to us at Auschwitz. What a terrible thing was done to the Jewish people. What terrible enemies we have.

DOCUMENT 22

From "Conversation with Shaul Ladany, an Olympian Who Survived the Holocaust and the Munich Massacre" (2020)[36]

Shaul Ladany was five years old when, in 1941, the German *Luftwaffe* bombed his family home in Belgrade. Ladany's parents hid him in a monastery, but he was captured by Nazi forces in 1944 and sent to the Bergen-Belsen concentration camp at the age of eight. He survived the war and emigrated to the new nation state of Israel in 1948. As a teenager, he took up marathon running and then race-walking, for which he qualified to compete at the 1972 Olympic Games in Munich. He wore a prominent Star of David on his jersey, "to show the Germans a Jew had survived." In this account, Ladany describes the attack on his team by members of the Black September faction of the **Palestine Liberation Organization**.

Palestine Liberation Organization: Founded in 1964, with the aim of ending the Israeli military occupation of the Palestinian Territories.

Most of the Israeli team stayed in 5 adjacent townhouse units at the Olympic village. Unit #1 housed the coaches, unit #2 housed me with 5 others, unit #3 housed another 6 athletes, unit #4 housed doctors, and unit #5 housed the chief of the delegation. I completed my race on September 3rd, and September 4th was a day off. In the early hours of September 5th, I was awakened by one of my housemates who told me that coach Moshe Weinberg from unit #1 was just shot and killed. Only a few hours earlier, Moshe asked me for an alarm clock so the team would be woken up early in the morning. Trying to see what was happening, I opened the front door of my unit for a peak outside and saw a few security guards talking to a man standing outside unit #1. I didn't know it at the time, but it was the start of the hostage situation, and the man was the terrorist ringleader. He refused to allow Red Cross aid to the wounded. A female security guard asked him "why should you be inhumane?," to which I heard him reply something like Jews or Israelis "are not humane either." At that point, I realized the danger. I put my training suit over my pajamas and was the last one to slip out from the terrace in the rear. Instead of just escaping, I went around the back to unit #5 to warn the delegation chief. In the end, I was lucky that the terrorists had raided units #1 and #3, but not #2 where I slept. It later turned out that the terrorists knew where each of the athletes was staying and my unit #2 housed two marksmen competitors and they didn't want to take the chance if the athletes had their rifles in the rooms.

36 "Conversation with Shaul Ladany, an Olympian Who Survived the Holocaust and Munich Massacre," *Sports History Weekly*, 12 July 2020.

Communist past: The Polish People's Republic was a one-party communist state in the Soviet-dominated Eastern Bloc from 1947 to 1989.

Solidarity movement: Founded at the Lenin Shipyard in Gdańsk in 1980, this trade union had more than ten million members by 1981 and ultimately played a prominent role in ending Soviet rule in 1989.

Tyminski: Stanisław Tymiński is a Polish-Canadian businessman who has run in elections in both Canada and Poland. In the 1990 Polish election, he promised to create wealth for everyone in the new capitalist state and sold himself as a Pole who had done well for himself abroad. He also carried around a briefcase that he said contained damaging evidence about his political opponents. He was a surprise second-place finisher in the first round of the presidential election.

Mazowiecki: In August 1989 Tadeusz Mazowiecki became the first non-Communist prime minister of Poland since 1946. He had previously been a well-respected political dissident and member of the Solidarity movement. Mazowiecki was a practicing Roman Catholic but faced rumors that he was Jewish, likely because some of his political advisors had Jewish parents.

Walesa: Lech Wałęsa is a Polish statesman and Nobel Prize laureate and was a prominent dissident, trade union activist, leader in the

DOCUMENT 23

"Anti-Semitism Continues to Mar Presidential Politics in Poland" (1990)[37]

In November 1990, following the collapse of the Soviet Union and decades of Communist rule, Poland held its first democratic presidential elections since 1926. Electoral rhetoric was influenced both by the recent **Communist past** and the anti-Communist **Solidarity movement** of the 1980s. Candidates also engaged in antisemitic rhetoric. As politicians once again used old stereotypes to smear their opponents, commentators wondered whether this wave of antisemitism was more indicative of a long history of prejudice in that country or was part of a more recent phenomenon of hatred against racialized others in the wake of the fall of the Berlin Wall.

Disturbing signs of anti-Semitism cropped up throughout Poland in the weeks preceding the country's first democratic presidential elections ever....

On Warsaw streets, vandals have taken to **Tyminski**'s posters. Green dollar signs obscure his eyes, and crude black letters mark words oft repeated in the campaign: "Juden raus!" (Jews out!)....

Most attribute Tyminski's political success to his personal fortune, which is attractive to many in this impoverished country. Others suggest that his victory stems from the widespread charges that **Mazowiecki** is of Jewish origin.

Mazowiecki, a former adviser to **Walesa** and Poland's first non-communist leader since the war, is, in fact, a devout Catholic. Nevertheless, the prime minister was dogged in his campaign by accusations that he and a "Jewish cabal" were running the country.

"There's no question anti-Semitism hurt us," said Piotr Rachtan, Mazowiecki's media spokesman. "These suspicions and fears represent a black hole. It is frightening."

Popular expressions of anti-Semitism, as well as obsessive curiosity about the origins of public figures, are a bizarre phenomenon in Poland, where only 10,000 people out of a population of 38 million are Jewish.

Before World War II, Poland was home to the world's largest Jewish population, numbering 3 million, or about 10 percent of the country. Only a few thousand survived the war, and most emigrated after

37 "Anti-Semitism Continues to Mar Presidential Politics in Poland," *Jewish Telegraphic Agency*, 4 December 1990.

government-sponsored anti-Semitic purges in 1968. The average age among those who stayed is 70.

Unlike the Soviet Union, where anti-Jewish groups harass a small but visible minority, the discussion of "who is a Jew" in Poland seems far removed from reality. For many Poles, images of Jews evoke shady characters who serve as scapegoats in hard times.

"Walesa is the only man who can lead our country," a Warsaw cab driver who refused to give his name said on the night of the first round of elections. "Mazowiecki is a Jew, and everyone knows that Jews are bad for Poland. All they ever want is money."

Indeed, the whole campaign took on ugly overtones. Last summer, Walesa said often that Jews in politics were hiding their origins, a comment that to many smacked of a "Jewish conspiracy" theory.

Asked by reporters whether Mazowiecki's supporters were mostly Jewish, Walesa replied: "Jews are great patriots, have done a lot for culture, but when they hide their nationality, they provoke attitudes of anti-Semitism.

"Why aren't Jews proud of the fact they're Jewish? I'm proud of the fact that I'm Polish and similarly would have been proud of my origin if I had been Jewish," Walesa said, according to a transcript provided by the Polish Press Agency.

Walesa later told the *New York Times* that his remarks were intended to squelch anti-Semitism, not inject it into the campaign. "I want the people of Jewish origin to be proud of their origin, and they are never satisfied, they never believe me."

Last week, however, Walesa expressed regret for his comment, saying he had misspoken. At a heated gathering of the divided Solidarity movement's former leaders—who were meeting to marshal forces behind Walesa for Sunday's second round—Walesa acknowledged that his remark was made "without foresight."

"I said this indeed. Out of 1,000 answers, one was bad," Walesa said. "But why can't you see my 999 correct ones?"

Many prominent Jews here do not believe Walesa is an anti-Semite. "I can tell you honestly, after many years of knowing him, that he is not," said Marianowicz, the writer.

But whatever the case, it seems his comments have taken root.

Solidarity movement, and to many, a national hero. He won the first round of voting in November 1990, but did not receive over 50 percent of the vote, as was needed for victory. In the second round, Wałęsa defeated Tyminski, and was president of Poland from 1990 to 1995.

PART 2

Racism against Muslim Peoples

INTRODUCTION

Islam was founded as the third major **monotheism** in the Middle East (after Judaism and Christianity) in the early seventh century CE by the Arabian merchant Muhammad (c. 570–632), who experienced a series of revelations from God (Allah) transmitted to him by the **archangel Gabriel** near Mecca. Convinced that he was the final prophet of the one true God, after Moses and Jesus, Muhammad began preaching to his fellow Meccans. While some converted, the elites resisted, and in 622 Muhammad and his followers were forced to move to Medina, where they received a much warmer welcome. By 629 Muhammad's forces had defeated all resistance, and Mecca was in their hands. By the Prophet's death in 632, all of Arabia had adopted the new faith, called Islam. Within decades the Prophet's successors had spread Islam across the Middle East, Persia, and North Africa, challenging Christian Western Europe and **Byzantium**. The result was over three centuries of **crusade** and conflict, but also in some places, such as the Middle East, Spain, and Southern Italy, a great deal of cultural interaction. Much of Spain in the Middle Ages was ruled by Muslim princes who followed the **dhimmi policy** of the Qur'an that allowed Christians and Jews to practice their faith if they paid extra taxes. It was only after three centuries of crusading (Reconquista) that the Christian princes King Ferdinand and Queen Isabella finally conquered the last European Muslim stronghold, Granada, in 1492. This was, incidentally, the same year they sponsored Christopher Columbus's voyage westward, leading to the conquest of the New World, and when they expelled all remaining Jews from Spain.

monotheism: A religion that believes in only one true God: the first was Judaism; Christianity and Islam are also monotheisms.

archangel Gabriel: A supernatural agent of God who delivered messages to humans in the Hebrew, Christian, and Muslim scriptures.

Byzantium: The Eastern Roman Empire with its capital of Constantinople (Istanbul); it was a Christian (Greek Orthodox) state that survived until its capture by the Ottomans in 1453.

crusade: A holy war proclaimed by the Catholic popes against unbelievers.

dhimmi policy: Policy relating to non-Muslim residents of Islamic territories.

Medieval European attitudes toward Muslims diverged in important ways from those directed at Jews. For one thing, most Christian Europeans had extremely limited contact with Muslims. For another, there were major principalities, including Granada in Spain, North Africa, and the Ottoman Empire to the East, which were governed by Muslim rulers. Europeans thus looked at Islam as a political and military competitor and threat, as well as a major religious rival. Yet, both Islam and Judaism presented the same potential threat to Christians: that of conversion, which gave the lie to the assumption that Christian Europeans had the superior or ultimate faith, that their version of god was the final one. Christian writers were therefore deeply concerned about the fact that far more Christians were converting to Islam—"turning Turke"—than the other way around; and much the same could be said about Judaism. Christian polemicists thus worked hard to discredit Islam, typically by telling malicious myths about Prophet Muhammad, and by implication they also sought to undercut the appeal of Judaism. The stories told by European Christian writers about Muhammad being influenced in the development of his new faith by some Jews was thus a strategy to demonize both faiths by association with each other (see Document 28).[1]

As can be seen in this part's documents, the practice of slandering the Prophet to discredit his movement continued through the early modern and modern eras. During the **Reformation**, the Ottoman military laid siege to Vienna twice, intensifying European anxiety that the **Turks** would conquer Christianity as a form of divine punishment. As Ottoman power weakened by the end of the seventeenth century, such fears dissipated. Even so, many Europeans captured on the Mediterranean by Muslim **corsairs** converted to Islam for what they hoped would be better treatment as an enslaved person, or out of sincere religious conviction. These converts were called Renegades or Renegados, and as **apostates** were liable to summary execution if captured by Christian sailors.[2] Such apostates challenged European notions of superiority well into the eighteenth century, when Enlightenment thinkers began to write about comparative religious movements around the world. The epitome of this was the *Religious Ceremonies and Customs of All the Peoples of the World*, an extraordinary collaborative work of nine volumes written by Jean Frédéric Bernard, a French bookseller in Amsterdam, and illustrated by Bernard Picart (1723–43).[3] Their portrayal of Judaism, Islam, various Christian sects, and other religions, such as Hinduism and Buddhism, was far less polemical than previous works, such as Hazart's (Document 32). This shift in attitude was made possible by growing contact with other cultures, although that could have deeply negative effects as witnessed by European colonization and exploitation of Indigenous populations, an activity that affected local Muslim peoples as well.

European imperialism had a major impact on Christian–Muslim relations. For instance, France invaded the city of Algiers in 1830 and occupied the

Reformation: The sixteenth-century movement of religious reform that divided Christendom into warring religious camps, in particular Catholicism, Lutheranism, and Calvinism.

Turks: Originally a nomadic people of the Eurasia Steppes who converted to Islam and created the powerful Ottoman Empire, a rival to the Byzantine and European states.

corsairs: Nimble, armed sailing vessels commanded by Muslim captains with often captive sailors. They hounded European shipping in the Mediterranean.

apostates: Those who leave their original religion for another; a capital offense in both Christian and Muslim states.

---

1 For further reading, see Waite, *Jews and Muslims*; Matthew Dimmock, *Mythologies of the Prophet Muhammad in Early Modern English Culture* (Cambridge: Cambridge University Press, 2013); Daniel Vitkus, *Turning Turk: English Theater and the Multicultural Mediterranean, 1570–1630* (Basingstoke, UK: Palgrave, 2003); and Nabil I. Matar, *Turks, Moors, and Englishmen in the Age of Discovery* (New York: Columbia University Press, 1999).

2 See Daniel J. Vitkus, ed., introduction by Nabil Matar, *Piracy, Slavery, and Redemption: Barbary Captivity Narratives from Early Modern England* (New York: Columbia University Press, 2001).

3 Lynn Hunt, Margaret Jacob, and Wijnand Mijnhardt, *The Book That Changed Europe: Picart and Bernard's "Religious Ceremonies of the World"* (Cambridge, MA: Harvard University Press, 2010).

country of Algeria for the next 132 years. Successive French governments put in place policies and laws aimed at controlling the territory, extracting valuable resources, imposing a racialized hierarchy on civil society, and violently reacting to those civilians who did not acquiesce to French colonial rule. Bureaucrats, educators, religious leaders, and others pursued a policy of de-Islamization that demanded Algerians denounce their religion in exchange for French citizenship. Christian ministers saw a "civilizing mission" as their responsibility, claiming the necessity of "raising up" colonial subjects around the globe. In their reasoning, the modernity of the West should be used to reform the traditional nature of the East. As part of this project, European imperialists, themselves part of deeply patriarchal societies, cited examples of veiling, child-marriage, widow immolation and seclusion, as evidence for the need to "save" Muslim women from repressive male-dominated societies. Authors wrote of Arabs as "a civilized people asleep," and of the necessity of their "moral recovery." At the same time, European travelers exoticized, and sometimes sexualized, aspects of Arab culture, including the veiled woman and the harem (see Document 36).

In Europe, the growth of Muslim communities was sometimes led by Christians who converted to the Islamic faith. Abdullah Quilliam (born William Henry) was born into a Methodist family but converted after an 1887 trip to Morocco, where he was struck by the Muslim focus on community and moral living, in contrast to what he saw as Christianity's failure to deal with the problems of Victorian society. Quilliam opened London's first mosque two years later, a site which served as a community religious site. Forty years later, Marmaduke Pickthall, another convert, completed the first English translation, by a believer, of the Qur'an.[4] In the city of Sarajevo, Muslim civil and religious communities existed alongside those of Catholics, **Orthodox Serbs**, and **Sephardic Jews**. Founded by the Ottomans in 1463 as a great Muslim city on the edge of Christian Europe, by the nineteenth century the regional council displayed political pluralism by guaranteed seats for each of these four groups. That status would change after the founding of the new state of Yugoslavia in 1919, when the new capital at Belgrade increasingly privileged Serbian voices within the government.[5] During the interwar period, hundreds of thousands of Muslim workers, students, and soldiers arrived in Europe, prompting new conversations on integration, community-building, and civil rights. When the Great Depression hit the Netherlands and the Dutch East Indies, for instance, many Indonesian migrant and domestic workers were deemed

Orthodox Serbs: Serbian members of the Eastern Orthodox Church, the world's second largest Christian denomination.

Sephardic Jews: A diasporic population who left Spain after 1492.

4 "The British Victorians Who Became Muslims," BBC News, 18 May 2019, https://www.bbc.com/news/uk-england-48069763.

5 Emily Greble, *Sarajevo, 1941–1945: Muslims, Christians, and Jews in Hitler's Europe* (Ithaca, NY: Cornell University Press, 2011).

ineligible for government benefits and were supported instead by Islamic community associations.[6] The growth of civil organizations, some of which also engaged in anti-colonialist activism led to European-wide organizing, such as the first European Muslim Congress meeting in Geneva in 1935.

European Muslim populations continued to play direct roles in European society into the twentieth century. When 80,000 Moroccans fought during the Spanish Civil War, Nationalist forces, including Francisco Franco, claimed a religious alliance between Muslim and Christian soldiers against their common atheist, Marxist enemy. Franco styled himself as a protector of Islam in Spain, and even ordered navy ships to transport Muslim soldiers to pilgrimage in Mecca in 1937. A 1940 paper stated, "below the rugged crust of these simple and brave Moroccan soldiers, beats a heart that is identical to the Spanish, which renders reverence to some other-worldly ideals, not very dissimilar to ours, and which feels the religious emotions which we feel, because it follows many of the Christian dogmas which we follow, and which atheist Marxism repudiates and persecutes."[7]

Thirty years later, and during a period of decolonization in Africa and Asia, Europeans continued to question issues of Muslim integration in Europe, even as they sought to hold power around the globe. As a response to the Algerian Revolution, French forces deployed military repression, bodily torture, and collective punishment to battle freedom fighters in Algeria and France (see Document 40). By July 1962, more than 1.5 million Algerian women, men and children were dead. The Algerian intellectual and novelist Mouloud Feraoun pointed to the hypocrisy of French writers who celebrated French World War II resistance fighters and Hungarians standing up to Russian occupation, but failed to see a parallel between these groups and Algerian "rebels": "Here I tell myself that in all these texts that the press publishes, each time the word Hungary is used, it could be replaced—without exaggeration—with the word Algeria, and yet it never is. Is it because the world that sees us suffer is not convinced that we are humans? It is true that we are only Muslims. That may be our unforgivable crime...."[8] Algerian communities continued to grow in France, increasing from 130,000 in 1930 to 600,000 in 1965, to 800,000 in 1983, with thousands more people emigrating

---

6 Klaas Stuje, "Indonesian Islam in Interwar Europe: Muslim Organizations in the Netherlands and Beyond," in *Muslims in Interwar Europe: A Transcultural Historical Perspective*, ed. Bekim Agai, Umar Ryad, and Mehdi Sajid (Edinburgh: Edinburgh University Press, 2017), 125–50.

7 Miguel Asín Palacios, as quoted in Ali Al Tuma, "Moros y Cristianos: Religious Aspects of the Participation of Moroccan Soldiers in the Spanish Civil War (1936–1939)," in *Muslims in Interwar Europe*, 156.

8 Mouloud Feraoun, *Journal 1955–1962: Reflections on the French-Algerian War*, trans. Mary Ellen Wolf and Claude Fouillade, ed. James le Sueuer (Lincoln, NE: University of Nebraska Press, 2000), 153.

from Morocco and Tunisia.[9] As part of West Germany's postwar "economic miracle," that government recruited guest workers from countries such as Italy, Spain, Greece, and Yugoslavia. Over the following decades, the largest number of workers arrived from Turkey. Many of these temporary workers decided to remain, and they formed the genesis of today's Turkish-German community. These largely Muslim families faced many forms of persecution in the postwar period, including forced health exams, segregated housing, and accusations of miscegenation as commentators used them as examples of the failure of integration and to question the viability of multicultural societies. Others have wondered about the compatibility of Islam with Christian values (see Document 41). In response to xenophobic attacks against her community, the young poet Semra Ertan, author of "My Name Is Foreigner," took her own life in a public act of self-immolation in 1982.

Muslims, in all their diversity, are currently the largest non-Christian minority group in Europe. In many ways, Muslims have become the stereotypical non-Europeans in Europe, whether the South Asian in Britain, the Turk in Germany, or the Arab in France. The difference, many scholars argue, is that Europe has a much longer history of Islamophobia on which to build, and as this volume seeks to illustrate.[10] The 9/11 attacks on the World Trade Center in New York City in 2001, the 2004 attacks in Spain, and the 2005 London Tube attacks have only intensified and radicalized anti-Muslim sentiment around the world. Now, and as states gave their police and security forces increased powers of surveillance and arrest, it became increasingly common for some Europeans to equate "Muslims" with "terrorists." The equating of Muslims with a security threat has lent fervor to right-wing rhetoric accusations of an unwanted Islamization of Europe, even as human rights organizations decry the rise in societal Islamophobia (see Documents 44, 45, 46).

---

9 Maud S. Mandel, *Muslims and Jews in France: History of a Conflict* (Princeton, NJ: Princeton University Press, 2014).

10 H.A. Hellyer, *Muslims of Europe: The "Other" Europeans* (Edinburgh: Edinburgh University Press, 2009), 2.

DOCUMENT 24

A Spanish Muslim, Ibn Ḥawqal, Comments on Sexual Relations between Muslim Men and Christian Women (10th century)[11]

Fatimid: A Muslim Shi'a Caliphate (political-religious state), which spread across North Africa with connections to Spain from the tenth through the twelfth centuries. Named after Muhammad's daughter Fatima.

Ibn Ḥawqal was originally from Southern Turkey, and served the **Fatimid** Muslims of North Africa, traveling extensively for them. He resided for a time in al-Andalus, the Arabic name for Spain, ruled by Muslims but with a large Christian population, as well as a significant Jewish minority. Here he writes about intermarriage between Muslim men and Christian women in al-Andalus.

mušaʿmiḏūn: Presumably Muslims.

alms: All Muslims are expected to pay alms to support the poor.

pilgrimage: Muslims are expected to perform the Haj, the pilgrimage to Mecca once in their lifetime.

Ramaḍān: The Muslim holy month when all Muslims must fast and pray from sun-up to sun-down; held in the ninth month of the Muslim calendar.

Most inhabitants of their fortresses, rural areas, and villages are **mušaʿmiḏūn**. I have seen that they enter into marriage with Christian women, which leads to the boys being assigned to their fathers as al-mušaʿmiḏūn and the girls becoming Christian women with their mothers. They do not pray, they do not perform acts of ritual purification, they do not give **alms**, and they do not go on **pilgrimage**. Some of them fast in the month **Ramaḍān** and thus achieve purification after great ritual impurity (al-ǧanāba). This [practice] is a curiosity they do not share with anyone else in the world, and with this trait they have won the trophy in the race of stupidity.

11 Ibn Ḥawqal, *Kitāb ṣūrat al-arḍ* (*Book of the Picture of the Earth*), produced in Germany in 1938 and translated into German in the Transmediterrane Geschichte (Trans-Mediterranean History) website project of the University of Constance. Translated from the German by Gary Waite.

DOCUMENT 25

Anonymous, *Here after Follows a Little Treatise against Mahumet and His Cursed Sect* (1530)[12]

This work was printed in London in 1530 and, based on the references within it to the pope and the **relics of saints**, likely originated from the continent before the Reformation. While little is known of Muhammad's life, most of the stories here are false. This account provides us with a window into late medieval attitudes toward Islam on the eve of the Reformation.

And for as much as by the falsehood and craft of a cursed man that was called **Mahumet** and by occasion of a false law that he and his disciples craftily imagined and feigned, more people have been deceived and more souls damned than ever have been by any **heretic** or cursed man since his time, and as some men have supposed more than have been deceived by all other heretics since the **passion of our Lord** unto this day: and yet the said falsehood and false law continues to this day as is openly known, so that many daily perish thereby. Therefore in this little treatise I have first shown the birth and some part of the wretched life of the said Mahumet that was the first beginner of that cursed law and after I have shown some of the contrary cited falsehood and open lies that be contained in the said law.... And I have thus set it in English to the intent that every man that can read English may the more lightly perceive the falseness of the said law, and finally to abhor it and despise it, and the rather to pray to our Lord that it may shortly come to an end....

[B]ut because he [Muhammed] could not lightly bring that about specially for that he had yet but few helpers and was but of **a low blood**, he used all the craft that he could, and dissimulated him self to be the prophet and messenger of god, trusting thereby in the end to obtain the dignity of a king. And when he had in this manner falsely taken upon him the name of a prophet he got unto him rude people that lightly might be deceived, ... and of them he sent vagabonds, murderers, and thieves, to lie by woods and hills to rob all that came that way, and he himself in the beginning of his prophecy came on a time to the city of Mecca and took away a poor man's camel, and under that manner he began his holy sect when he was about the age of 42 years. And there the people of Mecca perceiving his falsehood with great hatred and malice persecuted him, and so he went from thence

relics of saints: The physical remains of Christians identified by the Catholic Church as particularly holy and declared to be saints. At death they ascended to heaven, leaving their bodies behind as points of contact with believers.

Mahumet: The Prophet Muhammad's name was spelled a wide variety of ways; this was a popular variation.

heretic: Term used by the Catholic Church to identify those who dissented from approved doctrine.

passion of our Lord: The suffering and death of Jesus c. 33 CE on a wooden cross in Roman-controlled Palestine.

a low blood: Low born, or of ordinary lineage.

12 *Here after Followeth a Lytell Treatyse agaynst Mahumet and his Cursed Secte* ... (London, c. 1530), fols. Aiv–Axxiir. See Waite, *Jews and Muslims*, 83–84.

and came to an old city that was nigh destroyed ... and therefore he caused an old Jew to be strangled in his bed because he said he had rebuked him. How may it be therefore true that he wrote of himself that he was sent with mercy and pity that used nothing but fierceness and cruelty against the people....

But certain it is that he that denies the passion of Christ as this cursed heretic Mahumet does, denies all the mysteries of the church that take their effect of the said passion of our lord, and in that saying he agrees with the heretics that be called **Donatus** and he says further that **the devils may be saved** by the **Alcoran**, and that many of them when they heard it were glad and were made **Saracens** ... But if Mahumet had said that many Saracens were devils and himself also, I suppose he had said truth....

And thy cursed man Mahumet was so beastly and so wretched that he was not ashamed to say and to write it as a law that it is lawful for to use other men's wives indifferently as their own, wherein he follows the heretics that be called **Nicolatians**, and finally all his intent was to cut away all that was hard to believe and hard to do, and granted all that the people were ready and prone to use and endeavoured him to blind them with worldly delights and that might he anon do, especially the Arabs that much delight in gluttony, theft, and intemperance....

When the said cursed prophet Mahumet with his diabolical laws had perverted more people than ever did any other heretic before him, and also more than ever any holy man had converted, at the last he fell sick of the great disease and grievous sickness called **Epilepsia passio**, ... whereupon he fell many times and beat his head to the ground and lay foaming and spitting that it was an abominable sight to see.... He said therefore that many times the angel **Gabriel** came unto him and instructed him in many things, and that as often as he saw his clearness he might not bear it but as a carnal and a mortal man fainted and failed.... and the seventh day after the sickness took him again and therewith he yielded up his wretched spirit anon to be taken to the fiends of hell and forthwith his belly swelled and his little finger crooked together. And he died the Monday that was the 7th day of the first moon which among the Saracens is called **Rabeg** in the year of his age 63 ... in his life he commanded his disciples and friends that they should not bury him forthwith as he was dead, for he said that upon the **third day** after he should be taken into heaven, and so when he was dead they obeying his commandment, suffered him to lie still, ... 7 days to see when he should be taken in to heaven. And at the last they were weary with keeping of him, and perceiving in him nothing but an intolerable stink that daily increased in him, at the last with great indignation they threw his wretched body naked without any honour into the ground. This was the miserable end of Mahumet.

Donatus: Donatus Magnus (d. 355), leader of a North African Christian group who insisted on rebaptizing Christians who had apostacized to avoid persecution and now wanted to return.

the devils may be saved: The belief that at the Last Judgment God's forgiveness would extend even to demons. Traditional Christian teaching had sinners and demons suffering eternally in hell.

Alcoran: The Muslim scriptures, the Qur'an.

Saracens: A Western term for the Arabs of the Middle East.

Nicolatians: An alleged ancient heresy which denied the divinity of Jesus.

Epilepsia passio: Epilepsy, or the "falling sickness"; something Christian writers claimed Muhammad suffered from.

Gabriel: A leading angel (archangel) who spoke with Muhammad, as well as in Christian teaching announcing to the Virgin Mary that she would bear God's son.

Rabeg: The Prophet died 8 June 632; in the lunar Islamic calendar, twelfth day of Rabi-al-Awwal.

third day: In Christian teaching Jesus Christ rose from the dead on the third day.

And when he was soon dead all the people perceiving his falsehood, and seeing all that he had said proved untrue, returned again every man to the sect that they held before, except a few that were his kinsmen which trusted to succeed him in the kingdom. Among whom there was one that was most subtle and crafty in wit before all the other[s] that was called **Ebubeer** which after obtained the kingdom ... by all the ways that he could studied to bring them again to the law of Mahumet that were gone from it. And some he brought again for fear of pain, some for honour and some for rewards. But all that came, came under dissimulation, for none believed in Mahumet in their hearts.... [H]e made to Mahumet a precious temple in Mecca and the tomb wherein the bones of Mahumet should be lain he made to be set about with iron and set secretly **Adamites** in the higher part of the temple, and soon when the tomb was brought into the temple it was by the virtue of the said Adamant stones drawn up from the ground by little and by little as the property of the stones to do. Wherewith the people were soon deluded and deceived that they believed that the body for his holiness was soon lifted up into the air, and yet they abide in that error, and so they walk all in darkness and at the last shall be cast into the outward darkness in hell, but they forsake their error there to be always with their cursed prophet Mahumet.

Ebubeer: In Sunni tradition Muhammad's immediate successor as caliph was his friend Abu Bakr.

Adamites: Magnets. This became a very popular story among Christian writers, even though there is no evidence for it.

Sultan Suleiman: Sultan Suleiman the Lawgiver (the Magnificent) ruled the Ottoman Empire from 1520 to his death in 1566.

Buda: Modern-day Budapest.

scourge: A whip used to punish or discipline someone.

Antichrist: In Revelation, a human agent led by the devil to deceive humankind in the Last Days; the antithesis of Christ.

Turks: Christians typically labeled all Muslims as Turks, regardless of ethnic origin.

stupid preachers: Those who taught that since the Turks were God's instrument of punishment, they should not be resisted.

highwayman: An armed robber who waylaid travelers on the roads.

DOCUMENT 26

From Martin Luther, *On War against the Turks* (1529)[13]

The Protestant Reformer Martin Luther, whose opinions on Jews we have observed in Document 7, wrote this tract in 1528 in response to the march westward of the Ottoman Turks led by the great **Sultan Suleiman**; in 1526 they captured **Buda**, and in 1529 laid siege to Vienna. In 1518 Luther had written that since the Turks were acting as God's **scourge** to punish a sinful Europe, their invasion should not be resisted. By 1528 he had obviously changed his stance. Even so, the pope, who in Luther's mind is the **Antichrist**, comes in for more criticism than the Muslim Turks.

... [F]or the past five years certain persons have been begging me to write about war against the **Turks**, and to arouse and encourage our people. Now that the Turk is actually approaching, even my friends are urging me to do this, especially since there are some **stupid preachers** among us Germans ... who are making the people believe that we ought not and must not fight against the Turks.... Furthermore, some actually want the Turk to come and rule because they think our German people are wild and uncivilized—indeed, that they are half-devil and half-man.

... In the first place, the Turk certainly has no right or command to begin war and to attack lands that are not his. Therefore his war is nothing but an outrage and robbery with which God is punishing the world, as he often does through wicked scoundrels.... The Turk ... [is] like a pirate or **highwayman**, he seeks to rob and ravage other lands which do and have done nothing to him....

Since the Turk is the rod of the wrath of the Lord our God and the servant of the raging devil, the first thing to be done is to smite the devil, his lord, and take the rod out of God's hand, so that the Turk may be found only, in his own strength, all by himself, without the devil's help and without God's hand.... If the Turk's god, the devil, is not beaten first, there is reason to fear that the Turk will not be so easy to beat.

... For although some praise the Turk's government because he allows everyone to believe what he will so long as he remains the temporal lord,

13 Martin Luther, *On War against the Turks 1529*, excerpted from the *American Edition of Luther's Works*, vol. 46, *Christian in Society*, trans. Charles M. Jacobs, ed. Robert Schultz (Philadelphia: Fortress Press, 1967), 155–205. See Mark U. Edwards, *Luther's Last Battles: Politics and Polemics, 1531–46* (Philadelphia: Fortress Press, 2004); see also Andrew Cunningham and Ole Peter Grell, *The Four Horsemen of the Apocalypse: Religion, War, Famine and Death in Reformation Europe* (Cambridge: Cambridge University Press, 2000).

yet this reputation is not true, for he does not allow Christians to come together in public, and no one can openly confess Christ or preach or teach against Mohammed.[14] What kind of freedom of belief is it when no one is allowed to preach or confess Christ, and yet our salvation depends on that confession....

Since, therefore, faith must be stilled and held in secret among this wild and barbarous people and under this severe rule, how can it exist or remain alive in the long run, when it requires so much effort and labor in places where it is preached most faithfully and diligently? Therefore it happens, and must happen, that those Christians who are captured or otherwise get into Turkey fall away and become altogether Turkish, and it is very seldom that one remains true to his faith, for they lack the living bread of the soul and see the abandoned and carnal life of the Turks and are obliged to adapt themselves to it.

... In this connection the people should be told about the Turk's dissolute life and ways so that they may the better feel the need of prayer....

I have some parts of Mohammed's **Koran** which in German might be called a book of sermons or doctrines of the kind that we call pope's decretals. When I have time I must translate it into German so that everyone may see what a foul and shameful book it is.

Koran: The Qur'an was translated and printed in Latin in 1540; there was no complete German translation until the seventeenth century.

... Mohammed highly exalts and praises himself and boasts that he has talked with God and the angels, and that since Christ's office of prophet is now complete, he has been commanded to bring the world to his faith, and if the world is not willing to compel it or punish it with the sword; there is much glorification of the sword in it. Therefore the Turks think that their Mohammed is much higher and greater than Christ, for the office of Christ has come to an end and Mohammed's office is still in force.

From this anyone can easily see that Mohammed is a destroyer of our Lord Christ and his kingdom....

... Thus the Turk's faith is a patchwork of Jewish, Christian, and heathen beliefs.

... Thus when the spirit of lies had taken possession of Mohammed, and the devil had murdered men's souls with his Koran and had destroyed the faith of Christians, he had to go on and take the sword and set about to murder their bodies. The Turkish faith, then, has not made its progress by preaching and the working of miracles, but by the sword and by murder, and its success has been due to God's wrath....

14 Christians believed that their faith was superior to all others, and that it was their right to proselytize. While Jews and Christians were allowed by Muslim law to practice their faith in Muslim lands, they were not allowed to convert others. The same laws were applied in Christian lands toward Jews and Muslims.

... But just as the pope is the Antichrist, so the Turk is the very devil incarnate.

marriage: While the Qur'an does permit polygamy—the right of a husband to be married to more than one wife—it stipulates that the husband had to have the resources to support them.

... The third point is that Mohammed's Koran has no regard for **marriage**, but permits everyone to take wives as he will. It is customary among the Turks for one man to have ten or twenty wives and to desert or sell any whom he will, so that in Turkey women are held immeasurably cheap and are despised; they are bought and sold like cattle.

... It is said that among themselves the Turks are faithful, friendly, and careful to tell the truth. I believe that and I think that they probably have more fine virtues in them than that. No man is so bad that there is not something good in him.... Murderers and robbers are more faithful and friendly to each other than neighbors are, even more so than many Christians.

... Now we have heard above what kind of man the Turk is, that he is a destroyer, enemy, and blasphemer of our Lord Jesus Christ, a man who instead of the gospel and faith sets up his shameful Mohammed and all kinds of lies, ruins all temporal government and home life or marriage, and his warfare, which is nothing but murder and bloodshed, is a tool of the devil himself.

DOCUMENT 27

From Desiderius Erasmus of Rotterdam, *On War against the Turks* (*De bello turcico*) (1530)[15]

Desiderius Erasmus was the most famous **humanist** of Northern Europe. Prior to Luther he had sought ways to reform the church through his scholarship and humorous critiques of popular religiosity, such as **pilgrimages**. He did not like the division in Christendom that Luther had caused and he opposed unnecessary warfare. In this work, Erasmus responds to Luther's tract above (Document 26), although by the time it was printed in 1530, Suleiman's troops had returned to Istanbul (Constantinople).

humanist: Renaissance scholars who emphasized the humanities against scholastic philosophy.

pilgrimages: Travel to holy shrines or places, such as Jerusalem, out of devotion to Christ and the saints.

Let us not turn a deaf ear to the repeated warnings of the Lord; He is now calling out once again through the cruelty of the Turks, to which we have almost become accustomed; but this only makes our deafness the more unpardonable, in that, despite the frequency of these warnings, we have still not awoken to the danger. How many defeats have the Christian peoples suffered at the hands of this race of barbarians, whose very origin is obscure? What atrocities have they not committed against us? For how many cities, how many islands, how many provinces have they snatched away from the domain of Christ? See how they have confined the once world-wide power and influence of our religion to a narrow strip of Land! These early successes seem to suggest that, unless we are shielded by the right hand of God, in a few years the remainder of the Christian world will also be absorbed. Even if all these calamities occurred through no fault of our own the whole body of Christendom should be moved by Christian sympathy to grieve for one of its members in distress; but now there be no doubt that the Turks have won an immense empire less by their own merits than because of our sins, whose just reward has been the destruction of our empire. In view of this, all who acknowledge the name of Christ must now do more than grieve: we must give assistance to our brother nations in their time of distress. It is no longer a case of sharing these disasters because of our common religion, but because there is a danger now that we may soon share them in reality. "When your neighbour's wall is on fire, it becomes your business"; in fact, it becomes the business of the whole city, whenever a single house catches fire. Therefore we must give assistance if we are truly anxious to rid ourselves of this peril; but assistance of two kinds. Of course, we must make all the

15 Desiderius Erasmus of Rotterdam, *On War against the Turks* (*De bello turcico*), 1530, excerpted from Erika Rummel, ed., *The Erasmus Reader* (Toronto: University of Toronto Press, 1990), 315–33.

preparations necessary for such an arduous war, but before that we must make the preparations without which military strength will be in vain. We have frequently taken the field against the Turks, but so far with little success; either because we have still clung to all the things which have angered God and caused him to send the Turks against us ... or perhaps because we have relied upon our own strength for victory, and have forgotten that the battle is fought in the name of Christ....

While we have been endlessly fighting among ourselves over some useless plot of ground in what are worse than civil wars, the Turks have vastly extended their empire or, rather, their reign of terror.

... Can we attribute these successes to the Turks' piety? Of course not. To their valour? They are a race softened by debauchery and fearsome only as brigands. What, then, is the answer? They owe their victories to our sins; we have opposed them but, as the results plainly show, God has been angered against us. We assail the Turks with the selfsame eagerness with which they invade the lands of others. We are betrayed by our lust for power; we covet riches; in short, we fight the Turks like the Turks.... Now, if we had undertaken this legitimate war against the Turks in harmony among ourselves, with purer hearts, beneath the banners of Christ, and relying on his aid alone, Christendom would never have been reduced to its present straits....

Of course, not all wars against the Turks are legitimate and holy, yet there are times when failure to resist the Turks simply means the surrender of part of Christendom to these barbaric enemies, and the abandonment of those of our brethren who are already enslaved beneath their foul yoke.

On the other hand, whenever the ignorant mob hear the name "Turk," they immediately fly into a rage and clamour for blood, calling them dogs and enemies to the name of Christian; it does not occur to them that, in the first place, the Turks are men, and, what is more, **half Christian**; they never stop to consider whether the occasion of the war is just, nor whether it is practical to take up arms and thereby to provoke an enemy who will strike back with redoubled fury....

half Christian: The belief that Muslims were partly Christians since much of their teachings were drawn from Jewish and Christian scripture.

As far as Luther's argument is concerned, I may add that if it is not lawful to resist the Turks, because God is punishing the sins of his people through them, it is no more lawful to call in a doctor during illness, because God also sends diseases to purge his people of their sins. He uses the wiles of Satan for the same purpose, and yet we are commanded to resist them. It is therefore lawful to fight off the Turks, unless God manifestly prohibits it....

The mass of Christians are wrong, on the other hand, in thinking that anyone is allowed to kill a Turk, as one would a mad dog, for no better reason than that he is a Turk. If this were true then anyone would be allowed to kill a Jew; but if he dared to do so he would not escape punishment by the civil authorities. The Christian magistrate punishes Jews who break the state's laws, to which they are subject, but they are not put to death because of their religion; Christianity is spread by persuasion, not by force; by careful cultivation, not by destruction. This right, by which Jews are punished in the same way as Christians, was also exercised by pagan rulers against their Christian subjects; if, God forbid, we were living under the **laws of the Turkish empire**, they too could exercise this right. So any who believe that they will fly straight up to **heaven**, if they happen to fall in battle against the Turks, are sadly deluding themselves; they will reach heaven only if their conscience be pure, even though, for Christ's sake, they expose their lives to a tyrant who calls them to worship **idols**....

However, this triumph will be all the more acceptable to Christ if, instead of slaughtering the Turks, we manage to join them to us in a common faith and observance....

The best solution of all would be to conquer the Turkish empire in the way in which the **apostles** conquered all the peoples of the earth for their master, Christ; but the best alternative must be to have as the chief object of an armed campaign that the Turks will be glad to have been defeated. This task will be made easier if, firstly, they see that Christianity is not mere words, and can observe that our deeds are worthy of the Gospel; secondly, if honest preachers are sent in to reap the harvest, men will further Christ's interests, not their own. Thirdly, if any infidel cannot so quickly be persuaded, he should be allowed for a time to live under his own laws, until gradually he comes to agree with us.

laws of the Turkish empire: The Qur'an advocates the toleration of Jews and Christians, so the Ottoman Turks became a major place of refuge for Jews fleeing Christian lands.

heaven: Crusade preachers promised recruits that if slain in battle their sins would be forgiven and they could enter heaven.

idols: Images of gods to be worshipped. Muslims do not allow any such images of Allah or the Prophet Muhammad, fearing that these would be worshipped rather than the real divine.

apostles: I.e., through preaching the message of Christ to convert pagans.

DOCUMENT 28

From Henrick van Haestens and Christoffel von Sichem, *Abominations of the Foremost Head Heretics* (1608)[16]

Christoffel von Sichem was an engraver who produced a collection of portraits of heretics in 1606. A longer version with text was produced by the Leiden bookseller Henrick van Haestens. The Prophet Muhammad was not included in the first editions but was added in the 1623 version. In the original document the names of Muhammad's family are fictionalized.

In the year of our Saviour Jesus Christ **622** ... began the kingdom of the Saracens in the Orient on 15 July (on which date the Saracens have their annual **Alhigera**, that is pilgrimage and the first accounted to Mahomet), and their first Amiras or king was Machometh, the son of Abdalla.... He was born in Arabia, to **poor and mean parents**. In his youth he was captured and **sold by his enemies** to a rich merchant from Africa, named Abdimoneplis, with whom, due to his courage, he achieved so much credit and favor that he was not treated as a slave but as a free man in his master's family. And he became the foremost factor over all his business, by which he came into the great acquaintance of Christians and Jews. At the same time a certain monk named **Sergius** was banned out of Constantinople on account of the **Nestorian** sect. This one came to Africa, pressing himself into the household of Abdimoneplis, where he came to know Machometh, and became amazed at his sharpness and they got along. Under his [Muhammad's] name they began secretly to build a new sect, which would be neither entirely Jewish nor entirely Christian, but be collected out of both religions and made into one. Then Abdimoneplis died without children, leaving behind a rich widow, whom Machometh **bewitched** with strange arts to love him, so she married him and made him lord and master of all of the great wealth that her husband had left her. After she had given him the name of a prophet, thanks to unbelievable practices arising from his **falling sickness**, the woman passed away, and he thus inherited all of her possessions, having foreseen all. And having gathered around him a crowd of people, he finally declared himself publicly as a Prophet, further he proposed his false and perverse opinions to each one, verifying them with false miracles, and with the force of weapons

622: The Muslim calendar begins with the Prophet Muhammad's Hijrah (migration) from Mecca to Medina in 622 CE.

Alhigera: The Hijrah, the annual pilgrimage to Mecca in honor of the Prophet.

poor and mean parents: Muhammad's father, Abdullah ibn Abd al-Muttalib, was the son of a tribal leader; both he and Muhammad's mother, Amina bint Wahb, had died by the time Muhammad was six.

sold by his enemies: Another fabrication.

Sergius: Supposedly a monk of the Nestorian Christian sect, although there is no evidence of his actual existence.

Nestorians: An ancient Christian sect that denied the divinity of Jesus.

bewitched: Written at the height of the European witch-hunts, the author is clearly seeking to ascribe Islam's success to the devil.

falling sickness: A typical assertion that Muhammad's visions were the result of epileptic fits.

16 *Grouwelen der voornaemster Hooft-Ketteren Die voortijts ende in dese laeste tijden so in Duytslandt als oock in Nederlant hen opgheworpen hebben: haer Leere, Leven, begin ende eynde. Mits-gaders haere Afbeeldingen* (Abominations of the foremost Head Heretics which previously and in these last times have arisen in Germany and in the Netherlands, their doctrine, lives beginning and end) (Leiden: Henrick Lodewijcxsoon van Haestens, 1623), 26–31. Translated by Gary Waite.

made them accept and believe. His authority he made grow stronger over time, bringing various lands and peoples under his rulership. He was the author of the renowned book called the Alcoran ... which he had issued from God through the Angel Gabriel.... It is today regarded by the Turks as very holy, and as dictated from God, divided into many chapters which the Mahumetisten call **Azoaras**. ... That no doctrine is perfect except that which comes from the Old and New Testaments and this Alcoran. That its despisers will be punished and tortured into eternity.... That the power of this Book is so much, that if it were placed in a mountain, it would burst from it.

Azoaras: The Arabic term for the chapters dividing the Qur'an is surah.

... [The writer reiterates the false stories of Muhammad's death and burial in an iron coffin which levitated through magnets] whereby the simple people believed that he had entered into his sanctity, and had been resurrected, as he had prophesied.

The simple Arabs, Turks, and Saracens finished with this misunderstanding in 1470 when a lightning bolt struck a great part of this Temple at Mecca, together with the vaulted grave of Machomet, casting the iron coffin to the ground. But it was not long after that it was raised up again, and there it remains to delude the foolish and make credible the lies.... Since Machomet has, despite this, truly said that from the first establishment of his Law, a thousand years would pass, then his Alcoran ... would cease. May God in his foresight make this happen.

Morisco: Spanish Muslims forced to convert to Christianity; all were expelled from Spain between 1609 and 1614.

king: Morocco was an independent Muslim kingdom.

DOCUMENT 29
Ahmad bin Qasim (al-Hajari) in France, 1611–13: A Muslim Responds[17]

Ahmad bin Qasim (al-Hajari, b. 1569–70) was a former Spanish **Morisco** who escaped to Morocco, where he became **king** Mulay Zaydan's translator. He was sent on a mission to France and the Dutch Republic in c. 1612 and wrote this account in 1637–41. In his conversations with some French hosts, he discusses worship of saints' images, or idols, and the story of the magnets and the Prophet Muhammad told in many Christian biographies (Documents 25 and 28 above).

A girl from the nobility came from the city of Fontenay to visit an idol near the house where we were staying.... When she sat down, she looked disdainfully at me, and her face showed her hostility. Then she said:

"Are you a Turk?"

"A Muslim, praise be to God," I said to her.

"How come you do not know God?" she said.

"Muslims," I said to her, "know God better than you."

"Better than we?" she said.

"Yes," I said to her.

"What is your proof?" she said to me.

book under her arm: Likely a Christian prayer book that included the Ten Commandments (Exodus 20:2–17).

***ifranji*:** Arabic transliteration of "Frank," the general term used by Middle-Eastern Muslims to refer to Western Christians, the "Franks."

So I looked at her, and saw that she held a **book under her arm**, as is the custom among the daughters of wealthy ***ifranji*** merchants and nobility.... I said to her, "The proof of what you want is in the book you have. With it, I can prove what I said to you."

She took the book and laid it in my hands on the table. "Here is the book."

"Look at the ten divine commandments," I said to her.

So she searched in the book and said, "Here they are."

"Read the first of the ten about the religion of God," I said to her.

So she did and said, "The first commandment of the ten is: 'God almighty said, Do not carve statues, and do not worship them. Worship God alone.'"

After she had read it, I said to her, "Muslims don't carve statues and do not worship them; indeed, with God's help, they desist from making them. Even women who embroider decorations do not portray anything that has a spirit...."

"We do not worship the idols themselves," she said, "but what the idols represent."

---

17 Taken from Nabil Matar, ed. and trans., *In the Land of the Christians: Arabic Travel Writing in the Seventeenth Century*, First English Translations (Abingdon, UK: Routledge, 2003), 17–18, 24.

... "The divine commandment," I said to her, "in the text. [Did it not say] Do not make statues and do not worship them?"

"Yes," she said.

"Do you or do you not make idols?" I said to her.

She had to give in to reason and truth. So she looked at the women and said in their language:

"He won. I cannot find anything with which we can answer him."

So I looked at her, and found that she was now happy and relaxed, as if a veil had been removed from her heart. She then started talking with me in a friendly way, the anger and hostility she had felt for Muslims now gone....

I had other discussions like the one above in the city of Bordeaux with the judge named Fayrad ... [who said,] "I am amazed at you being a follower of the religion of the Muslims."

"Why?" I said.

"We have it in our books," he said, "that the Muslims visit Mecca to see their prophet in the middle of an iron ring hanging in the air. The ring is in the air because it is the center of a domed [building] with a magnet stone. It is known that the magnet draws iron and, inside the dome, it draws from all sides equally, which is why the ring stays in the air with your prophet. Muslims believe that to be a miracle of their prophet."

I said to him, "Is it permissible in your religion for someone to lie and insult the religion of another in order to glorify his own religion and magnify it before his own coreligionists?"

"Not at all!" he said.

"The Christians who said that committed a heinous sin [by the standards of] your religion," I said.

"How is that?" he said.

I said, "The prophet, God's prayer and peace upon him, is not in Mecca and is not in an iron ring. He is buried in Medina, and between it and Mecca there are ten [travel] days. The Muslims visit the **Ka'aba** because it is a blessed house built by our Sayyid Abraham, peace be upon him."

Ka'aba: The center of Islam's holiest mosque in Mecca, and which Muslims believed was constructed by Abraham.

DOCUMENT 30

From Henrick van Haestens, *Abomination of the Head Heretics* (1658)[18]

In 1658 John Davies translated Haesten's *Abomination of the Head Heretics* into English as *Apocalypsis: or, the Revelation of certain notorious Advancers of Heresie*. How is this version of the story of the Prophet Muhammad different from the Dutch original (Document 28)? It was included in the extremely polemical anti-heresy tome, *Pansebeia, or, a View of All Religions in the World*, by the Anglican royalist Alexander Ross in 1655. Ross also published a deeply polemical translation and edition of the Qur'an.

In the year six hundred twenty two, ***Honorius*** the fifth being Bishop of *Rome*, and ***Meraclius*** *Caesar* Emperor of the *East*, a transcendent Arch-heretic called *Mahomet*, exchanged Hell for earth; a *Prophet*, by Nation an *Arabian*, but most depraved and corrupt. He had sometimes been a Merchant extremely rich, and withal very subtle; to be short, he was a serious professor of **diabolical Arts**, a most ungodly instrument of Satan, the Viceroy of Antichrist, or his sworn fore-runner.... He with **Arrius** and **Eusebius**, most fervently and contumeliously held that Christ, was only a Man, and that he was only called God, *seconduin dici*, that is to say, according to a certain manner of speaking. He agrees with ***Carpocrates*** who denied that Christ was a God and a Prophet.... He imagined with the ***Manichees***, that it was not Christ, but some other that was fastened to the Cross. With the ***Donatists***, he condemned the purest **Sacraments** of the Church. With the most impure Origen he affirms that the devils shall be eternally saved according to an human, yet an invisible manner. He with ***Cerinthus*** placed eternal **Felicity** in the lust of the flesh. **Circumcision**, that was long since abolished and antiquated, he renewed. Upon his disciples he bestowed the privileges, of *Polygamy*, ***Concubines*** and *Divorce*, as *Moses* had done; and with such dreams and an imaginary frenzy was the miserable wretch ever troubled. This man when he died was put into an iron Tomb at *Mecca*, which by the strength of **Loadstones**, being as it were in the middle and centre of an arched edifice, hangs up to the astonishment of the beholders, by which means the miraculous sanctity of this Prophet is greatly celebrated. All the dominions of the Great *Turk*, profess this man's faith, whom they acquiesce in as a miracle.

Honorius: Pope Honorius I (r. 625–38).

Meraclius: Emperor Heraclius (r. 610–41).

diabolical Arts: Harmful magic under the command of the devil.

Arrius: A fourth-century church leader declared a heretic for denying the divinity of Jesus.

Eusebius: A fourth-century Christian bishop who allegedly supported Arius.

Carpocrates: A second-century leader of the Christian Gnostics who allegedly taught that Jesus was not divine.

Manichees: An ancient Christian sect that emphasized the duality between good and evil.

Donatists: A fourth-century Christian sect that emphasized that priests must be faultless if their sacraments were to be effective.

Sacraments: Christian rituals, such as baptism, to confer divine grace or power onto believers.

Cerinthus: A first century Gnostic Christian who supposedly taught that the divine Christ ascended onto Jesus only at his baptism and departed at the crucifixion.

Felicity: Happiness.

Circumcision: The ritual of cutting off the foreskin of infant boys as a sign of membership in Islam; also a practice in Judaism.

Concubines: Women who were used for sexual and

18 John Davies, *Apocalypsis: or, the Revelation of certain notorious Advancers of Heresie: Wherein their Visions and private Revelations by Dreams, are discovered to be most incredible blasphemies, and enthusiastical dotages: Together with an account of their Lives, Actions, and Ends* (London: John Saywell, 1658), 59. See Waite, *Jews and Muslims*, 99–100.

reproductive purposes but without the rights of marriage.

Loadstones: Magnets.

Mennonites: Religious descendants of the sixteenth-century Anabaptists, named after the leader Menno Simons.

DOCUMENT 31

From *Book of a Thousand Questions* (1657)[19]

In 1657 the Amsterdam translator Jan Hendriksz Glazemaker (1619–82) and his publisher friend Jan Rieuwertsz (1617–85) produced a Dutch translation of the Qur'an. Both liberal **Mennonites**, they were leaders in innovative thinking toward religion, Christian–Jewish relations, and philosophy, and supported the publication of the philosophical works by the ex-Jewish Enlightenment philosopher Baruch Spinoza.[20] Rieuwertsz's translation was from the French version by the gentleman Andrew du Ryer, published in 1647. In 1649 Alexander Ross produced an English translation from Du Ryer's. Glazemaker's is different from both in that he has surrounded the Qur'an text with various other accounts of Muhammad, some of which were positive toward the Prophet. Here we have an excerpt from one of these: the "Discussion of a Jew with Muhammad," which is actually a famous Muslim treatise, Book of a Thousand Questions.

Of a Jew with Mahomet, who gave him a reckoning of his life.

God's messenger, who has spread his blessing over him, sat once among his disciples in the city of **Jesrab**, when the Angel Gabriel appeared before him, and said to him: God greet you, oh Mahomet, who replied, "he is truly the Lord of all blessings and salvation, in order that you have come from him, and return hither...."

Jesrab: An early Arabic name for Medina.

[The Angel introduces Muhammad to four **Rabbis** from Israel, including one named Abdias ben Salon. They turn to discussing several points of comparison between Jewish and Muslim interpretations of the Hebrew law, concluding with the following:]

Rabbis: Jewish religious leaders and teachers.

"Listen to us, God's beneficent Messenger, great Prophet, and his universal servant. To whom, shall Moses say, do you mean to turn? Have I not given you a law, confirmed with so many miracles? And yet you will not believe in it. If you had believed me, then I would have been able to fulfil your request. But go and join you to Jesus Christ. You, turning to him, will say, 'O Jesus Christ, the spirit, the word, and the power of almighty God,

---

19 Jan Hendriksz Glazemaker, *Mahomets Alkoran, Door de Heer Du Ryer uit de Arabische in de Fransche Taal gestalt; Benevens een tweevoudige Beschryving van Mahomets Leven; En een verhaal van des zelfs Reis ten Hemel; Gelijk ook sijn Samenspraak met de Jood Abdias* (Amsterdam: Jan Rieuwertsz, 1657); excerpt taken from 1707 edition (Leiden: Hendrik van Damme), 518–19, 545–47. Translated by Gary Waite. See Waite, *Jews and Muslims*, 98–100.

20 Jonathan Israel, *Radical Enlightenment: Philosophy and the Making of Modernity, 1650–1750* (Oxford: Oxford University Press, 2001), 288–91.

that your mercy move you to pity, and know our disputation by God.' He shall say, You have lost the thing that you seek from me, through your own crime: for I have been sent to you in God's power and name, and in the word of the truth. But you have run off the track; and you have from me, your God, will make, the which is more, than I proclaimed to you. You have on this account fallen from my pleasure and approval but turn yourselves to the last Prophet. He who is saying this, O Abdias, know he is the one with whom you now speak. You, who turn to him, will say, 'O faithful messenger and friend of God, how greatly have we sinned, and done badly! ...'"

"O my misery!" Said Abdias to this, "what foolishness has possessed my spirit until now, that I have not seen the truth, which is clearer than light? But while it remains in your power to answer all my questions, so proceed, I beg you ... please tell me what groups shall be found in this day, and separate the believers from the unbelievers." Mahomet replied, "there are one hundred and twenty groups of all humans; but no more than three of [them] believers, and all the others of unbelievers. Each group shall take up as much space in the length as can be traveled in a thousand years, and in breadth, as far as one can go in five hundred years." "It is true, as you say," replied Abdias....

[Muhammad then describes Paradise and Hell for Abdias, the former filled with great joy, the latter with pain "and work without ceasing."]

The Jew, thereupon bursting into words with a loud voice, said, "Thou hast won, oh good Mahomet. Stay there, without proceeding any further, and receive my confession, for I believe, and see clearly that there are not many gods, but one singular God, who is almighty, of the which you, without doubt, are the true Messenger and Prophet."

The End

DOCUMENT 32

From Cornelius Hazart, *Church History of the Entire World* (1671)[21]

The Glazemaker translation (Document 31) was part of a growing trend to try to understand, and not just condemn, other religions and cultures in something approaching ethnographic studies. This excerpt is from the *Church History of the Entire World* by the Antwerp Jesuit priest P. Cornelius Hazart (1617–90). How is Hazart's work different from the earlier accounts?

The history writers are not of one opinion about the first origins of the Turks. Some believe that they originated from the **Tartars**, since these two nations do not differ much in either manners or in language.... Others believe that they came out of Turca, which was a large and rich city of Persia in earlier times, which managed to bring entirely under their authority lesser Asia. Others believe that the word Turk originated from the Hebrew word Tarac, which is to say, "abandoned by God," therefore the Turks do not like it when people use this name, but prefer Musselman [Muslim], that is "faithful to God," or "made blessed." Some believe finally that they originated from the city Turkestan, between Tartar and Meden. It is most likely that what **Augustinus Curio** has maintained is best, that the Turks sprouted from the Saracens of **Arabia Petreia** as a nation that previously never lived in cities, but always migrating, living without houses but in tents, tending to robbery and theft. They were also entirely differing among each other in religion, for some followed the old customs of the Jews, others were Christians, others idolatrous worshipping the sun and moon, trees, or serpents, namely the tower named **Alcaba**, which they believed had been constructed by Ishmael the son of Abraham.

Tartars: The term used by Europeans for the peoples of North and Central Asia, including the Mongols.

Augustinus Curio: The ancient Roman writer Coelius Augustinus Curio. His history of the Saracens was translated into English and printed in 1575.

Arabia Petreia: Latin term for Arabia.

Alcaba: The Kaaba, the center of Islam's holiest mosque in Mecca.

This Nation has spread so far that they dominate the greatest part of the world, for now they currently possess so many lands and provinces in the three parts of the world, Europe, Africa, and Asia....

Chapter II: Birth and Upbringing of Mahomet

Many years before the nation of the Turks had been established out of many different peoples, the cursed man Mahomet came into the world who spread his godless sect by the way through all of Turkey.

---

21 Cornelius Hazart, *Kerckelycke Historie Van de Gheheele Werelt Naemelyck, van Turckyen, Palestynen, Syrien Grieken-lant Moscovien Persien, Fez, Marocco, ende Tararien Het IV Deel* (Antwerp: Michiel Conbbaert, 1671), 1–11, and part II, chapter 1, "Het Tweede Deel Vande Religie der heden-daeghsche Turcken," 9–24, esp. 23–24. Translated by Gary Waite.

Mahomet had as his father a certain Abdalla, being an Arab and heathen; his mother was named Emine, being a Jewess, as most of the history writers have testified. He was born in the abandoned or desert lands of Arabia in 560, in the month of February, as Curio believed. Others say 561, as does **Elmacinus**, others the year 600, like Gregorius Monanchus, others the year 606, as Bredenbachius, others the year 612, like Sionita, others 620, like Petrus Messias, others the last year 622, like Joannes Hesronita, so that people cannot know anything certain about his birth.[22]

Elmacinus: Georgius Elmacinus, a thirteenth-century Coptic Christian in the employ of the Egyptian sultans. The other names mentioned here are Christian authors who had written on Islam.

In order to exalt and make their Prophet great, the Mahometans have embellished the stories of his birth with many wonderful things, such as:

1. That very quickly after his birth or as soon as he fell flat on his face on the earth to show honour to God, he said, "Oh my Mother," then raising his head, he is supposed to have said: "I testify that there is no more than one God, and I am his sent one": She said also that he came into the world circumcised.
2. They tell fables that his mother gave birth to him without pain.
3. That on the day of his birth thousands of churches collapsed, as a sign that when he reached his time he would break down Christendom.
4. That through the entire world all thrones and seats of justice would be cast down, in order to give him his place.
5. That with his birth the infertility of the earth, of humans, and of all other things has ceased.
6. That all false gods (idols) bowed down to him, that Lucifer fled out of fear, that the birds flew to him with shining beaks, and their light shed through the entire east and west.

They recount further another vision which is supposed to have happened at his birth: to know, there came a man clothed entirely in white, with three keys which were forged out of diamonds, with these he honoured the new-born child, saying with a loud voice: "Mahomet has received the key of victory, the key of the law, and the key of the prophets."

At this came three other men, whose faces were like suns. The first set before Mahomet a basin of **Carbuncle stone**, having four handles of pearl, and said, "this is the world; here is the East, there the West, here the South, and there the North, let us see which part the child grasps. The child took the basin by the middle, whereupon the man said: "Mahomet shall be lord of the entire world....

Carbuncle stone: A deep red gemstone.

22 Hazart cites a number of other medieval writers here.

From the Jews he had one who, as is said, was very learned in **Astrology**; from this one and some others of the same sect, he [Mahomet] learned the Jewish fables. From the Christians, he had a monk from Antioch by the name of Johan and the aforementioned Sergius a monk from Constantinople, and from these he learned the Christian habits, but with heresies intermingled. For with the heretics **Sabellius** and Arius he denied the most Holy Trinity.... One recounts [a story] of the aforementioned Sergius, that he, when Mahomet was speaking to the people, hid himself in an unknown corner from where he spoke as if he was an Angel from heaven, giving answers to Mahomet's questions.

Astrology: The art of interpreting the stars, arranged in twelve houses, to determine the future.

Sabellius: A third-century theologian who is alleged to have rejected the doctrine of the Trinity (one God in three persons).

Chapter IV: Of Mahomet's Scandalous Life, and of His Authority

Although Mahomet proclaimed himself as a Prophet and godly messenger, it is nevertheless the case that he lived so scandalously that he broke nearly all human and natural laws, pretending that everything that he did was the will of God. He took, as some say, seventeen women as his concubines. He strongly forbade all the others from marrying their relations, for he said that he alone had been granted this privilege by God to take whom he desired....

Chapter VII: Of the Death and Burial of Mahomet

This monster of all foolishness died in the year 630 or 632 in the city of Medina on the 8th of July, being a Monday ... for he at the time of his illness many times lay very thickly swollen, and at the last became so tired, that he was little more than skin over bones. He died on the 14th day of his illness, 63 or 64 years old, and in the seventh year of his foolish lordship.

His death became known and many of his disciples refused to believe it; the common people especially called, "how could he die since he was a witness to us of God? He has not died but taken up like Jesus." They therefore called out before the door, "do not bury him, for he has not died."

This **Omar**, one of his foremost disciples, confirmed this, calling: "Mahomet has not died, like the hypocrites say, but he has gone away, just as Moses had gone away." He therefore commanded that all who should say that Mahomet had died would have their feet and hands cut off. Though this dispute was finally put to rest by **Abubeker**, who proved from the Alkoran that Mahomet must die just as had the other Prophets; finally people believed that he was dead.

Omar: Umar, who succeeded Abu Bakr as caliph.

Abubeker: Abu Bakr, one of Muhammad's immediate successors as caliph.

People said that he had commanded that they should hold watch and not bury him, saying that he would be resurrected on the third day after his death into heaven. Though when they had watched him not only to the third day but indeed to the 14th, and they noticed nothing except for a horrible stink, they said that they should pick him up naked and throw him far from their houses. Whereupon some say that he was eaten by the dogs, apart from some bones. Ali, hearing this, wrapped up his bones and buried them at Mecca in an iron coffin: this, as is still believed to this day, would hang in the air between two large magnets which pulled against each other. But, this is a clear fable, which can be seen from numerous writers....

II Part, Chapter II: Of the Ceremonies, Prayers, and Fasts of the Turks

The second: they are deeply superstitious in washing and purifying themselves. Among the purifications they place the gargling or washing of the mouth, the cleaning of the nostrils, the shearing of the beard, the clamping of the hair, the rubbing of the teeth, the clipping of the nails, and more such acts of foolishness, which were commanded by Mahomet with a special law....

Chapter X: How the Turks Are Great Enemies of the Christians

The tyranny and nuisance the Turks show to Christians is so great, that they cannot be expressed with words, or described with the pen. For although they do allow the Christian religion to be practiced among them, since the professors of the same live nothing but peaceful lives, yet they are burdened with unbearable burdens, tolls, punishments, and difficulties.

Above all, they take away the third or fourth **child** from the Christians who are living in Europe under their authority, sometimes together. These are then instructed in the Mahometan doctrine and Turkish language and forced into hard labor. Some are then taken in by the **Janissaries**, that is, in the personal guard of the emperor. How sad this is can only be imagined. This happens, says the writer **Georgius**, not without bitter tears and pleas. For the father sees his son, whom he has raised for the service of Christ, taken away to the service of the devil in order to combat Christ. The son is torn away from his parents and all his friends so as to live in the strangest misery, and without father and mother....

child: The Ottomans would periodically demand Christian parents hand over a young son to be raised in the Muslim court.

Janissaries: The elite guard of the Sultan.

Georgius: Georgius Elmancinus cited above.

But there is no more miserable people as those who are captured by the Turks out of Christendom and taken away. These are made into slaves, are led in chains and barefoot through dry and rugged places, in hunger and thirst, like unreasoning beasts. On the way those who do not die are sold and bought to do heavy labor....

This makes the slavery of Christians frightening, that they are frequently pressed to deny their faith and confess the Mahometan religion. They must daily hear a thousand blasphemies against Christ, and must not speak, or say the least thing against the religion of the Turks. They are circumcised without their permission, if they kick against Mahomet, they are tossed into the fire.

DOCUMENT 33

From John Hughes, *The Siege of Damascus. A Tragedy* (1720)[23]

John Hughes was an English playwright and writer of historical works whose 1720 play, *The Siege of Damascus*, was his most popular. It is set during the 634 Siege of Damascus when the Muslim forces under Caliph Abu Bakr laid siege to the Byzantine Christian city of Damascus. Hughes was a proponent of toleration within Christian Britain, and in this play, he presents Muslim princes as human characters with foibles comparable to Christians; for example, while traditional treatments would have portrayed Muslim generals as bloodthirsty villains, Hughes has the general Khalid playing that role, with another, Abu Ubayda, making a treaty allowing Christians to leave the besieged city, for he was a man of his word as a Muslim. Here Caled, Abudah, and Daran are Muslim leaders in the battle, and Eumenes, Herbis, Artamon are the Byzantine Christians.

Scene changes to a Plain before the City. A prospect of Tents at a Distance.

Caled, Abudah, Daran.

Daran: To treat, my Chiefs?—What! Are we Merchants then, that only come to traffick with these Syrians, and poorly cheapen Conquest on Conditions? No; we were sent to fight the Caliph's Battles, 'till ev'ry Iron Neck bend to Obedience. Another Storm makes this proud city ours; What need to treat?—I am for War and Plunder.

Caled: Why so am I—and but to save the Lives of Mussulmans, not Christians, wou'd not treat. I hate these Christian Dogs; and 'tis our Task, as thou observ'st, to fight; our Law enjoyns it. Heav'n too is promis'd only to the Valiant. Our Prophet us'd to say, the happy Plains above, lye stretch'd beneath the Blaze of Swords.

Abudah: Yet Daran's loth to trust that Heav'n for Pay: This Earth, it seems has Gifts that please him more.

Caled: Check not his Zeal, Abudah.

23 John Hughes, *The siege of Damascus. A tragedy. As it is acted at the Theatre-Royal in Drury-Lane, by His Majesty's Servants. By John Hughes, Esq.*, 2nd ed. (London, 1721), 14–15. See "J. John Hughes," *Christian-Muslim Relations: A Bibliographic History*, vol. 13, *Western Europe (1700–1800)*, ed. David Thomas and John A. Chesworth (Leiden: Brill, 2019), 164–71.

Abudah: No; I praise it. Yet I cou'd wish that Zeal had better Motives. Has Victory no Fruits but Blood and Plunder? That we were sent to fight, 'tis true but wherefore? For Conquest, not Destruction. That obtain'd, the more we spare, the Caliph has more Subjects, and Heav'n is better serv'd.—But see, they come.

Enter Eumenes, Herbis, Artamon.

Caled: Well, Christians, we are met—and War awhile, At your Request, has still'd its angry Voice, to hear what you'll propose.

Eumenes: We come to know, after so many Troops you've lost in vain, if you'll draw off in peace and save the rest.

Herbis: Or rather to know first—for yet we know not—why on your Heads you call our pointed Arrows, in our own just Defence? What means this Visit? And why we see so many thousand tents rise in the air, and whiten all our fields?

Caled: Is that a Question now?—you had our Summons, when first we march'd against you, to surrender. Two Moons have wasted since, and now the third is in its wane. 'Tis true, drawn off a while, at **Aiznadin** we met and fought the Powers sent by your Emperor to raise our Siege. Vainly you thought us gone; we gain'd a Conquest. You see we return'd; our Hearts, our Cause, Our swords the same.

Aiznadin: Ajnadayn, Israel, where in 634 the Byzantines lost a battle to an Arab Muslim army.

Herbis: But why those Swords were drawn, and what's that Cause, inform us.

Eumenes: Speak your Wrongs, if wrongs you have receiv'd, and by what Means they may be now repair'd.

Abudah: Then, Christian, hear! And heav'n inspire you to embrace its Truth! No Wrongs t'avenge, but to establish Right. Our Swords were drawn: for such is Heav'n's command immutable. By us great Mahomet, and his successor Abubeker, invite you to the Faith.

Artman (aside): So—then it seems there's no Harm meant; we're only to be beaten into a new Religion,—If that's all, I find I am already half a convert.

DOCUMENT 34

From Voltaire, *Mahomet: The Impostor* (1796)[24]

François-Marie Arouet (pen name: Voltaire), was one of the most prolific French Enlightenment writers who was known for his critiques of Christianity and championed calls for freedom of speech and freedom of religion. In this play, Voltaire uses his own interpretation of the Prophet Muhammad's life to question the Prophet's character. The first translation was completed by James Miller in 1744, who changed "prophet" to "imposter" in the play's subtitle.

Act 1

Pharon: August and sacred chief of Ishmael's senate, this zeal of thine, paternal as it is, is fatal now—our impotent resistance controls not Mahomet's unbounded progress, but without weak'ning irritates the tyrant. When once a citizen you well condemn'd him as an obscure seditious innovator; but now he is a conq'ror, prince, and pontiff, whilst nations numberless embrace his laws, and pay him adoration—ev'n in Mecca he boasts his proselytes.... [p. 5]

Alcanor: Go, bring in pomp, and serve upon your knees this idol, that will crush you with its weight. Mark I abjure him: by his savage hand my wife and children perish'd, whilst in vengeance, I carry'd carnage to his very tent, transfix'd to earth his only son, and wore his trappings as a trophy of my conquest.... [p. 6]

Act 2

Mahomet: What crime! Dost say?—Learn all my frailty my life's a combat: keen austerity subjects my nature to abstemious bearings: I 'ave banish'd from my lips that trait'rous liquor that either works to practices of outrage or melts the manly breast to woman's weakness.... [p. 17]

Alcanor: Know me then Mahomet, I'd not admit a doubt to cloud my choice—Farwel.

---

24 Voltaire, *Mahomet: The impostor—A tragedy marked with the variations of the Manager's book at the Theatre-Royal in Drury-Lane*, trans. James Miller (London, 1796). We have removed the original line breaks.

Mahomet: Why, fare thee well then—churlish dotard! I will have great revenge; I'll meet thy scorn with treble retribution....

Mahomet: Those heart-chill'd paltry babblers plac'd on the bench of sloth with ease can nod and vote a man to death; why don't the cowards stand me in yonder plain?—with half their number I drove them headlong to their walls for shelter and he was deem'd the wisest senate.... [p. 21]

Act 3

Mahomet: Rash youth, beware; he that deliberates is sacrilegious, far, far from me those audacious mortals who for themselves would impiously judge, or see with their own eyes; who dares to think was never born a proselyte for me. Know who I am; know on this very spot I 'ave charg'd thee with the just decree of Heav'n, and when that Heav'n requires of. Thee no more than the bare off'ring of its deadliest foe, nay, thy foe too and mine, why dost thou balance, as thy own father were the victim claim'd! Go, vile idolater! False Musselman! Go seek another master, a new faith. [p. 28]

Act 4

Mirvan: ... Mecca's youth in vain lament their chief. To the mad crowd that gather'd round good Ali and myself (full of thy dauntless heav'nly-seeming spirit) disclaim'd the deed, and pointed out the arm of righteous Heav'n that strikes for Mahomet—think ye, we cry'd (with eyes and hands uprear'd) think ye our holy prophet would consent to such a crime, whose foulness casts a blot on right of nation, nature and our faith....

Palmira: ... Behold thy dearest blood spilt at thy feet, Mecca, Medina, all of our Asian world, join, join to drive th' Impostor from the earth, blush at his chains, and shake them off in vengeance.... [p. 44]

Mahomet: Paltry dastards! You fled the foe but can disarm your master. Angel of Death whose pow'r I 'ave long proclaim'd now aid me if thou canst.... [p. 51]

DOCUMENT 35

Charles Wesley, *Sun of Unclouded Righteousness* (1758)[25]

Charles Wesley was brother of John Wesley, the founder of the evangelical Christian denomination, Methodism. In 1758 he wrote the following hymn, as a call for Muslims to convert to Christianity. The hymn originally fell out of favor in the 1870s, but some scholars suggest it regained popularity after Great Britain declared war on the Ottoman Empire in 1914.

For the ***Mahometans***

Mahometans: Also, Muhammedans, followers of the Prophet Muhammad. Now replaced by "Muslims," as these earlier terms are now seen as offensive.

Sun of unclouded righteousness, 1
With healing in thy wings arise
A sad, benighted world to bless,
Which now in sin and error lies,
Wrapped in Egyptian night profound,
With chains of hellish darkness bound.
The smoke of the infernal cave, 2
Which half the Christian world o'erspread,
Disperse, thou heavenly Light, and save
The souls by that impostor led,
That Arab-thief, as Satan bold,
Who quite destroyed thy Asian fold.
O might the blood of sprinkling cry 3
For those who spurn the sprinkled blood!
Assert thy glorious Deity,
Stretch out thy arm, thou triune God,
the **Unitarian** fiend expel,
And chase his doctrine back to hell!
Come, Father, Son, and Holy Ghost, 4
Thou Three in One, and One in Three,
Resume thy own for ages lost,
Finish the dire apostasy;
Thine universal claim maintain,
And Lord of the creation reign!

Unitarian: Those who deny the Christian doctrine of the Trinity, affirming instead that God is one.

25 Charles Wesley, *Sun of Unclouded Righteousness* (1758).

DOCUMENT 36

Images: Jean-Léon Gérôme, *Pool in a Harem* (1876) and *Snake Charmer* (1879)

Romanticism: Cultural movement in the early nineteenth century that emphasized nature as an artistic subject, and the power of emotions over reason.

Edward Said: Said (1935–2003) was Professor of Literature at Columbia University and a prominent public intellectual who founded the academic field of postcolonial studies.

As an art movement, Orientalism was influenced by cultural **Romanticism** and Napoleon Bonaparte's military occupation of Egypt, 1798–1801. Orientalist painters created fantastical portrayals of life in the exotic East, including Turkey, Egypt, China, India, and Algeria. **Edward Said** argues "the Orient was almost a European invention … a place of romance, exotic beings, haunting memories and landscapes, remarkable experiments." This tendency is evident in two paintings by Jean-Léon Gérôme, a French painter who combined his own travel experiences with themes he thought would appeal to a late nineteenth-century European audience. Indeed, Professor Said used *Snake Charmer* as an example of Orientalism on the cover of his 1978 book.[26]

26 For more information on the historical concept of Orientalism, see Edward Said, *Orientalism* (New York: Pantheon Books, 1978) and for more examples, see "Orientalism," *WikiArt: Visual Art Encyclopedia.*

DOCUMENT 37

Eliza Fay, "Letter: On Board Ship, in the Red Sea, Near Suez," *Original Letters from India* (1779)[27]

Eliza Fay (1756–1816) was a British travel writer, who wrote letters to her friends and family to document her trip to India with her husband, Anthony. On her and her husband's first journey to the British colony, they were attacked by "bandits" as they traveled through Egypt and were later imprisoned by Hyder Ali, the king of Mysore. The couple eventually separated several years after settling in Calcutta (now Kolkata) and Fay returned to England. She traveled to and from India several more times before her death in 1816. Although not all are racist in nature, Fay's letters are representative of many British women's perceptions.

On Board Ship, in the Red Sea, Near Suez.

September 1st, 1779.

My Dear Friends.

heavenly Protector: Reference to the Christian God.

I have not a moment's time, for the boat is waiting, therefore can only beg that you will unite with me, in praising our **heavenly Protector** for our escape from the various dangers of our journey. I never could have thought my constitution was so strong. I bore the fatigues of the desert, like a Lion, though but just recovering from my illness. We have been pillaged of almost every thing, by the Arabs. This is the Paradise of thieves, I think the whole population may be divided into two classes of them; those who adopt force, and those who effect their purpose by fraud. I was obliged to purchase a thick cloak, and veil, proper for the journey, and what was worse, to wear them all the way hither, which rendered the heat almost insupportable.—Never was I more happy, than when I came on board; although the ship having been for six weeks in the hands of the natives, the reason of which I cannot enlarge on here, is totally despoiled of every article of furniture; we have not a chair or a table, but as the carpenter makes them, for there is no buying such things here. Our greatest inconvenience is the want of good water; what can be procured here, is so brackish, as to be scarcely drinkable. I have not another moment. God bless you! pray for me my beloved friends.

27 Eliza Fay, *Original Letters from India; containing a narrative of a journey through Egypt, and the author's imprisonment at Calicut by Hyder Ally. To which is added an abstract of three subsequent voyages to India. By Mrs. Fay* (Kolkata, 1821).

DOCUMENT 38

Image: Russian Anti-Turkish World War I Propaganda Poster, "Turkish Cowardice and Valiant Prowess" (1914)[28]

During World War I, all combatant nations used propaganda posters to influence popular opinion, at home and abroad. Many poster artists used racialized depictions of the enemy to sell war bonds, recruit soldiers and workers, boost morale, and persuade neutral nations to fight. This Russian poster used stereotypical images of "the Turk" to highlight their own cultural and military superiority. The caption reads, "Turkish cowardice and [Russian] valiant prowess."

ПРО ТРУСОСТЬ ТУРЕЦКУЮ ДА ПРО УДАЛЬ МОЛОДЕЦКУЮ.

28 "Turkish Cowardice and Valiant Prowess," Krasnoyarsk Museum of Regional Studies.

DOCUMENT 39

Correspondence about Moulvi Sadruddin, Imam of the Woking Mosque, and the Burial of Muslim Soldiers in England (1915)[29]

Sepoys: Indian soldiers recruited by European colonial powers. They were usually trained in "European" military tactics and were led by European officers.

One and half million men, including soldiers and non-combatants, were recruited into the British Indian Army between 1914 and 1919. **Sepoys** fought in battles around the world in this global conflict, yet have not until more recently received recognition on British war memorials, nor in history books. The tendency to devalue the service of some imperial soldiers is illustrated in the following 1915 document, where the Iman of the Shah Jahan Mosque in Woking, England, must fight for the right to bury the fallen with dignity.

This statement was made by Maulvi Sadr-Ud-Din at the Mosque, Woking, on August 27th, 1915. When the Indian soldiers were sent to the front, I—as head of the Mahommedan Church in England—was requested by the Government to bury any Mahommedan soldiers who might unfortunately die in England, from wounds or otherwise.

This I consented to do; a telegram being sent to the Viceroy who disseminated the news throughout the length and breadth of India, telling the native population that I should perform the obsequies according to the Mahommedan rite.

There arose the question of burial ground. Colonel Lucas, instructed by Colonial Sharman, of the Netley Hospital, and myself were called both to the War Office and India Office to discuss this question. The site suggested was part of the Christian cemetery within the confines of the Netley Hospital. I objected for three reasons. First, that it was not in accordance with Mahommedan ideas to be buried in a Christian cemetery; secondly, that any person desiring to visit the graves would first have to obtain permission from the War Office to pass into the grounds of Netley; and thirdly, on economic grounds that as there were six other hospitals with Indian soldiers in various parts of the country, there could not be six cemeteries and I could not possibly go from Woking to so many places. Therefore, I suggested that the burial ground should be near the mosque at Woking.

A great controversy arose and in the end a plot of land was provided through the kindness of Lord Onslow for the burial of the soldiers.

I then asked the Government whether they could not 1. Rail in the cemetery, 2. Make paths in the ground, 3. Provide a grave-digger, 4. Provide

29 Correspondence about Moulvi Sadruddin, Imam of the Woking Mosque, and the burial of Muslim soldiers in England, 27 August 1915, British Library, Mss Eur F143/80.

a caretaker, 5. Provide some place where the bodies could be left for the night, 6. Provide a decent waiting room, 7. Erect a gateway in Eastern style—however inexpensive—as a Memorial to the fallen Indian soldiers.

At first the Government blankly refused to do anything, and many months went past. I could not bury the dead soldiers in the marshy patch of unfenced ground over which people and dogs could stray; therefore, I buried twenty-five of them in the Mahommedan burial ground at Brookwood at my expense. This is now full, and I have already buried three in the new burial-place but, though it is fenced in, it is in such a disgraceful state that it would not be policy to allow the Indian soldiers to go and see the burial place of their comrades. They have frequently asked, but I have put them off because—being a loyal subject of his Majesty—I did not desire to raise the resentment which must inevitably be felt when the truth becomes known of the manner in which the British government have treated their dead heroes.

I have had bodies sent to me bearing the wrong names; bodies sent without any flowers; bodies sent to me at any hour of the day or night without any previous notice, and no respect shown for them whatever—not even any military demonstration at their graves.

No caretaker is provided for the Cemetery. If a visitor desires to go there, I myself—the head of the Mahommedan Church in England—is compelled to go with the key and admit the stranger, and already the cheap wooden doors are so warped that it is difficult to open them.

I desire to point out to the Government the very grave danger of allowing the impression to gain ground in India that England is not showing sufficient respect to the memories of her Indian heroes.

I need not enlarge upon the very serious effect which an exposure of this kind would make, both among the soldiers at the front, and the entire population throughout India.

DOCUMENT 40

From Mahfoud Rezigat, "It Was a Horrible Night" (1961)[30]

On October 5, 1961, during the Algerian War of Independence (1954–62), French police officials announced a nightly curfew from 8:30 p.m. to 5:30 a.m. for all Algerian Muslims and French Muslims living in Paris and its suburbs. Two weeks later, 30,000 people staged a protest against this mistreatment. French police responded violently, killing between 40 and 300 people, some of whom they threw into the river. A contemporary photograph shows graffiti on a bridge that reads, "ICI ON NOIE LES ALGERIENS," or "Here we drown Algerians." Only in 1998 did the French government acknowledge these killings. In the following passage, Mahfoud Rezigat describes his experiences during the Paris Massacre of 1961.

On October 17, I got back from work in Issy-les-Moulineaux [a suburb just south of Paris] with my friend Saâd and a group of Algerians from the hotel where we lived. It was 5pm. The **FLN** cell chief asked us to go to Charles-de-Gaulle-Étoile to demonstrate against the curfew. It had been in place since October 5, so all groups of Algerians were forbidden to be out on the street at night. I was often stopped by police.

FLN: The Front de libération nationale (National Liberation Front) was established in 1954 and became the central organization fighting for Algerian independence against French occupation forces. At the end of the war, the FLN was Algeria's sole ruling party until 1989.

The FLN's instructions were clear: we mustn't take a gun with us—and we had to be dressed in a way that showed pride in our Algerian identity. That was our state of mind as we set out for the demonstration. We took the metro to Corentin-Celton [just south of Paris]. When we arrived at the Porte-de-Versailles [an entry point to the city from the south], Algerians on their way back from Paris shouted at us: 'Don't go!' The police had already started arresting people.

We went back to our hotel. It was right in front of Vanves police station.... You could see from a distance that police were surrounding the hotel.

Saâd and I didn't know what to do. So, we went to the pub and had a drink. We went back to the hotel at 8.30pm, but the police were still there. We had to sleep in Vanves Park, which was just next door. At 6am, we went to work in Issy-les-Moulineaux.

30 Mahfoud Rezigat, "It Was a Horrible Night," Stories of an Unspeakable Night: October 17, 1961: A Massacre of Algerians in the Heart of Paris, France 24, https://webdoc.france24.com/october-17-1961-massacre-algerians-paris-france-police-history/chapter-2.html#rezigat.

On Friday, there was a terrible police raid on the hotel. I was by the window. A man was shot as he was doing his ablutions before prayers. He was shot. It was a horrible night.

The **harkis**—and I feel no hatred towards them—they were authorised to be very harsh. They'd shout: 'You want independence? You'll see, you dirty rebels, you stupid little rats!' There were insults, there was spitting. They set up a room at the back of the hotel and they'd take everyone they suspected there to be tortured.

harkis: A term used to identify Muslim Algerians who served as auxiliaries in the French Army during the Algerian War; it was also extended to include Algerians who supported the French over the National Liberation Front.

All the hotel's residents—including me—were taken to the Vincennes detention centre. It was well-known for its very harsh pre-trial detention, before the prisoners were taken somewhere else. There were two lines of police officers, and as we walked between them, they beat us with sticks, kicked us and spat at us. I was small, so I was on the receiving end of rather a lot of abuse. We weren't allowed to sleep. They'd throw water on us to wake us up.

The next day, they came and told me I was free to go. I was amazed. I left. They didn't know I'd spent three years in detention camps, otherwise they wouldn't have let me go.

There'd been attacks on the police that August. According to the FLN, they targeted officers who'd tortured Algerians. After that, **Papon** said: 'For every policeman killed, we'll kill ten Algerians' ["For every blow against us, we'll fight back with ten"]. It's also possible that this repression was aimed at squashing the talks between the French government and the FLN.

Papon: Maurice Papon was prefect of the Paris police during the 1961 Paris Massacre and during the February 1962 police attacks against Communist demonstrators, having previously participated in the deportation of Jews from Bordeaux during the Holocaust. Papon served in successive French governments into the 1980s and in 1998 was convicted of crimes against humanity. He died in 2004.

Now I expect President [Emmanuel] Macron to officially recognise that October 17 was a state crime and to grant access to the archives. Above all, I hope that on the 60th anniversary of Algeria's independence next year, he recognises colonialism as a crime against humanity. He said it was [a crime against humanity] when he was a presidential candidate [during the 2017 race]."

DOCUMENT 41

The Heidelberg Circle, "Heidelberg Manifesto" (1982)[31]

This document was written by conservative German academics to warn against Muslim immigration to Germany. It was largely in response to the post-World War II guest worker program, which encouraged the migration of workers from countries such as Turkey, Morocco, Italy, and the former Yugoslavia, to help rebuild the West German economy. The academics believed foreigners would taint the German people. This document was widely condemned due to its racist and xenophobic message.

With great concern, we observe the infiltration of the German people through an influx of millions of foreigners and their families, the infiltration of our language, our culture, and our national traditions by foreign influences. Despite the recruitment ban, the number of registered foreigners rose by 309,000 in the year 1980 alone; 194,000 of these foreigners are Turks. A little more than half of the number of children needed to maintain our [German] population are being born each year. In their neighborhoods and workplaces, many Germans already feel like foreigners in their own land.

The federal government promoted the influx of foreigners on the basis of [a policy of] unbridled economic growth that is now recognized as questionable. Up to this point, the German population has not been informed of the significance and consequences of these actions. For this reason, we are calling for the establishment of a politically and ideologically independent coalition whose task is to preserve the German **Volk** and its spiritual identity on the basis of our occidental Christian heritage. Standing firmly on the foundation of the **Basic Law**, we oppose ideological nationalism, racism, and every form of right- and left-wing extremism.

Volk: German term with a contentious history. The direct translation is "people," but it also represents a specific German nationhood and identity.

Basic Law: Refers to the 1949 constitution of the Federal Republic of Germany, which guaranteed fundamental human rights for most citizens.

In biological and cybernetic terms, peoples are living systems of a higher order with distinct system qualities that are passed on genetically and through tradition. The integration of large masses of non-German foreigners is therefore not possible without threatening the preservation of our people, and it will lead to the well-known ethnic catastrophes of multicultural societies.

Every people, including the Germans, has a natural right to preserve its identity and particular character in the place in which it resides. Respect for other peoples also necessitates their preservation, not their assimilation

31 "Heidelberger Manifest," *Frankfurter Rundschau*, 4 March 1982. Translated by Allison Brown for German History in Documents and Images.

("Germanization"). We perceive Europe as an organism of peoples and nations that are worthy of preservation and that share a common history....

What hope for the future do the hundreds of thousands of [guest-worker] children have if they are illiterate in both their native tongue and in the German language? What hope for the future do our own children have if they are being educated in classes with a preponderance of foreigners? Will the billions spent for the defense of our country have been worth it at the end of such a development?

Only active and viable German families can preserve our people for the future. Our own children alone are the sole basis for the German and European future.

Since technical advancement offers options (and will continue to offer more options) that make the employment of foreigners superfluous, the highest principle of economic management must be: do not bring people to machines, but machines to people.

Attacking the problem at its roots means offering focused development aid to improve the living conditions of guest workers in their home countries—and not here in our country. For the Federal Republic of Germany, one of the most densely populated countries in the world, returning foreigners to their ancestral homelands will not only provide social relief but environmental relief as well....

DOCUMENT 42

Image: Jochen Eckel, The Solingen Arson Attack (1993)[32]

Xenophobic sentiment continued after the fall of the Berlin Wall and was frequently accompanied by violent attacks against peoples considered foreign in **reunified Germany**. In May 1993, four German men, ages 16–23, and with ties to local **neo-Nazi organizations**, set fire to the home of a Turkish family living in Solingen, North Rhine-Westphalia. Three girls and two women died, and 14 other family members were injured. The perpetrators were all found guilty and sentenced to 10–15 years in prison. The murderous attack also prompted protests in support of the German Turkish community across the nation.

reunified Germany: Nation built after 1990 from the union of the Federal Republic of Germany and the German Democratic Republic. A rapid reunification process brought these peoples politically and economically together, but also triggered a series of societal problems, including a rise in violent attacks on racialized peoples.

neo-Nazi organizations: Part of a widespread movement to resurrect Nazi ideology after the 1945 death of Adolf Hitler. Neo-Nazis support white supremacy, and profess sexist, racist, and anti-democratic beliefs.

32 *Süddeutsche Zeitung*, 30 May 1993. Sueddeutsche Zeitung Photo/Alamy Stock Photo.

DOCUMENT 43

From "The Courage of a Mother: Kadefa Rizvanović" (1992–95)[33]

Kadefa Rizvanović was a victim of the Bosnian War. The war was fought following the dissolution of Yugoslavia in the early 1990s. Bosnia and Herzegovina was a proposed multi-ethnic community, composed of Muslim Bosniaks, Orthodox Serbs, and Catholic Croats. Following Bosnia and Herzegovina's declaration of independence in 1992, the region fell into violence as the Bosnian Serbs mobilized to ensure Serb territory. Conflict was accompanied by ethnic cleansing and genocide perpetrated against the Muslim Bosniaks. The Srebrenica massacre saw the mass murder of thousands of Muslim Bosnian men and boys. Following the end of the conflict, the United Nations created the International Criminal Tribunal for the former Yugoslavia to bring charges against the perpetrators of the conflict.

Before the war, I lived in Voljavica, in the municipality of Bratunac. My childhood was very happy. We didn't differentiate when it came to nationality: who was a Serb, who was a Muslim and who was a Croat. We socialized together, I had friends—we visited them when they were celebrating "**Slava**," they came to our homes during **Bajram**. I had a friend, Milada, a Serb, and I loved her like she was my sister. We were at school and spent our school days together. Later, we worked together at a sewing company, where we were just before the war.

Slava: An annual tradition in Serbian Orthodox Christian communities where families celebrate their patron saint.

Bajram: Also known as Eid al-Adha and the Feast of Sacrifice, an annual Muslim tradition involving family and friends and honoring Abraham's willingness to sacrifice his son Ishmael.

On the 17th April 1992 in Srebrenica, when I was coming back from work, Bratunac was blockaded. I was nine months pregnant. The people in Bratunac were already armed, walking around with insignia and beards, the Yugoslavian army, different paramilitary units, the police. Milada and I decided to go through the forests towards my settlement. We managed to get through the forests, she had lunch at our home in Voljavica and went back to her own home. We helped each other escape that day, but we never saw each other again after that.

On the 7th of May I went into labour. Everything was blockaded. I couldn't reach a hospital. My mother-in-law and her mother-in-law delivered my baby at home. There were already patrols around, they had asked people to surrender their weapons if they had them. Villages around us were burning. We were afraid for our lives. Some people surrendered. On the 12th of May, we finally had to leave. We headed off through the forest—my late

33 From Remembering Srebrenica, https://www.srebrenica.org.uk/survivor-stories/kadefa-rizvanovic/.

husband and his family, me and my two day old baby. As I had just given birth, I could hardly walk.

I begged them to leave me behind, so they did not risk their lives, to take my baby and leave me behind. My husband said: "I will carry you, but I won't leave you."

Twenty-two days later, through the tough and thorny paths of the forest, we reached Srebrenica.

When we arrived, we didn't have anywhere to go. We found an empty Serbian house and I was allowed to stay there because of the baby. Seventeen of us stayed in that house. We stayed there in terrible suffering until 1995, hungry and thirsty, exhausted, without clothes, electricity, or water.

As women, we had to fight like lions in order for our children to survive.

There was a huge food crisis. In such situations you are just struggling to feed your children, you're not important. Most of the women went through the territories under Serb control to find food, to bring it back in order to survive. There were women who were going and digging so they could feed their children. I was trying to plant something: carrots, or something to give to my child. It was a huge struggle to survive. It was hard, but we had to be strong.

In 1993, when the UN declared Srebrenica a safe zone, we felt some relief. The UN would protect us, at least some of our suffering would end, we wouldn't be hungry, we wouldn't be fired upon. We trusted in the UN forces. But they betrayed us.

In July 1995, Serbs started firing their weapons on the town. It was unbearable—we knew that they would break through the lines and enter the town. Masses of people from Srebrenica started moving towards Potočari. Nobody knew what was going on. The most difficult part for me was when we left the house, and arrived at my brother's place near the gas station. There were so many people there that we couldn't breathe.

My husband gave me a hug and told me: "Look after the children, I must go." I never saw him again.

I can never forget that scene, at the gas station in Srebrenica. Then the men started heading in a column, through the woods, under heavy fire. My daughter was three years old, and she walked all the way to Potočari with me. Her shoes were filled with blood from blisters, but she didn't cry, she didn't say a word. I was carrying my 14 month old son but I slipped and dropped him on the asphalt. He wasn't giving any signs of life, until my mother took a bottle of water and sprayed him.

When we arrived at Potočari, we could hear screaming in the distance. Then they started separating us. A Serbian soldier, unknown to me, came and tried to take a boy away. My mother said: "He's only a child; he's not even 10 years old." He kicked him with his foot and said: "No one's asking questions here." They never brought him back. Many men were taken like that. At that point I was really aware that things were not going to end in a good way. Then the trucks to transport us to the free territory of Kladanj arrived.

When we got to the trucks, they started separating men from women. We started moving towards Kladanj; we stopped every now and then: slowdowns, checkpoints, mistreatments, swearing, "they betrayed you," "nobody wants you," spitting, pouring water on us. We had to bear all of it.

When we finally got to Tuzla, I went to stay with my brother. Eleven of us stayed in his apartment. Then, we started to hear different information. Some were alive, some weren't. Or that all had been killed. Then some groups of people started arriving. I was begging my brother to go and seek information about my husband: did anybody see him, what happened? But no one knew anything. In 2003 they told me that they had found my husband. He was found in Pilica, Zvornik. What monsters are they? To drive him so many kilometers away, maltreat and hide him there. I simply cannot understand that another human could do something like that.

The war affected me a lot. They killed most of my family, over 20 close relatives of mine. They destroyed entire generations. I felt the effect on my health. After the fall of Srebrenica, I got an ulcer. I had surgery on my thyroid glands. Of course it affected my children, too. Not only my children, but most of the children. What were we doing, but sitting, crying, and talking about the subject? Of course it's going to affect our children. The war destroyed my soul, my heart; it took the joy from me. It took everything nice from me. They took it from me: the Serbs. They were all poisoned. Not all of them, but most of them were.

They took my youth, my joy, my home, my job. They took everything they could. They took all of my human rights.

It is important to talk, to write, to record, for the sake of history. Our children and youth, will learn the lessons from this war, from our stories. It's simple, ordinary people get hurt and lose everything. I appeal to the young people, to socialize together, to talk, and to build their futures and this country, in order for Bosnia to become the best country in the world. Actually, it is the best country in the world—it only needs more harmony and love.

DOCUMENT 44

"UN Rights Chief 'Appalled' at Recent Treatment of Refugees, Migrants by Hungarian Authorities" (2015)[34]

During 2015, 1.3 million people (many fleeing the Syrian War) requested asylum in European countries, which led to widespread debates about refugee policies across the continent. This report from the United Nations discusses practices at the Hungarian-Serbian border.

"The images of women and young children being assaulted with tear gas and water cannons at Hungary's border with Serbia were truly shocking," High Commissioner for Human Rights Zeid Ra'ad Al Hussein said in a news release.

"I am appalled at the callous, and in some cases illegal, actions of the Hungarian authorities in recent days, which include denying entry to, arresting, summarily rejecting and returning refugees, using disproportionate force on migrants and refugees, as well as reportedly assaulting journalists and seizing video documentation. Some of these actions amount to clear violations of international law."

The Hungarian Government has built a fence on its border with Serbia and closed border crossings. A new law criminalizing irregular entry into Hungary came into effect Tuesday, according to the High Commissioner's office.

Hungary has reportedly already begun returning refugees to Serbia, following very summary proceedings. The Government is also talking of building more fences along its other borders with Romania and Croatia.

Hungarian Prime Minister Victor Orban defended the measures, arguing that they concerned "defending our lifestyle," and contrasted this lifestyle with that of Muslims, the news release pointed out.

High Commissioner Zeid deplored the xenophobic and anti-Muslim views that appear to lie at the heart of current Hungarian Government policy.

"The package of measures brought in overnight between Monday and Tuesday is incompatible with the human rights commitments binding on Hungary," the High Commissioner said. "This is an entirely unacceptable infringement of the human rights of refugees and migrants. Seeking asylum is not a crime, and neither is entering a country irregularly."

---

34 "UN Rights Chief 'Appalled' at Recent Treatment of Refugees, Migrants by Hungarian Authorities," UN News: Global Perspective Human Stories, 17 September 2015, https://news.un.org/en/story/2015/09/509072.

"Many have made harrowing sea journeys to avoid other border fences," he added.

He also said he is extremely concerned at the "repeated failures" of the European Union to agree on firm and principled action to respond to the crisis in Hungary and elsewhere. "Current events highlight the urgent need for bolder and more human-rights driven migration and asylum policies in Europe."

DOCUMENT 45

Hillary Margolis, "Denmark's Face Veil Ban Latest in Harmful Trend" (2018)[35]

In the years following the 9/11 attacks in the United States, governments have increasingly sought to regulate and control the lives of Muslim individuals, especially women. For instance, there has been increased pushback in many European and North American countries against women's religious clothing. There are several articles of clothing that allow women to adhere to Islamic teachings on physical modesty. The *burqa* (or burka or paranja) is an outer garment that covers the wearer's entire body, including the face. *Niqāb* cover the face and body, but leave the eyes uncovered. A *hijab* usually refers to a scarf that covers the wearer's head, but not the face. This 2018 Human Rights Watch article discusses the situation in Denmark.

On Thursday, Denmark became the latest in a string of European countries to ban the wearing of full-face coverings in public. Parliament voted overwhelmingly (75 to 30) to adopt legislation that will have a disproportionate impact on one group only: Muslim women.

The law—which fines first-time offenders 1,000 kroner ($156 USD)—also bans fake beards, balaclavas, and other face masks. But those most likely to cover their faces in public are Muslim women who choose to wear the burqa or niqab, a veil that leaves only the eyes visible.

Discussion about the proposed law has had a decidedly anti-Muslim tone. The Danish Minister of Justice, Søren Pape Poulsen, argued that Islamic face coverings are "disrespectful" and "incompatible with Danish values." The spokesperson on immigration and integration of the **Danish People's Party** explicitly cited a decade of efforts to ban the burqa and niqab in public, and vowed to push for new measures against the "Islamicisation of Denmark."

Danish People's Party: A nationalist and populist political party in Denmark, which tends to oppose immigration and multiculturalism and the country's European Union membership. They have been losing political support since 2015.

Governments may restrict rights to freedom of expression or religion, such as expressed through clothing, but only when such restrictions are proportionate and on reasonable grounds. The Danish law is neither. Measures short of a complete ban can be instituted to address security concerns, such as allowing covered women to unveil in private spaces and be checked by female security officers. A total ban hardly seems warranted, and only fuels existing stigma and Islamophobic sentiment.

35 Hillary Margolis, "Denmark's Face Veil Ban Latest in Harmful Trend," Human Rights Watch, 1 June 2018, https://www.hrw.org/news/2018/06/01/denmarks-face-veil-ban-latest-harmful-trend.

For Muslim women who feel uncomfortable being uncovered in public, a ban can cut off their access to public transit, education, employment, and social services, isolating and blocking these women from opportunities to integrate into society. Arguments that banning the burqa or niqab helps liberate women also miss the point. Women choose to wear face coverings for many reasons. Telling women how to dress doesn't liberate them—it denies them the right to make their own choices.

Just as women should not be forced to wear the niqab, burqa or other religious dress, nor should they be punished for choosing to do so. Laws that do either are discriminatory. Denmark's ban is part of a worrisome trend that only marginalizes Muslim women in Europe and penalizes them for expressing their beliefs.

DOCUMENT 46

United Nations Secretary-General's Video Message on the International Day to Combat Islamophobia (2021)[36]

António Guterres took office as Secretary-General of the United Nations in 2017. On 15 March 2021, he marked the first International Day to Combat Islamophobia, after 60 UN Member-States adopted a resolution calling for a greater respect for human rights and religious diversity and stating, "terrorism and violent extremism cannot and should not be associated with any religion, nationality, civilization, or ethnic group."[37]

I thank the Organization of Islamic Cooperation for your timely focus on tackling the global challenge of Islamophobia, anti-Muslim bigotry and discrimination.

Just days ago, a report to the Human Rights Council found that suspicion, discrimination and outright hatred towards Muslims has risen to "epidemic proportions."

The report detailed a host of examples: disproportionate restrictions on the ability of Muslims to manifest their beliefs, the securitization of religious communities, limits on access to citizenship, socioeconomic exclusion and widespread stigmatization of Muslim communities.

The report also highlighted the intersectional dimensions of anti-Muslim bigotry—where Muslim women confront triple levels of discrimination because of their gender, ethnicity and faith.

Unfortunately, far too often, stereotypes are further compounded by elements of the media and some in positions of power.

Anti-Muslim bigotry is sadly in line with other distressing trends we are seeing globally—a resurgence in ethno-nationalism, neo-Nazism, stigma and hate speech targeting vulnerable populations including Muslims, Jews, some minority Christian communities as well as others.

Let us also remember that many acts of intolerance and suspicion may not appear in official statistics—but those acts degrade people's dignity and our common humanity.

Discrimination diminishes us all. It prevents people—and societies—from achieving their full potential.

36 "Secretary-General's Video Message on the International Day to Combat Islamophobia," United Nations, 17 March 2021, https://www.un.org/sg/en/content/sg/statement/2021-03-17/secretary-generals-video-message-the-international-day-combat-islamophobia.

37 "International Day to Combat Islamophobia 15 March," United Nations, https://www.un.org/en/observances/anti-islamophobia-day.

We must also place a special focus on safeguarding the rights of minority communities, many of whom are under threat around the world.

Minority communities are part of the richness of our cultural and social fabric.

Yet we see not only forms of discrimination but also policies of assimilation that seek to wipe out the cultural and religious identity of minority communities.

We must continue to push for policies that fully respect human rights and religious, cultural and unique human identity.

As the Holy Quran reminds us: nations and tribes were created to know one another.

Diversity is a richness, not a threat.

As we move toward evermore multi-ethnic and multi-religious societies, we need political, cultural and economic investments to strengthen social cohesion and tackle bigotry.

For all these reasons, fighting discrimination, racism and xenophobia is a priority for the United Nations.

And it is why we launched a first-of-its-kind UN Strategy on Hate Speech as well as a Plan of Action to Safeguard Religious Sites.

We also fully support vital work towards fostering interfaith harmony such as the Document of Human Fraternity co-authored by His Holiness Pope Francis and His Eminence the Grand Imam of Al Azhar Dr. Ahmed Al Tayyeb.

Let us keep working together to advance the shared values of inclusion, tolerance and mutual understanding—values that are at the heart of all major faiths and the United Nations Charter.

Once again, thank you for your efforts to stand up against anti-Muslim bigotry and for human rights. Let us keep striving for justice, dignity and inclusion. For our Muslim brothers and sisters—and for all humanity.

Thank you.

PART 3

Racism against Black Peoples

INTRODUCTION

Medieval Europeans based their understanding of the world and its peoples on two ancient sources: the Christian and Jewish Scriptures, which they believed were absolutely authoritative, if often difficult to interpret; and the ancient Greek and Roman philosophers, such as **Aristotle**, whom they believed were correct in everything apart from religion. The result was that medieval Christians inherited the ancient beliefs about ethnic differences and skin color, and it was only when Europeans began to engage in the African slave trade in the later fifteenth century that they began to develop a different understanding of blackness, one that over time fused Spanish notions of **blood purity** (see Document 5) and lineage with a racialized approach to skin color. As they became fixated on blackness as a negative characteristic, they increasingly came to see whiteness as the polar opposite, as identified with all of the positive characteristics that the ancients had associated with living in a moderate climate (see general introduction above).

Aristotle: Ancient Greek philosopher whose writings on philosophy and science were regarded as authoritative by Europeans well into the early modern era.

blood purity: A Spanish concept that only Christian blood was pure and that Jewish or Muslim blood would corrupt it.

The ancient Greek philosopher Plato (427–347 BCE) believed that as the mind rules over the body, the higher rules naturally over the lower. Those who were conquered by the Greeks proved by their defeat that they were lower, and thus deserving of conquest. Plato's student Aristotle (384–322 BCE) developed this concept further by arguing on behalf of "natural slavery," that the lower sort of people are by nature slaves, marked by subjugation by birth, just as animals were better off when tamed by humans. These, he believed, were the less intellectual people who were of a stronger build suitable for physical servitude.

While absorbing much of Greek philosophy and culture, the ancient Romans did not retain Aristotle's notion of natural slavery. Instead, they considered all foreigners as outsiders, as "barbarians" whose language and culture were incomprehensible and uncivilized. Those peoples they could conquer they often enslaved to keep their agricultural estates and households staffed. Yet, they did not believe that these captives were by nature slaves; instead, they could be civilized by taking on Roman language (Latin), culture, and civilization. They could in fact become free and be granted Roman citizenship, regardless of skin color or ethnic origin. Those who, like the Germans, could not be conquered, the Romans argued were too barbarian, but they could still make political and military deals with them. Those non-Roman peoples who were needed to defend the outer boundaries (*limes*) of the Empire, such as the **Gauls**, were granted some rights, but even in the early fifth century were still not admitted into the Roman Senate. Compromise and service to Rome were the key, and education the means to citizenship. Both the Romans and the Greeks explained variations in skin color as a result of the environment, that where on earth people lived determined their physical and intellectual characteristics. The sun's heat also played a major role in their understanding of coloration. Romans believed that Greeks, Egyptians, and Syrians, for example, were capable of intellectual activity, while Gauls and Germans were better suited to heavy labor. Black Ethiopians were typically viewed as best suited as household servants or bath attendants.

Gauls: A group of Celtic peoples resident in what is now France and Western Germany.

The Germans proved a problem for the Romans, and it was the Roman historian Tacitus (c. 56–c. 120 CE) who argued that they could not be conquered because they were a pure race, without the kind of ethnic mixture of the Roman Empire. They were strong, fierce, and tougher than the Romans, yet there was in Tacitus' account no mention of skin color, although here he described the Germans as "distinct, of pure blood, like none but themselves. Hence, too, are the same physical peculiarities throughout so vast a population. All have fierce blue eyes, red hair and huge frames, fit only for a sudden exertion. They are less able to bear laborious work. Heat and thirst they cannot in the least endure; their climate and soil inures them to cold and hunger."[1] As with Aristotle's concept of natural slavery, Tacitus's description of "pure blood" people would become important as Europeans interacted more actively with Black Africans. Medieval Europeans had very little contact with Black Africans, whom they typically called "Moors" or "Black Moors." Blacks in Europe were usually servants or members of Ottoman and North African embassies. There was a lot of ignorance as to what the peoples of the rest of the world, including Africa, were like, as seen in Documents 47 and 48, which were based, again, on an ancient Roman source, that by **Pliny**.

Pliny: Pliny the Elder (23–79 CE), Roman natural scientist and author of *Naturalis Historia* (*Natural History*).

As Iberians (Spanish and especially Portuguese) explored the African coast in the fifteenth century, they followed a generally Roman perspective toward these peoples as different, but still human, if uncivilized and inferior. These sailors searched for the mythical Prester John, an eastern Christian king of enormous wealth and power who could help them to defeat Islam, believing that his kingdom must be in Eastern Africa or Ethiopia. While they never found him, the Portuguese established diplomatic relations with the kings of Congo, in Western coastal Africa, converting them to Christianity.

1 Tacitus, *Germania*, chapter 4, https://www.unrv.com/tacitus/tacitusgermania.php.

This Roman-like relationship between Europeans and Africans would change dramatically over the course of the late fifteenth through the eighteenth centuries as Europeans moved from bit players in the African slave trade to the creators of the Atlantic slave trade which would force millions of Africans into lifelong slavery in Brazil, the West Indies (Caribbean), and the Americas (Document 58). There they were the principal laborers in the vastly profitable sugar, coffee, and tobacco plantations. It became necessary for the slave traders and their patrons to justify the permanent enslavement of these people. Writers thus engaged in a debate over the origins of blackness, increasingly favoring an interpretation of the Curse of Noah (Genesis 9:25–27) that would justify treating Africans as sub-humans. In this myth of a great Flood, Noah and his family had landed on dry land, when Noah was found by his sons naked in a drunken stupor; Cham laughed at him, while the other two covered him up. Noah heard of this, and cursed Cham (Ham), saying that his son Canaan and his descendants would forever be servants. There is no reference in this account of skin color or Africa, but early modern interpreters claimed that this was the true cause of the Black skin of sub-Saharan Africans. A divine curse and Aristotle's philosophy helped justify treating Black people as natural slaves. The Atlantic slave trade became one of the most lucrative forms of international business for all Western European nations, especially so for the Portuguese, British, French, Spanish, and Dutch. Some writers opposed it, especially those from religious nonconformist groups like the English Quakers (Document 55) who argued that Black Africans were like all other humans with a soul and the divine spark within. Others, like Edward Long (Document 56) used the Spanish pure blood laws to craft a chart of biological distinctions based on skin color. The Atlantic slave trade was the major factor in the racialization of skin color, broadening the biological racism inherent in antisemitism into a formal, scientific racism of the nineteenth century. It also brought thousands of Black Africans into European society.

The example of Angelo Soliman (c. 1721–96) illustrates many of the shifting perceptions of Black lives in modern Europe. Born in Western Africa in 1721, Soliman was taken as a slave to Vienna, where he served in multiple families as a "**House Moor**," a soldier, a tutor, an advisor, and a valet. He joined Austrian society, becoming a confident of **Emperor Joseph II**, and a member of the **Freemasons** with the composer Mozart. Despite having gained the respect of prominent Viennese citizens, upon his death Soliman's dead body was stuffed, mounted as an exotic trophy, and put on display. All this occurred over the written protests of his daughter.[2]

House Moor: A servant or enslaved person of a wealthy household; here African heritage is denoted by the designation "Moor."

Emperor Joseph II: Holy Roman Emperor, 1765–90; son of Empress Maria Theresa and brother of Marie Antoinette. He saw himself as an "enlightened" absolutist monarch.

Freemasons: Members of a fraternal organization that dates to the thirteenth century.

---

2 Jeff Bowersox, "Angelo Soliman (ca. 1721–96)," Black Central Europe, https://blackcentraleurope.com/sources/1750-1850/angelo-soliman-ca-1750/.

Indeed, increasingly after the **American Emancipation Proclamation of 1863**, African Americans began to visit Europe as tourists, students, activists, and musicians. Some viewed European countries as being freer and more equal than the United States, while others experienced the same types of prejudice as they had at home. The rise of **racial science** greatly impacted how some Europeans viewed Black peoples with authors such as **Samuel George Morton** arguing that physical appearance denoted cultural inferiority: "Characterized by a black complexion, and black, woolly hair; the eyes are large and prominent, the nose broad and flat, the lips thick, and the mouth wide.... In disposition the **Negro** is joyous, flexible, and indolent.... The Negroes are proverbially fond of their amusements, in which they engage with great exuberance of spirit; and a day of toil is with them no bar to a night of revelry. The Negroes have little invention, but strong powers of imitation, so that they readily acquire mechanic arts. They have a great talent for music, and all their external senses are remarkably acute" (see also Documents 62, 63, 67). Such intentional combining of traditional stereotypes with "modern" principles convinced increasing numbers of white Europeans of their own racial superiority, in ways like Tacitus' writings about Germans and Romans. Advertisers used these racist stereotypes to sell products (Documents 61, 65) and promoters sold tickets to ethnographic exhibits featuring human beings (Documents 60, 64)

Such assumptions supported European global expansion, especially in the latter part of the nineteenth century. The "**Scramble for Africa**" that followed the **1884–85 Berlin Conference** was justified by invented racialized hierarchies, whether by businessmen who sought to exploit "uncultivated" lands, missionaries who believed in their religious mission of saving souls, or philanthropists who implemented programs based on civilizing missions. Settler colonialism mandated that Europeans maintain racist power hierarchies if they wished to keep control of stolen lands.

Long before Nazi officials sought to reorder German society based on racial categories, European imperialists had used similarly constructed hierarchies as a tool to gain and maintain power among occupied peoples. Sexual race-mixing, or **miscegenation**, seemed to confuse these power structures. For instance, in 1908 anthropologist Eugen Fischer journeyed to German Southwest Africa (present-day Namibia) to conduct research on the Rehoboth Basters, a community descended from relationships between Afrikaner settlers and Indigenous Khoikhoi women. Fischer measured physical differences, traced genealogical lineages, and evaluated supposed moral characteristics, all to uncover the biological effects of racial mixture in humans. He concluded that miscegenation resulted in the degeneration of the "higher" race. Fischer conducted his anthropological fieldwork in the region most devastated by the German-Herero War of 1904–05, a genocidal

American Emancipation Proclamation of 1863: During the American Civil War, President Abraham Lincoln's proclamation declared "that all persons held as slaves" within the rebellious states "are, and henceforward shall be free." Despite the optimistic language, many African Americans remained enslaved or otherwise unfree.

racial science: Also known as biological racism and scientific racism, the false belief that racial difference, including hierarchies of superiority and inferiority, can be proven with empirical evidence.

Samuel George Morton: American physician and racial scientist who used his collection of a thousand skulls from around the world to argue against the idea that all humans have common ancestry.

Negro: A term historically used for persons of Black African heritage that comes from the Spanish/Portuguese word for black; it is no longer regarded as an appropriate term for use outside Black communities.

Scramble for Africa: The annexation and occupation of almost all African lands between 1881 and 1914. By the time of World War I, European powers controlled 90 percent of the continent, with only Liberia and Ethiopia remaining independent.

conflict that resulted in the deaths of at least 60,000 Herero, and 10,000 Nama peoples (see Document 66).[3]

Even while activists continued to showcase the vibrancy of Black culture in Europe (Document 68), racist thinking dominated high-level decision-making. Reflecting the Aristotelean attitudes toward natural slavery referenced above, French military general Charles Mangin similarly used racial characteristics to justify coercive action. In his 1910 *La Force Noire*, Mangin argued that European armies should harness the immense manpower pool of their African colonies, especially given Black men's status as "born soldiers," unspoiled by modern life, and who were especially good at soldiering because of their higher tolerance for physical pain. And, with the outbreak of the 1914–18 conflict, European military leaders used Black men as cannon fodder and laborers on the Western Front, while in the African sphere of war, they used Black men as porters and carriers, roles in which they literally transported the necessities of war on their backs. African civilians suffered from manmade famines and mass social dislocation. Historians estimate at least 250,000 men died while in the service of European armies, while the civilian death toll remains unknown.

Kande Kamara was working as a driver in the Guinean capital city, Bamako, when he heard about France's recruitment campaign for its European war. He immediately set off for home but found his village (**Kindia**) almost empty, with most men gone into hiding from the army recruiters.[4] He volunteered for military service against his parents' wishes, and following basic training was sent to a segregated camp for African soldiers on the outskirts of Bordeaux. From an interview Kamara gave in 1976, we know he often felt like a spectacle in the community: "When we arrived we were sent for parades. The people were roaring [as we walked past]. But if you turned left or right to look at them, you were slapped and you actually saw the fire of hell." Of the Germans he wrote: "Because of the colour of our skin, the Germans said we were shoes. The only people they respected and feared were white. We were black so we were nothing.... It hurt every black man. They actually underestimated us and disgraced us and dishonoured us." Though African units were segregated from European ones for most of the war, Kamara recalled noticing a gradual shift towards equality: "At the beginning of the war, the white people were always in the front

1884–85 Berlin Conference: Hosted by Otto von Bismarck of Germany, this meeting of 14 nations resulted in even greater European influence in Africa. Contemporary caricatures show imperialists "carving up the pie" of that continent.

miscegenation: Meaning sexual intercourse between people of different "races" and first coined by David Goodman Croly in *Miscegenation: The Theory of the Blending of the Races, Applied to the American White Man and Negro*. During the 1864 American presidential election, the term was frequently used by opponents of interracial relationships.

Kindia: Today, the fourth largest city in Guinea; can also refer to the Kindia Region of Western Guinea.

---

3 Lisa M. Todd, "Studying Sexual and Racial 'Mixture': Eugen Fischer and the Rehoboth Basters of German Southwest Africa, 1908–1913," in *After the Imperialist Imagination: Two Decades of Research on Global Germany and Its Legacies*, ed. Sara Pugach, David Pizzo, and Adam Blackler (Oxford: Peter Lang, 2020), 79–92.

4 This account is based on transcripts of an interview conducted by Joe Opala in 1976 in Bumbuna, Sierra Leone, and translated from the Susu by Abdul Kamara. Tapes and transcripts of the interview are deposited at the National Archives of Senegal. Svetlana Palmer and Sarah Willis, eds., *Intimate Voices from the First World War* (New York: HarperCollins, 2005).

line, but when we got to understand them and when they started trusting us that changed. At the very end of the war, we were all mixed, because by then everyone knew their mind and their heart and no one was afraid of colour except for the innocents." Kamara returned home in 1919.

Anti-Black racism remained multi-faceted in the 1920s. E.D. Morel illustrated (Document 69) how this form of prejudice was a central tenet of the so-called Black Horror on the Rhine, in which international audiences called for the protection of white women from the sexual advances of Black men. Anthropologists across the continent continued to study what they saw as the innate differences between peoples. At the same time, African American musicians, such as Josephine Baker, filled clubs and concert halls with European audiences who were by turns thrilled, or scandalized, by their performances. That European publics could simultaneously voice admiration for, and repulsion against, Black bodies illustrates a key interworking of white supremacy, one that continues in our culture today.

Black Germans suffered heightened persecution in the Third Reich (Document 70). Though not initially targeted for genocide like their Jewish and Romani neighbors, Black people were victims of Nazi racialized violence, including physical attacks, forced sterilizations, and concentration camp imprisonment. While in the camps, Black prisoners, including Allied prisoners-of-war were subjected to extreme brutality and medical experiments. German filmmakers used doctored footage of African POWs in their efforts to convince audiences that in using African soldiers, Allied governments were committing "crimes against the white race."[5]

The post-1945 period saw increased immigration to European nations. As illustrated by Document 72, the arrival to Britain of more than 500,000 people from the Caribbean to Great Britain resulted in conflicts between those citizens who wished to build a more tolerant multicultural society and those who worried about supposed "threats" to the "traditional British way of life." Communist states expressed solidarity both with African peoples (especially those in politically friendly communist states) and with African Americans during the civil rights movements. We now know these anti-racist ideological stances did not always play out on the ground. Decolonization movements led to freedom from imperial rule for tens of millions of people in Africa and to vibrant anti-racist movements across Europe (Document 71). As we continue to witness police violence against Black men and still read about bananas being hurled at Black soccer players, Black Europeans push back against systemic racism and advocate for postcolonial interpretations to be added to monuments, museum exhibits, school curricula and research agendas (Document 73).

---

5 See the video "1940 African POWs of the French Army Filmed by Nazis," Black Central Europe, https://blackcentraleurope.com/sources/1914-1945/prisoners-of-war-1939-40/.

DOCUMENT 47

Image: The "Blemmyes," a European Image of Africans (c. 1400s)[6]

This image is from a fifteenth-century manuscript account of the adventures of **Alexander the Great**, depicting Alexander's encounter with the "Blemmyes," the supposed headless people of Ethiopia, as described in Pliny.

Alexander the Great: Ancient Greek king of Macedonia, Alexander III of Macedon (356–23) whose conquests extended his empire from Greece to India.

6 A European image of Africans, British Library.

DOCUMENT 48

From George Best, *A True Discourse of the Late Voyage of Discovery* (1578)[7]

George Best sailed with the famed explorer **Martin Frobisher** on his second and third voyages. He apparently died while dueling in 1584. His travel account was later published by **Richard Hakluyt**.

Martin Frobisher: Frobisher (c. 1535–94) was an English seaman who sought the Northwest Passage through the Arctic Ocean, reaching Baffin Island.

Richard Hakluyt: Hakluyt (1553–1616) was an English Anglican priest and writer who promoted English colonization efforts in North America.

I myself have seen an Ethiopian as black as coal brought into England, who taking a fair English woman to Wife, begat a Son in all respects as black as the Father was, although England were his native Country, & an English woman his Mother: whereby it seems this blackness proceeds rather of some natural infection of that man, which was so strong, that neither the nature of the **Clime**, neither the good complexion of the Mother concurring, could anything alter, and therefore we cannot impute it to the nature of the Clime....

Clime: Climate.

It manifestly and plainly appears by holy Scripture, that after the general **Inundation** and overflowing of the Earth, there remained no more men alive, but **Noah** & his three sons, Sem, Cham, and Japhet, who only were left to possess & inhabit the whole face of the earth: therefore all the land that until this day hath been inhabited by sundry **descents**, must needs come of the offspring either of Sem, Cham, or Japhet, as the only sons of Noah, who all three being white, and their wives also, by course of nature, should have begotten and brought forth white children. But the envy of our great and continual enemy the **wicked Spirit** is such, that as he could not suffer our old Father **Adam** to live in the felicity & **Angelic state** wherein he was first created, but tempting him, sought & procured his ruin & fall: So again, finding at this flood none but a father and three sons living, he so caused one of them to transgress & disobey his father's commandment, that after him, all his posterity should be accursed. The fact of disobedience was this. When Noah at the commandment of God had made and entered the Ark, the floodgates of Heaven were opened, so that the whole face of the earth, every tree and mountain was covered with abundance of water, he greatly commanded his sons and their wives, as they should with reverence and fear behold the wise and mighty power of God, that during the time

Inundation: The flood of Genesis 6–8.

Noah: The mythic figure of the Abrahamic religions whom God commanded to build an ark (large boat) to save him and his family and the land animals from extinction during the Genesis flood.

descents: Descendants.

wicked Spirit: The devil.

Adam: According to Genesis 1–2, the first human created by God.

Angelic state: The creation story of Genesis 1 says that Adam and Eve were created in God's image, hence possessed of an angelic or heavenly nature, until the Fall.

7 Excerpts taken from George Best, *A Trve Discovrse of the late voyages of discouerie, for the finding of a passage to Cathaya, by the Northweast, vnder the conduct of Martin Frobisher Generall* (London: Henry Bynnyman, 1578), 29–32.

of flood, while they remained in the Ark, they should use continence, and abstain from carnal copulation with their wives....

Which good instructions and exhortations notwithstanding, his wicked son Cham disobeyed, being persuaded that the first child born after the flood (by right and law of nature) should inherit and possess all the dominion of the earth, he contrary to his father's commandment, while they were yet in the Ark, used company with his wife, and craftily went about, thereby to disinherit the offspring of his other two brethren, for the which wicked and detestable fact, as an example for contempt of Almighty God, and disobedience of parents, God would a son should be born, whose name was cursed, who not only it self, but all his posterity after him, should be so black and loathsome, that it might remain a spectacle of disobedience to all the World. And of this black and cursed **Chus** came all these black **Moores** which are in Africa, for after the water was diminished from off the face of the earth, and that the land was dry, Sem chose that part of the land to inhabit in which is now called Asia and Japhet had that which now is called Europe wherein we dwell, and Africa remains so cursed, and his black son Chus, and was called Chamesis after his father's name, being perhaps a cursed, dry, sandy, and unfruitful ground, fit for such a generation to inhabit in. Thus you see, the cause of the Ethiopian's blackness, is the curse and natural infection of blood, not the distemperature of the climate, which also may be proved by this example, that these black men are found in all parts of Africa, as well as without the Tropics, as within, even unto ***Capo d'buona Speranza*** southward, where, by reason of the sphere, should be the same temperature as is in Spain, **Laddigna**, and Sicily, where all be of very good complexion. Wherefore I conclude, that the blackness proceeds not of the hotness of the Climate, but as I said, of the infection of blood.

Chus: Cham's son.

Moores: Moors, the English term for North Africans.

***Capo d'buona Speranza*:** The Cape of Good Hope, a peninsula on the Atlantic side of South Africa.

Laddigna: Possibly Ladinia, a mountainous area in Northern Italy.

DOCUMENT 49
Elizabeth I, "An Open Letter to the Lord Mayor of London" (1596)[8]

This letter from the Queen of England from 1596 deals with the perceived problem of growing numbers of Blacks in England; it does not explicitly expel all Black peoples from the realm and should be read in the context of the **Iberian slave trade**.

Iberian slave trade: The Spanish and Portuguese were the first to develop the Atlantic Slave Trade.

An open letter to the Lord Mayor of London and the Alderman his brethren, And to all other mayors, sheriffs, etc. Her Majesty understanding that there are of late diverse **Blackamoors** brought into this Realm, of which kind of people there are already here too many, considering how God hath blessed this land with great increase of people of our own nation as any country in the world, whereof many for want of Service and means to set them on work fall to Idleness and to great extremity; Her Majesty's pleasure therefore is that those kind of people should be sent forth of the Land. And for that purpose there is direction given to this bearer **Edward Banes** to take of those Blackamoors that in this last voyage under **Sir Thomas Baskerville** were brought into this realm the number of Ten, to be transported by him out of the realm. Wherein we require you to be aiding and assisting unto him as he shall have occasion, and thereof not to fail.

Blackamoors: Typical term used by English writers for Black Africans.

Edward Banes: A merchant whom the Queen appointed to deliver the letter and ensure that its orders were carried out.

Sir Thomas Baskerville: Baskerville (d. 1597) was a general in Queen Elizabeth's army who as commander of the Indian armada traveled to the West Indies.

8 Transcribed from the UK National Archives, Open Government Licence v3.0. See Emily Weissbourd, "'Those in Their Possession': Race, Slavery, and Queen Elizabeth's 'Edicts of Expulsion,'" *Huntington Library Quarterly* 78, no. 1 (2015): 1–19.

DOCUMENT 50

Odoardo Lopez, *A Report of the Kingdom of Congo* (1597)[9]

In 1597 Abraham Hartwell edited and translated the 1591 account of a visit to Africa by the Portuguese traveler Odoardo Lopez, who was a contemporary of George Best (Document 48).

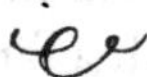

The men are black, and so are the women, and some of them also somewhat inclining to the colour of the wild Olive. Their hair is black and curled, and some also red. The stature of the men is of an indifferent bigness; and excepting their blackness they are very like to the **Portingalles**. The **apples of their eyes** are of diverse colours, black and of the colour of the tea. Their lips are not thick, as the **Nubians** and other Negroes are and so like wise countenances are some fat, some lean, and some between both, as in our countries there are, and not as the Negroes of Nubia and **Guinea**, which are very deformed....

All the ancient writers have certainly believed, that the cause of black colour in men is from the heat of the Sun. For by experience it is found, that the nearer we approach to the countries of the South, the browner and blacker are the inhabitants therein. And contrariwise, the farther you go towards the north, the whiter shall find the men, as the French, and the Dutch, and the English, and others. Notwithstanding it is as certain a thing as may be, that under the **Equinoctiall**, there are people which are born almost all white, as in the kingdom of **Melinde** and **Mombara** situate under the Equinoctiall, and in the **Isle of San Thomas** which lieth also under the same Climate, and was at the first inhabited by the Portingalles, though afterwards it was uninhabited, and for the space of a hundred years and upwards their children were continually white, yea and every day still become whiter and whiter. And so likewise the children of the Portingals, which are born of the women of Congo, do somewhat incline towards white. So that Signor Odoardo was of [the] opinion, that the black color did not spring from the heat of the Sun, but from the nature of the feed, being induced thereunto by the reasons above mentioned. And surely this his opinion is confirmed by the testimony of **Ptolome**, who in his description of the innermost parts of Libya makes mention of white Ethiopians which he calls ... white Moors....

Portingalles: Portuguese.

apples of their eyes: The pupil.

Nubians: Residents of the ancient kingdom of Nubia along the Nile River in North Africa, extending as far south as Central Sudan.

Guinea: A coastal region of West Africa.

Equinoctiall: Equator.

Melinde: Malindi, a coastal town of Kenya.

Mombara: Presumably Mombasa, in coastal Kenya.

Isle of San Thomas: Possibly Santo Tomas, Batangas, Philippines, which was colonized by the Portuguese.

Ptolome: Ptolemy (c. 100–170 CE), the ancient Greek mathematician, geographer, and astronomer.

---

9 Odoardo Lopez, *A Reporte of the Kingdome of Congo, a Region of Africa*, trans. Abraham Hartwell (London: John Wolfe, 1597), 14, 18–19, 32, 34–35, 125.

The men are very active and nimble; and leap up and down the mountains like Goats. Courageous they are and condemn death: men of great simplicity, loyalty and fidelity, and such as the Portingalles do trust more than any other. In so much as Signor Odoardo was wont to say, that if these **Anzichi** would become Christians, (being of so great fidelity, sincerity, loyalty and simplicity, that they will offer themselves to death, for the glory of the world, and to please their Lords will not stick to give their own flesh to be devoured) then would they with a far better heart and courage endure martyrdom; for the name of our redeemer Jesus Christ, and would most honourably maintain our faith and religion, with their good testimony, and examples against the **Gentiles**.

Anzichi: Residents of pre-colonial West Central Africa.

Gentiles: Generic term for people not members of Christianity, Judaism, or Islam.

Moreover, the said Signor Odoardo did likewise affirm, that there was no conversing with them, because they were a savage and a beastly people, saving only in respect that they come and traffic in Congo, bringing thither with them slaves both of their own nation, and also out of Nubia (whereupon they do border)....

They used to circumcise themselves: and another foolish custom they have, both men and women, as well of the nobility, as of the commonalty, even from their childhood to mark their faces with sundry flashes made with a knife, as in due place shall be further shown unto you.

They keep a **shambles** of man's flesh as they do in these countries for beef and other victuals. For their enemies whom they take in the wars, they eat, and also their slaves, if they can have a good market for them, they sell: or if they cannot, then they deliver them to the butchers to be cut into pieces, and so sold, to be roasted or boiled. And (that which is marvellous history to report) some of them being weary of their lives, and some of them even for valour of courage, and to shew themselves stout and venturous, thinking it to be a great honour onto them, if they run into voluntary death, thereby to show that they have a special contempt of this life, will offer themselves to the butchery, as faithful subjects to the Princes, for whose sake, that they may seem desirous to do them noble service, they do not only deliver themselves to be devoured by them, but also their slaves, when they are fat and well fed, they do kill and eat them. True it is that many nations there are, that feed upon man's flesh as in the east Indies, and in **Bresill**, and in other places: but that is only the flesh of their adversaries and enemies, but to eat the flesh of their own friends and subjects and kinsfolk, it is without all example in any place of the world, saving only in this nation of the Anzichi....

shambles: An archaic word for a butcher's slaughterhouse.

Bresill: Brazil.

And a wonderful thing is to be noted, that within less the one month [from a decree forbidding superstition], all the Idols, and Witcheries and Characters, which they worshipped and accounted for Gods, were sent and brought unto the Court. And certainly the number of these toys were infinite: for every man adorned and reverenced the thing that best liked him, without any order, or measure, or reason at all, so that there was among them a huge multitude of Devils, in sundry strange and terrible shapes. Many there were, that carried a devotion to Dragons with wings, which they nourished and fed in their own private houses, giving unto them for their food the best and most costly viands that they had. Others kept Serpents of horrible figures: Some worshipped the greatest Goats, they could get, some tigers, and other most monstrous Creature, yea the more uncouth and deformed the beasts were, the more they were honoured....

They had moreover their Witches,[10] which made the foolish people to believe, that their Idols could speak: and so deceived them: and if any man being in sickness or infirmity would recommend himself unto them, and afterwards that man recovered his health, the Witches persuade him that the Idol had been angry with him, but now was appeased and had healed him.

10 Hartwell was likely telling these stories to oppose the remnants of Catholicism in England, for Protestants viewed the statues of saints and of Christ as idols, while the English were still trying women as witches.

DOCUMENT 51

From Johan Isaksson Pontanus, *Historical Description of the Very Widely Famed Merchant City of Amsterdam* (1614)[11]

Johan Isaksson Pontanus was a resident of Amsterdam whose history of the city takes the reader from its streets and warehouses to the far-flung reaches of its merchant fleets as they traveled to the West and East Indies. Here he describes the Dutch merchant sailors encountering some of the Indigenous peoples of South Africa in 1595.

Here lived a sort of people that are best described as barbarian than human.... They go around mostly naked, wearing [animal] hides with the hair next to their body,[12] with wide belts of the same around their middle, the one end hanging before their shameful [parts] ... Some have concluded that these people are cannibals because they eat raw meat; and they grab the **tripe** and other innards, shaking the dung greedily from them, and finally gnaw at the legs like dogs. Because of this they have a stinking breath.... They have no houses, but holes and caverns.

tripe: Edible stomach lining of farm animals.

11 Johan Isaksson Pontanus, *Historische Beschrijvinghe der seer wijt beroemde Coop-stadt Amsterdam* ..., trans. Petrus Montanus (Amsterdam: Judocus Hondius, 1614), 181–84. Courtesy of Allard Pierson, Amsterdam. Translated by Gary Waite.

12 European Christians would have thought of the hair shirt worn by those who wanted to punish their flesh as a form of penance.

DOCUMENT 52

Pieter Jansz Twisck's Story of the Black Moor and the Jesuit, from *History of the Fall of Tyranny* (1620)[13]

Pieter Jansz Twisck (1565–1636) was a member of one of the Dutch Republic's dissenting religious groups, the Mennonites. A widely read man, he wrote major works promoting religious freedom and praising the Republic's informal policy allowing religious diversity, which included Jews. He also records the visits of Moroccan and Turkish ambassadors to Holland. Here he tells a joke.

A Slanderous Jesuit terrified by a Moor.

When the **Jesuit Franciscus Costerus** in his writings spoke terribly against the **Geusen**, saying about them that they were damned, and for confirmation of this he affirmed that if it were not just so, then he should be cast into the eternal fire by Lucifer. Whereupon **Pieter Cock van Enkhuizen** warned Costerus, saying, "let him observe well that he does not go as far as a Jesuit named Father Joost, who in his sermon called out in a manner that **Luther**, **Melanchthon**, **Calvin**, etc., were all damned, and if that was not true (he says), then **Satan** should immediately take him away and lead him into hell. It happened that the young Count of **Mansvelt** came into the Church. This one went to sit immediately next to the **pulpit**, and he had a Moor with him who remained standing under the pulpit, without the Jesuit seeing him. The Jesuit seeing that a great gentleman had arrived at his sermon, began repeating his previous lesson, becoming so zealous that he banged upon the pulpit, not noticing that his book fell onto the floor close to the Moor.... This one picked up the book, and looking to his master, saw his wink. By this he understood that he should bring the Jesuit's book back onto the pulpit. As the Moor began to climb the stairs to the pulpit, the Jesuit suddenly saw him coming towards him, and seeing the terribly black Moor, he became terrified beyond measure, believing that Satan had come to take him away due to his pledge. He thrust his hands into his hair and cried out for whatever help there was, saying further that he had given bad testimony about the aforementioned [Protestant] men and their teaching; they were sincere. The Jesuit soon died afterwards of fright.

Jesuit: A Catholic religious order established in 1540 by Ignatius Loyola to preach against Protestantism and spread Catholicism around the world.

Franciscus Costerus: A late sixteenth-century Flemish Jesuit polemicist.

Geusen: The "Beggars" who led the Dutch revolt against the Spanish Habsburgs.

Pieter Cock van Enkhuizen: A Dutch Calvinist who engaged in a published polemic with Costerus.

Luther: The German Reformer whose critique of the Catholic papacy began the Protestant Reformation. See Documents 7 and 26 above.

Melanchthon: Philip Melanchthon (1497–1560) was Martin Luther's most important colleague.

Calvin: Another major Protestant leader whose theology was adopted by the Dutch rebels.

Satan: The devil.

Mansvelt: Peter Ernst of Mansfelt (1517–1604), governor of the Spanish Netherlands from 1592 to 1594.

pulpit: A raised platform at the front of the church for preaching.

---

13 Pieter Jansz Twisck, *Chronijck vanden onderganc der tijrannen ofte Jaerlycklche Geschiedenissen in Werltlycke ende Kercklijke saecken*, vol. II (Hoorn: Isaac Willemssz, 1620), 1544. Translated by Gary Waite. See also Waite, *Jews and Muslims*, 55–67, 107–08.

DOCUMENT 53

From Sir Thomas Herbert, *A Relation of Some Years Travel ... into Africa and the Greater Asia ...* (1634)[14]

Thomas Herbert (1606–82) was an English lord, traveler, and writer. In the late 1620s he served, with Robert Shirley, as English ambassador to Persia, traveling around Africa into the Indian Ocean to Persia. During the English Civil War, he served in Oliver Cromwell's government in Ireland. Readers might notice some obvious borrowings from earlier travel accounts.

Angola: A Portuguese colony on the West coast of Southern Africa.

In **Angola** the people are fearful black, their Religion is Ethnic, their Idols are of great esteem amongst them ... generally they are so wedded to Superstition, that some adore the Devil in form of a bloody Dragon. Others a Ram-goat, a Leopard, a Bat, an Owle, a Snake or Dog, to whom they ceremoniously kneel and bow unto, groveling then upon the Earth, they throw dust on their faces, and offer Herbs, Rice, Roots, Fruits and such like, which is devoured by the Witches, a Monster not a little feared and esteemed of amongst these Devilish Savages.

Dame Cynthia: Greek goddess of the moon, Selene.

monthly Fluxes: Menstrual cycle.

The Female Sex against the appearing of the New Moon, assemble upon a Mountain, where turning up their bare bums, they contemptuously defy **Dame Cynthia**, who hath this despite, only for being causer of their **monthly Fluxes**. They esteem much of novelties, amongst which, Dogs are of especial value with them, Insomuch, that twenty slaves have been sold, for an European Dog....

Amazigues: Transliteration of a Portuguese term for Central Africa: see **Anzichi** above.

Next these, inhabit the **Amazigues**, a Nation endued with many temporal benefits, as wealth, health; gold, strength, valour, and the like, yet want these the virtue to make them civil, for though they abound with Nature's blessings, yet they delight in eating man's flesh, more than other food. And whereas other people, infesting them, content their appetites with the flesh of their Enemies. These barbarous Anzigui covet their friends, whom they [dis]embowel with a greedy delight, saying, they can no way better express a true affection, than to incorporate their dearest Friends and Cousins into themselves, as in love before, now in body uniting two in one, a bloody Sophistry.

They have Shambles of men and women's flesh, jointed and cut in several Morsels, and some (weary of life) voluntarily proffer themselves unto the bloody Butchers, who accordingly are sold and eaten....

---

14 Sir Thomas Herbert, *A Relation of Some Yeares Travaile, Begvnne Anno 1626. Into Afrique and the Greater Asia ... Of their Religion, Language, Habit, Discent, Ceremonies, and other matters concerning them* (London, 1634), 8–10.

Although they trouble themselves but little in devotion, yet do they **circumcise** Males and sometimes Females.

In adding to their beauties, they have two or three slashes in the face, and (if to any) they give reverence to those glorious Planets, Sun, and Moon, whom they suppose to live in matrimony.

These and other black-faced Africans, are much addicted to **rapine** and thievery, they will commit a villainy sooner in the day than night, lest Moon and Stars give testimony against them. The Devil is no stranger amongst them, whose Oracles they use, to offend an **Amazonian** people near them, valiant, though naked, and not fearing them....

circumcise: While male circumcision is a ritual in both Judaism and Islam, female circumcision, or female genital mutilation, is practiced in some African, Asian, and Middle Eastern communities, although it is mostly now outlawed.

rapine: Plunder.

Amazonian: The Amazon is of course in South America; the term was used more widely to refer to a barbarian society ruled by women.

DOCUMENT 54

From *A True Relation of the Inhumane and Unparallel'd Actions, and Barbarous Murders of Negroes or Moors: Committed on Three English-men in Old Calabar in Guinny* (1672)[15]

This is a sensationalistic pamphlet account of an incident on the African coast from 1668. After the author tells how some of the crew were caught and cannibalized by Africans near **Parrot Island**, an African leader provides an explanation for this alleged cruelty.

Parrot Island: An island on the southwest coast of Nigeria, above Cameroon.

Upon discourse after with this Arauna or Master he began to understand the reason of their barbarous dealing with him and his friends, he telling him that naturally the people were civil and simply honest, but if provoked, full of revenge; and that this cruelty was occasioned by some unhandsome action of carrying a Native away without their leave about a year before; they resolving if any came ashore they should never go off alive....

The People are very careless, idle, sluggish, given wholly to ease, going stark naked (only some of the chiefest having a little apron to cover their nakedness) not exercising themselves either in work or play; free from having any tillage whatsoever, (a small part only for **Tobacco**, for their own use, excepted) having no thought for tomorrow. Their stature and bigness not near so big as our English....

Tobacco: Leaves of a plant dried and smoked by Native Americans and adopted by Europeans in the later sixteenth century.

The Slaves they sell to the English are prisoners taken in war: the Kings war much against one another. They have no Holds, Castles, nor Prisons; but for keeping those they have taken, until the next Ship comes in, with which they fasten them to a pole, that they cannot untie themselves, and get home. They are also persuaded that they go to help that King to fight against his enemy, and that they shall live idly, and eat good victuals, drink good liquor, and have clothes, and that the King will give them great rewards. But if half were performed that is promised, they would be more ready to go, than we to fetch them.

15 *A True Relation of the Inhumane and Unparallel'd Actions, and Barbarous Murders of Negroes or Moors: Committed on Three English-men in Old Calabar in Guinny* ... (London, 1672) 6, 12, and 16.

DOCUMENT 55

From George Keith, *An Exhortation and Caution to Friends Concerning Buying or Keeping of Negroes* (1693)[16]

George Keith was a member of the English religious nonconformist group, the Society of Friends, or **Quakers**, who opposed slavery on the principle that all humans possessed the divine spark within them and were thus equal before God.

Quakers: The Society of Friends, a religious group founded by George Fox in the 1640s that emphasized the light of God within all humans, hence of the equality of all.

An Exhortation and Caution to Friends Concerning buying or keeping of Negroes.

Seeing our Lord Jesus Christ has tasted death for every man, and given himself a ransom for all, to be testified in due time, and that his Gospel of peace, liberty, and redemption from sin, bondage and all oppression, is freely to be preached unto all, without exception, and that Negroes, Blacks, and **Tawnies** are a real part of mankind, for whom Christ has shed his precious Blood, and are capable of salvation, as well as any white men; and Christ the Light of the World has (in measure) enlightened them, and every man that comes into the world; and that all such who are sincere Christians and true believers in Christ Jesus, and followers of him, bear his image, and are made comfortable unto him in love, mercy, goodness and compassion, who came not to destroy men's lives, but to save them, nor to bring any part of mankind unto outward bondage, slavery or misery … but to ease and deliver the oppressed and distressed, and bring into liberty both inward and outward.…

Tawnies: Those of a lighter brown skin color.

Therefore, in true Christian Love, we earnestly recommend it to all our Friends and brethren, not to buy any Negroes, unless it were on purpose to set them free, and that such who have bought any, and have them at present, after some reasonable time of moderate service they have had of them, or may have of them, that may reasonably answer to the charge of what they have laid out, especially in keeping negroes' children born in their house, or taken from that house, when underage, that after a reasonable time of service to answer that charge, they may set them at liberty, and during the time they have them, to teach them to read, and give them a Christian education.…

But what greater oppression can there be inflicted upon fellow creatures, than is inflicted on the poor Negroes! They being brought from their own

16 George Keith, *An Exhortation and Caution to Friends Concerning Buying or Keeping of Negroes* (New York: William Bradford, 1693).

country against their wills ... to the American plantations, and [sold] ... the husband from the wife, and the children from the parents; and many that buy them do exceedingly afflict them and oppress them, not only by continual hard labour, but by cruel whippings; and other cruel punishments, and by short allowance of food, some **Planters** in Barbados and Jamaica, it is said, keeping one hundred of them, and some more, and some less, and giving them hardly any thing more than they raise on a little piece of ground appointed to them, on which they work for themselves the seventh day of the week in the afternoon ... and the remainder of their time being spent in their master's service; which doubtless is far worse usage than is practiced by the Turks and Moors upon their slaves. Which tends to the great reproach of the **Christian profession**.... Surely the Lord does behold their oppressions and afflictions, and will further visit for the same by his righteous and just judgements, except they break off their sins by repentance, and their iniquity by showing mercy to these poor afflicted, tormented miserable slaves!

Planters: Owners of large plantations producing sugar, cotton, or tobacco, and worked by enslaved peoples.

Christian profession: The Christian faith.

DOCUMENT 56

From Edward Long, *The History of Jamaica* (1774)[17]

Edward Long (1734–1813) was a British administrator in Jamaica, where he was born. His discussion of Africans and Indigenous peoples in Jamaica explicitly applied the Spanish concept of blood purity and lineage with respect to Jewish and Muslim converts (see Document 5 above) onto Black and Indigenous peoples of Jamaica. The terms Mulatta, Terceron, Quateron, Quinteron, refer to the percentage of mixture: half, third, quarter, fifth, etc. A Venter is a woman who is the source of offspring.

The inhabitants of this island may be distinguished under the following classes: Creoles, or natives; Whites, Blacks, Indians, and their varieties; European and other Whites; and imported or African Blacks.

The intermixture of Whites, Blacks, and Indians has generated several different **casts**, which have all their proper denominations, invented by the Spaniards, who make this a kind of science among them. Perhaps they will be better understood by the following table.

casts: Castes, a form of social stratification where one's place in society is predetermined by birth.

DIRECT lineal Ascent from the Negroe Venter.

White Man, = Negroe Woman.
|
White Man, = Mulatta.
|
White Man, = Terceron.
|
White Man, = Quateron.
|
White Man, = Quinteron.
|
WHITE

MEDIATE OR STATIONARY, neither advancing nor receding.

Quateron, = Terceron.
|
Tente-enel-ayre.

RETROGRADE.

Mulatto, = Terceron. → Saltatras.

Negroe, = Mulatta. → Sambo de Mulatta, } = Negroe. → NEGROE.

Indian, = Mulatta. → Mestize.

Negroe, = Indian. → Sambo de Indian, } = Sambo de Mulatta. → Givero [*o*].

17 Edward Long, *The History of Jamaica. Or, General Survey of the Antient and Modern State of That Island: with Reflections on its Situation, Settlements, Inhabitants, Climate, Products, Commerce, Laws, and Government*, vol. 2 (London, 1774), 260–74.

In the Spanish colonies, it is accounted most creditable to mend the breed by ascending or growing whiter; insomuch that a Quateron will hardly keep company with a Mulatto; and Mestize values himself very highly in comparison with a Sambo. The Giveros lie under the imputation of having worst inclinations and principles; and, if the cast is known, they are banished. These distinctions, however, do not prevail in Jamaica; for here the Terceron is confounded with the Quateron; and the laws permit all, that are above three degrees removed in lineal descent from the Negro ancestor, to vote at elections, and enjoy all the privileges and immunities of his majesty's white subjects of the island. The Dutch, I am informed, transcend the Spaniards very far in their refinement of these complexions. They add drops of pure water to a single of dusky liquor, until it becomes tolerably **pellucid**. But this needs the apposition of such multitude of drops, that, to apply the experiment by analogy to the human race, twenty or thirty generations, perhaps, would hardly be sufficient to discharge the stain.[18] …

pellucid: Transparently clear.

With all these praise-worthy qualities, the **Creoles** have some foibles in their disposition. They are subject to frailties in common with the rest of mankind. They [are] possessed with a degree of supineness and indolence in their affairs, which renders them bad economists, and too frequently hurts their fortune and family. With a strong natural propensity to the other sex, they are not always the most chaste and faithful of husbands. They are liable to sudden transports of anger; but these fits, like hurricanes, though violent while they last, are soon over and subside into calm: yet they are not apt to forget and forgive substantial injuries.…

Creoles: A person of mixed European and Black African descent, especially in the Caribbean.

The planters of this island have been very unjustly stigmatized with an accusation of treating their Negroes with barbarity. Some allege, that these slave-holders (as they are pleased to call them, in contempt) are lawless **bashaws**, West-India tyrants, inhuman oppressors, bloody **inquisitors**, and a long [list], etc. of such pretty names. The planter, in reply to these bitter invectives, will think it sufficient to urge, in the first place, that he did not make them slaves, but succeeded to the inheritance of their services in the same manner as an English squire succeeds to the estate of his ancestors; and that, as to his Africans, he buys their services from those who have all along pretended a very good right to sell; that it cannot be for his interest to treat his Negroes in the manner represented; but that it is so to use them well, and preserve their vigour and existence as long as he is able.…

bashaws: A person of high rank.

inquisitors: Originally Dominican friars tasked with conducting heresy trials; by the eighteenth century, a term used widely to refer to any oppressive system.

The planters do not want to be told, that their Negroes are human creatures. If they believe them to be of human kind, they cannot regard them … as no better than dogs and horses. But how many poor wretches, even

18 The Dutch were, like the English, French, and Spanish, heavily engaged in the slave trade and colonizing of the world.

in England, are treated far less with far less care and humanity than these brute animals! ... Amongst three or four hundred Blacks, there must be some who are not to be reclaimed from savage, intractable humour, and acts of violence, without the coercion of punishment. So, among the whole body of planters, some may be found of naturally austere and inhuman tempers. Yet they, who act up to the dignity of man, ought not to be confounded with others, whose odious depravity of heart has degraded them beneath the rank of human beings....

Many of the good folks in England have entertained the strange opinion, that the children born in Jamaica of white parents turn swarthy, through effect of the climate; nay, some have not scrupled to suppose, that they are converted into black-a-moors. The truth is, that the children born in England have not, in general lovelier or more transparent skins, than the offspring of white parents in Jamaica.

DOCUMENT 57

William Cowper, *The Negro's Complaint: A Poem* (1788)[19]

The English author William Cowper wrote this poem from the perspective of a Black slave, in support of the Committee for the Abolition of the Slave Trade. The poem became popular in England, was later published as an illustrated children's book and was sometimes put to music and sung as a ballad. When reading the poem, consider how the imagery may have appealed to a white abolitionist audience.

Forced from home and all its pleasures
Afric's coast I left forlorn,
To increase a stranger's treasures
O'er the raging billows borne.

Men from England bought and sold me,
Paid my price in paltry gold;
But, though slave they have enrolled me,
Minds are never to be sold.

Still in thought as free as ever,
What are England's rights, I ask,
Me from my delights to sever,
Me to torture, me to task?

Fleecy locks and black complexion
Cannot forfeit nature's claim;
Skins may differ, but affection
Dwells in white and black the same.

Why did all-creating Nature
Make the plant for which we toil?
Sighs must fan it, tears must water,
Sweat of ours must dress the soil.

Think, ye masters iron-hearted,
Lolling at your jovial boards;

---

19 William Cowper, *The Negro's Complaint: A Poem* (London: Harvey and Darton, 1826; orig. 1788), 1–15.

Think how many backs have smarted
For the sweets your cane affords.

Is there, as you sometimes tell us,
Is there one, who reigns on high?
Has he bid you buy and sell us,
Speaking from his throne, the sky?

Ask him, if your knotted **scourges**,
Matches, blood-extorting screws,
Are the means that duty urges
Agents of his will to use?

scourges: Whips to punish captives.

Hark! he answers!—wild tornadoes
Strewing yonder sea with wrecks,
Wasting towns, plantations, meadows,
Are the voice with which he speaks.

He, foreseeing what vexations
Afric's sons should undergo,
Fixed their tyrants' habitations
Where his whirlwinds answer—no.

By our blood in Afric wasted
Ere our necks received the chain;
By the mis'ries that we tasted,
Crossing in your barks the main;

By our sufferings, since ye brought us
To the man-degrading mart,
All, sustain'd by patience, taught us
Only by a broken heart:

Deem our nation brutes no longer,
Till some reason ye shall find
Worthier of regard and stronger
Than the colour of our kind.

Slaves of gold, whose sordid dealings
Tarnish all your boasted pow'rs,
Prove that you have human feelings,
Ere you proudly question ours!

DOCUMENT 58

Olaudah Equiano Describes Conditions on a Slave Ship Crossing the Atlantic, in *The Interesting Narrative of the Life of Olaudah Equiano* (1789)[20]

According to his own account, Olaudah Equiano was born in Essaka, Africa, in 1745. When he was 11 years old, he says that he and his sister were kidnapped from Guinea and forced onto a slave ship. He arrived in England in 1757, a country to which he would return many times over the course of his enslavement. In one of the first influential slave autobiographies of the eighteenth century, Equiano recounts the cruelty he experienced during this time, and his attempts to attain freedom. In this passage, Equiano describes conditions on a slave ship crossing the Atlantic.

pestilential: An environment that causes the spread of disease.

At last, when the ship we were in had got in all her cargo, they made ready with many fearful noises, and we were all put under deck, so that we could not see how they managed the vessel. But this disappointment was the least of my sorrow. The stench of the hold while we were on the coast was so intolerably loathsome, that it was dangerous to remain there for any time, and some of us had been permitted to stay on the deck for the fresh air; but now that the whole ship's cargo were confined together, it became absolutely **pestilential**. The closeness of the place, and the heat of the climate, added to the number in the ship, which was so crowded that each had scarcely room to turn himself, almost suffocated us. This produced copious perspirations, so that the air soon became unfit for respiration, from a variety of loathsome smells, and brought on a sickness among the slaves, of which many died, thus falling victims to the improvident avarice, as I may call it, of their purchasers. This wretched situation was again aggravated by the galling of the chains, now become insupportable; and the filth of the necessary tubs, into which the children often fell, and were almost suffocated. The shrieks of the women, and the groans of the dying, rendered the whole a scene of horror almost inconceivable. Happily perhaps for myself I was soon reduced so low here that it was thought necessary to keep me almost always on deck; and from my extreme youth I was not put in fetters. In this situation I expected every hour to share the fate of my companions, some of whom were almost daily brought upon deck at the point of death, which I began to hope would soon put an end to my miseries.

20 Olaudah Equiano, *The Interesting Narrative of the Life of Olaudah Equiano, or Gustavus Vassa, The African. Written by Himself* (1789).

One day, when we had a smooth sea and moderate wind, two of my wearied countrymen who were chained together (I was near them at the time), preferring death to such a life of misery, somehow made through the nettings and jumped into the sea: immediately another quite dejected fellow, who, on account of his illness, was suffered to be out of irons, also followed their example; and I believe many more would very soon have done the same if they had not been prevented by the ship's crew, who were instantly alarmed.

DOCUMENT 59

Society for the Friends of Blacks in Paris, "Address to the National Assembly for the Abolition of the Trade in Blacks" (1790)[21]

Society of the Friends of Blacks: An abolitionist society active during the French Revolution, which sought to end slavery in all French overseas holdings.

Declaration of the Rights of Man and the Citizen: Inspired by the 1776 American Declaration of Independence, this 1789 French document demanded freedom and equality for all men, but left out women and Black and Jewish peoples.

French National Assembly: A revolutionary political assembly founded by members of the Third Estate in the Estates-General during the early phase of the French Revolution.

On 5 February 1790, during the French Revolution, the **Society of the Friends of Blacks** used the language of the new **Declaration of the Rights of Man and the Citizen** to address the **French National Assembly** to call for the abolition of the slave trade in the French colonial empire. Although that body had previously granted citizenship to French Jews, they waited five more years to abolish the enslavement of Black peoples. Napoleon Bonaparte then reinstituted slavery in the French Caribbean in 1802, meaning enslavement for an estimated 300,000 people until France legally ended the practice in 1848. As with the Cowper poem, consider here the authors' use of language, and concepts such as equality and freedom.

THE HUMANITY, the justice and the magnanimity which have guided you to reform the most deeply rooted abuses, make the Society of the Friends of the Blacks hope that you will welcome with benevolence its demands in favor of the large part of humanity that has been cruelly oppressed for two centuries. This Society, which has been cowardly and unjustly slandered, derives its mission from the humanity that urged it to defend the Blacks from despotism in the past. Oh! Can there be a more respectable title in the eyes of this august Assembly, which has so often in its decrees defended the rights of man?

You declared these rights; you have engraved them on an immortal monument, that all men are born & remain free & equal in rights. You have returned these rights to the French people, after the despotism had stripped and ignored them.... [Y]ou have broken the bonds of feudalism which still degrade many of our fellow citizens; you announced the destruction of all the stigmatizing distinctions which religious or political prejudices had introduced into the great family of the human race. The men, whose cause we defend, do not have higher pretensions, although, as citizens of the same Empire and men like us, they have the same rights as us. We are not asking that you restore to the French Blacks these political rights, which were, however, to attest to and maintain the dignity of man; we are not even asking for their freedom. Slander, no doubt prompted by the greed of Shipowners, has attributed that plan to us, so that planters and their many creditors who are afraid of even gradual emancipation, turn against us.

---

21 Society of the Friends of Blacks, *Adresse à l'Assemblée Nationale pour l'abolition de la traite des noirs, par la Société des Amis des Noirs* (Paris, 1790), 1–6. Translated by Lisa Todd.

They want to alarm all Frenchmen, in whose eyes the prosperity of the Colonies is painted as inseparable from the slave trade and the perpetuity of slavery.... [Instead, we believe] the immediate emancipation of the Blacks would not only be a fatal operation for the Colonies; it would even be a fatal gift for the Blacks, given the state of abjection and nullity to which **cupidity** has reduced them. It would leave them as helpless beings, like children in a cradle. It is therefore not yet time to ask for their freedom; we merely ask vehemently that we cease to cut the throats of thousands of Blacks every year, in order to make hundreds of captives. We ask that you stop the prostituting and profaning of the French name by the continued acceptance of thefts, atrocities, and murders. In short, we demand the abolition of the slave trade, and we beg you to promptly take this important subject into consideration. To convince you, must we give you examples of this horrible trade? Shall we paint for you the infamous maneuvers employed by shipowners and captains, to procure Blacks?

cupidity: A greed for money or possessions.

Shall we cite for you those bargains in human flesh, made in the middle of a premeditated orgy, where for a few flasks of an intoxicating liquor ... one forces a Prince to beat his subjects as wild beasts, to steal them, to sell them? Are we going to cite those trials commissioned by Europeans, where the injustice of the Prince condemns so many innocent people to a slavery from which his avarice must draw the fruit? Shall we cite to you those bloody wars, where Princes are still forced to capture and chain their peaceful neighbors to pay artificially imposed debts? You would be revolted, if we exposed your eyes to all the circumstances of this atrocious robbery; if we told you, for example, that when they caught the Blacks in their huts, their inhuman drivers snatched their children from their arms? Or, of the children, whom parents must abandon in flight to hunger, to death, because their too weak arms would make them useless and costly to their executioners! And we consider the men who feed this brigandage, who command it, who live from it, to still be human! Hey! if you fled to these floating prisons in these cesspools whose space is measured by avarice, where one piles these unfortunate Africans one on top of the other, would you not feel pain at this dreadful affair? Imagine these unfortunate people, furious at being torn from their fatherland, from their children, whom they will never see again, believing themselves delivered to the hands of cannibals and destined for butchery, piled up in narrow between-decks, whose infection and stifling heat are increased by a devouring folly; chained two by two, condemned by the chains & this entanglement to the dreadful torture of immobility; immobility which is interrupted only in storms, by the still more cruel torments of violent rolling. Imagine those captives violently crumpled against each other, torn by the friction of their chains, suffocated in rainy weather ... gnawed by infectious diseases, calling for death.... Ah! whoever contemplates this spectacle must shiver with horror and be revolted to see men treated with this inhumanity....

DOCUMENT 60

Image: Advertisement, Just Arrived from London … the Hottentot Venus: The Only One Ever Exhibited in Europe (c. 1810)[22]

Hottentot: A derogatory term misused by Europeans to refer to peoples from Southern Africa.

Venus: Roman goddess associated with love, beauty, sexuality, and fertility, a counterpart to the Greek goddess Aphrodite. When paired with Hottentot, it became a derogatory way of mocking Sarah Baartman's female body.

Sarah Baartman (1789–1815) was a young Khoisan woman from Southern Africa who was recruited from her home to England where she was exhibited in stage shows and at private parties as an example of "savage" womanhood. She was given the stage name "The **Hottentot Venus**," which capitalized on the fascination, disgust, and eroticism expressed by white people in her audiences at seeing a body that was allegedly different than their own. When reading the advertisement below, consider not only the language it uses to describe Baartman, but also her audiences. Baartman's body was exploited for entertainment and profit and also studied by medical doctors and scientists. Even after she died alone in Paris in 1815, Baartman's body was dissected, studied, and used in medical school classes. The Museum of Man in Paris exhibited parts of Baartman's body until 1975. Her remains were repatriated to South Africa only after Nelson Mandela made the request in 2002.[23]

22 Just arrived from London, and, by permission, will be exhibited here for a few days at Mr. James's Sale Rooms, corner of Lord-street: that most wonderful phenomenon of nature, the Hottentot Venus: the only one ever exhibited in Europe, Wellcome Collection.

23 For more on Sarah Baartman's experiences in Europe, see Robin Mitchell, *Vénus Noire Black Women and Colonial Fantasies in Nineteenth-Century France* (Athens, GA: University of Georgia Press, 2020) and the film *Vénus Noire* [*Black Venus*], directed by Abdellatif Kechiche (MK2 Productions, France 2 Cinéma, CinéCinéma, 2002).

JUST ARRIVED
FROM LONDON,

And, by Permission, will be Exhibited here for a few Days,

At Mr. James's Sale Rooms, Corner of Lord-street,

THAT MOST WONDERFUL

Phenomenon of Nature,

THE

HOTTENTOT
VENUS,

The only One ever exhibited in Europe.

In viewing this Wonderful LIVING Production of Nature, the Public have a perfect Specimen of that most extraordinary Tribe of the Human Race, who have for such a Length of Time inhabited the most Southern Parts of Africa, whose real Origin has never yet been ascertained, nor their Character, which has been so differently described by every Traveller who has visited those remote Regions of the World; and considering the natural morose Disposition of those People (who are scarcely ever observed to laugh) she is remarkably mild and affable in her Manners. She has had the Honor of being visited by His Royal Highness the PRINCE REGENT, and several Branches of the ROYAL FAMILY, also the principal NOBILITY, of both Sexes, in England, and declared to be a great natural Curiosity, well worthy the Attention of the Public. She is particularly obliged to the Female Sex who have so liberally patronized her Exhibition, and more especially after the malicious Reports circulated to her Disadvantage after her Arrival in this Kingdom; but which have been long since proved to be groundless. Over her Clothing, which is suitable to this Climate, is worn all the rude Ornaments used by that tribe on Gala Days.

N. B. Elegant Engravings of the Venus, by Lewis, sold at the Room.

ADMITTANCE—ONE SHILLING.

CHESTER, PRINTED BY J. FLETCHER.

DOCUMENT 61

Image: Advertisement, A Black Man Buying Some of J. Morison's Pills, Hoping They Will Make Him White (c. 1825)[24]

quack doctor: A person who pretends to have medical knowledge or training, usually to sell a product or service.

Massa: A term used by some enslaved African Americans in place of "master"; here a mockery of stereotypical Black speech patterns.

James Morison was an early nineteenth-century **quack doctor** who marketed vegetable laxative pills as a "cure all" for a variety of ailments and diseases. This advertisement promotes the idea that Morison's customers thought his pills could do anything—in this case, the man hopes the pills will turn his Black skin white. The text reads, "**Massa** doctor you tink I get more vite for taking you pills?" "Decidedly sir! about two thousand boxes more will without doubt render you as white as a lily!" The use of language here, coupled with the man's aristocratic clothing, were meant to humorously highlight the fantastical nature of the pills' claims. Another advertisement in this series shows vegetables growing out of a man's body, implying that act to be as likely as a Black man changing his skin color.

24 A Black Man Buying Some of J. Morison's Pills, Hoping They Will Make Him White, colored lithograph (c. 1825), Wellcome Collection.

UNIVERSAL PILLS No1.

Massa Doctor you tink I get more wite for taking you Pills?
Decidedly Sir! about two thousand boxes more will without doubt render you as white as a Lily!

London W Spooner 377 Strand.

DOCUMENT 62

Image: From Josiah Clark Nott and George Gliddon, *Types of Mankind or Ethnological Researches, Based upon the Ancient Monuments, Paintings, Sculptures, and Crania of Races, and upon the Natural, Geographical, Philological and Biblical History* (1854)[25]

Josiah Nott (1804–73) was an American surgeon, anthropologist, and owner of nine slaves. He once claimed "the negro achieves his greatest perfection, physical and moral, and also greatest longevity, in a state of slavery." George Gliddon was an English-born American Egyptologist, who used skulls to study changes in humans over time. In their book, they argued in favor of the polygenism theory, which stated that the races of mankind did not originate from a single pair (Adam and Eve), but that instead God created distinct races and placed them in different parts of the world. When Charles Darwin wrote his *The Descent of Man* in 1871, he argued against Nott and Gliddon's polygenism, instead supporting evolutionary theory, monogenism, and the single-origin hypothesis.

25 J.C. Nott and G.R. Gliddon, *Types of Mankind or Ethnological Researches, Based upon the Ancient Monuments, Paintings, Sculptures, and Crania of Races, and upon the Natural, Geographical, Philological and Biblical History* (Philadelphia: Lippincott, Grambo, & Co., 1854), 458–59.

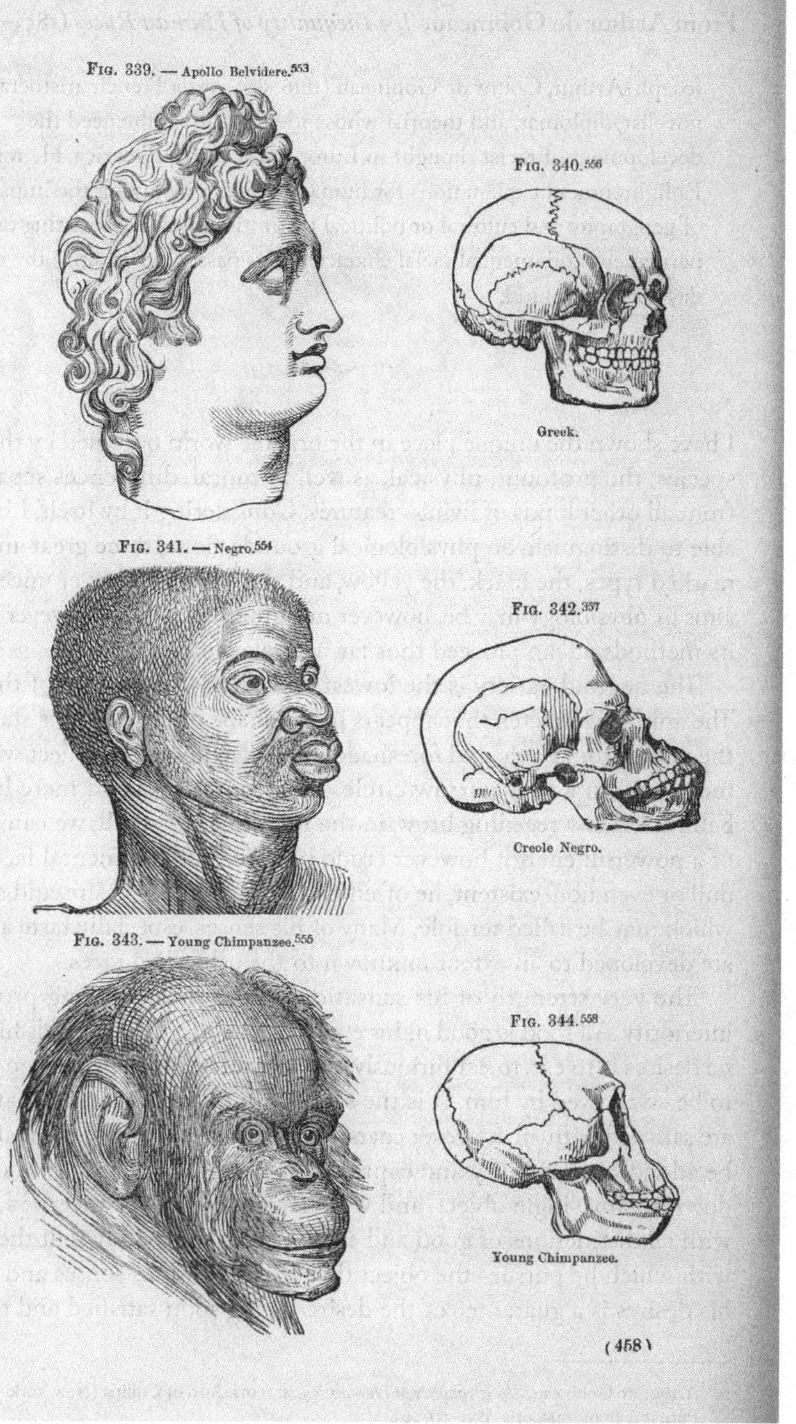
Fig. 339. — Apollo Belvidere.553
Fig. 340.556
Greek.
Fig. 341. — Negro.554
Fig. 342.557
Creole Negro.
Fig. 343. — Young Chimpanzee.555
Fig. 344.558
Young Chimpanzee.
(458)

DOCUMENT 63

From Arthur de Gobineau, *The Inequality of Human Races* (1853–55)[26]

Joseph-Arthur, Count de Gobineau (1816–82), was a French aristocratic novelist, diplomat, and theorist whose ideas greatly influenced the development of racist thought in Europe and North America. He rejected Enlightenment explanations for human diversity, including the impact of geography and cultural or political institutions, instead insisting on permanent and unequal racial characteristics passed down since the earliest days of humankind.

I have shown the unique place in the organic world occupied by the human species, the profound physical, as well as moral, differences separating it from all other kinds of living creatures. Considering it by itself, I have been able to distinguish, on physiological grounds alone, three great and clearly marked types, the black, the yellow, and the white. However uncertain the aims of physiology may be, however meagre its resources, however defective its methods, it can proceed thus far with absolute certainty.

The negroid variety is the lowest and stands at the foot of the ladder. The animal character, that appears in the shape of the pelvis, is stamped on the negro from birth, and foreshadows his destiny. His intellect will always move within a very narrow circle. He is not however a mere brute, for behind his low receding brow, in the middle of his skull, we can see signs of a powerful energy, however crude its objects. If his mental faculties are dull or even non-existent, he often has an intensity of desire, and so of will, which may be called terrible. Many of his senses, especially taste and smell, are developed to an extent unknown to the other two races.

The very strength of his sensations is the most striking proof of his inferiority. All food is good in his eyes, nothing disgusts or repels him. What he desires is to eat, to eat furiously, and to excess; no carrion is too revolting to be swallowed by him. It is the same with odours; his inordinate desires are satisfied with all, however coarse or even horrible. To these qualities may be added an instability and capriciousness of feeling, that cannot be tied down to any single object, and which, so far as he is concerned, do away with all distinctions of good and evil. We might even say that the violence with which he pursues the object that has aroused his senses and inflamed his desires is a guarantee of the desires being soon satisfied and the object

26 Arthur de Gobineau, *The Inequality of Human Races*, trans. Adrian Collins (New York: G.P. Putnam's Sons, 1915; orig. 1853–55), 205.

forgotten. Finally, he is equally careless of his own life and that of others: he kills willingly, for the sake of killing; and this human machine, in whom it is so easy to arouse emotion, shows, in face of suffering, either a monstrous indifference or a cowardice that seeks a voluntary refuge in death.

DOCUMENT 64

Image: Advertisement for the Zulu Kaffirs, or WILD MEN! of Africa: Maxos and Nonswenzo ... Will Go through Their Wonderful and Extraordinary Performances at Each Exhibition (1861)[27]

George Wombwell was a shoemaker in London when he began buying wild animals off ships arriving at port and then exhibiting them to the public for a profit. By 1805 Wombwell's business had grown so successful he took his **menagerie** on the road, drawing large audiences, including **Queen Victoria** and her family. This poster advertises the show "Wild Men of Africa," which took place after Wombwell's death in 1850, as part of the Edmonds' Late Wombwell's **Royal Windsor Castle** Menagerie. The accompanying excerpt from the ***London Illustrated News*** calls the show a "complete picture of **Kaffir** life," in which three male actors, perform as a "band of wild but interesting savages," who wear the "costume of their tribe" to "hunt, eat, sing, dance, make love, and fight." The author admitted that "Natives of South Africa" had been exhibited in London before but especially praised the comedic value of this show.

menagerie: A display of "exotic" animals. Traveling menageries date to the early eighteenth century, and were a precursor to zoos and circuses.

Queen Victoria: Monarch of the United Kingdom, 1837–1901.

Royal Windsor Castle: Windsor Castle has been a home to British monarchs for more than a thousand years.

***London Illustrated News*:** The world's first illustrated newspaper and published in the UK from 1842 to 2003.

Kaffir: A racial slur for Black people, especially those from Southern Africa. The term is legally defined as hate speech in South Africa and people often replace it with 'K-word.'

27 Important notice! Edmonds' late Wombwell's Royal Windsor Castle Menagerie, will exhibit at Shrewsbury, on Friday, Saturday, and Monday, August 23rd, 24th, and 26th, and at Wellington, on Tuesday, August 27th, 1861, accompanied by that extraordinary race of men, the Zulu Kaffirs, or WILD MEN! of Africa: Maxos and Nonswenzo—who will go through their wonderful and extraordinary performances at each exhibition ... (1861), Wellcome Collection.

IMPORTANT NOTICE:

Edmonds' late Wombwell's

ROYAL WINDSOR CASTLE MENAGERIE,

WILL EXHIBIT AT

SHREWSBURY,

On FRIDAY, SATURDAY, and MONDAY, August 23rd, 24th, and 26th,

AND AT WELLINGTON, ON TUESDAY, AUGUST 27TH, 1861,

Accompanied by that extraordinary race of men, the ZULU KAFFIRS, or

WILD MEN!

OF AFRICA—**Maxos** and **Nonswenzo**,—who will go through their wonderful and extraordinary performances at each Exhibition, representing in their Native Costume the MANNERS and CUSTOMS of KAFFIR LIFE, viz:—

The War Signal, Modes of Warfare, War Dances, Club Dances and Exercises, Songs of War, Peace, &c., &c.

THE WAR SIGNAL

OF THE KAFFIRS!

Extracts from the "Illustrated London News."

ZULU KAFFIRS.—A complete picture of Kaffir life is exhibited at St. George's Gallery, Hyde-park corner, with such admirable accessories in the way of scenic illusion, that it may rather be described as a picturesque drama illustrative of Kaffir manners and customs. The actors are a party of Zulu men, who, in the costume of their tribe, hunt, eat, sing, dance, make love, and fight, in a series of scenes which charm by their spirit and *vraisemblance*. The performance has its comic features; for the Zulu poet-laureate wears a leopard's head and collar of tigers' tails, when he chants the king's praises; and the entrance of the witch-doctor, in pursuit of the sorcerer who has caused the illness of a sick man—for the Zulus believe that all illness is the result of witchcraft—is more amusing than anything in a farce. The cries, songs, and dances of these extraordinary people are extremely amusing; and the pencil of Mr. C. MARSHALL enables the visitor to realize the scenery of Port Natal, Pietermaritzburg, the Basuta Country, &c.

THE ZULU KAFFIRS AT THE ST. GEORGE'S GALLERY, KNIGHTSBRIDGE.—This band of wild but interesting savages are taking such high rank among the metropolitan exhibitions of the present season, and represent so faithfully the manners, habits, and costume of their tribe, that we give an illustration of a scene in their performances. A number of huts, such as they occupy, are placed upon the stage, with an African landscape in the background; and, one by one, the savages make their appearance, engaged in the pursuits of their every-day life. After a supper of meal, of which the Kaffirs partake with their large wooden spoons, an extraordinary song and dance are performed, in which each performer moves about on his haunches, grunting and snorting the while like a pair of asthmatic bellows. We mentioned one or two of the more ludicrous scenes last week: but no description can give an idea of the cries and shouts—now comic, now terrible—by which the Kaffirs express their emotions. The scene illustrative of the preliminaries of marriage and the bridal festivities might leave one in doubt which was the bridegroom did not that interesting savage announce his enviable situation by screams of ecstacy which convulse the audience.

The Zulus must be naturally good actors, for a performance more natural and less like acting is seldom if ever seen upon any stage. The hunting expedition and the fight between hostile tribes, have each an interest of their own: and the glimpse of the Bushmen in their trees is exceedingly interesting.

We stated last week that the exhibition is illustrated by some excellent panoramic scenery, painted by MARSHALL, from sketches made in Kaffirland; and that the various scenes in the entertainment are explained by an intelligent young lecturer.

Natives of South Africa have been before exhibited in the metropolis, but we do not recollect to have seen the people either so numerously or so efficiently represented as in the present exhibition. These Kaffirs have been brought from Natal, by Mr. A. T. CALDECOTT, who, for this purpose, memoralized the colonial authorities at Natal for permission to ship the natives, which application was complied with, on Mr. CALDECOTT having entered into a recognizance—himself in a sum of £500, and two sureties in £250 each, that such natives as were willing to accompany him to England would be properly treated on the voyage, duly reported, and, if required, produced to the Secretary of State for the Colonies, and finally brought back to Durban; and the natives were further, previous to their embarking, taken before the Diplomatic Agent to testify their full and voluntary concurrence.

MAXOS, the chief of the party, stands 5 feet 9 inches without his shoes, and he has been twelve months from the Zulu country. He was, before his desertion, a soldier in one of King Panda's regiments; he is the son of a Zulu Chief, under Chaka and Dingaan, who was slain in an engagement between the Maswazwas and Zulus, in the reign of Acugaan. The son Maxos has also been in battle, and has been wounded several times: an assaigai wound above the left eye, and one in the back, are still to be seen.

Next is NONSWENZO, a cousin of Faku, the Chief of the Umopondas. He stands 6 feet without his shoes, and is a very powerful man, and of violent temper, if excited. He left his country nine months ago; he talks little; and, though he appears to be a man who has seen and done much in his time, he will never speak of his past life; his age is about twenty-nine.

UMLOW (the Wizard Doctor), a middle sized man, is active, and of a very excitable disposition. He, like Maxos, was formerly a soldier in one of King Panda's regiments. He is famous for using the knob-kerry or short club, a weapon used by the Zulus in war, which he throws with great accuracy and force.

A variety of implements displayed during the performances of the troupe add much to their interest. Thus, one of the Zulus, in the prefixed illustration, bears a large oval war-shield, 4 feet 6 inches high, and 2 feet 3 inches wide across the middle; it is made of ox-hide. Their hunting shield is 3 feet high, 18 inches across the middle, and of the same material and form as the war-shield. The assaigai, of which there are specimens, is a wooden rod or lath, 3 feet 4 inches long, into which the spear is fixed; the point being ground sharp, and fixed to the wood with cat-gut: the spear is from 12 to 15 inches long. There are also wooden assaigais, beautifully carved, but these are used only for courting purposes.

Next are baskets for carrying their produce. These are made of common grass, strongly plaited together. Their calabashes consist of a vegetable of the pumpkin kind, scooped out, and the shell dried used for carrying water and beer. Their pots are made of black clay, baked in an oven. The Zulu Huts are constructed of twigs, thatched with grass, 7 feet high in the centre, and about 14 feet in diameter.

STAFFORD & CO., PRINTERS TO THE ESTABLISHMENT, CHURCH GATE, NOTTINGHAM.

DOCUMENT 65

Image: Advertisement for Pears' Soap: Matchless for the Complexion (c. 1880)[28]

Commodity racism refers to the use of racist imagery and stereotypes to sell products. In the late nineteenth century, European companies sometimes relied on images of Empire to convince consumers that their products were innovative, exciting, and exotic. Images of colonized peoples in Africa and Asia appeared in advertisements for cocoa, cookies, cigarettes, and boot laces, while they also seemed to offer visual proof of racial differences and hierarchies. This soap advertisement is based on Aesop's fable, "Washing the Blackamoor [or Ethiopian] White," the message of which is that just as you can't wash the black off a person, you cannot change moral character traits [the modern equivalent might be "a leopard never changes his spots"]. Note the similarity with the earlier Morison's Pills advertisement, and indeed, a focus on the importance of skin color throughout these sources.

28 Pears' Soap: Matchless for the Complexion/Pears (A. & F.) Limited [between 1880 and 1889?], Wellcome Collection.

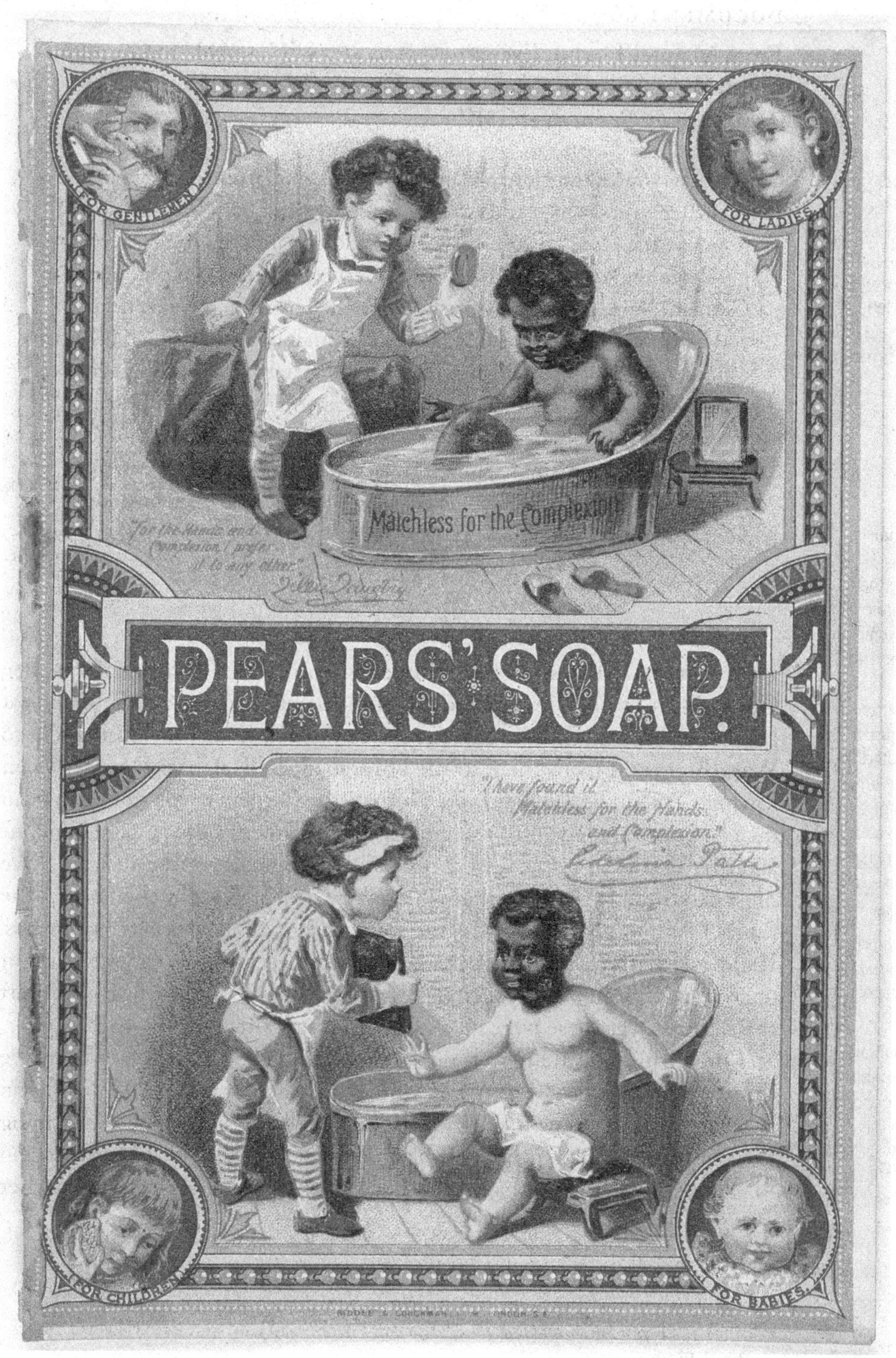
FOR GENTLEMEN
FOR LADIES
Matchless for the Complexion
PEARS' SOAP.
"I have found it Matchless for the Hands and Complexion."
FOR CHILDREN
FOR BABIES

DOCUMENT 66

From Manuel Timbu, Eyewitness Account of Genocide in German South West Africa in *Report on the Natives of South-West Africa and Their Treatment by Germany* (1918)[29]

Samuel Maharero: A Paramount Chief of the Herero people, and now recognized as a national hero in Namibia. In a letter to Namaqua Chief Hendrik Witbooi, Maharero said of the war with the Germans, "Let us die fighting!"

General von Trotha: German military commander during the genocide of the Herero and Nama peoples. His infamous extermination order read in part: "Any Herero found inside the German frontier, with or without a gun or cattle, will be executed. I shall spare neither women nor children. I shall give the order to drive them away and fire on them. Such are my words to the Herero people."

Okahandja: A city in central Namibia, often referred to as the Herero Capital of Namibia.

Waterberg: A mountain range in central Namibia. One of the sites of genocidal killing described in this document, it is now a popular national park.

In January 1904, the Herero people, led by **Samuel Maharero**, organized a campaign of resistance against German settlers in South West Africa. In response, the German government sent additional troops to the colony, to put down the "rebellion." The ensuing German–Herero War, and then the German–Nama War, were devastating to the Herero and Nama peoples, and constituted the crime of genocide. Community members and historians estimate that German soldiers killed approximately 80,000 Herero people, 10,000 Nama people, and an unknown number of San people. Debates over proper memorialization and restitution for these crimes continue in Namibia and Germany today. In this account, Manuel Timbu describes some of the things he saw, while working for the German commander, **General von Trotha**.

I was sent to **Okahandja** and appointed groom to the German commander, General von Trotha. I had to look after his horses and to do the odd jobs at his headquarters. We followed the retreating Hereros from Okahandja to **Waterberg**, and from there to the borders of the Kalahari Desert. When leaving Okahandja, General von Trotha issued orders to his troops that no quarter was to be given to the enemy. No prisoners were to be taken, but all, regardless of age or sex, were to be killed. General von Trotha said, "We must exterminate them, so that we won't be bothered with rebellions in the future." As a result of this order the soldiers shot all natives we came across. It did not matter who they were. Some were peaceful people who had not gone to rebellion; others, such as old men and old women, had never left their homes; yet these were all shot. I often saw this done.

Once while on the march near Hamakari beyond the Waterberg, we came to some waterholes. It was winter time and very cold. We came on two very old Herero women. They had made a small fire and were warming themselves. They had dropped back from the main body of Hereros owing to exhaustion. Von Trotha and his staff were present. A German soldier

29 *Report on the Natives of South-West Africa and Their Treatment by Germany. Prepared in the Administrator's Office, Windhuk, South-West Africa, January 1918* (London: His Majesty's Stationery Office, 1918). Republished as *Words Cannot Be Found: German Colonial Rule in Namibia—An Annotated Reprint of the 1918 Blue Book*, ed. Jeremy Silvester and Jan-Bart Gewald (Leiden: Brill, 2003), 115–16.

dismounted, walked up to the old women and shot them both as they lay there. Riding along we got to a **vlei**, where we camped. While we were there a Herero woman came walking up to us from the bush, I was the Herero interpreter. I was told to take the woman to the General to see if she could give information as to the whereabouts of the enemy. I took her to General von Trotha; she was quite a young woman and looked tired and hungry. Von Trotha asked her several questions, but she did not seem inclined to give information. She said her people had all gone towards the east, but as she was a weak woman she could not keep up with them. Von Trotha then ordered that she should be taken aside and bayoneted. I took that woman away and a soldier came up with a bayonet in his hand. He offered it to me and said I had better stab the woman. I said I would never dream of doing such a thing and asked why the poor woman could not be allowed to live. The soldier laughed, and said, "If you don't do it, I will show you what a German soldier can do." He took the woman aside a few paces and drove the bayonet through her body. He then withdrew the bayonet and brought it, all dripping with blood and poked it under my nose in a jeering way, saying, "You see, I have done it." Officers and soldiers were standing around looking on, but no one interfered to save the woman. Her body was not buried, but like all others they killed, simply allowed to lie and rot and be eaten by wild animals.

vlei: In Southern Africa, a temporary lake that collects water in the wet season and then acts as a waterhole.

A little further ahead we came to a place where the Hereros had abandoned some goats which were too weak to go further. There was no water to be had for miles around.... I was an eyewitness of everything I have related. In addition, I saw the bleeding bodies of hundreds of men, women and children, old and young, lying along the roads as we passed. They had all been killed by our advance guards. I was for nearly two years with the German troops and always with General von Trotha. I know of no instance in which prisoners were spared.

DOCUMENT 67

From Karl Pearson, *National Life from the Standpoint of Science* (1905)[30]

Karl Pearson (1857–1936) was an English mathematician who founded the world's first university statistics department at University College London, in 1911. Pearson supported the ideas of Social Darwinism and eugenics and was a student of **Francis Galton**. He gave the following address in Newcastle, England, during the Second Boer War. He used the occasion to illustrate his view that civilization can only progress through struggle, war, and the eventual domination of an inferior race by a superior race.

Francis Galton: A British polymath, now best known for his work in racial anthropology, Social Darwinism, and eugenics.

Now, if you have once realized the force of heredity, you will see in natural selection—the choice of the physically and mentally fitter to be the parents of the next generation—a most **munificent** provision for the progress of all forms of life. Nurture and education may immensely aid the social machine, but they must be repeated generation by generation; they will not in themselves reduce the tendency to the production of bad stock. Conscious or unconscious selection can alone bring that about.

munificent: Something which is larger or more generous than is considered necessary.

What I have said about bad stock seems to me to hold for the lower races of man. How many centuries, how many thousands of years, have the **Kaffir** or the negro held large districts in Africa undisturbed by the white man? Yet their intertribal struggles have not yet produced a civilization in the least comparable with the **Aryan**. Educate and nurture them as you will, I do not believe that you will succeed in modifying the stock. History shows me one way, and one way only, in which a high state of civilization has been produced, namely, the struggle of race with race, and the survival of the physically and mentally fitter race....

Kaffir: A racist slur, referring to a Black person from Southern Africa

Aryan: An ancient culture of Indo-Iranians; the myth of the "Aryan race" first appeared in the nineteenth century to describe an alleged distinct and superior race of fair-skinned peoples from Northern Europe.

If you bring the white man into contact with the black, you too often suspend the very process of natural selection on which the evolution of a higher type depends. You get superior and inferior races living on the same soil, and that coexistence is demoralizing for both. They naturally sink into the position of master and servant, if not admittedly or covertly into that of slave-owner and slave. Frequently they intercross, and if the bad stock be raised the good is lowered....

The struggle means suffering, intense suffering, while it is in progress; but that struggle and that suffering have been the stages by which the white

30 Karl Pearson, *National Life from the Standpoint of Science*, 2nd ed. (London: A. & C. Black, 1905), 20–22, 26, 36–37, 64.

man has reached the present stage of development, and they account for the fact that he no longer lives in caves and feeds on roots and nuts....

There is a struggle of race against race and of nation against nation. In the early days of that struggle it was a blind, unconscious struggle of barbaric tribes. At the present day, in the case of the civilized white man, it has become more and more the conscious, carefully directed attempt of the nation to fit itself to a continuously changing environment....

Mankind as a whole, like the individual man, advances through pain and suffering only. The path of progress is strewn with the wreck of nations; traces are everywhere to be seen of the hecatombs of inferior races, and of victims who found not the narrow way to the greater perfection. Yet these dead peoples are, in very truth, the stepping-stones on which mankind has arisen to the higher intellectual and deeper emotional life of today.

DOCUMENT 68

"A Plan to Highlight the Academic and Professional Accomplishments of 'Coloured' Men" (1913)[31]

The *African Times and Orient Review* was first published in 1912 by Duse Mohamed Alu, an Egyptian-British actor, journalist, and political activist. Educated at King's College London, Alu was inspired by the **1911 Universal Races Congress** and sought to build solidarity among non-white peoples of the world. The British government banned the journal in India and in several British-held African colonies, for fear its authors might encourage unrest. In the May 1913 edition, Dr. John Kunst lays out his plans to promote knowledge of the academic and professional achievements of "coloured" men, to which he received conflicting responses from German newspaper editors.

1911 Universal Races Congress: An anti-racism conference attended by more than 2,000 people and hosted by the University of London.

Sir,
I take the liberty of asking your opinion on the following subject—

I have the intention of creating together with some educated Negroes, Arabs, Indians, etc., a committee for the purpose of collecting information about members of the Black, Red, Malayan, and certain parts of the **Mongol races** who have attained Academical degrees in European or North American Universities; also of inventions patented by coloured men. It may be stated, without any danger of exaggeration I think, that in Germany fully 99 percent of even the educated men have not the slightest knowledge of the existence of University-trained coloured people; a state of things that cannot be without influence upon the coming into existence or maintenance of race prejudices. Combating the latter, is the purpose of our undertaking. We intend to publish every month or so, a compilation of news of the description above hinted at, and we take the liberty of asking you whether your paper would aid us in its promulgation....

Mongol races: A racist slur, most likely referring to peoples from the region of Mongolia. 'Mongoloid' has also been used to describe people who are either of mixed heritage or developmentally delayed.

The following are the replies received by the Doctor:

From the *Kölnische Volkszeitung* of Cologne, **Centre Party**:

Centre Party: A German conservative political party, whose members were typically members of the Catholic faith.

31 "Dr. Kunst's Scheme," *The African Times and Orient Review—A Monthly Journal Devoted to the Interests of the Coloured Races of the World* 1, no. 11 (May 1913): 329–30. See also C.L. Innes, *A History of Black and Asian Writing in Britain, 1700–2000*, 2nd ed. (Cambridge: Cambridge University Press, 2008).

The Conference of our editors held yesterday has dealt with your offer, for which we offer you our heartiest thanks. Now, the Conference is of the opinion that, through the exigencies of space, we are unable to publish a regular series of news articles on coloured men who have obtained any academical degree, etc. but we would be glad to publish an article giving intelligent information on the matter. The editors are therefore expecting such an article from your pen.

From the *Germania*, of Berlin, Centre Party:

We would agree to publish every month a report of the kind described by you, if you would engage to make it as *brief as possible*.

From the *Triennik Poznanski* of Posen, Polon Party:

In reply to yours of the 14th inst., we are forced to state that reports on reaching Academical degrees by Blacks, Red Indians, etc., would not be of considerable interest to our readers, though evidently, they are so from a broad cultured point of view.

From the *Vorwaerts*, of Berlin—party official Gazette of the **Socialists**:

Socialists: A German left-wing political party whose members at this time were most often part of the working classes.

We regret we cannot give way to your proposition, as such things are hardly adapted to a daily paper. Perhaps you might go to the *Documents of Progress*. In America there are special Institutes devoted to the civilization of coloured people, which would aid an undertaking like yours. We have published occasional hints and will continue to publish them later on.

From the *Freisinnige Zeitung*, of Berlin—Party Official Gazette of the Liberals:

On principle, we would agree to publish your list, provided that it would not be too large. We beg you to send us a list, that we may know what space it will require.

From the *Allgemeine Rundshau*, of Munich, Centre Party, a weekly of very large circulation:

Your proposed undertaking is much to be welcomed from the most divergent points of view, but the underlying idea on account of its newness must be promulgated vividly.... It would be a very good thing in our opinion, to give short, interesting biographies of the most interesting savants of the coloured races not omitting the creed of each individual dealt with.

From the *Augsburger Postzeitung*, of the Bavarian Centre Party:

We shall by pleased to publish your reports under the heading of "News from High Schools," and we welcome your understanding as very well adapted to the requirements of the age.

From the *Schlesische Volkszeitung* of Breslau, Centre Party:

We are not averse to take your plan into consideration, and to take notice of each of your reports, under the conditions mentioned by you, and in a manner adapted to the requirements and interest of our paper. Recently we read in a periodical a statement regarding the fact on which you lay stress, viz., that it is much too little known how many members of the coloured races obtain degrees, etc., in European or North American universities, and are holding highly esteemed positions at home. We fully sympathise with the intention underlying your understanding, viz., to contribute to the enfeeblement of certain prejudices.

DOCUMENT 69

From E.D. Morel, *The Horror on the Rhine* (1921)[32]

As part of the **Treaty of Versailles**, following the end of World War I, Allied troops occupied parts of a defeated Germany. The French military included African colonial troops as part of their occupation army, a fact which prompted some Germans to produce "Black Horror on the Rhine" propaganda that depicted Black men as rapists and carriers of disease, as described here by British journalist E.D. Morel. Some Europeans later viewed the children of these relationships as threats to the purity of the white race. In *Mein Kampf*, Hitler combined two strands of his virulent racism by proclaiming, "the Jews had brought the Negroes into the Rhineland with the clear aim of ruining the hated white race through miscegenation." Approximately 700 of these children, known by the derogatory phrase, Rhineland Bastards, were forcibly sterilized by Nazi doctors in 1937.

Treaty of Versailles: The terms of surrender forced upon the Germans after the end of World War I.

Danger lurks everywhere for women and girls in the French area of occupation. Women are afraid to walk alone after sunset. Strolling in the woods is no longer possible. Girls doing agricultural work in the fields often need the protection of their men-folk. Girls and boys are molested on their way to and from school. The towns and villages and the roads leading to them are alike unsafe. In ones and twos, sometimes in parties, big, stalwart men from warmer climes, armed with sword-bayonets or knives, sometimes with revolvers, living unnatural lives of restraint, their fierce passions hot within them, roam the countryside. Woe to the girl returning to her village home, or on the way to town with market produce, or at work alone hoeing in the fields. Dark forms come leaping out from the shadows of the trees, appear unexpectedly among the vines and grasses, rise from the corn where they have lain concealed....

32 E.D. Morel, *The Horror on the Rhine* (London: Union of Democratic Control, 1921), 26.

DOCUMENT 70

Image: Poster for a Degenerate Music Exhibition in Nazi Germany (1938)[33]

Black Europeans were targeted for racialized persecution in the Third Reich both because of their skin color and because of their assumed association with so-called degenerate art and culture. Hilarius (Lari) Gilges, a dancer by profession, was murdered by the SS in 1933, probably because he was Black. This poster advertises one of a series of exhibitions designed to show how un-German music, such as jazz, and art were damaging to the "Aryan" race. Note the Star of David on the musician's lapel. As with Hitler's writings on the Rhineland occupation, here the artist equates Blackness and Jewishness as two dangers facing the German people.

33 Nazi propaganda poster for the *Entartete Musik* (Degenerate Music) exhibition showing stereotype caricature of Black man playing saxophone. From Dusseldorf Exhibition, 1938, artist unknown. Lebrecht Music & Arts/Alamy Stock Photo.

Entartete
MUSIK
EINE ABRECHNUNG VON
STAATSRAT Dr. H.S. ZIEGLER
Preis 40 Pfennig

DOCUMENT 71

From Frantz Fanon, *Black Skin, White Masks* (1952)[34]

Free French Army: Military forces who fought alongside the Allies following the World War II German occupation of France.

Frantz Fanon was among the most vocal critics of colonialism and racism during the twentieth century. He was born in 1925 in Fort-de-France, Martinique, then a French colony. During World War II, Fanon joined the **Free French Army** and was stationed in both Algeria and France. Following the end of the war, Fanon studied medicine and psychiatry, and wrote several influential books. In the years following the publication of *Black Skin, White Masks*, a psychological study of the effects of colonialism and racism on Black people in white majority societies, Fanon became a vocal supporter and advocate for the decolonization of Algeria and was a member of the Algerian National Liberation Front. Following his death in 1961, Fanon's work continued to have a lasting impact, especially in global decolonization movements. The following represents only a few excerpts from a fulsome work.

Chapter 1: The Negro and Language

The black man has two dimensions. One with his fellows, the other with the white man. A Negro behaves differently with a white man and with another Negro. That this self-division is a direct result of colonialist subjugation is beyond question.... No one would dream of doubting that its major artery is fed from the heart of those various theories that have tried to prove that the Negro is a stage in the slow evolution of monkey into man. Here is objective evidence that expresses reality.

But when one has taken cognizance of this situation, when one has understood it, one considers the job complete. How can one then be deaf to that voice rolling down the stages of history: "What matters is not to know the world but to change it."

This matters appallingly in our lifetime....

The problem we confront in this chapter is this: The Negro of the Antilles will be proportionately whiter—that is, he will come closer to being a real human being—in direct ratio to his mastery of the French language....

Every colonized people—in other words, every people in whose soul an inferiority complex has been created by the death and burial of its local cultural originality—finds itself face to face with the language of the civilizing nation; that is, with the culture of the mother country. The

34 Frantz Fanon, *Black Skin, White Masks*, trans. Charles Lam Markmann (London: Pluto Press, 1986), 8–9.

colonized is elevated above his jungle status in proportion to his adoption of the mother country's cultural standards. He becomes whiter as he renounces his blackness, his jungle....

DOCUMENT 72
Enoch Powell, "Rivers of Blood" Speech (1968)[35]

British Nationality Act: 1948 Act of Parliament that created the status "Citizen of the United Kingdom and Colonies," which replaced "British subject."

The 1948 **British Nationality Act** granted citizenship and right of abode in the United Kingdom to all members of the British Empire. Between 1948 and 1971, nearly half a million people moved from the Caribbean to Great Britain, to fill jobs left open by a severe postwar labor shortage. Known as the Windrush generation after HMT *Empire Windrush*, one of the first ships to bring Caribbean migrants to the UK, they built lives, careers, and families, while also facing discrimination from people who believed that an increasingly multicultural society was threatening the British way of life. The following speech by politician Enoch Powell, delivered to a Conservative Association meeting in Birmingham, displays some of these prejudices.

A week or two ago I fell into conversation with a constituent, a middle-aged, quite ordinary working man employed in one of our nationalised industries.

After a sentence or two about the weather, he suddenly said: "If I had the money to go, I wouldn't stay in this country." I made some deprecatory reply to the effect that even this government wouldn't last for ever; but he took no notice, and continued: "I have three children, all of them been through grammar school and two of them married now, with family. I shan't be satisfied till I have seen them all settled overseas. In this country in 15 or 20 years' time the black man will have the whip hand over the white man."

... Here is a decent, ordinary fellow Englishman, who in broad daylight in my own town says to me, his Member of Parliament, that his country will not be worth living in for his children.

I simply do not have the right to shrug my shoulders and think about something else. What he is saying, thousands and hundreds of thousands are saying and thinking—not throughout Great Britain, perhaps, but in the areas that are already undergoing the total transformation to which there is no parallel in a thousand years of English history.

In 15 or 20 years, on present trends, there will be in this country three and a half million Commonwealth immigrants and their descendants. That is not my figure. That is the official figure given to parliament by the spokesman of the Registrar General's Office....

---

35 Enoch Powell, "Rivers of Blood" speech, delivered to a Conservative Association meeting in Birmingham on 20 April 1968. Immigration speeches, 1968–02 to 1976–10, GBR/0014/POLL 3/2/1/20, Churchill Archives Centre, https://archivesearch.lib.cam.ac.uk/repositories/9/archival_objects/468927.

It almost passes belief that at this moment 20 or 30 additional immigrant children are arriving from overseas in **Wolverhampton** alone every week—and that means 15 or 20 additional families a decade or two hence. Those whom the gods wish to destroy, they first make mad. We must be mad, literally mad, as a nation to be permitting the annual inflow of some 50,000 dependants, who are for the most part the material of the future growth of the immigrant-descended population. It is like watching a nation busily engaged in heaping up its own funeral pyre. So insane are we that we actually permit unmarried persons to immigrate for the purpose of founding a family with spouses and fiancés whom they have never seen....

Wolverhampton: A city in the West Midlands, England, in which large numbers of Black and Asian immigrants settled in the 1940s–1960s. It was also the home riding of Enoch Powell.

Nothing is more misleading than comparison between the Commonwealth immigrant in Britain and the American Negro. The Negro population of the United States, which was already in existence before the United States became a nation, started literally as slaves and were later given the franchise and other rights of citizenship, to the exercise of which they have only gradually and still incompletely come. The Commonwealth immigrant came to Britain as a full citizen, to a country which knew no discrimination between one citizen and another, and he entered instantly into the possession of the rights of every citizen, from the vote to free treatment under the National Health Service....

For these dangerous and divisive elements the legislation proposed in the **Race Relations Bill** is the very pabulum they need to flourish. Here is the means of showing that the immigrant communities can organise to consolidate their members, to agitate and campaign against their fellow citizens, and to overawe and dominate the rest with the legal weapons which the ignorant and the ill-informed have provided. As I look ahead, I am filled with foreboding; like the Roman, I seem to see "the River Tiber foaming with much blood."

Race Relations Bill: A 1968 British law making it illegal to refuse employment, housing, or public services to a person on the grounds of color, race, ethnicity, or nationality.

Only resolute and urgent action will avert it even now. Whether there will be the public will to demand and obtain that action, I do not know. All I know is that to see, and not to speak, would be the great betrayal.

DOCUMENT 73

Afrophobia in European School Curricula, *European Network against Racism Shadow Report 2014–2015* (2015)[36]

European Network against Racism: Founded by activists in 1998, it aims to "work to put an end to structural racism and discrimination across Europe and make a real difference in ethnic and religious minorities' lives."

Since 1998, the **European Network against Racism** has conducted annual surveys and studies on the experiences of minority groups in the contemporary European Union. This 2015 report suggests the persistence of Afrophobia, or anti-Black attitudes and prejudices, here demonstrated in school curriculum content.

Several Member States report negative representations of Black people in the curriculum and teaching materials, as well as the absence of positive and empowering images. In Germany children's books play a major role in introducing and reinforcing negative stereotypes of Black people. Scholars, civil society and parent initiatives have campaigned against the use of racist language in schoolbooks and in 2013 there was a high-profile debate in Germany around the use of the N-word. A schoolbook study published by the anti-discrimination governmental agency shows that new editions of schoolbooks still contain racist and discriminatory content in which Black people are stereotyped but states that the N-word is no longer used.

Hairspray: American musical set in 1962 Baltimore that follows the story of a white girl who works to desegregate a dance show. Productions have frequently been criticized for featuring all-white casts, some of whom have performed in blackface.

The curriculum in Ireland does not take into account or reflect the full diversity of students and a clear example of inadequate cultural sensitivity was displayed in 2014 when one school performed the musical ***Hairspray*** with White students in blackface playing the roles of the African American teenagers. In the Netherlands a strong link has been made between the role of education, historiography and blackface used for the Black Pete character during the annual St. Nicholas celebrations. Since 2011 there has been a high-profile debate around White Dutch people dressing up as the character in blackface with red lipstick and gold earrings, which are elements of racist stereotypes. The debate has revealed the lack of historical perspective in the Netherlands and limited collective memory of the Dutch colonial past. It highlights the gaps in the history curriculum and its impact on the current lives of people of African descent.

PAD/BE: People of African Descent/Black Europeans.

The absence of Europe's role in the slave trade and the colonization of Africa in curricula impacts on contemporary relationships between White Europeans and **PAD/BE**. As highlighted by the Netherlands questionnaire

36 Ojeaku Nwabuzo, *Afrophobia in Europe: ENAR Shadow Report 2014–2015* (Brussels: European Network against Racism, 2015), https://www.enar-eu.org/wp-content/uploads/shadowreport_afrophobia_final_with_corrections.pdf.

response, the lack of attention paid to slavery and colonialism in history books can cause a rupture in the understanding of the concept of race and racial inequality. It enables some European countries to justify their capitalist exploitation by decoupling it from their presence in the colonies.

Where slavery is included in history books, for example in the Netherlands, Africans are often essentialized and racialized as strong and violent and lacking humanity, while racialized White people are portrayed as good traders and businessmen. As reported in Italy, colonialism has very little space in the curriculum or history textbooks. The total lack of knowledge of the history of the Italian slave trade and its colonial past contributes to modern-day racism. In Portugal, the secondary school curriculum does not include Africa's role in the economic and cultural construction of the country. Recognising the past abuses of White Europeans is a significant element of history that needs to be included in the curriculum, however Black history did not start, nor end with slavery and colonialism. There are many more positive contributions from Black people that are simply omitted from textbooks. For example, the national curriculum for English in the UK fails to include a single non-White author at Key Stage 4 (14- to 16-year-olds). Prior to the change students were able to study the works of Black authors including **Chinua Achebe**. Furthermore the issue of race in World War I is not explored and there is a general lack of awareness and recognition of the role and contribution of ethnic minorities, including people of African descent, in the UK's history. The marginalisation and misrepresentation of Black people in the history of Europe can alienate Black Europeans and lead to disengaged students within national European countries. The "White washing" of history through the education system adds to the notion of White superiority and misleads the majority population in Europe into thinking ethnic diversity in Europe is new.

Chinua Achebe: Achebe (1930–2013) was a famous Nigerian author and critic whose 1958 *Things Fall Apart* remains one of the most widely read works of African literature.

PART 4

Racism against Asian Peoples[1]

INTRODUCTION

Europeans knew little of the Far East before the **Mongol** invasion of the thirteenth century. Until then, they relied on information from the ancient Romans and their Middle Eastern Muslim competitors to develop an image of the region and its peoples. Most of what they wrote in the Middle Ages was pure fantasy, as was their imagining of a powerful Christian king (Prester John) to the East of the Islamic realms whom they sought to reach in order to unite against the **Saracens** and Turks. When the Mongols, a nomadic people from the Gobi Desert region, under the leadership of Genghis Khan began the conquest of their neighbors, they demolished all opposition in their path. This would eventually include China and the Turkish forces of the Middle East. By the 1220s they had in fact reached Eastern Europe, and by the 1240s were in control of much of Hungary and Russia, extracting enormous tribute from the local rulers and governing the region known as the Golden Horde. Over time absorbing much of the culture of their Chinese subjects, the Mongols impressed the Europeans who expressed considerable hope that the Mongol Khans (emperors) would convert to Christianity to play the role of Prester John. They never did so, although the Khans were tolerant of a variety of religions, including an ancient form of Christianity called Nestorianism, and several of their wives were Christians.

Mongol: An East Asian ethnic group with historical origins in Mongolia and Western China.

Saracens: European name for Muslims of the Middle East.

The account of the voyage of Marco Polo (Document 74) brought new information to Europe about the Far East, and it emphasized that the Mongolians and Chinese were a civilized and powerful people with rich cities and a large population. This encouraged further travels eastward, and as they interacted more with Mongolian traders and officials, it became clear to Europeans that they could not easily conquer these lands. The desire for the riches of China and India, however, spurred numerous efforts to reach the Far East, but since the Muslims and Mongols controlled the overland passageways, Europeans sailed westward to reach those shores. They of course

1 For continental Europeans, Asian typically refers to peoples originating from Japan, China, or the countries near them, while in the UK, Asian refers to someone from India, Pakistan, or Southeast Asia. This Reader uses a broad historical interpretation and includes European sources that describe various communities of people.

did not expect the large land masses of the Americas and assumed that these were the coasts of India and China. Readers can certainly observe significant contrast between how Europeans described their visits to Africa, such as Documents 47, 48, 50, 51, and 53 above, with their interpretation of Asia.

In the sixteenth and seventeenth centuries, European trading vessels were establishing colonies along the western shore of India and in the East Indies and used intermediaries to contact Chinese and Japanese officials. These contacts were followed by **Jesuit** and **Franciscan** missionaries who sought to learn the local languages and to convert the inhabitants to Christianity. Such efforts proved largely unsuccessful, yet the reports sent back to Europe by these mendicants further informed western writers. As can be seen from the first several documents, Europeans focused on elements of Asian culture that they could critique, such as religion, philosophical sophistication, or hygiene, since China and Japan both proved formidable powers that Europeans could not readily subdue, at least until the late eighteenth century. Otherwise, European writers expressed some elements of surprise at the sophistication of Chinese and Japanese culture. As Europeans developed their concept of whiteness as superior to other skin colors, however, it would not be long before they would view Asians with the same kind of racializing lens they had been turning on Jews, Muslims, Blacks, and other outsiders. And, since many Asians had converted to Islam, European prejudicial attitudes toward Arabian and Turkish Muslims were also transferred onto them.

Jesuit: Members of the Society of Jesus, a Catholic religious order founded to counteract Protestantism and to missionize the world.

Franciscans: Members of the mendicant order founded in the thirteenth century by St. Francis of Assisi to preach against heresy and live like the 12 apostles.

In the eighteenth and nineteenth centuries, racial scientists debated the origins of the races of the world. For instance, some anthropologists and linguists believed Hindus represented a branch of the so-called Aryan race, while others viewed the peoples of the subcontinent as brown or black peoples. Pseudo-scientific studies "proving" that Northern Indians had sullied their **Aryan** heritage by mixing with lesser peoples reconciled these two erroneous views. Other commentators used technological innovation and industrial advancement as a measure of national and racial status; they argued for example, that while the Chinese had a long and rich history, they had stalled as a modern people because of centuries of despotic political rule (see Documents 82, 83). By the early twentieth century, biological racism negated the need for such distinctions; instead, it became more convenient for Europeans to insist that whiteness guaranteed superiority. Such assumptions led educational experts to question whether Indian children could ever master an English school curriculum, and whether Chinese workers could ever rise to supervisory positions (Document 84). The assumption that Asian peoples were largely incapable of learning Western ways fit nicely with imperialist plans to seize and hold territorial power around the globe.

Aryan: Ancient culture of Indo-Iranians; the myth of the "Aryan race" first appeared in the nineteenth century to describe an alleged distinct and superior race of fair-skinned peoples from Northern Europe.

Europeans had long viewed Asia as an important source of raw materials and as an untapped market for Western goods—by the 1830s, British traders were dealing in Indian **opium** and Chinese luxury goods such as silks, tea, and porcelain. Conflicts over markets and tariffs led to the **Opium Wars**. The Chinese opium addict became a key anti-Asian stereotype, one that was frequently connected to sexually predatory men who allegedly preyed on vulnerable white women (a prejudice also leveled at Jewish and Black men, as we have seen in Documents 14 and 53). In North America, these prejudices, coupled with anti-immigration policies became known as the **Yellow Peril**. The 1842 **Treaty of Nanking** increased trade access and placed Hong Kong under British control and treated Chinese in concession areas as foreigners in their own lands. Christian missionaries saw Chinese men, women, and children as heathens in need of saving. Anti-imperialist sentiment, exacerbated by military defeat to Japan in 1895, led to increasingly violent attacks against Europeans; the ensuing military conflict known as the **Boxer Rebellion** led to widespread loss of civilian and military life, and further cemented prejudices that saw Asian people as insubordinate, weak, and linked to supernatural and irrational forces (see Document 87). By 1900, European powers had divided up most of the Pacific region with the British in India and Burma, Holland in Indonesia, France in Indochina, Russia in Central Asia, Germany in the Samoan Islands, and American in the Philippines. Only Japan remained truly independent.

During both World War I and World War II, European militaries used Indian and Chinese soldiers and laborers to augment their own troop numbers and perform tasks deemed below those expected of white men (see Documents 88 and 90). The military restricted entry into the British Army to men of pure European descent, though other branches could recruit "aliens" for specific jobs and ranks. However, the British military did relax its **color bar**, allowing more than two and a half million Indian citizens to serve in the armed forces. Historians still debate whether they did so out of military expediency, as a deliberate act of anti-racism, or because they did not wish to answer public accusations of prejudice while fighting Nazi Germany. Non-white veterans spent decades seeking adequate pensions, recognition, and to have their comrades' names included on national memorials.

In the 1950s and 1960s, South Asians from India and Pakistan were recruited to work in European industries, especially in Italy and Britain. These programs paralleled the West German guest worker programs we described in Part 2. Many migrants were educated, middle-class professionals who were then forced to work in lower-paying factory jobs. Their children, as second-generation immigrants, often faced discrimination in their schools and communities. Even as Indian food became accepted as British cuisine, anti-Asian sentiment impacted generations of families. Prejudice sometimes

opium: A drug obtained from the seed pods of opium poppies; it has been used legally and illegally in global societies since at least 3400 BCE.

Opium Wars: Two conflicts fought in China between the Qing Dynasty (1644–1912) and British and French forces. In both cases, in 1839–42, and in 1856–60, the foreign powers used their victories to gain greater imperial control over Chinese territories.

Yellow Peril: A racist belief used extensively in Europe and North America that Asian peoples (both individually and collectively) pose a threat to non-Asian peoples; specifically, it harnessed anxieties held by some white peoples of being "taken over by foreigners."

Treaty of Nanking: The 1842 agreement ending the First Opium War. The treaty mandated that China pay Britain a financial sum, cede the territory of Hong Kong, and allow European merchants to access more Chinese ports.

Boxer Rebellion: An uprising that sought to drive Westerners out of China in 1900 that led to an invasion by a 19,000-strong international military force. As many as 100,000 people died in the resulting war, which ended in Chinese defeat.

color bar: Systematic discrimination, based on "racial" distinctions.

French bans on symbols of faith: A 2004 law that uses the constitutional requirement to separate church and state to prohibit the wearing of certain items of clothing deemed religious.

turban: A head covering made by winding cloth, variations of which have been worn in diverse cultures for thousands of years. In the Sikh faith, men wear turbans to cover uncut hair and as a symbol of equality, honor, spirituality, courage, and friendship.

turned violent, especially as South Asians were frequently scapegoated for the industrial decline of the 1970s.

The postwar period has also seen increasing clashes over the Europeanness of wearing non-Christian religious symbols in public. **French bans on symbols of faith**, aimed at preserving French secularism, have largely been aimed at Muslim hijabs and burqas, Christian crucifixes, Jewish skullcaps, and Sikh **turbans**. Sikh leaders protested the law's application to their community, stating turbans represent cultural rather than religious traditions.

Elizabeth Chan, a British actress of Chinese descent, wrote the following in a 2012 newspaper article about anti-Asian racism in her country—"Shouts of 'Jackie Chan!' and kung-fu noises from random strangers continue to greet me in the street, perhaps followed by a 'konichiwa!' Just a few days ago, a friend was having a post-hangover drink in a trendy east London pub, only to be accused by the manager of being a DVD peddler hassling his clients." In her opinion, such prejudice is worsened by continuing stereotypes in mainstream media. Chan writes, "Chinese characters rarely appear on our television screens, but when they do, you can bet they'll be DVD sellers, illegal immigrants, spies or, in the case of last year's Sherlock, weird acrobatic ninja types. Many Chinese viewers were outraged at the portrayal of east Asians in this show, but typically, few complained."[2] Indeed, Chan argues that British Chinese communities tend to be more reluctant to speak up about the treatment they receive, resulting in less public knowledge about anti-Asian racism. As Document 91 well illustrates, misconceptions about the origin and spread of the COVID-19 pandemic have only intensified racist stereotypes about Asian peoples around the world.

2 Elizabeth Chan, "Chinese Britons Have Put Up with Racism for Too Long," *Guardian*, 11 January 2012.

DOCUMENT 74

Marco Polo's Account of Mongolian China, from "The Travels of Marco Polo" (c. 1295)[3]

Marco Polo (1254–1324) was a son of a Venetian merchant who, with his uncle and father, traveled the merchant route known as the Silk Road to China, where he served Kublai Khan, the Mongol ruler, for nearly a quarter century. Returning to Venice in 1295, Polo was imprisoned by Venice's competitor Genoa, where he recounted his tale to a fellow prisoner, Rustichello da Pisa. While Polo likely embellished many parts of his account, he had traveled to China, as did many other Christian merchants. "The Travels of Marco Polo" shaped how Europeans viewed the Far East for centuries. Readers should compare the significant differences in attitude between Polo's travelogue compared to those relating to Africa above and Indigenous peoples below.

After you have travelled thirty days through the Desert as I have described, you come to a city called Sachiu lying between north-east and east; it belongs to the Great **Kaan**, and is in a province called **Tangut**. The people are for the most part **Idolaters**, but there are also some Nestorian Christians and some **Saracens**. The Idolaters have a peculiar language, and are no traders, but live by their agriculture. They have a great many abbeys and **minsters** full of idols of sundry fashions, to which they pay great honour and reverence, worshipping them and sacrificing to them with much ado. For example, such as have children will feed up a sheep in honour of the idol, and at the New Year, or on the day of the Idol's Feast, they will take their children and the sheep along with them into the presence of the idol with great ceremony. Then they will have the sheep slaughtered and cooked, and again present it before the idol with like reverence, and leave it there before him, whilst they are reciting the offices of their worship, and their prayers for the idol's blessing on their children. And if you will believe them the idol feeds on the meat that is set before it! … And you must know that all the Idolaters in the world burn their dead.…

Kaan: Khan, the supreme Mongolian ruler.

Tangut: A tribe of Northwest China conquered by the Mongols.

Idolaters: People who worship images of gods.

Saracens: Medieval European term for Muslims of the Middle East.

minsters: English term for cathedrals, here applied to Chinese temples.

Camul is a province which in former days was a kingdom.… The people are all Idolaters, and have a peculiar language.… They are a people who take things very easily, for they mind nothing but playing and singing and dancing and enjoying themselves. And it is the truth that if a foreigner comes to

Camul: Name given to a region in inland China south of Tangut.

3 Excerpted from Sir Henry Yule, ed., *The Book of Ser Marco Polo, the Venetian, Concerning the Kingdoms and Marvels of the East*, 2 vols. (London: John Murray, 1871), vol. 1: 184–86, 189, 224, 265, 404; vol. 2: 171, 185.

lists: Desires; the implication is that they allow male guests to have sexual relations with their wives.

wittols: Husbands who are acquiescent cuckolds.

thurible: A metal censer for the burning of incense.

incense: Aromatic material that is burned for its fragrance; used in religious services in East Asian culture as well as Polo's own Roman Catholic Church.

Natigay: A household god of the Tartars who guards over families and agricultural fertility.

enchanters: Sorcerers or magicians.

astrologers: Those who read the movement of the stars and planets to determine future events.

necromancy: The summoning of demons to perform acts or provide knowledge for the necromancer. Illegal in Europe, but widely practiced by learned clergy and others.

Tebet: Presumably Tibet, in Southwestern China.

Kesimur: Presumably Kashmir, a region south of China, portions of which are currently governed by Pakistan, India, and China.

Devil: A supernatural creature of evil within Christian teaching; Christians like Polo interpreted anything they saw that was contrary to Christian theology as arising from the devil.

the house of one of these people to lodge, the host is delighted, and desires his wife to put herself entirely at the guest's disposal, whilst he himself gets out of the way, and comes back no more until the stranger shall have taken his departure. The guest may stay and enjoy the wife's society as long as he **lists**, whilst the husband has no shame in the matter, but indeed considers it an honour. And all the men of this province are made **wittols** of by their wives in this way. The women themselves are fair and wanton....

This is the fashion of their religion. They say there is a Most High God of Heaven, whom they worship daily with **thurible** and **incense**, but they pray to Him only for health of mind and body. But they have [also] a certain [other] god of theirs called **Natigay**, and they say he is the God of the Earth, who watches over their children, cattle, and crops. They show him great worship and honour, and every man hath a figure of him in his house, made of felt and cloth; and they also make in the same manner images of his wife and children. The wife they put on the left hand, and the children in front. And when they eat, they take the fat of the meat and grease the god's mouth withal, as well as the mouths of his wife and children. Then they take of the broth and sprinkle it before the door of the house; and that done, they deem that their god and his family have had their share of the dinner....

But I must now tell you a strange thing that hitherto I have forgotten to mention. During the three months of every year that the Lord resides at that place, if it should happen to be bad weather, there are certain crafty **enchanters** and **astrologers** in his train, who are such adepts in **necromancy** and the diabolic arts, that they are able to prevent any cloud or storm from passing over the spot on which the Emperor's Palace stands. The sorcerers who do this are called **Tebet** and **Kesimur**, which are the names of two nations of Idolaters. Whatever they do in this way is by the help of the **Devil**, but they make those people believe that it is compassed by dint of their own sanctity and the help of God. (They always go in a state of dirt and uncleanness, devoid of respect for themselves, or for those who see them, unwashed, unkempt, and sordidly attired.) These people also have a custom which I must tell you. If a man is condemned to death and executed by the lawful authority, they take his body and cook and eat it. But if any one die a natural death then they will not eat the body.

... Description of the Great City of Kinsay [Hangzhou], which is the Capital of the Whole Country of Manzi [China].

Certain of the streets are occupied by the women of the town, who are in such a number that I dare not say what it is. They are found not only in the vicinity of the market places, where usually a quarter is assigned to them, but all over the city. They exhibit themselves splendidly attired and abundantly perfumed.... These women are extremely accomplished in all the arts of allurement, and readily adapt their conversation to all sorts of persons, insomuch that strangers who have once tasted their attractions seem to get **bewitched**, and are so taken with their blandishments and their fascinating ways that they never can get these out of their heads. Hence it comes to pass that when they return home they say they have been to Kinsay or the City of Heaven, and their only desire is to get back thither as soon as possible....

bewitched: One of the most commonly attributed forms of magic in medieval Europe was love magic.

DOCUMENT 75

From a Translated Spanish Pamphlet Called "News from China" (1577)[4]

By the middle of the sixteenth century, printers were churning out popular **newssheets** and pamphlets for an eager readership. This example is about Mexico, which the writer says is under the rule of China and was under attack by Turkish ships. Neither of these statements is true.

newssheets: Short, cheap, news reports, predecessor to newspapers.

In the month of March, 1577 a certain Merchant dwelling in the famous city of Mexico, which is situated in the west India, now called **new Spain**, writes among other things to his friend dwelling in the Province of **Andoluzia**, the particular news, which at that instant were come from the great dominion of China, which adjoins unto the East India, saying as follows....

new Spain: Called such by the Spanish.

Andoluzia: Andalusia, South-central Spain.

Two ships came from China, in one of the which came a credible person, who as a present witness does declare, that the Spaniards which were inhabited in certain Islands which stand distant from that firm land, [discovered that] the people are of small stature. Their women when they are born, they use to wrest one of their legs, whereof they ever remain lame,[5] because they should continually keep their houses: & are kept so close, that none may see them, except those of the household. For our learned men being there, as is said, six months, could not describe five women.

The men use their nails of their hands very long, for they find it a profitable thing for the wars.

This people do worship their Gods, that is to say, the Sun, the Moon, and an Idol with three heads.... They believe that the Sun is God of the wars, and the Moon is the God of temperature, which is lesser in substance, than the Sun. They also believe that all 3 Gods are as one in Godhead, although they rule severally every one by himself.

And having now understanding by our learned men, of the blessed **Trinity**, they allow very well thereof, thinking that it is similtude of their three Gods.

Trinity: The Christian doctrine that God is both one and three persons: the Father, Son, and Holy Spirit.

This guard of five thousand men was sent to defend our learned men from the Turks, because at that time were **ten Sail of Turks** on the Coast, who did great hurt unto them. These Turks gave chase to our men, and their company, and slew thirty Christians, and many Indians. The Christians slew of the Turks above five hundred. And the next day following,

ten Sail of Turks: Ten Turkish sailing vessels.

4 [Thomas Nicholas], *The strange and marueilous Newes latelyh come from the great kingdome of Chyna, which adioyneth to the East Indya. Translated out of the Castlyn tongue* (London, c. 1577), fols. Aiiir–Aviir.

5 Presumably the foot binding of women practiced in China. See Document 82.

our men & their Indians having refreshed themselves, set again upon the Turks, and slew their king, and near two thousand persons of his army, and drove the residue to flight.[6]

When the Indians that went to accompany our men, returned with that news, all the Citizens rejoiced, and chiefly the King of China, who was abiding in an other City farther within the main land.[7] And forthwith he sent a present unto them for their King, which was a statue of God, in token of victory: and advertised him of the valiantnesse of his subjects, which had slain the mighty Turk King of **Brazer** ... with this fleet of Indians and 300 Spaniards, they proceeded to seek the Turks Navy, which they met not, but they conquered in that return homewards, other 3 Islands, the which they left in subjection, to the King our Master.

Brazer: Derived from the Spanish *bracero* referring to the region of Mexico.

And when the Indian Fleet returned from the Island toward China, two Ships departed from the new Spain, for those parties in the which went 12 learned men, to preach the Gospel unto those Indians, and to instruct them of the mystery of the holy trinity, I beseech God that the fruit thereof may ensue, as we trust it will, and coming so to pass, it will be the richest Land that ever was known.

We do now look for other two Ships, that the Viceking pretended to send for 1000 men, to attempt the Conquest of China, for he says that his heart serves him to finish that enterprise with so many men, because the Indians are of small courage, yea, and though they have **Arquebuses** and other Artillery, yet they know not how to use them.... And all the citizens of Mexico are moved with desire to go thither, with love of the great quantity of Gold that is there.

Arquebus: An early matchlock gun.

6 There is of course no evidence that a Turkish fleet had reached Mexico.

7 An obvious misunderstanding reflecting that the author still believed that the Americas were really the coast of China.

DOCUMENT 76

From Peter Martyr d'Anghiera, *The History of Travel in the West and East Indies, and Other Countries Lying Either Way* (1577)[8]

Peter Martyr d'Anghiera (1457–1526) was an Italian historian who worked as chaplain for King Ferdinand II of Aragon and Queen Isabella I of Castile, the sponsors of Christopher Columbus's voyages in 1492. Martyr wrote his account based on the writings of Columbus and other European explorers. Here he writes about China.

close stools: Toilets.

dungfermers: Procurers of human waste.

Hen: Chicken.

Portugalles: English term for Portuguese.

***Chineans*:** Chinese.

The country is so well inhabited, that not one foot of ground is left untilled.... Here be sold the voidings of **close stools**, although there wants not the dung of beasts: & the excrements of man are good merchandise throughout all China. The **dungfermers** seek in every street by exchange to buy this dirty ware for herbs and wood. The custom is very good for keeping the city clean.... And if this country were like unto India, the inhabitants whereof eat neither **Hen**, beef, nor pork, but keep that only for the **Portugalles** and Moors, they would be sold here for nothing. But it so falling out, that the ***Chineans*** are the greatest eaters in all the world, they do feed upon all things, specially on pork, the fatter that is, unto them the less loathsome.... Frogs are sold at the same price that is made of Hens, and are good meat amongst them, as also Dogs, Cats, Snakes, and all other unclean meats....

***Loutea*:** Martyr is referring to Chinese nobility; perhaps he is also subtly satirizing European nobility?

I shall have occasion to speak of a certain order of gentlemen that are called ***Loutea*** ... who, along with all the people of China, are wont to eat their meat sitting on stools at high tables as we do, and that very cleanly, although they use nether tablecloths nor napkins. Whatsoever is set down upon the board, is first carved, before that it be brought in: they feed with two sticks, refraining from touching their meat with their hands, even as we do with forks, for the which respect, they less do need any tablecloths. Nor is the nation only civil at meat, but also in conversation, and in courtesy they seem to exceed all other.... The *Louteas*, are an idle generation, without all manner of exercises and pastimes, except it be eating and drinking.

... The inhabitants of China, be very great Idolaters, all generally do worship the heavens: and as we are wont to say, God knows it: so say they

8 Pietro Martire d'Anghiera, *The history of travayle in the West and East Indies, and other countreys lying eyther way, towardes the fruitfull and ryche Moluccaes As Moscouia, Persia, Arabia, Syria, AEgypte, Ethiopia, Guinea, China in Cathayo, and Giapan: with a discourse of the Northwest passage. Gathered in parte, and done into Englyshe by Richarde Eden*, ed. Richard Wills (London: Richarde Jugge, 1577), fols. 238v–242r.

at every word, *Tien Tautee*, that is to say, *The heavens do know it.* Some do worship the Sun, and some the Moon, as they think good, for none are bound more to one than to another. In their temples, the which they do call *Meani*, they have a great **altar** in the same place as we have, true it is that one may go round about it. There set they up the Image of a certain *Loutea* of that country, whom they have in great reverence for certain notable things he did.[9] At the right hand stands the devil, much more ugly painted than we do use to set him out, whereunto great homage is done by such as come into the temple to ask counsel, or to draw lots: this opinion they have of him, that he is malicious and able to do evil. If you ask them what they do think of the souls departed, they will answer, that they be immortal, and that as soon as any one departs out of this life, he becomes a devil if he have lived well in this world, if otherwise, that the same devil changes him into a buffalo, ox, or dog. Wherefore to this devil do they much honour, to him do they sacrifice, praying him that he will make them like unto himself, and not like other beasts.

... The greatest fault we do find in them is **Sodomy**, a vice very common in the meaner sort, & nothing strange amongst the best.

altar: A raised platform used in religious ceremonies, originally to make animal sacrifices upon it; Catholic Churches have altars at their center for the celebration of the Mass, often with statues of the crucified Christ hanging above them.

Sodomy: A generic term used by Europeans to describe same sex relations between men, which was a crime in Europe.

9 Likely the Buddha.

DOCUMENT 77

From Jan Huyghen van Linschoten, *His Discourse of Voyages into the East and West Indies* (1598)[10]

Jan Huyghen van Linschoten (1563–1611) was a Dutch traveler who served in Portuguese India (western coastal India) from 1583 to 1589 and wrote a description of Asian trade routes, from which this passage is excerpted. His accounts inspired Dutch merchants to set off for the East.

The Island or the land of *Japan* ... is a great land.... In some places the land is very hilly and unfruitful, they eat no flesh but the flesh of wild beasts, and such as is hunted, wherein they are very expert, although there are Oxen, Cows, Sheep, and such like Cattle good store, yet they use them to other things about their labours, and because it is tame flesh, which they cannot **brook**, they refuse it as we do horse flesh, they do likewise refuse to eat Milk, as we do blood, saying that Milk although it is white, yet it is **very** blood. They have much Fish, whereof they are very desirous, as also all kinds of fruits, as in China.

brook: Tolerate.

very: Truly, in actual fact.

The ***Japens*** are not so curious nor so clean as the men of China, but are content with **a mean**, yet for the most part they go very well appareled in Silk, almost like the ***Chinos***. The country has some mines of silver, which from thence is by the Portingals yearly brought unto China, and there bartered for Silk, and other Chinese wares, which the Japans have need of.... They have among them very good handicrafts men, and cunning workmen in all kind of handy works, they are sharp witted, and quickly learn anything they see, as by experience it is found in those parts which the Portingales have discovered.

Japens: Japanese.

a mean: A mean or simple life.

Chinos: Chinese.

The common people of the land are much different from other nations, for that they have among them as great courtesy and good policy, as if they had lived continually in the **Court**, they are very expert in their weapons as need requires, although they have little cause to use them, for that if any of them begin to brawl or to draw his sword, he is put to death, they have not any prisons, for that whosoever deserves to be imprisoned, is presently punished, or banished [from] the country. When they mean to lay hold upon a man, they must do it by stealth and by deceit, for otherwise he would resist and do much mischief. If it be any **Gentleman** or man of great authority, they beset his house about with men, and whether he chance to slay himself

Court: The Imperial Court where rules of etiquette dominated.

Gentleman: For Europeans, a member of the aristocracy and nobility, originally members of the military elites. In Japan, such gentlemen were called the daimyo.

10 John Huyghen van Linschoten, *His Discours of Voyages into the Easte and West Indies Devided into Foure Bookes* (London: John Wolfe, 1598), 44–45.

or not, they enter the house by force, and kill all they find therein. Which to avoid, he suffers himself often times to be killed by his servants. And it is often seen that they rip their own bellies open, which often times is likewise done by their servants for the love of their Masters, therein to show their Masters the love they bear unto them, so little esteeming their own lives, to pleasure and serve them. The like do young Boys in presence of their parents, only for grief or some small anger. They are in all their actions very patient and humble, for that in their youths they learn to endure hunger, cold, and all manner of labour, to go bare headed, with few clothes, as well in Winter as in Summer, and not only the common people, but the principal Gentlemen and Nobles of the country. They account it for great beauty to have no hair, which with great care they do pluck out, onely keep a bunch of hair on the crown of their heads, which they tie together.

... [T]here is so great envy and hatred between them and the men of China, that they hate each other to the death, and do all the mischief one unto the other that they can imagine or devise, even until this time. The men of *Japan* have done much mischief unto the men of China, and many times fallen upon their coasts, and put all to fire and sword, and now at this present have not any conversation with them, but only they traffic with the Portingales ... and as among other nations it is a good sight to see men with white and yellow hair and white teeth, with them it is esteemed the filthiest thing in the world, and seek by all means they may to make their hair and teeth black, for that the white causes their grief, and the black makes them glad. The like custom is among the women, for as they go abroad they have their daughters & maids before them, and their men servants come behind, which in *Spain* is clean contrary, and when they are **great with child**, they tie their girdles so hard about them, that men would think they should burst, and when they are not with Child, they wear their girdles so slack, that you would think they would fall from their bodies, saying that by experience they do find, if they should not do so, they should have evil luck with their **fruit**, and presently as soon as they are delivered of their children, instead of cherishing both the mother and the child with some comfortable meat, they presently wash the child in cold water, and for a time give the mother very little to eat, and that of no great substance.

great with child: Pregnant.

fruit: Fetus.

DOCUMENT 78

From José de Acosta, *The Natural and Moral History of the East and West Indies* (1604)[11]

José de Acosta (1539–1600) was a Spanish Jesuit missionary to Peru and Mexico whose *Historia natural y moral de las Indias* was published in 1590, and excerpts of which are taken from the 1604 English translation. Comparing the **Old World** to the New, he suggested that human migration to the Americas was via an Asian land bridge.

Old World: Europeans regarded Eurasia as the Old World in contrast to the Americas, which they termed the New World.

fathers of our company: Jesuit priests.

religious men: Monks.

***Boncos*:** Presumably Buddhist monks.

Orders: Catholic monastic organizations devoted to prayer, preaching, and service. Here de Acosta is interpreting Chinese religious groups through this Catholic lens.

make profession: When Catholics joined religious orders, they took vows of poverty, chastity, and obedience.

***Paquin*:** Presumably Peking, the European transcription of Beijing, now the capital of China.

It is well known, by Letters written by the **fathers of our company** from *Japan* the number and multitude of **religious men** that are in those Provinces, whom they call ***Boncos***, and also their superstitious customs and lies. Some fathers that have been in those countries, report of these *Boncos* and religious men of China, saying, that there are many **Orders**, and of diverse sorts, some came unto them clad in white, bearing hoods, and others all in black, without hair or hood, and these are commonly little esteemed, for the *Mandarins* or ministers of Justice whip them, as they do the rest of the people. They **make profession**, not to eat any flesh, fish, nor any thing that hath life, but only Rice and herbs; but in secret they do eat anything, and are worse than the common people. They say the religious men which are at the Court, which is at ***Paquin***, are very much esteemed. The *Mandarins* … little esteem idols, and do hold it for a vain thing, and worthy to be laughed at: yea they believe there is no other life, nor Paradise, but to be in the office of the Mandarins, nor any other hell, than the prisons they have for offenders. As for the common sort, they say, it is necessary to entertain them with idolatry.…

There are many which think, and it is the most common opinion, that the writings which the *Chinois* used, are letters, as those we use in Europe.… But it is not so, for they have no Alphabet, neither write they any letters, but all their writing is nothing else but painting and ciphering: and their letters signify no parts of distinctions, as ours do, but are figures and representations of things, as of the Sun, of fire, of a man, of the sea, and of other things.… So as things being of themselves innumerable, the letters likewise or figures which the *Chinois* use to signify them by, are in a manner infinite: so as he that shall read or write at China (as

11 José de Acosta, *The Naturall and Morall Historie of the East and West Indies Intreating of the Remarkable Things of Heaven, of the Elements, Mettalls, Plants and Beasts which are Proper to that Country: Together with the Manners, Ceremonies, Lawes, Governments, and Warres of the Indians … translated into English by E.G.* (London: E. Blount and W. Aspley, 1604), 197–98, 440–43.

the *Mandarins* do) must know and keep in memory at the least **fourscore** and five thousand characters or letters, and those which are perfect herein, know above sixscore thousand.... For this reason learned men are so much esteemed in China, for the difficulty there is to conceive them....

fourscore: A score is 20, so fourscore is 80.

Of **divine sciences** they have no knowledge, neither of natural things, but some small remainders of strayed propositions, without art or method, according to every man's wit and study. As for the Mathematics, they have experience of the celestial motions, and of the stars. And for **Physics**, they have knowledge of herbs, by means whereof, they cure many diseases, & use it much ... in effect all the knowledge of the *Chinois*, tends only to read and write, & no farther: for they attain to no high knowledge.... But in the end with all their knowledge, an Indian of *Peru* or *Mexico*, that has learned to read and write, knows more than the wisest *Mandarin* that is amongst them: for that the Indian with four and twenty letters which he has learned, will write all the words in the world: and a *Mandarin* with his hundred thousand letters, will be troubled to write some proper name, as of *Martin*, or *Alonso*, & with greater reason he shall be less able to write the names of things he knows not.

divine sciences: Theology and philosophy.

Physics: Medicine.

DOCUMENT 79

Image: From Johan Isaksson Pontanus, *Historical Description of the Very Widely Famed Merchant City of Amsterdam* (1614)[12]

Buddha: Gautama Buddha, the South Asian ascetic of the sixth or fifth century BCE whose teachings formed the basis for Buddhism. Regarded as fully enlightened, his statues are revered across Eastern Asia, and his teachings maintained by communities of Buddhist monks.

As noted in Document 51, Johan Isaksson Pontanus was a resident of Amsterdam who described the travels of its merchants. Here he has an engraving of Chinese worshipping an image of a demonic figure, but which was likely originally a statue of the **Buddha**.

218 Historische beschrijvinge van Amsterdam

29

12 Johan Isaksson Pontanus, *Historische Beschrijvinghe der seer wijt beroemde Coop-stadt Amsterdam*, trans. Petrus Montanus (Amsterdam, 1614), 218. Courtesy Allard Pierson, Amsterdam.

DOCUMENT 80

From Cornelius Hazart, *Church History of the Entire World* (1671): A Netherlandic Jesuit's Perspective on the Mongols (Tartars)[13]

As noted in Document 32, Cornelius Hazart (1634–90) was a Southern Netherlandic Jesuit priest who opposed **Calvinism**. His *Church History of the Entire World* was popular among Jesuits who missionized around the globe. Here he writes about the Mongols, whom he also calls Tartars, who were a neighboring ethnic group conquered by the Mongols.

Calvinism: A movement founded by the sixteenth-century Protestant Reformer John Calvin. The Dutch Republic was officially Calvinist, yet informally allowed other faiths.

The inhabitants of Tartaria are divided into twelve nations, each standing under a special Cham or ruler, and they claim their ancestry to be from the Patriarch **Abraham**, which leads some writers to be of the opinion that the twelve captains are those which God promised in Genesis 17, that they would blossom from the blood of **Ishmael**. …

Abraham: Regarded as the ancient father of Judaism, Christianity, and Islam.

Ishmael: The son of Abraham and his wife's slave, Hagar. Muslims regard him as their ancestor, as Abraham's other son Isaac, whom he conceived with his wife, Sarah, was the ancestor of the Jews.

The Tartars are of average build, but strong and pious, with large protuberant eyes and which cover themselves with thick and raw **wine-brewed** clothing. Their faces are flat and wide with little beard but long mustaches.

wine-brewed: Rough, raw tanned hides.

They rarely walk, but sit almost always on horses, and regard it a particular magnificence if they have a bell hanging on the neck of the horse.

When they drink, they do not separate until they are completely drunk, otherwise they regard it as shameful.

Many of them do not live in cities or villages, but outside on the land under tents. In the winter they stick to the valleys, in the summer on the hills. Many have no use for bread, yes, they don't even know how to bake.

They despise all nations that they look upon, so that they also regard the Christians as dogs. They are greatly inclined to **sorcery**, and to interpreting dreams. They are great **usurers**, and never give any **alms**, although if someone comes over while they are eating and drinking they will distribute some very mildly.

sorcery: *Tooverijen*, which can also be translated as witchcraft.

usurers: Those who charge interest on loans; a sin in the Old Testament, and a charge often made against Jews (see Documents 7 and 9).

alms: Charity as a religious act.

They eat horse flesh, although half raw, and regard this as so tasty, that the **Duke of Moscow** served this to them whenever he had to feed some emissaries. They use the hide of the horses still fresh to sit on in the place of benches. They drink mare's milk like costly wine.

Duke of Moscow: Ruler of Russia after the expulsion of the Mongol horde, which was defeated by Ivan III, the Grand Prince of Moscow, in the later fifteenth century.

They gather so many people from Russia, Poland, Moldavia, Walachia and from wherever they can, to make them slaves, that there is a certain

13 P. Cornelius Hazart, *Kerckelycke Historie van de Gheheele Werelt. Het vierde deel* … (Antwerp, 1671), 319–22. Translated by Gary Waite.

Jew, sitting over the tolls, who once asked if there were still any people left to find in those regions.

By some this cruel custom is common that they seize the prisoners captured in war and roast them before the fire, and then in great numbers they come together in order to tear up the body with their teeth, just like raging wolves.

They surrender other prisoners to their slaves to kill them like animals with a spike or axe, in order to frighten those who witness it: out of each thousand they select one, which they hang head down on a long stake, to be terrified of those who lay killed before his eyes; many suck the blood from the wounds when they are still fresh.

... When they journey through large moors or wildernesses, they guide themselves by the north star, for they are particularly well versed in astrology.

Whenever any of their kings die, those who drag the body to the grave strike dead all of the men they meet, saying "go, and serve our king in the other life." As proof of this, **Paulus Venetus** reports when he was in Tartaria, that when their king Mongul Khan died, over ten thousand soldiers were killed....

There is great diversity in religion within this nation: many follow the sect of **Mahomet** which they encountered in the year of Christ 1246. They maintain the **books of Moses** and some of the commandments of the Old Testament, calling daily Iahi illo Illoloth, that is, "there is no God but one God."

Among the Tartars of **Cathay** there are indeed many **Mohametans**, but even more idolaters, those among them who have any feelings for worship. They believe that there are two gods, the one of heaven, the other of the earth: of the first, which they daily honor with incense, asking for nothing more than that they might have good health in a healthy body. Of the second, they ask for plentiful animals and riches....

So as often as they eat they take a thick piece of meat and smear the mouth of the idol, and of his wife, and children, which statues they always have in their houses. The sop that the meat was cooked in they pour out outside the house, so that through the smell the spirits, I do not know which, are fed.

They believe indeed that the **souls** of people are immortal, but that they are housed in one body then another, now in one comfortable, in another uncomfortable, according to the things that they have done in their life.

Among other proofs they also have great honor for the Sun, Moon, and the **four elements**, to which they perform special sacrifices. They make their idolatrous statues mostly of thick cloth and put clothing on them. They regard all the days as equally holy, and never **fast**. The Jews, which live among them, say that they have originated from the lineage of Israel, but many have fallen to the sect of Mahomet. Christendom in this region is

Paulus Venetus: Early fifteenth-century Catholic philosopher and Augustinian general who served as ambassador to the Republic of Venice.

Mahomet: The Prophet Muhammad.

books of Moses: The Talmud, or the first five books of the Hebrew Scriptures (Genesis, Exodus, Numbers, Deuteronomy, and Leviticus).

Cathay: Cathay, which many early-modern Europeans thought was separate from China; it became an alternate term for China.

Mohametans: Muslims.

souls: Christians believed that humans were made of a perishable body and an immaterial soul that would survive the death of the body.

four elements: Ancient Greeks believed that all things consisted of a combination of earth, air, water, and fire.

fast: To do without food for a period of time, usually as part of religious devotion.

corrupted into many pieces. They burn the dead bodies to a powder, gathering the ashes, and mixing them daily with their food noon and evening. In the rest they follow the heresy of **Nestorius**, and do their worship in **Chaldean**.

Nestorius: A fifth-century Christian bishop who denied the divinity of Jesus, and whose followers moved to Persia where they established the Church of the East.

Chaldean: Aramaic, the common language of the Middle East in the Ancient and Medieval periods; the language spoken by Jesus.

DOCUMENT 81

From Louis de Gaya and Thomas Brown, *Marriage Ceremonies* (1703)[14]

Louis de Gaya was a historian and nobleman from France who wrote books on war, genealogy, and nobility in addition to marriage. It is unclear if de Gaya traveled to Asia and witnessed the ceremonies he described or received this information from someone else.

Polygamy: The practice of allowing more than one wife for a husband. Permitted in Islam (as it had been in ancient Israel) but forbidden in Christianity.

Pegu: Bago, Myanmar.

Pudenda: External genitalia.

Siam: Thailand.

In Bengala they allow **Polygamy**, according to their Abilities to maintain them, but keep them in close custody.

... In **Pegu** they have extraordinary Ceremonies in their Marriages. As they were heretofore much addicted to an unnatural Vice, their Queen made very severe Punishments for those that should be Convicted of it, even to Burning them alive: And to divert the Fury of this infamous Lust, she Commanded the Women should go almost naked, to attract Men's Love to them. When they marry, they must pay the Father of the young Woman a certain Sum agreed on, which he pays back if he will have his Daughter home, from any ill Usage of her Husband, who may likewise leave her, only he is to keep and Educate the Children. The Women being naturally extremely Amorous, the Men are very nice in Marrying them, making the strictest Enquiries before they engage. And from hence it is, that many Fathers, to preserve their Daughters Virgins, sow up their **Pudenda**, and in that Condition deliver them to their Husbands, that they may be ascertain'd of their Honesty. The King, and those of greatest Quality, lie not the first Night with their Wives, but admit others, and pay them bountifully, that will give themselves the Trouble.

... In **Siam**, after the manner of Pegu, they may Marry many wives. But the Mahometans of these Countries observe not their ridiculous Ceremonies, fit only for a Nation blinded with Idolatry.

... The Heathen Tartars have many Wives, who Live together in great quiet. They give Money to their Wives' Mothers, as a Recompence for the Advantages receiv'd from them. The first Wife is look'd upon most Lawful and so are the Children born of her. When the Father dies, the Son may Marry all his Wives, excepting his Mother, and her Sisters: They Marry their Half-Sisters, after their Brother's Death; and make very great Entertainments at these Marriages.

14 Louis de Gaya and Thomas Brown, *Marriage ceremonies as now used in all parts of the world ... Written originally in Italian, by Seignior Gaya*, 3rd ed. (London, 1703), 114–16, 121–22.

... The people of Tangut and Cathay marry as many Wives as they can keep: And if any poor young Woman be beautiful, a rich Man marries her presently, and gives her Mother and Family a Reward to have her; as, Cattel, Slaves, and oftentimes Money; they valuing only Beauty. They have to Thirty Wives, more or less, according to their Abilities; but the first is always chiefest. And if any is infirm or not agreeable, they send her home. They Marry their Relations, as the Tartars do, even to their Step-mothers.

DOCUMENT 82

Leaflet Advertising Appearances by "Two Chinese Ladies" in Elaborate National Costume, Singing and Playing Traditional Chinese Instruments (1826)[15]

Twenty years after Sarah Baartman was exhibited in London, this leaflet advertised the exhibition of 24-year-old Attoi Whoatoy, the "scarcely 18" Powyuen Guatuoa, and their interpreter, Ayong-chongtie, as the "only female natives of the celestial empire ever seen in Europe!" This leaflet describes the women's appearance, clothing, jewelry, and musical skills. It further tells us that a "profusion of Chinese Curiosities" were arranged alongside the women and that visitors could buy souvenirs. The accompanying article appeared in a London literary magazine and allegedly presents Whoatoy and Guatuoa's impressions of the English people, as well as the author's comparison of female beauty types.

Pall Mall: A street in central London, well known in the nineteenth century for gentlemen's clubs and high end shops.

minnikin feet: Likely refers here to the Chinese custom of foot binding in which young girls' feet were broken and bound so they would remain small. Also known as "lotus feet," bound feet were regarded as a beautiful symbol of social class. By the time this article was written, many Chinese reformers and Western missionaries were beginning to challenge this practice, though it continued in some areas into the twentieth century.

Canton: Today the city of Guangzhou in southern China, and a major port of interest to European businessmen in the nineteenth century. Indeed, the British captured Canton during the First Opium War of 1839.

pettitoes: Pig's feet when they are consumed as food.

Sights of London

We have been much interested with the novelty of two Chinese females, who are at present visible in the **Pall Mall**. It is not precisely long nails and **minnikin feet** that attract curiosity; but the physical and moral attributes of these fair Tartars possess considerable interest. They are from the country some fifty miles above **Canton**, and represented to be of respectable station. The eldest, Attoi Whoatoy, is twenty-four years of age, and the youngest Powyuen Guatuoa, scarcely eighteen; the former stout and inclined to be lusty, and the latter petite and less corpulent. From the pleasure of a *tête-a-tête* or two, we can state, that they hold the people of this boasted country in the most celestial contempt; having respect neither for their dresses, their manners, nor their endowments. Indeed they consider us to be very odd, and perhaps very foolish animals. Why our ladies strangle themselves about the waists, is one of the absurdities that astonishes them most. Attoi Whoatoy, whose abdomen is not unlike a paunchy alderman's is peculiarly disgusted with our unnatural and screwed-in beauties. Then again, with respect to limbs: how shapeless are the taper ankles of England! On the contrary, a Chinese lady has **pettitoes** about three inches long, and one and

15 "Two Chinese ladies" in elaborate national costume, singing and playing traditional Chinese instruments in the Grand Saloon at 94 Pall Mall, London, Wellcome Collection. "Sights of London," *The London Literary Gazette and Journal of the Belles Lettres, Arts, Sciences, &c* 517, 16 December 1826, 797.

No. 94, PALL MA[LL]

TWO Chinese Ladies!

THE ONLY FEMALE NATIVES OF THE

CELESTIAL EMPIRE,

EVER SEEN IN EUROPE!

N. B. The Public are respectfully informed, than on account of the INTENDED DEPARTURE OF THE CHINESE LADIES, the price of Admission is now reduced to ONE SHILLING, to afford every one the high gratification of viewing those enterprising Strangers, whose visit to this Country has already excited such intense interest and curiosity amongst the higher classes of Society.

THESE MOST INTERESTING and ELEGANT OBJECTS OF PUBLIC CURIOSITY, are Natives of the Province of Congsee-Laang-Lin Foo: The eldest (ATTOI WHOATOY) 24 years of age—the youngest (POWYUEN GUATUOA) scarcely 18; their STATURE is about the general standard of their Country-women, and their COUNTENANCES are highly expressive of affability and gentleness, with a pleasing cast of pensiveness, so characteristic in all representations of Chinese Ladies. Their very DIMINUTIVE FEET, being little more than three inches in length; and remarkably LONG FINGER NAILS, of nearly the same extent, are with them, not only reckoned beauties of the first order, but also the most significant tokens of PERSONAL CONSIDERATION and RANK! Their Dresses, which are in the richest Costume of their Country, are of the finest Silks, Taffeta, and Crape, beautifully Embroidered and Embossed with Gold, Silver, and Colours, in the richest profusion and variety. The peculiar mode of attiring their Hair, is in the most esteemed fashion of Pekin; ornamented with costly Jewellery, Artificial Flowers, &c. Their Bracelets are massive Orbs of Gold, Coral, Agate, and other precious Materials; and their Rings, Ear-drops, and Necklaces of the same.

The pleasing countenance of the Interpreter, Ayong-chongtie, from Canton, (attired in the Dress of a Mandarin,) gives great interest to the Group; which, with the characteristic embellishments, exhibit in the most correct manner, the Apartments, and Costume of the *Fashionables of China*!

☞ *The Saloon* is enriched with a profusion of *Chinese Curiosities*, in elegant *Lanthorns, Skreens*, fine *Jars*, and other *Ornaments* of the *richest Porcelain*; also a great variety of the most curious *Paintings* and *Drawings*, in *Portraits, Fancy*, and *Mythological* subjects, *Landscapes, &c.* Likewise a complete *Altar*, or *Joss-House*, with the customary offerings presented to their HOUSEHOLD DEITY!!

Descriptive Catalogues, 6d each, may be had at the Saloon. Also, (just Published,) a fine Print of the Chinese Ladies and their Interpreter.

OPEN FROM 11 TILL 6.

ADMITTANCE, ONE SHILLING.

E COLYER, Printer, 105, Leadenhall Street.

a half broad, surmounted by ankles about the shape of **Chuny** the elephant's and gradually tapering upwards to the knee. A wonderful improvement!

Chuny: An Indian elephant exhibited in a London menagerie; his violent death in 1826 caused a public scandal.

These females are, however, very cheerful and good-tempered, and well deserve a visit from the curious. They eat twice a day, according to the custom of China, preferring pork to all other meats (beef is a forbidden food) and liking fish fried with leeks. Of tea they drink very little, and only black. Our malt liquor is most unpalatable to them; not so wine, and brandy and whiskey are in high esteem—not to excess. Great care seems to be taken of them, and they are in good health. Their hair is beautiful, and beautifully arranged; but we must have another *tête-a-tête*, or perhaps we may tell what ought not in Chinese gallantry to be told—and then what could we expect but to catch a Tartar?

DOCUMENT 83

Arthur de Gobineau on Characteristics of the "Yellow Race" in *The Inequality of Human Races* (1855)[16]

As noted in Document 63, Joseph-Arthur, Count de Gobineau, was a French aristocratic novelist, diplomat, and theorist whose ideas greatly influenced the development of racist thought in Europe and North America. Here he compares the characteristics of the "yellow race" to that of the "negroid" and the "white."

The yellow race is the exact opposite of this type [the "negroid type"]. The skull points forward, not backward. The forehead is wide and bony, often high and projecting. The shape of the face is triangular, the nose and chin showing none of the coarse protuberances that mark the negro. There is further a general proneness to obesity, which, though not confined to the yellow type, is found there more frequently than in the others. The yellow man has little physical energy and is inclined to apathy; he commits none of the strange excesses so common among negroes. His desires are feeble, his will-power rather obstinate than violent; his longing for material pleasures, though constant, is kept within bounds. A rare glutton by nature, he shows far more discrimination in his choice of food. He tends to mediocrity in everything; he understands easily enough anything not too deep or sublime. He has a love of utility and a respect for order and knows the value of a certain amount of freedom. He is practical, in the narrowest sense of the word. He does not dream or theorize; he invents little but can appreciate and take over what is useful to him. His whole desire is to live in the easiest and most comfortable way possible. The yellow races are thus clearly superior to the black. Every founder of a civilization would wish the backbone of his society, his middle class, to consist of such men. But no civilized society could be created by them; they could not supply its nerve-force or set in motion the springs of beauty and action.

We come now to the white peoples. These are gifted with reflective energy, or rather with an energetic intelligence. They have a feeling for utility, but in a sense far wider and higher, more courageous and ideal, than the yellow races; a perseverance that takes account of obstacles and ultimately finds a means of overcoming them; a greater physical power, an extraordinary instinct for order, not merely as a guarantee of peace and tranquility, but as

16 Arthur de Gobineau, *The Inequality of Human Races*, trans. Adrian Collins (London: William Heinemann, 1915; orig. 1853–55).

an indispensable means of self-preservation. At the same time, they have a remarkable, and even extreme, love of liberty, and are openly hostile to the formalism under which the Chinese are glad to vegetate, as well as to the strict despotism which is the only way of governing the negro....

The white races are further distinguished by an extraordinary attachment to life. They know better how to use it, and so, as it would seem, set a greater price on it; both in their own persons and those of others, they are more sparing of life. When they are cruel, they are conscious of their cruelty; it is very doubtful whether such a consciousness exists in the negro. At the same time, they have discovered reasons why they should surrender this busy life of theirs that is so precious to them. The principal motive is honour, which under various names has played an enormous part in the ideas of the race from the beginning. I need hardly add that the word honor, together with all the civilizing influences connoted by it, is unknown to both the yellow and the black man. On the other hand, the immense superiority of the white peoples in the whole field of the intellect is balanced by an inferiority in the intensity of their sensations. In the world of the senses, the white man is far less gifted than the others, and so is less tempted and less absorbed by considerations of the body, although in physical structure he is far the most vigorous.

DOCUMENT 84

From Joseph Salter, *The Asiatic in England: Sketches of Sixteen Years' Work among Orientals* (1873)[17]

Joseph Salter (1822–99) was a British missionary at the Strangers' Home for Asiatics, Africans and South Sea Islanders in London, England. In this passage, Salter writes of working with lascars, sailors usually from Southeast Asia or the Indian subcontinent, who were employed on European ships. Salter also worked with Ayahs, women and girls from the Indian subcontinent who worked as nannies for British families. Ayahs often traveled between colony and metropole with their employers and were sometimes abandoned in Great Britain. Like other missionaries, Salter claimed to be concerned about the spiritual well-being of the people he encountered and endeavored to "save" them.

A home for receiving and lodging Asiatic, African, or other foreign sailors visiting the Port of London, is one of those institutions which so exactly meets a pressing want, that when it is once established, we are apt to wonder that it had not been long since provided. The habits of strangers are so different from those of our own countrymen, that those excellent institutions which bear the name of "**Sailors' Homes**" are unsuitable for them.... At a monthly conference held by the secretaries of the various **Missionary Societies** of London, it was a matter of discussion whether, while we are sending missionaries at a great cost into foreign lands, something ought not be done by Christians for the inhabitants of those lands that occasionally visit this country.... The sight of **Hindoos**, Chinamen, Negroes, and other heathens in the streets of London, suggested this question to the consciences of more than one member of that conference, and it was determined to ascertain, by inquiry, what the effect of a visit to this Christian country had upon these heathen visitors.... The erection of such a Strangers' Home in the neighbourhood of the Docks became from this time an object of earnest desire to the Secretaries of various Missionary Societies.

Sailors' Homes: Institutions providing international sailors with inexpensive and safe lodging while in port. Their proprietors often provided "moral" entertainment to keep the men away from taverns, brothels, and gambling establishments.

Missionary Societies: Religious organizations seeking to solve the moral problems associated with large numbers of sailors visiting London, as detailed above.

Hindoos: An older spelling of Hindus (followers of Hinduism), which today is inappropriate.

... They may live or die; no one around them cares about the life of a Lascar; and as for the soul, who gives a moment's thought about that? The heathens of the heathen land associate here with the heathens of Christian London; and, truly, they both dwell in the valley of the shadow of death. Between these waifs from the banks of the Indus and the Ganges, and the

17 Joseph Salter, *The Asiatic in England: Sketches of Sixteen Years' Work among Orientals* (London: Seeley, Jackson, and Halliday, 1873), i–v, 26–27, 30–33. See Fred Halliday, *Britain's First Muslims: Portrait of an Arab Community* (London: I.B. Tauris, 2010); and Humayun Ansari, *The Infidel Within: The History of Muslims in Britain, 1800 to the Present* (London: C. Hurst & Co., 2004).

reputable white man brought up on the banks of the Thames, there is a great gulf fixed, and this gulf is crossed by very few. The difficulty of colloquial communication is one barrier that stands in the way; but far more formidable, as a division, is the foul atmosphere of human depravity in which these Orientals live and suffer: this is too forbidding and appalling for any but a sturdy Christianity and an earnest love to penetrate. The heathen mind is dark, and the vices of the various heathen systems in which the **Asiatic** is so brought up, as to form part of his nature, are bad enough when unmingled with European sin in his own land of superstition; but here is an interchange of sin and an unholy compound of both. Who will stretch forth his hand to pluck the brand from the fire? Who will descend into the pit of mire and clay to rescue these perishing ones from inevitable death?

Asiatic: An older term referring to a person of Asian descent, which today is inappropriate.

... Let us now visit the chief rendezvous of these men. We are about to enter Satan's stronghold, and shall observe how shamelessness has its premium and admirers, and honesty, truth, and self-respect are trampled in the dust.... Here disease and death, decked in gaudy tinseled robes, allure the victim to the grave.

... We are now fairly in the **Oriental** quarter; there are several houses devoted to Asiatics, presided over by Chinese, Malays, and Indians, according to the country of the Asiatic seeking companionship. Each of the proprietors is assisted by an English mistress, some of whom have lived so long in this element that they use the Oriental vernacular, and have even been to act as interpreters at the Police-courts when the oft-repeated quarrels of Asiatics have brought them into trouble.... Let us enter the first house on this colony of evil spirits.... This is a Chinese gambling-house, and these celestials are so earnest in their dangerous play, that they are by no means troubled by our presence. At one end of the table they are gambling with dice, which they cast with much energy into a glass, whirl it violently round, and toss the dice out again with fevered excitement. The money is rapidly changing hands, poverty and destitution will soon be the heritage of the gamblers.... Here is another house, the rendezvous of another class of Asiatics. It is known by all the Lascars that visit England, for it has an unenviable reputation for many years past.... We might go upstairs, if time had allowed, and see them reclining on beds, smoking the insidious opium. Most likely we should find some victims half or quite stupefied by its effects, lying on a miserable bed, or on the floor, till the effects of the poisonous smoke had passed off.... There is another house we must enter before retiring from the neighbourhood. It is the public house, with its **skittle-ground** extending along a narrow court of two-roomed houses.... It is like a glimpse into a pandemonium, and the fumes of smoke which envelope passing figures as they whirl around the room, come into collision and tumble over each other.... We wonder, as we leave this sickening scene, if this is all that Asiatics know of England's Christianity.

Oriental: As above, an older term referring to a person of Asian descent, which today is inappropriate; or an object or practice that is from the Orient (Asia).

skittle-ground: Skittles was the precursor to modern bowling, and could be played indoors or out.

DOCUMENT 85

From Fanny L. Rains, Travel Writings on Domestic Life in Singapore (1878)[18]

Fanny L. Rains was a female British travel writer. As a woman, Rains was privy to the domestic sphere, a realm from which European men were typically excluded. In this space, Rains was able to interact with people on a more intimate level. However, this familiar interaction did not exempt her from the dominant European racist discourse regarding Asian people. Note the similarities in language usage between Rains and Gobineau.

Malay: A blanket term used to refer to peoples from modern Malaysia, Indonesia, Thailand, and Singapore.

betel-nut: Also known as the areca nut, used for chewing in a way similar to tobacco.

coolie: A hired laborer. The derogatory term became synonymous with the East and South Asian workers throughout the British Empire.

The **Malay** women dress very picturesquely, with one exception—the nose ornament. Pieces of bright coloured stuff are thrown round their shoulders and fall in graceful folds to their ankles, round which are fastened anklets. On their arms they wear bracelets. Neither the men nor the women are tall, and I do not think I was particularly struck with their beauty! They chew the **betel-nut**, which stains their teeth and lips a bright red, and is a great disfigurement. Their huts are most uninhabitable-looking hovels. The Malays are cowardly and superstitious, and a lazy people, especially the men, from two causes—one being the climate, the other that they are able to live on so little they need not greatly exert themselves to earn sufficient for the necessaries of life: five cents a day, about two pence farthing, being enough to supply them with food. They delight to loll and squat about on the ground just outside their dwellings or by the wayside, smoking and chattering, in what would be to us a most fatiguing position. To sit down seems almost, if not entirely, an unknown posture to them, as even at meals they often range themselves like so many monkeys on a bench, their feet on the top, and their bodies resting on their heels. The Chinese adopt the same fashion, and all are innocent of a superabundance of clothing.

The better class of Chinese live in one or two-storied houses with the fronts gaily decorated, which gives them a very gaudy and pasteboard appearance, reminding one forcibly of such as are seen on the stage, and through the doorways one can catch glimpses of carved furniture. The hire of a **coolie** per diem is only 30 cents, and for that they do the roughest and heaviest work. They are very strong and can carry weights for long distances. They are, in fact, the hewers of wood and drawers of water, for work that is

18 Fanny L. Rains, *By Land and Ocean, or The Journal of a Young Girl Who Went to South Australia with a Lady Friend, then Alone to Victoria, New Zealand, Sydney, Singapore, China, Japan, and Across the Continent of America Home* (London: Sampson Low, Marston, Searle and Rivingston, 1878), 90–92.

considered beneath the dignity of a Malay is shunted off to an unfortunate coolie. For example, our washerman, or "dobie," as he is called, is a Malay, and when he comes for the linen, he brings a coolie with him to carry it. They attach their burdens to each end of a bamboo stick, which they put across their shoulders, and then move along at a kind of ambling pace or trot, indeed it is called "the coolie trot." The Chinese are plodding and industrious and make wonderfully good gardeners. As a rule, truthfulness is not their greatest virtue, and with an immovable countenance they will tell a lie if that be most convenient. One must therefore learn to possess one's soul in patience; and should you in righteous indignation reprove any of them for lying, they will probably preserve a stolid indifference, and even consider you pay them a compliment in telling them that they are not speaking the truth....

DOCUMENT 86

Image: French Political Cartoon by Henri Meyer, "China—the Cake of Kings and … of Emperors" (1898)[19]

China had managed to stave off European attempts to claim its land, resources, and people for centuries. However, England, Germany, and France continued to seek a foothold in the nation. The two opium wars, 1839–42 and 1856–60, resulted in the French and English gaining concessions in China. These concessions forced the Chinese to relinquish many of their sovereign and territorial rights. This image illustrates the imperialist tendencies other world powers harbored against China, who in this political cartoon is represented by a stereotypical and racialized image of a **Qing** official.

Qing: The Qing dynasty governed China for nearly three centuries, from 1636 to 1912.

19 Henri Meyer, "En Chine—Le gâteau des Rois et … des Empereurs," *Le Petit Journal*, 16 January 1898.

DOCUMENT 87

From Pierre Loti, *Carmen Sylva and Sketches from the Orient* (1912)[20]

Pierre Loti (1850–1923) was the pseudonym of French author and naval officer Louis Marie-Julien Viaud. He was best known for his written work that glamorized and exoticized the East. With the French Navy, he traveled to French Polynesia and throughout Asia, visiting other European colonies as well as Japan and China. It was during one of these trips that he found inspiration for this description of Japanese women, written from the perspective of **Carmen Sylva**, Queen of Romania.

Carmen Sylva: Pauline Elisabeth Ottilie Luise zu Wied (1843–1916) was the Queen Consort of King Carol I of Romania and was widely known by her literary name of Carmen Sylva.

I do not believe that a European can write anything absolutely correct or exact about the Japanese woman, if he insists on investigating beneath the surface of things. Only a Japanese could do this, or, perhaps, *à la rigueur*, a Chinese, for between these two nations, though so different from each other, there exists the most undeniable affinities of soul.... The yellow race and our own are the two opposite poles of the human species; there exists the widest difference even in our ways of perceiving external objects, whereas our ideas on things in their essence are frequently the reverse of each other. We can never fully penetrate the mind of a Japanese or a Chinese; there suddenly comes a time when, with mingled feelings of terror and mystery, we find ourselves checked by intellectual barriers beyond which we cannot pass; these nations feel and think the very opposite of ourselves. Consequently what I am about to say now will be very superficial, and from the outset I prefer to state frankly that it would be impossible for my description to be anything else.

Very plain-looking are these poor little Japanese women! I will say this from the beginning, in all its brutality, for later on I shall mitigate this impression by speaking of their mincing daintiness and graceful drollery, of their adorable little hands, and finally, of ***poudre de riz***, of the pink and gold spread on the lips, and of artifices of every kind.

***poudre de riz*:** The French translation of rice powder, used on the face to absorb oil and extend the longevity of make-up.

Scarcely any eyes at all—nothing worth mentioning; two thin, slanting, divergent slits, deep sunk, in which roll a pair of cunning or wheedling eyeballs—such as may be seen between the half-open eyelids of a tabby, which cannot endure the full glare of daylight.

There is no country in the world in which feminine types form such distinct contrasts between the different castes. Dark peasant women as

20 Pierre Loti, *Carmen Sylva and Sketches from the Orient*, trans. Fred Rothwell (New York: Macmillan, 1912), 180–84.

bronzed as Hindus, with tiny, dainty, well-dressed figures, their limbs plump and muscular beneath their eternal blue cotton dresses. Languishing diminutive townswomen, white and pallid as unhealthy Europeans, with that something furrowed and worn away, so to speak, in the very flesh itself, which is indicative of too old a race. And all the artisan women in the large towns seem as though they have been hereditarily worn out, used up even before birth by too long and continuous labour, their minds ever directed on the most minute details of things.... Lastly, in the princesses, aristocratic refinement, going back into the remote past, has come to form astonishing little artificial persons, with the hands and bodies of children, and whose painted faces, more pink and white than a fresh *bonbon*, give no indication of age; in their smile there is a distant expression such as one sees in the smile of an old idol, whilst the reserved look in their eyes may be described as both youthful and dead at the same time.

DOCUMENT 88

From P. Daryl Klein, Second Lieutenant in the World War I Chinese Labour Corps (1919)[21]

During World War I the British Army recruited the Chinese Labour Corps to complete support work such as digging trenches and repairing railways. This was done to free up white soldiers to fight on the front lines. By the end of 1917, over 50,000 Chinese laborers were working in France and, by the 1918 Armistice, the number had nearly doubled. Second Lieutenant Daryl Klein recruited men and accompanied them to Europe. Klein clearly felt affection for the men but was deeply patronizing and called the workers by the racist term "coolies."

The diary, which is printed practically as I wrote it, covers the training period in China (two months) and crossing the Pacific.... This long journey gave me many an opportunity to observe the mental shock and change which a coolie suffers as he leaves the placid East and is shown the brilliant wonders of the West. He does not appear to be greatly interested in anything; he seldom gives way to an expression of surprise, but, like a child, he is taking it in all the time, he is changing under the influences of a new vision, and there is not a coolie in France today who, when the war is over, will not go back to his country a better man for his exploits abroad, a progressive spirit, and the possessor of clean habits.

That is not to say that he left China a barbarian. If this little work in the least modifies the popular conception of the "Chinese coolie" it will have done much. As children we were taught to believe that both Cain and coolies were murderers from the beginning; no coolie was to be trusted; he was a yellow dog; he would stick a knife into you in a dark alley on a dark night. He was treacherous. To-day we have outgrown this **puerility**, but still retain a deep distrust of the coolie and his ways. Nothing could be more unfair. The coolie whom we trained and brought to France is a simple, jolly fellow. He is content with the simplicities of life; he steals, but not overmuch; he is to be trusted. He is extraordinarily happy; he grins and grins; he is good to his fellow-creature. In the following pages I have often compared him to a child because of his simplicity, his playfulness, his frank delight with life, his quaintness and his affectionate character.

puerility: Childishness or immaturity.

21 Daryl Klein, *With the Chinks* (London: John Lane, 1919), vii–ix, 7, 31, 182–83, 247–48. Chinks is a highly offensive term that is no longer appropriate to use in any context.

Sausage Machine: A slang expression meaning a process that aims to make everyone the same.

Spent the morning overseeing certain functions of the **Sausage Machine**:

1. The hair-cutting function.
2. The cleansing function.

These are midway functions of a process which turns an ordinary uninviting workaday coolie into a clean, well-clothed and smartly active human being. An astonishing process which is doing a great good for a corner of China. If the whole nation, male and female, could pass through the Sausage Machine it would make the people anew, as it is making them, two to three hundred a day, in this camp....

Our children (a paternal attitude towards the coolies is recommended) are passionately fond of playing the fool. They are a race of Peter Pans, never having grown up. Nightly I thank God they are not going to be soldiers. Never a man would reach the trenches alive. I see their fate at the hands of a colonel ignorant of their psychology. They would be shot at dawn by battalions....

[Trip to the sea, to swim.] It was a great day for them; and it was a great day for us. We who had so often compared the coolies to children now quite unmistakably saw that they were children. They had no foolish dignity of men. They lost themselves in the moment's joy. They lived for that sunlit hour. And, like children, they weren't afraid of giving themselves away; they had no false reticence, no false notions of nudity. And, that spring morning, they seemed to inherit the earth....

Remember, practically every coolie who goes to France releases an able-bodied man to go into the trenches. I'm not sure, though, that the coolie himself wouldn't like a turn in the trenches! ... If the war goes on long enough I don't see why they shouldn't bring over a few hundred thousand of these splendid fellows. Probably they would make good fighters—almost as good fighters as they are labourers. At all events, if they don't get a **Tommy**'s chance in this war, they will get it sooner or later in their own country. It will be a war of their own—a civil war—not flesh and blood against flesh and blood, but clean, clear open minds again the dirt and truck and turgidness of centuries. When these men go back to China they won't be satisfied with the old life, the constricted and congested village life; they will want an existence more akin to our Western ideas and ideals of life; they will want more order, more open spaces, more cleanliness, and they won't want to stick in one place their whole lives. They will want to move from one part of the country to the other and mix and throw light into one another's lives. In a word they will be progressive.

Tommy: Colloquial term for a British soldier.

"Not surely as we have been progressive," commented the young collegian. "Look where our progress has led us."

DOCUMENT 89

From George Orwell, *Burmese Days* (1934)[22]

Burmese Days was English writer George Orwell's first published novel and was loosely based on his own experiences as a police office in British-controlled **Burma** (now Myanmar). Set in the fictional district of Kyauktada in the 1920s, the novel is a scathing attack on the imperial system of the **Raj**. The central character, John Flory, is an unmarried teak salesman with few friends in the expat community. He has a Burmese mistress, but seeks an English wife, so is delighted by the arrival of Elizabeth Lackersteen. In the following excerpts, Orwell first describes the segregated geography of Flory's neighborhood, and next details a conversation between Flory and Lackersteen about the appearance of the Burmese peoples. The novel was unevenly received by audiences in the 1930s (and was harshly critiqued by pro-imperialists) but has since become an important source in the history of British imperialism. In 2013, the government of Myanmar bestowed on the novel one of its highest literary awards.

Burma: Today Myanmar, a country in Southeast Asia. Britain controlled the territory from 1885 to 1948.

Raj: Extensive British rule of the Indian subcontinent from 1858 to 1947.

Flory's house was at the top of the **maidan**, close to the edge of the jungle. From the gate the maidan sloped sharply down, scorched and khaki-coloured, with half a dozen dazzling white bungalows scattered around it. All quaked, shivering in the hot air. There was an English cemetery within a white wall half-way down the hill, and near by a tiny tin-roofed church. Beyond that was the European Club, and when one looked at the Club—a dumpy one-story wooden building—one looked at the real centre of town. In any town in India the European Club is the spiritual citadel, the real seat of the British power, the Nirvana for which native officials and millionaires pine in vain. It was double so in this case, for it was the proud boast of Kyauktada Club that, almost alone of the Clubs in Burma, it had never admitted an Oriental to membership. Beyond the Club, the **Irrawaddy** flowed huge and ochreous glittering like diamonds in the patches that caught the sun and beyond the river stretched great wastes of paddy fields, ending at the horizon in a range of blackish hills.

The **native town**, and the courts and the jail, were over to the right, mostly hidden in green groves of peepul trees. The spire of the pagoda rose from the trees like a slender spear tipped with gold. **Kyauktada** was a fairly typical Upper Burma town, that had not changed greatly between the days of Marco Polo and 1910 and might have slept in the Middle Ages for a century more

maidan: A term with several meanings; here, likely referring to an open space.

Irrawaddy: Myanmar's most important commercial waterway.

native town: A reference to the highly segregated nature of most European imperial societies, where the indigenous communities would live and work separately from the settler population.

Kyauktada: Township in the center of downtown Yangon, Myanmar; Orwell used the name for the fictional setting of his novel.

22 George Orwell, *Burmese Days* (New York: Harper and Brothers, 1934), 14–15, 104.

if it had not proved a convenient spot for a railway terminus. In 1910 the Government made it the headquarters of a district and a seat of Progress—interpretable as a block of law courts, with their army of fat but ravenous pleaders, a hospital, a school and one of those huge durable jails which the English have built everywhere between Gibraltar and Hong Kong. The population was about four thousand, including a couple of hundred Indians, a few score Chinese and seven Europeans. There were also two **Eurasians** named Mr. Francis and Mr. Samul, the sons of an American Baptist missionary and a Roman Catholic missionary respectively. The town contained no curiosities of any kind, except an Indian **fakir** who had lived for twenty years in a tree near the bazaar, drawing his food up in a basket each evening.

Eurasians: Today refers to the peoples living in the geographical landmass that comprises the continents of Europe and Asia; historically, also used to refer to people of mixed European and Asian heritage.

fakir: A Muslim or Hindu person who renounces wealth and worldly possessions for religious reasons.

* * *

The subject cropped up in a hundred ways. A knot of Burmans would pass them on the road. She, with her still fresh eyes, would gaze after them, half curious and half repelled; and she would say to Flory, as she would have said to anybody:

"How REVOLTINGLY ugly these people are, aren't they?"

"ARE they? I always think they're rather charming-looking, the Burmese. They have such splendid bodies! Look at that fellow's shoulders—like a bronze statue. Just think what sights you'd see in England if people went about half-naked as they do here!"

"But they have such hideous-shaped heads! Their skulls kind of slope up behind like a tom-cat's. And then the way their foreheads slant back—it makes them look so WICKED. I remember reading something in a magazine about the shape of people's heads; it said that a person with a sloping forehead is a **CRIMINAL TYPE**."

"Oh, come, that's a bit sweeping! Round about half the people in the world have that kind of forehead."

"Oh, well, if you count **COLOURED** people, of course—!"

Or perhaps a string of women would pass, going to the well: heavy-set peasant girls, copper-brown, erect under their water-pots with strong marelike buttocks protruded. The Burmese women repelled Elizabeth more than the men; she felt her kinship with them, and the hatefulness of being kin to creatures with black faces.

"Aren't they too simply dreadful? So COARSE-LOOKING; like some kind of animal. Do you think ANYONE could think those women attractive?

"Their own men do, I believe."

"I suppose they would. But that black skin—I don't know how anyone could bear it!"

CRIMINAL TYPE: Reference used by criminologists to describe the alleged link between physical appearance and moral attributes. The terms "lowbrow" and "highbrow" entertainment originate from this false idea that people with higher brows/foreheads are of higher intelligence.

COLOURED: This term has been used in multiple racist ways. At times, it has referred to non-white, and specifically Black peoples, while in other societies, such as apartheid-era South Africa, it was used specifically to denote peoples of mixed ethnicity.

"But, you know, one gets used to the brown skin in time. In fact they say—I believe it's true—that after a few years in these countries a brown skin seems more natural than a white one. And after all, it IS more natural. Take the world as a whole, it's an eccentricity to be white."

"You DO have some funny ideas!"

DOCUMENT 90

Images: British Anti-Japanese Sentiment from World War II (1943–45)[23]

During World War II, German-allied Japan attacked several British colonies, including Singapore. British women and children were sent to Japanese prison camps, which were plagued by overcrowding and sickness. As word reached Britain about the treatment of their citizens in the camps, civilians rallied to provide their support in factories and farms, and to express their hatred of the Japanese, as illustrated in these wartime images.

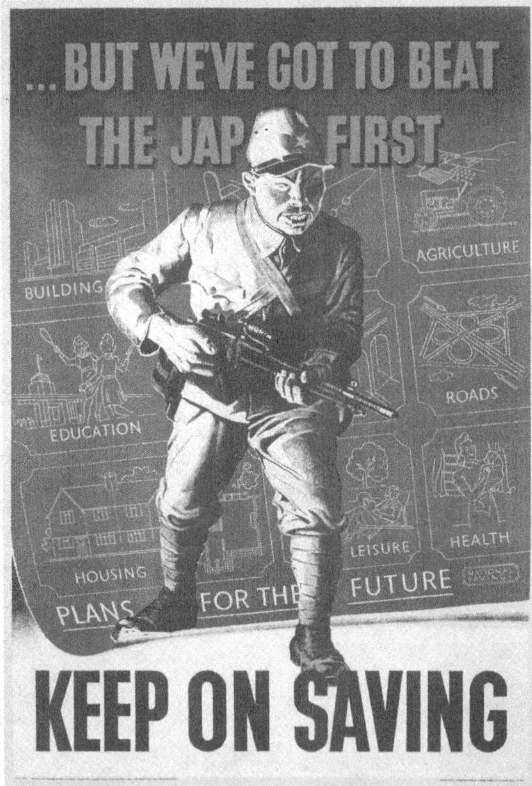

23 Issued by the National Savings Committee, London; the Scottish Savings Committee, Edinburgh; and the Ulster Savings Committee, Belfast. Imperial War Museum Collections, Object 29035.

DOCUMENT 91

Susanné Seong-Eun Bergsten, "Abused and Shunned—Being of Asian Descent in Sweden during COVID-19" (2020)[24]

As the COVID-19 virus spread around the world in 2020, many people speculated that it had originated in a Chinese wet market. Especially after US President Donald Trump tweeted about "the Chinese virus," anti-Asian sentiment spiked around the world. These at times violent attacks prompted UN Secretary-General António Guterres to issue a statement in May that read in part, "COVID-19 does not care who we are, where we live, what we believe or about any other distinction. We need every ounce of solidarity to tackle it together. Yet the pandemic continues to unleash a tsunami of hate and xenophobia, scapegoating and scare-mongering."[25] Here, Susanné Seong-Eun Bergsten, of Human Rights Watch, details her experiences as a Swedish-Korean.

Recently when I was heading home from work, a man on the bus pushed me up against the bus window and asked if I was from China. Physically trapped and scared, I told him that I'm Swedish-Korean. Thankfully, that's when another passenger on the bus intervened.

I wish I could say that this is the only instance in which I have been singled out during the COVID-19 pandemic for being of Asian descent. But it's not. Sometimes it's people covering their mouths when I get on the subway, other times shuffling away to the end of the train, as far away from me as physically possible.

In Sweden, a country that prides itself on tolerance and liberal attitudes, COVID-19 has increasingly become an excuse for **xenophobic** and racist attacks and **microaggressions** against people of Asian descent. Individuals have reportedly been yelled at, harassed, asked to leave public transportation, and shunned. There have been reports of children being bullied, even by children at kindergarten.

xenophobic: From xenophobia, fear of foreigners.

microaggressions: Commonplace and frequent slights, in this case communicating negative attitudes toward stigmatized groups.

Similar abuses have occurred in other European countries; people of Asian descent have experienced verbal and physical attacks, vicious beatings, online harassment, and even boycotts of their businesses. Unfortunately, this is part of a rise in Europe—and globally—in anti-Asian abuses spurred by

24 Susanné Seong-Eun Bergsten, "Abused and Shunned—Being of Asian Descent in Sweden during COVID-19, 2020," Human Rights Watch, 6 April 2020, https://www.hrw.org/news/2020/04/06/abused-and-shunned-being-asian-descent-sweden-during-covid-19.

25 United Nations, press release by Secretary-General António Guterres, 8 May 2020, https://press.un.org/en/2020/sgsm20076.doc.htm.

derogatory language used by politicians and media. In Sweden, politicians have not fueled this abuse, but the government response has been too weak.

Racism has sometimes spilled over to other groups. Following reports that several Swedish-Somalian people were among the country's first COVID-19-related deaths, this community was the target of racist abuse online by people expressing happiness about the deaths.

Sweden and Europe have never been free from racism, as evidenced by the rise of far-right political parties across the region and xenophobic responses to the recent arrival of significant numbers of migrants. But there seems to have been a significant increase as COVID-19 spreads around the world.

The heads of three pan-European human rights institutions recently called on governments to protect victims of hatred triggered by the pandemic. European Union and international law imposes obligations on states to combat racism and xenophobia.

Governments, including Sweden, should act immediately to protect individuals and communities who may be targets of COVID-19-related racist abuse, and should investigate all reported incidents and hold perpetrators accountable. Politicians should not just avoid spreading slurs but should debunk racist misconceptions about COVID-19 and explicitly condemn racist responses to the pandemic.

DOCUMENT 92

"Six Years a Slave: Indian Farm Workers Exploited in Italy" (2021)[26]

As is the case in many wealthy economies, the Italian agricultural sector is largely dependent on the seasonal labor of migrant workers, many of whom come from Africa and Asia. While some work under legal conditions, tens of thousands more are brought to Europe each year on false promises of high wages and decent living conditions. Once they arrive the women and men find dangerous working conditions, threats of violence, and rates of pay well beneath the minimum wage.

When Balbir Singh refers to his ordeal, he uses the Italian word "macello," which roughly translates as "mess"—but it is hardly enough to convey what the migrant Indian farm worker has endured. For six years, he lived in what can only be described as slave-like conditions tending cattle in the province of Latina, a rural area south of Rome that is home to tens of thousands of Indian migrant workers like him. "I was working 12–13 hours a day, including Sundays, with no holidays, no rest," Singh told AFP. The farm owner paid him 100 to 150 euros ($120 to $175) a month, he said, which amounts to less than 50 cents an hour. The legal minimum for farm workers is around 10 euros an hour.

Singh was rescued by a police raid on March 17, 2017 after appealing for help via Facebook and WhatsApp to local Indian community leaders and an Italian rights activist. Officers found him living in a **caravan**, with no gas, hot water or electricity, and eating the leftovers that his boss either threw in the bin or gave to chickens and pigs. Singh had to wash in the stables, with the same hosepipe he used to clean cattle, and it was made clear to him he should not complain. "When I found a lawyer ready to help me, (the owner) told me ... 'I'll kill you, I'll dig a hole, throw you in it, and fill it up' ... he had a gun, I saw it," he recalled. Singh said he was beaten up a couple of times and had his identity papers taken away. His former employer is now on trial for labour exploitation, while Singh is living in a secret location for fear of retribution.

caravan: Referred to in North America as camper vans or trailers.

Singh's story is extreme, but it fits into a wider picture of brutal exploitation of migrant farm labourers in the Agro Pontino—the Pontine Marshes, the plain around Latina—and elsewhere in Italy. The UN's special rapporteur on contemporary forms of slavery estimated in 2018 that more

26 "Six Years a Slave: Indian Farm Workers Exploited in Italy," France 24, 11 July 2021, https://www.france24.com/en/live-news/20210711-six-years-a-slave-indian-farm-workers-exploited-in-italy.

than 400,000 agricultural workers in Italy risk being exploited and almost 100,000 likely face "inhumane conditions." Last month, a 27-year-old from Mali collapsed and died in the southeastern Apulia region after working a day in the fields in temperatures of up to 40 degrees Celsius (104 degrees Fahrenheit).

In the Agro Pontino, a major hub for greenhouse farming, floriculture and buffalo mozzarella production, Indians have been a presence since the mid-1980s. They work on land drained from marshes in the 1930s, one of the biggest public works projects enacted under dictator **Benito Mussolini**. Sociologist Marco Omizzolo, the rights activist who helped free Singh, says between 25,000 and 30,000 Indians live in the Agro Pontino, mostly Sikhs from the Punjab region. Under an illegal but well-established system, they live under the thumb of "caporali," the gangmasters who recruit farm labourers on behalf of land owners. Typically, they are offered contracts but then are paid for only a fraction of their work. "You may work 28 days, but they'll mark only four on your pay slip, so at the end of the month you may get 200, 300 euros," Omizzolo told AFP. "Formally, it is all by the book," he added.

Benito Mussolini: Fascist dictator of Italy, 1922–43.

The reality is far grimmer, as shown by a recent police investigation that offered fresh evidence of widespread opioid abuse among the Indian community. That operation led to the arrest of a doctor in the beach town of Sabaudia. He was accused of illegally prescribing more than 1,500 boxes of Depalgos, a powerful painkiller containing Oxycodone and given to cancer patients, to 222 Indian farm workers. "The drug presumably allowed them to work longer in the fields by relieving pain and fatigue," Latina chief prosecutor Giuseppe De Falco told AFP.

The problem of exploitation of farm workers has not gone unnoticed in parliament. It was under an anti-caporali law passed in 2016 that Singh's employer was prosecuted. But unions say there are still too few checks and labour inspectors to enforce the law properly. Sociologist Omizzolo, who works with the Eurispes think tank, spent years researching farm labour abuse in the Latina area—some of it undercover. He lived for three months in Bella Farnia, a village mostly occupied by Indians, working incognito in the fields. He, too, now lives under police protection, after several death threats. In 2019, he was given a knighthood by President Sergio Mattarella in recognition of his "courageous work." In 2016, the sociologist was instrumental, along with the **Flai Cgil trade union**, in organising the first-ever strike of the Agro Pontino's Indian workers. Since then, their hourly pay has risen from three euros or less per hour to around five euros—although this is still only half the legal minimum. Omizzolo recognises the working conditions are still far from ideal. But the protest, he said, made the Indians understand that "it pays to fight for your rights."

Flai Cgil trade union: Organizes workers in the Italian agricultural and food processing industries.

PART 5
Racism against Romani Peoples

INTRODUCTION

While long a part of European society, the **Roma** and **Sinti (Romani)** did not really enter the Western European cultural consciousness until about the fifteenth century. Originating from India around the tenth century, the Roma migrated westward into Persia and the **Byzantine Empire**, while some communities continued westward into the Balkans and Eastern Europe. There was a large community in the Byzantine Peloponnese, and Italian merchants and Christian pilgrims described the residents of "poor huts" surrounding the city of Methoni (Modon) as "Zigeuner" ("Gypsies") who allegedly called themselves "Little Egyptians." This self-designation was not necessarily a reference to Egypt, as later European writers assumed, but to a region near "Gyppe" called "Tzingania" near Methoni.[1] Whatever the origin of the legend of Egyptian ancestry, the name stuck, as did the association with the so-called mysteries of Egypt. Some Roma musicians, performers, **palm readers** and fortune tellers would later use these stereotypes to their advantage to play up their "mysterious" origins for white audiences. Roma communities were often encouraged to settle in European communities due to their skills in smithing.

When these Romani migrants arrived in various European locales in the fifteenth century, the leader of each band, calling himself a duke, count, or *voivode*, typically carried letters of safe travel from the **Holy Roman Emperor** or the **Pope**, some of which were authentic. To ensure safe treatment, they told their hosts a story that they had been compelled to perform a seven-year **pilgrimage**, and thus they were initially treated as pilgrims. This positive response soon changed to suspicion, and terms such as "ugly," "black," "distrustful," and "thieves" came to fill writings referring to them. Many European rulers considered the Roma as their own property, and some treated them as slaves. Since the Roma had arrived from the

Roma: This Reader uses the identifiers Roma, **Romani**, and **Sinti** to speak about diverse communities of people. Historically, Europeans have also used the terms "gypsy," and "travelers" to refer to the Roma.

Byzantine Empire: The Eastern Roman Empire centered on Constantinople (Istanbul) which survived into the middle of the fifteenth century.

palm readers: People who practiced palmistry, the interpretation of the lines on the palm of the hand to predict the future.

Holy Roman Emperor: The titular head of the various German states.

Pope: Head of the Roman Catholic Church.

pilgrimage: A trip made for religious reasons; in the Catholic tradition, a form of penance that revealed that one had indeed repented of one's sin.

---

1 Council of Europe, "Education of Roma Children Factsheet: From India to Europe," https://rm.coe.int/from-india-to-europe-factsheets-on-romani-history/16808b18ed.

Turks: Residents of the Ottoman Empire. Europeans often used the term Turk to refer more generally to Muslims.

gypsies: An archaic and derogatory name for the Roma.

East, many European writers assumed that they were acting as spies for the **Turks**, who, as seen above in Documents 26 and 27, were pressing in on Europe's borders. Christian writers often also associated the Roma with Jews, with harmful consequences.[2] We just need to recall Martin Luther's recommendation in Document 7 above, that the Jews "might be lodged under a roof or in a barn, like the **gypsies**," associating the peripatetic lifestyle of the Roma with the alleged rootlessness of the Jews, and thereby inviting further comparisons at a critical moment in the history of the Roma (see Document 93 below).

galleys: Mediterranean sailed vessels that relied on prisoners to row in light winds.

While some lords protected the Roma, the negative stereotyping implying that all Roma were by nature untrustworthy or thieves led many rulers to issue edicts of expulsion, such as the English ones included here (Documents 94–96, and 99). In 1500 the Holy Roman Emperor Maximilian I issued an edict in which he ordered that all "Gypsies" leave by Easter 1501, after which, if any German harmed a Roma, they would not be held legally responsible.[3] Such decrees became more draconian over time; in many of these decrees, Roma could be punished, often with enslavement in the **galleys**, without trial, suggesting that they were targeted for their ethnic identity rather than criminal activity. Well over a hundred of these decrees were passed by the various states of the German Empire between 1500 and 1750, not to mention numerous other countries. In 1619, five years after the Moriscos (New Christians of Muslim ancestry) had been expelled from Spain, King Philip III ordered the expulsion of all Roma from the country, although those who abandoned their traditional "dress, name and language of the Gitanos [i.e., Roma]," were permitted to stay. While this might imply a non-racialized view of the Roma in Spain, it must be remembered that similar allowances had been made toward Jews and Muslims should they convert to Christianity, only to find that the Old Christians refused to regard these **Conversos** and Moriscos as truly Christian, or Spanish.[4] The same "racialization" process was making it difficult for the Roma—who were typically described as **heathen**—to be viewed as anything other than an unassimilable minority, as had Jews and Muslims. Escalating in harshness over the early modern period, such orders led to the infamous Gypsy hunts of the eighteenth century in German states like Saxony or Hesse, the Netherlands, France, and elsewhere during which the authorities placed a bounty on the Roma, in many cases stipulating only that the reward would

Conversos: Jews who had converted to Christianity and their descendants.

heathen: People not members of Judaism, Christianity, or Islam.

2 See, for example, Miriam Eliav-Feldon, "Vagrants or Vermin? Attitudes towards Gypsies in Early Modern Europe," in *The Origins of Racism in the West*, ed. Miriam Eliav-Feldon, Benjamin Isaac, and Joseph Ziegler (Cambridge: Cambridge University Press, 2009), 276–91.

3 Council of Europe, "Education of Roma Children Factsheet: Western Europe," https://www.coe.int/t/dg4/education/roma/Source/FS2/2.4_western-europe_english.pdf.

4 Miriam Eliav-Feldon, "Vagrants or Vermin?," 283.

be halved if the captured were killed.[5] Language used about the Roma that suggested they, like Jews, were a "plague" or "vermin" or possessed particular physical characteristics, was particularly powerful in these circumstances.[6] Such physiological stereotyping would, in fact, by the seventeenth century become ubiquitous, as Europeans increasingly used skin color or alleged physical characteristics to distinguish themselves from others.

During the late eighteenth century, European governments sought different ways to "solve" the **Gypsy Problem**. **Ferdinand VI** ordered a mass round-up of Gypsies in Spain in 1749, leading to the well-orchestrated and violent expulsion of 10,000–12,000 people, in what has since been remembered as "Black Wednesday." The **Marquis of la Ensenada** was discussing the importance of finding an appropriate destination for these deported people when he stated his desire for "this category of people" to "disappear." Other leaders implemented **assimilationist policies** aimed at forcing families into abandoning their so-called roving and vagabond ways. Austrian officials decreed that Roma were prohibited from owning wagons and horses, and instead were given plots of land and encouraged to become farmers. They restricted Roma from marrying one another and could be caned for speaking their languages. Children were forcibly removed from their families—contemporary accounts describe them being ripped from their desperate mothers' arms. Such attempts at "civilizing" Romani peoples could parallel settler colonial efforts to civilize Indigenous populations, especially in the residential schools of North America and Oceania.

By the nineteenth century, and during the **Age of Nationalism**, societal persecution of the Roma continued to center on challenges **semi-nomadic peoples** allegedly posed to modern notions of citizenship. Their lack of permanent addresses seemed at odds with the obligations of national citizens. Increasingly, local and national governments identified a Gypsy problem in their societies and instituted separate laws and regulations aimed at forcing the Roma to settle. Longstanding stereotypes held they were lazy, dirty, sexually promiscuous, and prone to criminal lifestyles. At the same time, some nineteenth-century Europeans proclaimed a fascination with Romani folk traditions, and sometimes an admiration for the alleged ability of Roma and Sinti communities to live outside industrializing society. Again, we see some parallels with authors and artists who depicted Indigenous people as close to nature. Popular culture artefacts illustrate a range of attitudes: they celebrated Romani subjects for their "exotic" looks, fine musical talents, and fortune-telling skills, while simultaneously warning of their proclivity toward

Gypsy Problem: Phrase used to indicate that Romani persons were a problem that needed to be solved; similar in tone and intent to the Jewish Problem.

Ferdinand VI: Spanish monarch, 1746–59.

Marquis of la Ensenada: Spanish Secretary of State, 1748–54.

assimilationist policies: Plans to instill cultural homogeneity into a population by encouraging or forcing groups to give up their own culture and language in favor of that of the dominant group.

Age of Nationalism: The rise of the nation state and the concept of nationalism as an organizing principle in the late eighteenth and nineteenth centuries.

semi-nomadic peoples: Peoples whose cultural heritage determines they move from location to location, most often for economic reasons.

5 Council of Europe, "Factsheet: Western Europe," 3.
6 Miriam Eliav-Feldon, "Vagrants or Vermin?," 286–91.

crime, violence, and kidnapping children (see Documents 100–104). This fear certainly paralleled child murder accusations leveled at Jewish communities.

The Roma became targets of the burgeoning fields of racial anthropology and criminology as social scientists and governments sought ways to classify the Roma as a distinctive race (Document 105). Expanding police forces took up the challenge of ensuring Romani peoples followed an increasing number of laws and regulations aimed at forcing them to live and work like "normal" people. In 1899, Bavarian police established a central office for "Gypsy affairs," with the goal of coordinating the surveillance of Roma populations. Much of this information was subsequently published in the 1905 *Zigeuner-Buch* (Gypsy Book), which listed the names of thousands of the people they arrested. This accumulation of data laid the groundwork for further persecution and eventual mass murder.

By the 1920s, anti-Romani prejudice was becoming even more pronounced in some municipalities. In 1926, Bavarian officials opened the Munich Center for the Fight Against Gypsies in Germany; a law against "Gypsies, travelers, and the **workshy**" cemented the traditional prejudice of the Roma and Sinti as lazy and frequently unemployed. After 1933, the Nazis saw Romani peoples as both racial and asocial obstacles to harmony in the Third Reich (Document 106). German police arrested, and sent to internment camps, Roma and Sinti communities to "clean up the streets" in the lead up to the 1936 Olympic Games. A series of laws stripped them of citizenship rights. Doctors used coercive medical practices against thousands of Roma and Sinti peoples, including Joseph Muscha Mueller, who was **forcibly sterilized** by the state at the age of 12. Across **Occupied Europe**, Romani women, men, and children were subjected to racial laws, **forced labor**, and deported to concentration and death camps (for an example, see Document 108). At least 250,000–500,000 Roma and Sinti were murdered as part of Nazi genocidal programs, a tragedy often referred to as the *Porrajmos*; the "devouring."

In the postwar period, Romani survivors continued to face persecution, and for decades received no compensation for, and little recognition of, crimes committed against their communities. While the German government provided some compensation for Jewish Holocaust victims beginning in the 1950s, they neglected to provide the same for Roma and Sinti Holocaust victims until the 1980s and 1990s. In doing so, they relied on centuries of prejudice and said they suffered Nazi persecution because of their "**asocial**" classification, rather than their race. Officially, Socialist Bloc countries proclaimed an end to societal racism; in practice, the Soviet Union passed a law banning anyone from leading an **itinerant** way of life in 1956, with several other countries following suit (Document 109). States such as Czechoslovakia implemented **sedentarism policies** that sought

workshy: Term used to describe a person who is chronically unemployed and/or someone who is lazy or disinclined towards hard work.

forcibly sterilized: Procedures performed without informed consent on women (tubal ligations or hysterectomies) and men (vasectomies) to ensure they could not reproduce.

Occupied Europe: Countries and regions under German military control during World War II.

forced labor: Millions of people were conscripted by the Nazis during World War II to labor in agriculture, manufacture, construction, and mining. Millions died of overwork, malnutrition, disease, and intentional violence.

asocial: Today a synonym for anti-social behavior; previously used as a quasi-legal term to denote people who seemed not to fit into dominant society. The Nazis accused many groups of being asocial, including Romani, queer women, criminals, and political opponents.

itinerant: A person who travels from place to place.

sedentarism policies: Policies such as mandatory public education, meant to dissuade people from living semi-nomadic lifestyles.

to restrict nomadic lifestyles. Some Roma maintain they benefited from these policies, while others remember them as coercive and damaging to community structures.[7]

Anti-Roma prejudice continues today, perpetrated by police forces, government officials, and neighbors (Documents 110–112). In 2020, the European Commission called on member states to "end racism and discrimination, which blatantly affects our large ethnic Roma minorities."[8] Roma leaders and educators continued the work of counteracting negative stereotypes about their communities and highlighting the richness of Roma history. For instance, due to decades-long activism we now commemorate Roma Holocaust Memorial Day on 2 August and Resistance Day on 16 May, the latter to remember the Roma prisoners in Auschwitz who resisted Nazi efforts to send them and their families to the gas chambers. Institutions such as the Documentation and Cultural Centre of German Sinti and Roma welcome visitors from around the world.[9]

---

7 Elena Marushiakova and Veselin Popov, "State Policies under Communism," Council of Europe, https://rm.coe.int/state-policies-under-communism-factsheets-on-romani-history/16808b1c58.

8 Suki Haider, "The Historical and Ongoing Persecution of Europe's Gypsies," The Open University, https://www.open.edu/openlearn/history-the-arts/history/the-historical-and-ongoing-persecution-europes-gypsies.

9 https://dokuzentrum.sintiundroma.de/en/.

DOCUMENT 93

Image: Colored Pen and Ink Illustration of the First Roma in Bern, Switzerland (1484)[10]

chronicle: A form of history writing that recorded in chronological order key or sensational events, often with little obvious analysis.

Depicted in 1484 by Diebold Schilling the Elder (c. 1445–86) in a **chronicle,** the caption above the Romani reads "Of the black baptized heathens who arrived in Bern together." Note their clothing and weapons, which are reminiscent of European depictions of Middle Eastern Muslims and of Jews (see Document 6).

10 Diebold Schilling the Elder (1445–86).

DOCUMENT 94

From King Henry VIII of England's Statute against Egyptians (1530/31)[11]

This source suggests that "Egyptians" or "gypsies" could not be English and were illegal aliens. Passed by the **Parliament of England** in 1530/1531, the Act accused "Egyptians" of purposely deceiving people and being criminals. It prohibited further Gypsy immigration and told those already residing in England to leave. This act was unsuccessful, for Parliament later passed the Egyptians Act of 1854 allowing Roma to live in England if they did not practice their traditional nomadic lifestyles. Henry VIII's act was repealed in 1856 by the Repeal of Obsolete Statutes Act.

Parliament of England: England was a parliamentary monarchy, with a House of Commons and House of Lords, although most power remained with the Crown.

An Act concerning Egyptians

Forasmuch as before this Time diverse and many outlandish People, calling themselves Egyptians, **using no Craft** nor Feat of Merchandise, have come into this Realm, and gone from **Shire** to Shire, and Place to Place in great Company and used great, subtle, and crafty Means to deceive the People, bearing them in hand, that they by Palmistry could tell Men's and Women's Fortunes, and so many Times by Craft and Subtilty have deceived the People of their Money, and also have committed many heinous Felonies and Robberies, to the great Hurt and Deceit of the People that they have come among: Be it therefore by the King our Sovereign Lord, the **Lords Spiritual and Temporal**, and the Commons, in this present Parliament assembled, and by the Authority of the same, ordained, established, and enacted, That from henceforth no such Person be suffered to come within this the King's Realm; and if they do, then they and every of them so doing, shall forfeit to the King our Sovereign Lord all their Goods and **Chattels**, and then to be commanded to avoid the Realm within Fifteen Days next after the Commandment, upon Pain of Imprisonment; and it shall be lawful to every Sheriff, Justice of Peace, and **Escheator**, to seize to the Use of our Sovereign Lord, his Heirs and Successors, all such Goods as they or any of them shall have, and thereof to make Account to our said Sovereign Lord in his Exchequer; and if it shall happen any such Stranger hereafter to commit within this Realm any Murder, Robbery, or any other Felony, and thereof

using no Craft: Not practicing a craft such as shoemaking; most crafts required membership in a craft guild, which were forbidden to foreigners.

Shire: England was divided into shires responsible for policing such regulations.

Lords Spiritual and Temporal: Members of the House of Lords, which included ecclesiastical and secular lords.

Chattels: Animals, such as horses and cattle.

Escheator: Exchequer, the royal treasurer.

11 "Public Acts 1530 Anno vicesimo secundo Henrici VIII / 22 Hen. VIII, 10, An Act Concerning Egyptians (passed in 1531)," in *The Statues at Large, of England and of Great-Britain: From Magna Carta to the Union of the Kingdoms of Great Britain and Ireland*, vol. III, *From I Hen. VIII A.D. 1509–10 to 7 Edw. VI A.D. 1553*, ed. John Raithby (London, 1811), 89–90.

intriable: Subject to judicial trial.

***Medietatem Linguae*:** Latin term used when the crown allowed foreigners to be tried in their own language.

be **intriable** by the Country, that then the Inquest that shall pass between the King and any such Party, shall be altogether of Englishmen, albeit that the Party so indicted pray ***Medietatem Linguae***, according to the Statue of Anno 8 Henrici VI or any other Statute thereof made,

"Proclamation shall be made for Departure of Egyptians, which if they obey they shall not forfeit their Goods."

DOCUMENT 95

From King Philip and Queen Mary of England, Egyptians Act (1554)[12]

The Egyptians Act of 1554 was passed by **Queen Mary**'s parliament as a modification to the previous act. Attempting to hinder the illegal immigration of the Romani people, the act imposed fines and sentenced Roma caught in England to either death or deportation. However, those who gave up their nomadic lifestyle could be spared persecution. The Roma could assimilate into the Christian realm, leave England, or be punished. Note that Mary and her husband, King Philip II of Spain, were also harsh opponents of Protestantism.

Queen Mary: King Henry VIII's daughter by his first wife, Catherine of Aragon; Mary (ruled 1553–58) married King Philip II of Spain, but he held no real power in England.

An Act for the Punishment of certain Persons calling themselves Egyptians.

Where in a Parliament held at **Westminster** in the 22nd Year of the Reign of our late Sovereign Lord King Henry the Eighth, for the avoiding and banishing out of this Realm of certain outlandish People [here the text repeats the 1530 Act up to "Pain of Imprisonment;"] and such Persons calling themselves Egyptians, as were then within this Realm, should depart within Sixteen Days next after Proclamation of the said Act, upon Pain of Imprisonment, and Forfeiture of all their Goods and Chattels, with divers other Clauses and Articles contained in the said Act, as by the said Act more at large it appears: Forasmuch as diverse of the said Company, and such other like Persons, not fearing the Penalty of the said Statute, have enterprised to come over again into this Realm, using their old accustomed, devilish and naughty Practices and Devices, with such abominable Living as is not in any Christian Realm to be permitted, named or known, and be not duly punished for the same, to the perilous and evil Example of our Sovereign Lord and Lady the King and Queen's Majesties most loving Subjects, and to the utter and extreme undoing of diverse and many of them, as evidently does appear:

Westminster: The Parliament buildings in London.

II. For Reformation whereof, be it ordained and enacted by the King and Queen our Sovereign Lord and Lady, the Lords Spiritual and Temporal, and the Commons, in this present Parliament assembled, and by the Authority of the same, That if any Person or Persons after the last Day of January next coming do willingly transport, bring or convey into this Realm of England or

12 Egyptians Act 1554 (1 & 2 Philip & Mary, c. 4), in John Raithby, *The Statutes at Large, of England and of Great-Britain*, vol. IV, *From I Mary, A.D. 1553 to 16 Charles I A.D. 1640* (London: G. Eyre and A. Strahan, 1811), 32–34.

Wales: Nation to the West of England which was under the control of the English crown.

Pounds: The standard currency of Britain: pounds, shillings, and pence.

Felons: Criminals.

Sanctuary: The right when pursued by the law to take sanctuary in a church.

Wales, any such Persons calling themselves, or commonly called Egyptians, that then he or they so transporting, bringing or conveying in any such Persons, contrary to the true Meaning of this Act, shall forfeit and lose for every Time so offending, Forty **Pounds** of lawful Money of England.

III. And be it further enacted by the Authority aforesaid, That if any of the said Persons called Egyptians, which shall be transported and conveyed into this Realm of England or Wales as is aforesaid, do continue and remain within the same by the Space of one Month, that then he or they so offending shall by virtue of this Act be deemed and judged a Felon and **Felons**, and shall therefore suffer Pains of Death, Loss of Lands and Goods, as in Cases of Felony, by the Order of the Common Law of this Realm, and shall upon the Trial of them or any of them therein so tried in the County, and by the Inhabitants of the County or Place, where they or he shall be apprehended or taken, and not *per medictatem linguae*, and shall lose the Benefit and Privilege of **Sanctuary** and Clergy....

V. And be it also enacted by the Authority aforesaid, That if the Egyptians, and other Persons commonly called Egyptians, and every of them, now being within this Realm of England and Wales, do not depart out and from the same within 40 Days next after Proclamation shall be made of this Act ... shall be judged and deemed according to the Laws of this Realm of England, a Felon and Felons, and shall suffer therefore Pains of Death, Loss of Lands and Goods, as in other Cases of Felony, and shall be tried as is aforesaid, and without having any Benefit or Privilege of Sanctuary or Clergy....

VII. Provided always, and be it enacted by the Authority aforesaid, that this present Act, nor any Thing therein contained, shall not extend or be hurtful to any of the said Persons commonly called Egyptians, which within the said Time of 20 Days next after the said Proclamation to be made as is aforesaid, shall leave that naughty, idle and ungodly Life and Company, and be placed in the Service of some honest and able Inhabitant or Inhabitants within this Realm, or that shall honestly exercise himself in some lawful Work or Occupation, but that he or they so continuing in Service, or other lawful Work or Occupation, shall during such Time as he or they shall so continue be discharged of all Pains and Forfeitures contained in this Act.

VIII. Provided also, and be it enacted by the Authority aforesaid, That this Act shall not in any wise extend to any Child or Children, being not above the Age of Thirteen Years, nor to any of the said Persons, being now in Prison, so that he or they so being in Prison do depart out of this Realm within Fourteen Days next after his or their Delivery out of Prison; nor shall extend to charge any manner of Person or Persons as accessary to any Offence or Offences contained or specified in this Statute.

DOCUMENT 96

Queen Elizabeth I of England, "For the Punishment of Vagabonds Calling Themselves Egyptians" (1563)[13]

Unlike the Egyptian Acts of 1531 and 1554, this statute passed early in the reign of Queen Mary's half-sister **Elizabeth I** (r. 1558–1603) recognized Gypsies as natives of England. At the same time, it criminalized anybody found in their company, or caught counterfeiting or disguising themselves as **vagabonds** via their dress, language, or other behavior. Though this statute was repealed in 1783, vagrancy laws continued to be enforced.

Elizabeth I: Henry VIII's daughter by his second wife, Anne Boleyn, restored England to a Protestant faith, but with some Catholic elements and royal control over the Church of England.

vagabonds: Those who wander from place to place without a permanent home or job.

An act for further punishment of vagabonds, calling themselves Egyptians.

WHEREAS since the act made in the first and second years of the late King and Queen, King Philip and Queen Mary, for the punishment of that false and subtle company of vagabonds calling themselves Egyptians, there is a scruple and doubt risen, whether such persons as being born within this realm of England, or other the Queen's highness dominions, and are or shall become of the fellowship or company of the said Vagabonds, by transforming or disguising themselves in their apparel, or in a certain counterfeit speech or behaviour, are punishable by the said act in like manner as others of that sort are, being strangers born and transported into this realm of England:

II. Therefore for the avoiding of all doubts and ambiguities in that behalf, and to the intent that all such sturdy and false vagabonds of that sort, living only upon the spoil of the simple people, may be condignly met withal and punished, be it enacted ... that the said statute made in the first and second years of the said late King and Queen concerning those vagabonds calling themselves Egyptians, shall continue, remain and be in full force, strength and effect.

III. And yet moreover, be it enacted by the authority aforesaid, That all and every person and persons, which from and after the first day of May now next ensuing shall be seen or found within this realm of England or Wales, in any company or fellowship of vagabonds, commonly called or calling themselves Egyptians, or counterfeiting, transforming or disguising themselves by their apparel, speech or other behaviour, like unto such vagabonds, commonly called or calling themselves Egyptians, and so shall do or continue and remain in the same, either at one time or at several times, by

13 5 Elizabeth C.20, 1563, in *The Statutes at Large, from the First Year of Q. Mary, to the Thirty-fifth Year of Q. Elizabeth, inclusive*, ed. Danby Pickering (Cambridge: Joseph Bentham, 1763), 211–12.

the space of one month: that then the said person or persons, shall by virtue of this act be deemed and judged a felon and felons; and shall therefore suffer pains of death, loss of lands and goods, as in cases of felony by the order of the common laws of this realm; and shall upon the trial of them, or of any of them therein, be tried in the county and by the inhabitants of the county or place where they or he shall be apprehended or taken, and not *per medietatem lingua*; and shall lose the privilege and benefit of sanctuary and clergy.

IV. Provided always, and be it enacted by the authority aforesaid, That this act shall not in any wise extend to any child or children being within the age of fourteen years, nor to any of the said persons being in prison the last day of this present parliament; so that he or they so being in prison, do within fourteen days next after his or their delivery out of prison, either depart out of this realm of England and Wales, or put him or themselves to some honest service, or exercise some lawful work, trade or occupation, and utterly forsake the said idle and false trade, conversation and behaviour of the said counterfeit and disguised vagabonds, commonly called or calling themselves Egyptians.

V. Provided also, and be it enacted by the authority aforesaid, That the said act made in the first and second years of the said late King and Queen, shall not extend to compel any person or persons born within any the Queen's majesty's dominions, to depart out of this realm of England or Wales, but only to constrain and bind them and every of them to leave their said naughty, idle and ungodly life and company, and to place themselves in some honest service, or to exercise themselves at home with their parents, or elsewhere, honestly in some lawful work, trade or occupation; anything mentioned in the said former act to the contrary hereof in any wise notwithstanding.

DOCUMENT 97

From Thomas Dekker, *Lanthorne and Candle-Light. Or The Bell-Mans Second* (1609)[14]

Thomas Dekker (c. 1572–1632) was a popular English playwright and **pamphleteer**. In this work Dekker's lead character is a demon who visits his various human followers, including the so-called Gypsies, which he links with the moon that was believed to be associated with madness.

pamphleteer: Writer of short, cheap, publications aimed to persuade readers of a particular polemical position.

Moon Men

A discovery of a strange wild people, very dangerous to towns and country villages.

A Moon-man signifies in English, a mad-man, because the Moon has greatest domination (above any other Planet) over the bodies of **Frantic persons**. But these Moon-men ... are neither absolutely mad, nor yet perfectly in their wits. Their name they borrow from the Moon, because as the Moon is never in one shape two nights together, but wanders up & down Heaven, like an **Antic**, so these changeable-stuff-companions never tarry one day in a place, but are the only, and the only base **Ronnagats** upon earth. And as in the Moon there is a man, that never stirs without a bush of thorns at his back, so these Moon-men lie under bushes, & are indeed no better than Hedge creepers.

Frantic persons: Mental illness was not well understood by early modern people, and they called people who behaved in unusual or frenzied ways mad or frantic.

Antic: Someone who behaves in a bizarre fashion.

Ronnagats: A runaway, or vagabond.

They are a people more scattered than Jews, and more hated: beggarly in apparel, barbarous in condition, beastly in behavior: and bloody if they meet advantage. A man that sees them would swear they had all the yellow **Jaundice**, or that they were **Tawny Moors** bastards, for no **Red-oaker man** carries a face of a more filthy complexion, yet are they not born so, neither has the Sun burnt them so, but they are painted so, yet they are not good painters neither: for they do not make faces, but mar faces. By name they are called Gipsies, they call themselves Egyptians, others in mockery call them Moon-men.

Jaundice: A medical condition that causes the skin to take on a yellowish hue.

Tawny Moors: North Africans whose skin color was a light brown.

Red-oaker man: A reference to the Indigenous people of North America.

If they be Egyptians, sure I am they never descended from the tribes of any of those people that came out of the Land of *Egypt: **Ptolomy*** (King of the Egyptians) I warrant never called them his Subjects: no nor ***Pharaoh*** before him. Look what difference there is between a civil citizen of Dublin

***Ptolomy*:** Presumably Pharaoh Ptolemy XIII (62–47 BCE) who co-ruled with his sister, the famed Cleopatra.

***Pharaoh*:** The ancient rulers of Egypt.

14 Thomas Dekker, *Lanthorne and candle-light. Or The bell-mans second* ... (London, 1609), fols. H1r –H3r.

Kerne: From Middle Irish ceithern, a group of fighting men.

Rogue: A person who flouts social norms.

four-score: Four times twenty.

boot-halers: Soldiers who forage and steal from local populations.

harlots: Pejorative term for the women who resided with and serviced soldiers in their camps.

panniers: A type of basket used to transport foodstuffs.

quartered: A form of execution that had the victim hung, then tied by their limbs to horses which were driven in different directions, thus pulling the body apart. A sentence reserved for treason against the crown.

rents: Rips, tears.

Callico: Calico, a plain textile made from cotton.

Morris-dancers: English folk dancers who wear bells and carry staffs at festivals.

knaveries: Deeds done by a rascal or dishonest person.

Skeanes: Celtic daggers.

mantles: Cloaks.

Heath: A shrubland, typically of poor soil and low-growing vegetation.

***Hamlet*:** The lead character in Shakespeare's *The Tragedy of Hamlet, Prince of Denmark* (c. 1601) who seeks revenge for the murder of his father.

& a wild Irish **Kerne**, so much difference there is between one of these counterfeit Egyptians and a true English Beggar. An English **Rogue** is just of the same livery.

They are commonly an army about **four-score** strong, yet they never march with all their bags and baggages together, but (like **boot-halers**) they forage up and down countries, 4, 5, or 6 in a company ... these vagabonds have their **harlots** with a number of little children following at their heels: which young brood of Beggars, are sometimes carried (like so many green geese alive to a market) in pairs of **panniers**....

One Shire alone & no more is sure still at one time, to have these Egyptian lice swarming within it ... let them be scattered worse than the quarters of a traitor are after he's hang'd drawn and **quartered**, yet they have a trick (like water cut with a sword) to come together instantly and easily again: and this is their policy....

Their apparel is odd, and fantastic, though it be never so full of **rents**: the men wear scarfs of **Callico**, or any other base stuff, *hanging* their bodies like **Morris-dancers**, with bells, & other toys, to entice the country people to flock about them, and to wonder at their fooleries or rather rank **knaveries**. The women as ridiculously attire themselves, and like one that plays the Rogue on a Stage wear rags, and patched filthy mantles uppermost, when the under garments are handsome and in fashion.

The battles these Out-laws make, are many and very bloody. Whosoever falls into their hands never escapes alive, & so cruel they are in these murders, that nothing can satisfy them but the very heart blood of those whom they kill. And who are they (think you) that thus go to the pot? Alas! Innocent Lambs, Sheep, Calves, Pigs, etc. poultry-ware are more churlishly handled by them, than poor prisoners are by keepers in the counter with the Poultry.... The bloody tragedies of all these, are only acted by the Women, who carrying long knives or **Skeanes** under their **mantles**, do thus play their parts: The Stage is some large **Heath**: or a Fir bush Common, far from any houses: Upon which casting them-selves into a King, they enclose the Murdered, till the Massacre be finished. If any passenger come by, and wondering to see such a conjuring circle kept by Hell-hounds, demand what spirits they raise there? One of the Murderers steps to him, poisons him with sweet words and shifts him off, with this lie, yet one of the women is fain in labour. But if any mad ***Hamlet*** hearing this, smell villainy, & rush in by violence to see what the tawny Devils are doing: then they excuse the fact, lay the blame on those that are the Actors, & perhaps (if they see no remedy) deliver them to an officer, to be had to punishment: But by the way a rescue is surely laid and very valiantly (though very villainously) do they fetch them off, & guard them.

The Cabins where these Land-pirates lodge in the night, are the Outbarns of Farmers & **Husband-men** (in some poor Village or other) who dare not deny them, for fear they should in the morning have their **thatched houses** burning about their ears....

These Barns are the beds of Incests, **Whoredoms**, Adulteries, & of all other black and deadly-damned *Impieties*; here grows the Cursed *Tree* of ***Bastardy*** that is so fruitful: here are written the *Books* of all *Blasphemies, Swearing* & *Curses*, that are so dreadful to be read. Yet the simple country people will come running out of their houses to gaze upon them whilst in the meantime one steals into the next Room, and brings away whatsoever he can lay hold on. Upon days of pastime & liberty, they Spread themselves in small companies amongst the Villages: and when young maids & bachelors (yea sometimes old doting fools, that should be beaten to this world of villainies, & forewarn others) do flock about them, they then profess skill in Palmistry, & (forsooth) can tell fortunes which for the most part are infallibly true, by reason that they work upon rules, which are grounded upon certainty: for one of them will tell you that you shall shortly have some evil luck fall upon you, & within half an hour after you shall find your pocket picked, or your purse cut. These are those *Egyptian Grasshoppers* that eat up the fruits of the Earth, and destroy the poor corn fields: to sweep whose swarms out of this kingdom, there are no other means but the sharpness of the most infamous & basest kinds of punishment.

Husband-men: Farmers.

thatched houses: Small houses with roofs made of straw or rushes layered to shed water away from the inner roof.

Whoredoms: An old term for sexual improprieties.

***Bastardy*:** Offspring born out of wedlock who typically lack the legal and economic benefits of children born within a marriage.

DOCUMENT 98

From Samuel Rid, *The Art of Juggling or Legerdemain* (1612)[15]

In this source Jacobean writer Samuel Rid identifies street illusionists in England as Gypsies. Legerdemain, referring to dexterity of the hands, or the art of deception, is associated with magical acts, specifically card magic, and theft. In this work Rid plagiarizes (a not uncommon feature of early modern publishing) from the famous 1584 book by Reginald Scot, *Discoverie of Witchcraft*, in which Scot expresses profound skepticism toward belief in witchcraft. Despite their activities as fortune tellers, Roma were not typically tried as witches, who were most often fellow Christian neighbors of the accused.

These kind of people about an hundred years ago, about the twentieth year of King *Henry* the eight,[16] began together an head, at the first here about the Southern parts, and this (as I am informed) and as I can gather, was their beginning.

Certain Egyptians banished their Country (belike not for their good conditions) arrived here in England, who being excellent in quaint tricks and devises, not known here at that time among us, were esteemed and had in great admiration, for what with strangeness of their attire and garments, together with their sleights and legerdemains, they were spoke of far and near, insomuch that many of our English loiterers joined with them, and in time learned their craft and **cozening**. The speech which they used was the right Egyptian language, with whom our Englishmen conversing, at last learned their language. These people continuing about the country in this fashion, practicing their cosening art of **fast and loose**, and legerdemain, purchased to themselves great credit among the country people, and got much by Palmistry, and telling of fortunes: insomuch they pitifully cosened the poor country Girls, both of money, silver spoons, and the best of their apparel, or any good thing they could make, only to hear their fortunes.

cozening: Acts of fraud or deception.

fast and loose: An old carnival game in which a player seeks to snare a leather loop with a stick (to make fast, or firm), but the operator rigs it so that it remains loose.

This *Giles Hather* (for so was his name) together with his whore *Kit Calot*, in short space had following them a pretty train, he terming himself the King of the Egyptians, and she the Queen, riding about the country at their pleasures uncontrolled: at last about forty years after, when their knavery began to be **espied** ... it pleased the Council to look more narrowly

espied: Spied or spotted.

15 Samuel Rid, *The art of iugling or legerdemaine Wherein is deciphered, all the conueyances of legerdemaine and iugling, how they are effected, and wherein they chiefly consist.* ... (London: George Eld, 1614), fols. B1v–B3r; Reginald Scot, *The Discoverie of witchcraft* (London, 1584).

16 See Document 94 above.

into their lives, and in a Parliament made in the first and second years of *Phillip* and *Mary*,[17] there was a strict Statute made, that whosoever should transport any Egyptians into this Realm, should forfeit forty pounds: [Rid summarizes the statute in Document 95 above]. These Acts and Statutes now put forth, and come so their hearing, they divide their bands and companies into diverse parts of the realm: for you must imagine and know that they had above two hundred rogues and Vagabonds in a **Regiment**: and although they went not altogether, yet would they not be above two or three miles one from the other, and now they dare no more be known by the name of Egyptians, nor take any other name upon them than poor people. But what a number were executed presently upon this statute, you would wonder: yet notwithstanding all would not prevail: but still they wandered, as before up and down, and meeting once in a year at a place appointed: sometimes at the **Devils arse** in peak in Derbyshire.... Then it pleased Queen *Elizabeth* to revive the Statute before mentioned, in the twentieth year of her happy reign,[18] endeavouring by all means possible to root out this pestiferous people, but nothing could be done you see until this day they wander up and down in the name of Egyptians, colouring their faces and fashioning their attire, and garment like unto them, yet if you ask what they are, they dare no otherwise than say, they are Englishmen, and of such a shire, and so are forced to say contrary to that they pretend.

Regiment: A military unit typically recruited from a single region and led by a local notable; consisting of about 800 soldiers.

Devils arse: A cavern in in Castleton, Derbyshire, England, alleged to have been the abode of criminals, such as Giles Hather.

... [T]hese fellows seeing that no profit comes by wandering, but hazard of their lives, do daily decrease and break off their wonted society, and take themselves many of them, some to be **Peddlers**, some **Tinkers**, some Jugglers, & some to one kind of life or other, insomuch that Juggling is now become common ... which I must needs say, that some deserve commendation for the nimbleness and agility of their hands, & might be thought to perform as excellent things by their Legerdemain, as any of your wizards witches or magicians whatsoever. For these kind of people do perform that in action, which the other do make show of: and no doubt many when they hear of any rare exploit performed which cannot enter into their capacity, and is beyond their reach, straight they attribute it to be done by the devil, and that they work by some familiar spirit, when indeed it is nothing else but mere illusion, cosoning, or Legerdemain.... But when these experiments grow to superstition and impiety, they are either to be forsaken as vain, or denied as false: howbeit, if these things be done for recreation and mirth, & not to the hurt of our neighbour, nor to the profaning & abusing of God's holy name: then sure they are neither impious nor altogether unlawful, though herein or hereby a natural thing be made to seem supernatural.

Peddlers: Traveling vendors of goods.

Tinkers: Those who traveled about fixing metal vessels.

17 See Document 95 above.

18 See Document 96 above.

DOCUMENT 99
From King George III of Great Britain, Repeal of the Egyptians' Act (1783)[19]

The aforementioned act "For the Punishment of Vagabonds calling themselves Egyptians" passed by Queen Elizabeth I (Document 96 above) was repealed by King George III (r. 1760–1820) in 1783 on the grounds that it was too severe.

Anno 23rd Georgii III, c.51, A.D. 1783

An Act to repeal an Act made in the Fifth Year of the Reign of Queen Elizabeth, intituled, An Act for further Punishment of Vagabonds calling themselves Egyptians.

Whereas an Act, made in the Fifth Year of the Reign of Queen Elizabeth, intituled, An Act for further Punishment of Vagabonds calling themselves Egyptians, is and ought to be considered as a Law of excessive Severity; Be it therefore enacted by the King's Most Excellent Majesty, by and with the Advice and Consent of the Lords Spiritual and Temporal, and Commons, in this present Parliament assembled, and by the Authority of the same, That from and after the First Day of August One thousand seven hundred and eighty three, the said Act shall be and the same is hereby repealed.

19 William Andrews, *Legal Lore: Curiousities of Law and Lawyers* (London: William Andrews, 1897), 174. The excerpt is from *The Statutes at Large, of England and of Great-Britain: From Magna Carta to the Union of the Kingdoms of Great Britain and Ireland*, vol. XV, *From 20 George III A.D. 1780 to 24 George III A.D. 1784*, ed. John Raithby (London: George Eyre and Andrew Strahan, 1811), 450.

DOCUMENT 100

"The Gipsies" (1816)[20]

By the early nineteenth century, non-Roma Europeans held conflicting and often contradictory views on their Roma neighbors, as is illustrated in this series of questions and answers from the *Times*. The "gipsies" of England and Scotland are said here to be indifferent to moral restraints, have peculiar habits and anti-religious attitudes, and do not value education.

Of late years some attempts have been made to reduce the numbers, or at any rate to civilize the habits, of that vagabond and useless race, the Gipsies. In pursuance of such purpose, a society of gentlemen have been making all the preliminary inquiries requisite to a proper understanding of the subject. A series of questions have been proposed to competent persons in the different countries of England and Scotland; and answers have been received.

From whence is it said the Gipsies first came?

All Gipsies suppose the first of them came from Egypt.

How many is it supposed that there are in England?

They cannot form any idea of the number in England.

What is your circuit in summer?

The Gipsies of Bedfordshire, Hertfordshire, parts of Buckinghamshire, Cambridge, and Huntingdonshire, are continually making revolutions within the range of those counties.

How many Gipsy families are supposed to be in it?

They are either ignorant of the number of Gipsies in the counties through which they travel, or unwilling to disclose their knowledge.…

What proportion of their number follow business, and what kind?

More than half their number follow no business, others are dealers in horses and asses; **farriers**, smiths, tinkers, **braziers**, grinders of cutlery, basket-makers, chair-bottomers, and musicians.

farriers: People who trim and shoe horses' hooves.

braziers: Those who make or repair metal objects.

How do they bring their children up?

Children are brought up in the habits of their parents, particularly to music and dancing, and are of dissolute conduct.

What do the women employ themselves in?

The women mostly carry baskets with trinkets and small wares; and tell fortunes.

From how many generations can they trace their descent?

20 "The Gipsies," *Times (London)*, Issue 9891, 19 July 1816.

Too ignorant to have acquired accounts of genealogy, and perhaps indisposed to it by the irregularity of their habits....

How long have they lived in this part?

It cannot be ascertained whether, from their first coming into the nation, attachment to particular places has prevailed.

Have they any speech of their own, different to that used by other people? What do they call it? Can anyone write it? Is there any writing to be seen any where?

When among strangers, they elude inquiries respecting their particular language, calling it gibberish. Don't know of any person who can write it, or of any written specimen of it.

Have they any rules of conduct which are general to their community?

Their habits and customs in all places are peculiar.

What religion they mostly profess?

Those who profess any religion represent it to that of the country in which they reside; but their description of it seldom goes beyond repeating the Lord's prayer; and only a few of them are capable of that. Instances of their attending any place for worship are very rare.

Do they marry, and in what manner?

They marry for the most part by pledging to each other, without any ceremony. A few exceptions have occurred when money was plentiful.

How do they teach their children religion?

They do not teach their children religion.

Do any of them learn to read? Who teaches them?

Not one in a thousand can read.

What proportion of them, is it supposed, live out of doors in winter, as in summer?

Some go into lodgings in London, Cambridge, &c. during the winter; but it is calculated three fourths of them live out of doors in winter as in summer.

DOCUMENT 101

From Victor Hugo, *The Hunchback of Notre Dame* (1831)[21]

Victor Hugo's novel *The Hunchback of Notre Dame*, published in 1831, but set in 1482, features a French girl named Agnès, whose name was changed to La Esmeralda after being raised by Romani. A "wanderer," she allegedly attracts men with her seductive dancing, shapely body, and dark, golden skin. Quasimodo, the "hunchback," protects Esmeralda through the law of sanctuary, to which she is not entitled because of her Romani status. She is ultimately wrongfully convicted, tortured, and killed for murder and the charge of witchcraft. Hugo's novel relies on long-held anti-Romani stereotypes, including that of the exotic Gypsy woman to provide entertainment to his audience.

In an extensive space left open between the crowd and the fire, there was a young female dancing.

Whether this young female was a human being, a fairy, or an angel, **Gringoire**, skeptical philosopher and satirical poet as he was, could not at the first moment decide, so completely was he fascinated by the dazzling vision. She was not tall, though she appeared to be so, from the slenderness and elegance of her shape. Her complexion was dark, but it was easy to divine that by daylight her skin must have been the beautiful golden tint of the Roman and **Andalusian** women. Her small foot, too, was Andalusian. She danced, whirled, turned round on an old Persian carpet carelessly spread on the pavement, and every time her radiant face passed before you as she turned, her large black eyes flashed lightning.

Gringoire: Pierre Gringoire, a character in the novel, who was in an arranged marriage with Esmeralda, and eventually fell in love with her.

Andalusian: People from Southern Spain.

Every eye was fixed upon her, every mouth open; and in truth, while she was thus dancing, what with the sound of the tambourine, and which her two plump, exquisitely shaped arms held above her head, her bodice of gold without folds, her spotted robe which swelled with the rapidity of her motions, her bare shoulders, her finely turned legs, which her petticoat now and then discovered, her black hair, her eyes of flame, she was a supernatural creature.

"Verily," thought Gringoire, "it is a salamander, a nymph, a goddess, a bacchanal of **Mount Menalaeus**!" At that moment one of the tresses of the salamander's hair got loose, and a piece of brass which had been fastened

Mount Menalaeus: A place in Classic Greek mythology.

21 *The Valjean Edition of the Novels of Victor Hugo* (New York/London: The Co-Operative Publication Society, 1900; orig. 1831), 54–55.

to it dropped to the ground. "Ha! No," said he; "'tis a gypsy!" The illusion was at an end.

She began dancing again. She picked up from the ground two swords, which she balanced on their points upon her forehead, and made them turn round one way, while she turned the other. She was, in fact, a gypsy, neither more nor less. But though the spell was dissolved, still the whole scene was not without fascination and charm for Gringoire; the bonfire threw a crude, red, trembling light on the wide circle of faces and on the tawny brow of the girl, and, at the extremity of the place, cast a faint tinge, mingled with their wavering shadows, upon the ancient, black and furrowed façade of the Maison-aux-Piliers on the one hand, and upon the stone arms of the gibbet on the other.

DOCUMENT 102

Image: *A Family of Gypsies Sit in Their Camp with a Child They Have Stolen* (1840)[22]

This engraving was published to accompany a poem entitled *The Stolen Child*; or, *The Gipsy Encampment* by H.J. Shepherd, which begins with the stanza, "The swarthy tribe, the wild mysterious crew, / A doubtful race, that wander Europe through, / Whom, in his turn, each neighbour views with fears, / The wise, as wandering rogues—the fool, as seers— / Beneath the rocks have pitch'd their evening tent, / Pleased with the morning's prize, and well content / With what their wits have won, or casual fortune lent. / Or both conspiring brought when they beguiled / From his neglectful nurse the unconscious child."

The myth that Romani kidnapped Christian children was widespread in nineteenth-century Europe and continues, in some regions, to the present day. In 1999, for instance, Italian authorities interrogated a Roma mother about the legitimacy of her child because she was "too pretty to be a Gypsy."[23]

22 *A Family of Gypsies Sit in Their Camp with a Child They Have Stolen*. Engraving by W. & F. Holl, 1840, after F.P. Stephanoff, Wellcome Collection.

23 Kathryn Carlisle, "Stealing Children: Institutionalizing Romani Children in Italy," European Roma Rights Centre, 3 October 2000, http://www.errc.org/roma-rights-journal/stealing-children-institutionalising-romani-children-in-italy.

DOCUMENT 103

Image: The Gypsy Fortune Teller, a Trading Card for Dr. Jayne's Expectorant (c. 1870–90)[24]

This collectible trading card was also an advertisement for a cold medicine, Dr. Jayne's Expectorant. The image relies on long-held cultural stereotypes of Romani peoples and fortune-telling or palmistry (as seen in documents above). The owl, though often a symbol of wisdom, could also denote dangerous occult knowledge when paired with a woman.

24 Drug advertising ephemera, Box 31, Wellcome Collection.

DOCUMENT 104

From "Gypsies of Hungary" (1909)[25]

This excerpt further catalogs several anti-Romani prejudices, this time regarding early twentieth-century Hungarian society. Note the possible comparison between this categorization of Romani women as "unspoilt by civilization" with anti-Indigenous racism, which also implied they were "closer to nature" and therefore not as civilized as white Europeans.

One word of the Gypsies of Hungary, those lazy kings and queens of solitude who the Hungarians alone welcomed when in the rest of Austria they were reckoned among "Turks and infidels." Free and wayward as the wind, the women of the gipsies keep their "splendid vices" and are untouched by the manners and customs of the Hungarians. Unspoilt by civilization the women of the purely nomadic tribes feel no need for the shelter of clothes so long as they are in the country, and are content with the most scanty covering, even in the villages and towns. They are fortune tellers, the jugglers, the dancing girls of the country, and whether nomads or settlers are full of the language which the Hungarians have caught from them, the language of music.

25 Athol Joyce and N.W. Thomas, *Women of All Nations. A Record of Their Characteristics, Habits, Manners, Customs, and Influence* (London: Cassell and Co., 1909), 696.

DOCUMENT 105

From Cesare Lombroso's Criminological Classification of Romani as Atavistic Criminals in *Criminal Man* (1911)[26]

Criminal biologists followed on from racial anthropologists in seeking "scientific" evidence to support traditional prejudices. Cesare Lombroso, the so-called father of criminology, argued that **hereditary criminality** had biological causes, and could be traced in individual families, regions, and in specific races. Further, Lombroso believed that criminals could be identified by specific physical features such as large ears, sloping foreheads, long arms, and asymmetrical faces. In some cases, he equated these physical characteristics of criminality to those of apes and lower primates, which in his mind was evidence that some humans still bore savage looks and tendencies. Lombroso was not alone in categorizing the Romani as "natural born criminals" and habitual reoffenders, as he illustrates in the following excerpt.

hereditary criminality: Theory posits biological links between criminal behavior and genetics. Criminologists previously studied genealogical charts to determine how criminality traveled through the generations, usually with little attention to social or economic conditions.

Pathological Origin of Crime. The **atavistic** origin of crime is certainly one of the most important discoveries of criminal anthropology, but it is important only theoretically since it merely explains the phenomenon. Anthropologists soon realized how necessary it was to supplement this discovery by that of the origin or causes which call forth in certain individuals these atavistic or criminal instincts, for it is the immediate causes that constitute the practical nucleus of the problem, and it is their removal that renders possible the cure of the disease....

atavistic: Reverting to ancestral or ancient traits or behaviors.

Heredity is the principal organic cause of criminal tendencies. It may be divided into two classes: indirect heredity from a genetically degenerate family with frequent cases of insanity, deafness, syphilis, epilepsy, and alcoholism among its members; direct heredity from criminal parentage....

Race. This is of great importance in view of the atavistic origin of crime. There exist whole tribes and races more or less given to crime, such as the tribe **Zakka Khel** in India. In all regions of Italy, whole villages constitute hot-beds of crime, owing, no doubt, to ethnical causes.... The frequency of homicide in **Calabria, Sicily, and Sardinia** is fundamentally due to African and Oriental elements.

In the gipsies we have an entire race of criminals with all the passions and vices common to delinquent types: idleness, ignorance, impetuous fury, vanity, love of orgies, and ferocity. Murder is often committed for some trifling gain.

Heredity: The genetic transmission of characteristics down through generations.

Zakka Khel: A clan of the Pakhtun tribe of the Northwest Frontier province of British India which resisted British rule. In 1908 British military forces put down the rebellion.

Calabria, Sicily, and Sardinia: The southernmost portions of Italy whose residents in the nineteenth century were largely poorly educated and impoverished, and where organized crime groups dominated local governance.

26 *Criminal Man, According to the Classification of Cesare Lombroso*, ed. Gina Lombroso Ferrero, with an introduction by Cesare Lombroso (New York/London: G.P. Putnam's Sons, 1911), 137, 139–40.

The women are skilled thieves and train their children in dishonest practices. On the contrary, the percentage of crimes among Jews is always lower than that of the surrounding population; although there is a prevalence of certain specific forms of offences, often hereditary, such as fraud, forgery, libel, and chief of all, traffic in prostitution; murder is extremely rare.

Heinrich Himmler: Leading member of the Nazi Party and a central organizer of the European-wide Holocaust.

Reich Central Office for Combating the Gypsy Nuisance: Established in 1937 to coordinate Nazi anti-Romani policies and actions but based on a similar center that opened in Munich before the Third Reich.

DOCUMENT 106
Heinrich Himmler, "Fighting the Gypsy Plague" (1938)[27]

Heinrich Himmler argued that Gypsies were a threat to national morale and should be required to register with Germany's centralized **Reich Central Office for Combating the Gypsy Nuisance**. After the registration procedure documented below, many Romani were interned, deported, subjected to forced labor or murdered in extermination camps.

(1) The experience gained so far in combatting the gypsy plague and the knowledge gained through racial biological research make it seem appropriate to tackle the regulation of the Gypsy Question from the nature of this race. Experience has shown that the mixed breeds make up the greatest share of the criminality of the gypsies. On the other hand, it has been shown that attempts to make the gypsies sedentary have failed in the racially pure population due to their wandering instinct. It is therefore necessary, in the final solution to the Gypsy Question, to treat the pure race Gypsies and the mixed breeds separately.

(2) To achieve this goal, it is first necessary to determine the racial affiliation of the individual gypsies living in the German Reich and that of the people who move about in a "gypsy way" [*Zigeunerart*].

(3) I order therefore that all sedentary and non-sedentary gypsies, as well as the persons roaming in the manner of gypsies, are to be registered with the Reich Criminal Police Office—Reich Central Office for Combating the Gypsy Nuisance.

(4) Accordingly, the police authorities will report all persons, who by their appearance, customs, and morals, are identified as gypsies or mixed breeds, as well as those people who move about like the gypsies, to the Reich Criminal Police Office—Reich Central Office for Combating the Gypsy Nuisance.

(5) The report must be made on an index card, and according to the detailed instructions of the Reich Criminal Police Office.

27 "Bekämpfung der Zigeunerplage," 8. Dezember 1938, Ministerialblatt des Reichs- und Preußischen Ministeriums des Innern, 1938, Nr. 51, Spalten 2105–2106, original reproduced at Die Verfolgung der Sinti und Roma im Nationalsozialismus–Materialien aus Niedersachsen Erlasse: 1938 Bekämpfung der Zigeunerplage. Translated by Lisa Todd.

DOCUMENT 107

Image: Anthropologist Eva Justin Creating a Plaster Cast on a Romani Man (1938)[28]

Nazi racial ideology, based on centuries of prejudice, stated that Roma and Sinti peoples posed a threat to Germany, both because of their non-Aryan racial status and their tendency to exhibit hereditarily criminal, or asocial, traits. However, some Nazi ideologues also exhibited a fascination with "pure-blooded Gypsies." It fell to social scientists to sort and classify Romani peoples according to their physical characteristics, health, genealogy, and behavior. As a PhD student in the 1940s, Eva Justin used 39 Romani children as research subjects to determine whether institutions could assimilate and "civilize" biracial children. After she defended her dissertation, Nazi officials deported the children by train to Auschwitz-Birkenau, where all but four died. In this pre-war photo, Justin takes a plaster cast of a man's face, which she would later use in her research.

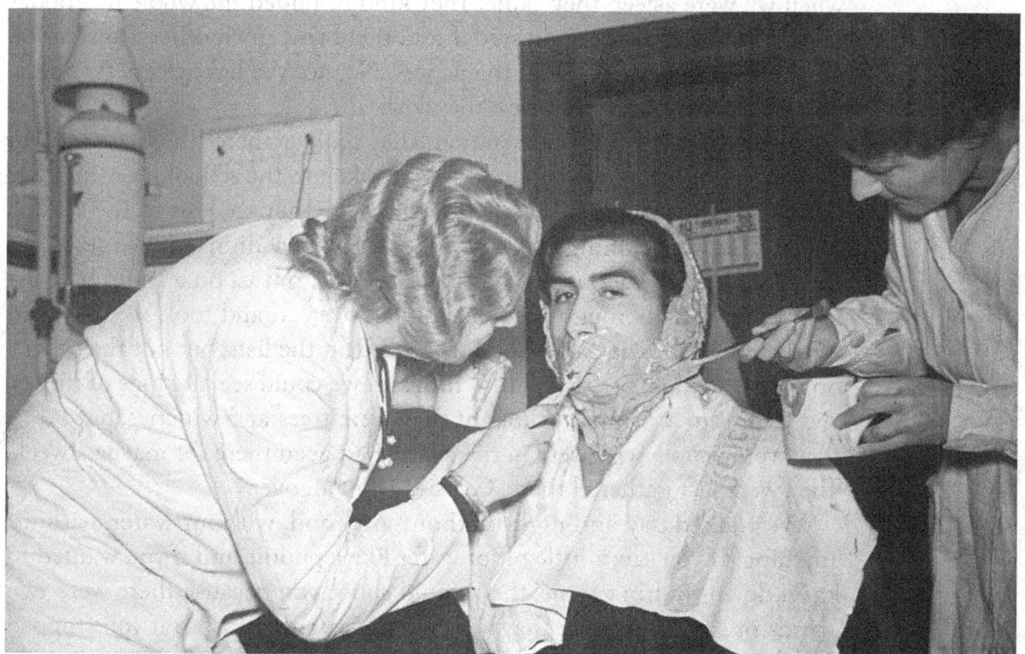

28 Used under CC BY-SA 3.0 DE DEED.

DOCUMENT 108

Holocaust Biographies of Maria Sava Moise and Stefan Moise (1943)[29]

Between 1939 and 1945, between 250,000 and 500,000 Sinti and Roma men, women, and children were murdered by Nazis, and their accomplices, as part of their genocidal plans for the racial reordering of occupied Europe. The following testimonies come from interviews conducted by the United States Holocaust Memorial Museum with the married couple Maria and Stefan Moise. Maria and Stefan were both born in Moldavia, Romania; their childhood neighborhoods were comprised of both Roma and non-Roma Romanians. In 1942, when Iasi's Roma community was rounded up by the Romanian police, the couple were sent east to **Transnistria**. There, they were left to die of hunger in the elements. Stefan managed to escape, and the two were reunited after the war. In this source Maria and Stefan discuss their persecution and survival during the Holocaust.

Transnistria: During the Holocaust, a disputed region of Romania that contained ghettos and concentration camps; today a breakaway state officially recognized as part of Moldova.

Maria Moise: The police came in the morning ... one or two in the morning when we were asleep they came. They kind of raided the whole neighborhood. We got up. We got dressed. I told them that my mother was drafted. My mother showed them all the papers. No, no. We have to go. And they picked us up ... They only took the gypsies....

They took us to the police station. They took us there. The first roundup ... we were in the first roundup. We were taken to the school. Then another batch of people came and then a third one... They took us to the school. My mother was coming, crying, to let us go. They didn't.... We stayed at the school maybe about two days and then ... put us on a train. It was a long train. It had brought people from all over, ... and took all of us who were there in that neighborhood who were on the lists, but not the others. So they loaded us in cars... From the train we could see all kinds of things, and we got to a point... I thought they were trees and wineries, but no ... they were people who were in this place, had been there for maybe a week. They were just gathered there. Gypsies from all over.

We walked day and night without any food, without water, without anything. If you saw a little bit of water like a puddle and if you wanted to kneel down to drink some, they would shoot you because there were two guards or something like that with weapons, with arms, so if you stopped

29 Interview with Maria Moise, 9 September 1991, United States Holocaust Memorial Museum, RG-50.030*0165; Interview with Stefan Moise, 14 April 1991, United States Holocaust Memorial Museum, RG-50.030*0164.

to drink the water, they would shoot you right there. So we just continued walking ...

Stefan Moise: All night long until in the morning, they kept bringing in people from Iasi, gypsies. At a certain point they used to call our name and take us to the cell and they used to take information ... ask us information about our address, the parents, where I was born ... so anyway they filled up all kinds of forms. There were many many people. And we stayed there maybe about two days, until they finished the forms for all the people. After everything was done, they formed small groups and they took us to the train station. There were trains waiting for us, freight cars, empty. They were freight cars, yes. We had to climb into the cars. We were too many of us in a car.... [W]e stayed in these freight cars maybe another day, one night, in the train station until they brought other trains from other parts of the country, also a train full of gypsies.

It was not a train that could climb mountains. So there were trains there, but they brought some carts and they took some of the luggage, some old women and children, and put them in the carts, but not many of them. Most of us had to walk and we walked. It was September which is very hot. The sun was burning. We would go by wells, by running water, brooks, rivers ... we were not allowed to stop to drink. We were not allowed to drink anything.... We were left out there in the field and we no longer saw any soldiers or no one whatsoever. We were just left alone without any guards, no one to talk to us. They just left, left us there alone without telling us anything. We just stayed on this field. On the right there was a stone quarry or a stone mine. There were some pits. How should I call them ... pits, you know, stone pits, no longer in use, so all we could see was the place, you see, open pits. And we just stayed there on the field. When it rained, we would go down the quarry. And we just stayed there on the fields until November. Some people already started to die off.

DOCUMENT 109
Great Britain House of Commons Debate on Gypsies in Dartford (1962)[30]

Racism against the Roma extended well past the end of World War II and the dissolution of the Nazi racial state. It remained alive and well into the Cold War, in all parts of Europe, as government and neighbors continued to view Traveler (Roma) communities with suspicion. The following is an excerpt from a British House of Commons debate in 1962.

Darenth Woods: A 300-acre forested area in Kent, on route from the Dover ferry terminal to London.

Dover: Major port in Southeast England and point of departure for the ferry to France.

Guardian: British daily newspaper, published since 1821.

On 20th January this year, the Dartford Rural District Council evicted from the **Darenth Woods** at Dartford nearly 300 gypsies and other travellers, with about 80 caravans, 26 horses, one donkey, and sundry other things. With few exceptions, those 300 people are still living now, three-and-a-half months later, with their caravans parked on the grass verge of one of Britain's busiest roads, the A.2. On their way to London, visitors arriving at **Dover** from the Continent see one of the most appalling sights which anyone could ever see in any country of Europe. Indeed, I doubt that such a sight can be … seen in any other European country.

These people have been without lavatories, dustbins or litter bins. There is one water pipe for most of them about a mile away. Early-morning workers have told me that they have seen these human beings moving half a mile or a mile away from their caravans in order to attend to the requirements of nature. Many of them, of course, cannot do even that.

There is, in fact, no sign of anything being done to improve the situation….

… It is obvious from this case that people, not of their own volition, can have their homes taken from them and sold. Where will it lead to? I urge the Minister to look at this again because in the **Guardian** on 17th April last, under the headline "Council clears gypsy camp," and the subheading, "Hundred moved on by police," appeared the paragraph: Police and bailiffs stood by at an encampment on Eastern Avenue, Ilford, yesterday, when more than a hundred gypsies were moved from the site. An Essex County Council solicitor, Mr. E. Peel, told the gypsies at 9 a.m. that they had to leave immediately, but three hours later several families were still there. Among them was a man who was lying seriously ill in his caravan, but in

30 Great Britain House of Commons Debate, Orders of the Day, 2 May 1962, A.2 Road, Dartford (Gypsies) HC Deb 02 May 1962 vol 658 cc1163–72. Parliamentary information licensed under the Open Parliament Licence v3.0.

spite of pleas by his wife to let him stay, the vehicle was moved to a lay-by on the main London to Southend Road. From the backwoods, where they were not required, they were moved—and this seems to be becoming the policy—to the main road. The article continued: In another caravan there was a woman expecting a baby. A doctor visited her and told officials that she was due to be in labour at any time and should not be moved far. She and her family were also transferred to the lay-by....

These people are not welcome when they are near built-up areas, and they are not welcome in the wide open spaces. One must come to the conclusion that the only possible solution would be that which Hitler used, namely, that they should be put into gas chambers.

I ask the Minister of Transport to recognise that he has a big stake in this business of gypsies and other travellers. I am not weakening. This thing is going to be won in the next few months, and there is only one way in which it can be done, and that is by pressure. If I am blamed for being emotional it is because I have seen so much. I am disgusted at this country, that this sort of thing can happen here. This cannot be seen in any other country in Europe—only in England and Wales, and nowhere else. We should be ashamed of ourselves.

DOCUMENT 110

Elena Gorolová Describes Her Forced Sterilization by the Czechoslovakian Government (2009)[31]

From the 1970s to the 1990s, women were subjected to coercive, forced, and involuntary sterilization in the Czech Republic (now Czechia). Roma women like Elena Gorolová made up 36.6 percent of these sterilized women, even though they comprised less than 2 percent of the Czech population. This state policy was driven by eugenics. According to the *Health and Human Rights Journal*, the "active targeting of Romani women was an element of population policy, driven by the state's eugenic concern over public health. Because the list of medical indications for sterilization included a 'social' indicator, medical records sometimes even listed 'gypsy origin' as the indication for sterilization." Since 1989, at least 300 Romani women have come forward to authorities or doctors because they were illegally sterilized without their informed consent. Elena Gorolová gave the following account to the **Durban Review Conference** and in 2018 was named to the BBC 100 Women list for her continuing work as a social worker and activist.[32]

Durban Review Conference: Held in Geneva in 2009, this UN-sponsored conference evaluated progress towards the goals set by the 2001 World Conference against Racism, Racial Discrimination, Xenophobia and Related Intolerance in Durban, South Africa.

Elena Gorolová and her husband had always dreamed of having a little girl. Blessed with the birth of two sons, they looked forward to the next—until she was told she had been sterilized without her knowledge by the very doctor who delivered her son.

The horrifying discovery led to the slow realization that she was not alone, and that many Roma women like herself had been involuntarily sterilized in hospitals in the Czech Republic. Pleas to officials not only fell on deaf ears but added insult to injury.

"My husband and I visited the social services department to demand an explanation and asked if this had happened because we are Romani and the staff were extremely rude to us and threw us out," Gorolová told a gathering at the United Nations in Geneva, on the sidelines of the Durban Review Conference.

Gorolová recalls that the birth of her second child in a hospital in Ostrava in 1990 was a difficult one.

31 "The Story of Elena Gorolova," Durban Review Conference, Geneva, 20–24 April 2009, United Nations, https://www.un.org/en/durbanreview2009/story24.shtml#:.

32 "BBC 100 Women 2018: Who Is on the List?" BBC News, 19 November 2018, https://www.bbc.com/news/world-46225037.

"I was in labour, it was very confusing and there were many doctors all around me," she said. "A nurse came to me with a paper and I signed it. At the time I had no idea what that meant as I was in great pain."

"The next day, the head physician of the maternity ward told me I would never be able to have children again. I began to cry. I was only 21 years old and we wanted to have a little girl. My husband began to cause a scene and for a long time he could not bear the thought that we could not have more children."

Gorolová went on to discover that her fallopian tubes had been severed, making the operation irreversible.

"The nurse told me that previously the method had been to tie the tubes, but that some women had become pregnant despite this," she said. "They didn't want any more Roma children to be born.... I have experienced discrimination since I was a child ... they just don't like the Roma people."

DOCUMENT III

European Roma Rights Centre, "Mob Violence against Roma in Poland," *Roma Rights Journal* (1997)[33]

American Civil Rights movement: Mass campaign against racial segregation and discrimination against African Americans that lasted from 1954 to 1968, characterized by non-violent protest, civil disobedience, sit-ins, and boycotts.

Activists inspired by legal victories in the **American Civil Rights movement** and a landmark victory involving a Romani man winning a police brutality case in Bulgaria, founded the European Roma Rights Centre (ERRC) in the 1990s. An online database contains thousands of news articles detailing the treatment of Roma peoples in the past three decades, including the one excerpted below. Other headlines, such as "18-year-old Romani woman shot dead by security guard in Bulgaria," "UN 'deep alarm' over racism in Hungary as new fascist militia targets Roma" (2019) and "Roma purged from World Cup as Moscow undergoes 'clean-up'" (2018), provide vivid examples of the continuation of anti-Romani violence.

Świebodzice: Town in south-western Poland, close to the German border, that dates to 1279.

Recent research conducted by the ERRC revealed that several Roma communities in Poland are systematically subjected to violent attacks by the local non-Romani population. One such attack took place in the south-western town of **Świebodzice** just before last Christmas. Late in the evening of December 23, 1996, a mob of approximately fifty masked local youths threw burning bottles filled with petrol at houses inhabited by Roma. Mrs. E.S., one of the victims, told the *ERRC*: "I was preparing for Christmas in the kitchen. My two grandchildren who stayed with me were already in bed. All of a sudden, I heard something smashing in the living room and I ran there to see what was happening. I saw that one of the windows was broken and that my curtain was on fire. Then, another burning bottle came in through the second window and my 5-year-old grandson's pajamas caught fire. Luckily enough, my son was here and he quickly took the boy outside and threw him in the snow."

According to Mrs. E.S., violent attacks against Roma in Świebodzice started around two years ago and have since occurred regularly: "They have attacked our houses at least 20 times for the past two years. I can't even count how many times I have changed the windows here. They stand in a long row outside the house and start throwing burning bottles filled with petrol in through the windows. They have also destroyed several cars. There are always a lot of them, at least 20, and sometimes, like in December, there are up to 50 of them. They scream, 'Poland for Poles' and 'We don't want

33 European Roma Rights Centre, "Mob Violence against Roma in Poland," *Roma Rights Journal*, 15 July 1997.

Gypsies here.' I think they are always the same people, but they are difficult to identify, first of all because they come at night when it is dark but also because they often wear masks."

... Romani inhabitants told the *ERRC* that the local police have remained passive despite numerous official complaints on their part. During the attack on December 23, 1996, a few police officers allegedly arrived half an hour after they had been called and did nothing but state that the Roma "should cover the broken windows with something so that their children don't catch a cold over night."

According to the Polish daily ***Gazeta Wyborcza***, which reported the December incident in a local issue on January 20, 1997, Świebodzice Vice-Mayor, Henryk Sawa, stated that, "Nowadays, these young Gypsies are spoiled. Before, they used to know their place. I am not talking about segregation, but they knew where they could play. They did not flash their money around." Mr. Sawa reportedly added, "Such a small community and so much trouble with them." ...

***Gazeta Wyborcza*:** Polish daily newspaper based in Warsaw; founded in 1989 shortly after the collapse of the communist regime.

Roma in the southern town of **Dębica** have also been subjected to similar attacks by groups of local non-Roma. Although the last two years have been relatively peaceful, Miecryslaw Sadowski, a Romani resident of Dębica, remembered at least six violent attacks against the Romani population during the period between 1993 and 1995: "Each time there is a special event of some sort in the town, I know we are in trouble. The worst such events are football matches. After the game is over, they come to attack our houses."

Dębica: A town in Southeastern Poland.

A particularly violent attack against the Dębica Roma took place in June 1994. This started when his nephew, then 13-year old Gniewko David Sadowski, was attacked and severely beaten by a group of around thirty skin heads on the central square at around four in the afternoon. Mr. Sadowski told the *ERRC*: "They broke his ribs and put a trash-can over his head. He walked home in a state of shock and collapsed when he got home. I took him to the hospital and left him there."

Upon his return from the hospital, Mr. Sadowski was met by a big group of people screaming in the street outside the houses inhabited by Roma: "They were armed with bricks and stones and were throwing them at the houses facing the street. I managed to drive my car inside the courtyard and found all our men standing outside the houses, in the courtyard facing the street. They were trying to prevent the mob from getting inside." ...

According to Mr. Sadowski, the police did not react properly: "The police had already been called by the time I got home, but they didn't come until much later, and then they only drove back and forth in their car. They didn't really do anything. Then, finally, when they came inside, we had already caught five of the attackers and we handed them over to the police. The police took them to the police station and told us to come and give testimony."

According to the *ERRC*'s information, an investigation was launched into the incident, but the case seems to have been dropped before it reached the court. Allegedly, four of the suspects escaped to Germany and have not returned to Dębica since, while the fifth was released without being formally charged....

DOCUMENT 112

Bernard Rorke, "A Spectre Is Haunting Europe—Spike in Anti-Roma Pogroms as EU Election Campaigns Kick Off" (2019)[34]

The European Roma Rights Centre wrote this article to draw attention to violence perpetrated against Roma communities during campaigning for the 2019 European Parliament elections. It is illustrative of continuing links between far-right politicians and the instigation of street violence against racialized peoples.

Just one month ago, the **European Roma Rights Centre** (ERRC) published a fact sheet on mob violence and collective punishment and warned of the threats facing Roma communities in countries where **antigypsyism** has been mainstreamed as an "acceptable form of racism." Tragically this warning proved to be all too prescient. Mob violence against Roma in Bulgaria, Italy and France has not occurred in a vacuum—it is politically orchestrated. Antigypsyism is an obscenity, a stain on the European Union and democratic values. It's time to call it out and combat it more forcefully. The message to mainstream political parties is simple: to remain silent is to be complicit.

European Roma Rights Centre: A Roma-led legal organization working to combat anti-Romani racism and human rights abuses.

antigypsyism: Anti-Roma discrimination.

Last week's shocking attacks on Roma homes and property in the Bulgarian town of Gabrovo by gangs of young men following "spontaneous" protests, are the latest incidents of mob violence against Roma in the run up to the European elections. Together with the vicious assaults on vulnerable Roma in Paris and Rome, these outrages serve as a grim reminder that antigypsyism won't be wished away. As the far right mobilizes for votes and against "ethnic replacement," multiculturalism and minorities, one thing is certain, Roma lives will be further endangered between now and election day.... The chilling scenario is that these elections hold the prospect of dramatic gains for right wing extremist forces across Europe....

There is a clear link between **Matteo Salvini**'s talk of deporting irregular Roma and "a mass cleansing street by street, piazza by piazza," and the later events in the rundown Torre Maura suburb of Rome. Screaming "those bastards must burn," a 300-strong far right mob, backed by neo-fascist groups **CasaPound and Forza Nuova**, set fire to dumpsters and cars to prevent the placement of 70 Roma in a local **reception centre**.

Matteo Salvini: Italian politician who has served as deputy prime minister and a member of the European Parliament. He opposes illegal immigration and the European Union and remains a vocal supporter of Vladimir Putin.

CasaPound and Forza Nuova: Italian neo-fascist organizations who espouse social conservatism, extreme nationalism, Euroskepticism, and anti-LGBTQIA+ rights.

reception centres: Institutions that provide housing, food, and medical attention to recently arrived migrants or refugees; conditions vary widely.

34 Bernard Rorke, "A Spectre Is Haunting Europe—Spike in Anti-Roma Pogroms as EU Election Campaigns Kick Off," European Roma Rights Centre, 15 April 2019, http://www.errc.org/news/a-spectre-is-haunting-europe---spike-in-anti-roma-pogroms-as-eu-election-campaigns-kick-off.

... Antigypsyism has been "mainstreamed," for it is no longer the preserve of Nazi sociopaths. Government ministers in Sofia get acquitted of hate speech charges for describing Roma as "brazen, feral, human-like creatures." Recent "spontaneous" attacks on Roma neighbourhoods have been coordinated by a combination of far-right militants and football ultras....

Video footage of this latest violence in Gabrovo shows the mob attacking houses, throwing rocks through the windows and demolishing their chimneys, to the vehement applause of bystanders. On the back of protests bizarrely billed as "say no to aggression," this terror has forced Romani children to stay home from school for their own safety, and families to flee to other towns to stay with relatives....

In France, government spokesman Benjamin Griveaux condemned the series of 25 attacks against Roma between 25 March and 9 April around the outskirts of Paris as an "absolutely unacceptable targeting of the Roma community." This "Gypsy hunt" was sparked by coordinated hoax reports on social media alleging that Roma people in a "white van" were abducting children and planned to rape them or sell their organs.

But many vividly remember that the official face of "the Gypsy hunt" in France was former **President Sarkozy**, whose policy of dawn raids and demolitions of camps followed by swift mass deportations prompted condemnation from the European Parliament in 2010 for "the inflammatory and openly discriminatory rhetoric lending credibility to racist statements and the actions of extreme right-wing groups." ...

President Sarkozy: Nicolas Sarkozy served as President of France from 2007 to 2012. He was convicted on two counts of corruption in 2021.

Beyond the violence, the beatings, burnings, and murders, it is the everyday racism, the routine segregation in schools, towns, and villages; the policies that forcibly evict and push Roma beyond the city limits, out of sight and out of mind, that cultivates complete indifference to their privations and suffering. This indifference amounts to complicity and nourishes what some call the "last acceptable form of racism" in Europe....

PART 6

Racism against Indigenous Peoples

INTRODUCTION

How white Europeans have seen themselves as the "chosen people" or the "best race" is perhaps most obvious in their interactions with Indigenous peoples[1] around the globe, whether close to home, as with the Irish or the Sámi people of the North, or in the East and West Indies and Americas starting in the late fifteenth century. While themselves the descendants of ancient migratory peoples like the Franks and Goths who settled into the Roman Empire, medieval Europeans believed that as Christians they were God's chosen people, superior to all others. While it became difficult for them to maintain this myth in the face of other powerful empires, such as the **Ottoman** or the Chinese, when it came to peoples that Europeans could identify as culturally unsophisticated or as "pagan," their attitude of superiority came to the fore, often, as we have seen in the preceding parts, with deeply negative consequences. Apart from some devout missionaries, such as Bartolomé de las Casas (Document 113) and the Quakers (Document 55), most Europeans believed it to be their inherent right to exploit non-Christian peoples. Beginning with Christopher Columbus in 1492, European sailors forced Indigenous peoples to provide the gold and silver the Europeans believed were abundant in the Indies, and then enslaved them to work in the bullion mines. Columbus and other early explorers saw themselves as crusaders or conquistadors searching for a route to the riches of India and China that would bypass the Muslims who controlled the overland trade routes. They believed they had in fact landed on the eastern coast of India, hence named the inhabitants "Indians." While the Spanish

Ottoman: The Turkish empire centered at Istanbul (formerly Constantinople) that defeated the Byzantine Empire in the fifteenth century.

1 This part adopts a broad definition of the term "Indigenous," and one that acknowledges overlap with other parts of this volume. According to the United Nations Permanent Forum on Indigenous Issues, there are currently more than 370 million Indigenous people in more than 70 countries worldwide. They retain political, economic, cultural, and social practices that are "distinct from those of the dominant societies in which they live." We have included here for comparison sources that reflect European attitudes toward various disparate global populations, including in Northern Europe, Ireland, and Wales, North and South America, and Oceania. See https://www.un.org/esa/socdev/unpfii/documents/5session_factsheet1.pdf.

Aztec: The dominate socio-political power in Mexico prior to European conquest.

smallpox: An infectious virus with a high mortality rate and which disfigured many survivors.

Oceania: Geographical region that includes Australasia, Melanesia, Micronesia, and Polynesia.

conquistadors were at first deeply impressed with the urban civilization of the **Aztec** peoples, they soon discovered they could overcome their significant numerical disadvantage by recruiting the disgruntled Indigenous subjects of the Aztecs. The use of horses and gunpowder weapons was also decisive.

The result was devastating to Indigenous peoples, as were the European diseases such as **smallpox** that wiped out roughly 90 percent of the Indigenous populations of Central and North America. When the Italian explorer Giovanni Caboto (John Cabot) sailed to the coast of North America in 1497/98 on behalf of the English King Henry VII, he saw evidence of large Indigenous communities; when in 1604 the French explorer and colonist Samuel de Champlain arrived in what would be known as New France, these settlements were gone, and the region sparsely populated. This gave Europeans the confidence to settle the region, believing that these lands were virtually empty, and the remaining peoples could be easily accommodated or displaced. In all cases European sailors believed they had the divine right to claim the "newly discovered" lands—the "New World"—for their respective kings or corporations, since they did not regard the local inhabitants as fully human. Over the seventeenth and eighteenth centuries many Indigenous peoples joined with one or the other of the warring European nations, particularly France and England. What is of importance for this Reader is not the specific history of those intertwined relationships, but the attitudes of the Europeans who forced Indigenous peoples to fit into their conceptual schema wherein the colonizers possessed the divine right to conquer and dispossess peoples who were regarded as pagan, soulless, or as inferior peoples by nature suited to slavery, as Aristotle would have it. With the Enlightenment of the eighteenth century came the perspective that Indigenous Peoples were noble savages who remained untouched by the evils of European civilization and therefore lived in a state of innocence (Document 121). Yet this attitude did not improve actual treatment of local peoples by Europeans.

The European exploitation of Indigenous lands, resources, and cultures continued with the nineteenth-century expansion of settler colonial societies, especially in North and South America and **Oceania**. Using stereotypes of "Indians" as lazy, uneducated, heathen, immoral, and dangerous, European bureaucrats, missionaries, and educators pursued aggressive assimilationist policies designed to remove Indigenous autonomy and power. They parceled territories into reservations, removed civil liberties, and restricted fishing and hunting rights. Residential schools in North America and training schools in Australia took hundreds of thousands of children from their families and communities, with the stated aim of "removing the native from the child." Racial scientists continued to debate the efficacy of these programs into the twentieth century. University of London eugenicist Reginald Ruggles

Gates's 1938 research project used blood samples, physical measurements, and photographs of the eye, hair, and skin color, of one hundred children at the **Shubenacadie Indian Residential School** to determine whether any "pure blood" **Mi'kmaq** people survived in Nova Scotia (see also Document 132).[2] An Australian education conference that same year saw teachers debate how the "lesser races" should be educated, whether Aboriginal intelligence was more akin to early man or the mentally unfit, and whether it was "even fair" to make Indigenous students compete with white children in the school system. Identity cards from that period still characterized the "breed" of Indigenous peoples by **full blood, half-caste, and quadroon**.

Shubenacadie Indian Residential School: More than a thousand Mi'kmaq children were removed from their families and placed in this Nova Scotia institution from 1930 to 1967.

Mi'kmaq: Peoples who are part of the Wabanaki Confederacy and live on territories that are now the Atlantic Provinces, the Gaspé region of Quebec, and northern Maine.

full blood, half-caste, and quadroon: Derogatory and outdated terms used to describe a person's ethnic lineage and to delineate whether they had "mixed" with other "races." See Document 56 above.

The Irish and the Welsh continued to be viewed as second-class citizens within the United Kingdom. The English sought control of Ireland since the twelfth century; by the nineteenth century, the Gaelic-speaking population was still dependent on the mainly wealthy English landowning elite. To justify their status, settlers and legislators used anti-Irish stereotypes of people who were unproductive, lazy, dirty, unmodern, rebellious, and ungrateful, while caricatures often mirrored racialized representations of Black and Indigenous peoples (Document 128). Generations of English settlement had also resulted in poverty for much of the Irish population. The 1841 Census found that two-fifths of all families lived in fourth-class accommodations. When a blight led to an 1846 potato crop that was 75 percent smaller than usual, the people of Ireland faced a crisis. Starvation conditions, and diseases related to malnutrition such as typhus, dysentery, and cholera, ravaged the population until 1852. The worst natural disaster in nineteenth-century Europe resulted in at least one million dead and one million emigrants leaving Ireland—a combined 25 percent population loss in six years.[3]

In European popular culture, we see a dichotomy between a fascination with, and a condescension towards, global Indigenous cultures. Several of the documents that follow illustrate instances when Indigenous peoples have been used for entertainment (such as in so-called human zoos) or to sell products—"Eskimos" to promote cold weather products, and "Indians" to advertise tobacco (Documents 122, 124–126). This fascination continues to the present day and often plays out in ways that would be largely unacceptable to a North American audience. In Germany, for instance, there remains a subculture of adults who playact life in the Wild West, complete with costumes, teepees, powwows, and an ongoing obsession with the novels of Karl May, the nineteenth-century author who made the character Winnetou famous.

2 Reginald Ruggles Gates, "The Blood Groups and Other Features of the Micmac Indians," *Journal of the Royal Anthropological Institute of Great Britain and Ireland* 68 (July–December 1938): 283–98.

3 Karen Sonnenlitter, *The Great Irish Famine: A History in Documents* (Peterborough: Broadview Press, 2018).

Sámi: Indigenous people who live in what is now Sweden, Norway, Finland, and parts of Russia. The Sámi have also historically been called Laplanders, a term they consider derogatory.

Ainu: Indigenous people, who before the arrival of Japanese and Russian settlers, lived around the Sea of Okhotsk.

Nivkh: Indigenous people who live on the northern half of Sakhalin Island and on adjacent Russian coast.

At the same time, the Indigenous peoples of northern Europe, including the **Sámi**, the **Ainu**, and the **Nivkh**, have continued to face state-sponsored persecution and assimilationist measures in the modern period. They have responded by forming human rights activist groups to fight for national self-determination, civil rights, and long-held claims to the land, as we see in Documents 133 and 134.

DOCUMENT 113

Spanish Bishop Condemns Spanish Treatment of Indigenous Peoples: Bartolomé de las Casas, *The Spanish Colony* (1552, 1583)[4]

This work, first written in Spanish in 1542 by the **Dominican friar** and bishop of Chiapas, Mexico, Bartolomé de las Casas (1484–1566), describes the cruel treatment of Natives in the New World by his fellow Spaniards. It was subsequently extensively translated and published by Protestant writers as anti-Spanish propaganda. However, in his efforts to show the cruelty of Spanish colonizers, de las Casas described the Indigenous peoples as innocent children, unintentionally encouraging further exploitation. In 1550 de las Casas was called to Spain to account for his criticism, and he responded that Christ called his disciples to preach the gospel gently, not to slaughter the inhabitants.

Dominican friar: A mendicant (itinerant) monk of the Dominican Order established in the thirteenth century to disseminate Catholic teaching.

The Indies were discovered the year one thousand, four hundred, ninety-two, and inhabited by the Spanish the year next after ensuing.... And the first land that they entered to inhabit, was the great and most fertile Isle of **Hispaniola**, which contained six hundred **leagues** in compass. There are other great and infinite Isles round about and in the confines on all sides: which we have seen the most peopled, and the fullest of their own native people, as any other country in the world may be. The firm land lying off from this Island [are] all full of people.... It seems that God has bestowed in that same country ... the greatest portion of mankind.

Hispaniola: Now the island of the Dominican Republic and Haiti.

leagues: A pre-modern measurement indicating the distance that a person could walk in an hour, about five to six kilometers.

God created all these innumerable multitudes in every sort, very simple, without subtlety, or craft, without malice, very obedient, and very faithful to their natural **liege Lords**, and to the Spaniards, whom they serve, very humble, very patient, very desirous of peace making, and peaceful, without brawls and strugglings, without quarrels, without strife, without rancor or hatred, by no means desirous of revenge.

liege Lords: A term arising from medieval feudalism in which a tenant (vassal) of a landlord made an oath to obey his feudal lord in exchange for the lord's protection.

They are also people very gentle, and very tender, and of a complexion, and which can sustain no travel, and do die very soon of any disease whatsoever, in such sort as the very children of Princes and Noble men brought up amongst us, in all commodities, ease, and delicateness, are not more soft than those of that country: yea, although they be the children of labourers. They are also very poor folk, which possess little, neither yet do so much

4 Bartolomé de las Casas, *The Spanish Colonie, or Briefe Chronicle of the Acts and Gestes of the Spaniardes in the West Indies, Called the Newe World, for the Space of xl. Yeeres: ... And nowe First Translated into English, by M.M.S.* (London, 1583), fols. A1r–A4r, Q3r.

as desire to have much worldly goods, & therefore neither are they proud, ambitious, nor covetous.... Their apparel is commonly to go naked: all save their shamefast parts alone covered.... They have their understanding very pure and quick, being teachable and capable of all good learning, very apt to receive our holy Catholic faith, and to be instructed in good and virtuous manners, having less incumbrances and disturbances to the attaining there unto, than all the folk of the world besides, and are so enflamed, ardent, and importune to know and understand the matters of the faith after they have but begun once to taste them.... Undoubtedly these folks should be the happiest in the world, if only they knew God.

Upon these lambs so meek, so qualified & endowed of their maker and creator, as has been said, entered the Spanish incontinent as they knew them, as wolves, as lions, & as tigers most cruel of long time famished ... tear them in pieces, kill them, martyr them, afflict them, torment them, & destroy them by strange sorts of cruelties never neither seen, nor read, nor heard of the like ... so far forth that of above three Millions of souls that were in the Isle of *Hispaniola*, and that we have seen, there are not now two hundred natives of the country. The Isle of *Cuba*, the which is in length as far as from *Valladolid* until *Rome*, is at this day as it were all waste. St. Johns isle, and that of *Jamaica* both of them very great, very fertile, and very fair: are desolate.... For they have been all of them slain, after that they had drawn them out from thence to labour in their minerals in the isle of *Hispaniola*, where there were no more left of the inborn natives of that island....

We are able to yield a good and certain account, that there is within the space of the said 40 years, by those said tyrannies & devilish doings of the Spaniards do to death unjustly and tyrannously more than twelve Millions of souls, men, women, and children. And I verily do believe, and think not to mistake therein, that there are dead more than fifteen Millions of souls....

The cause why the Spanish have destroyed such an infinity of souls, hath been only, that they have held it for their last scope and mark to get gold, and to enrich themselves in a short time, ... or, for to say in a word, the cause hereof hath been their avarice and ambition, which hath seized them the exceedingest in the world in consideration of those lands so happy and rich, and the people so humble, so patient, and so easy to be subdued. Whom they have never had any respect, [esteeming them as] less than of the mire of the streets, and even as much care is it that they have had of their lives and of their souls. And by this means have died so many Millions without faith and without sacraments.

It is a certain verity, and that which also the tyrants themselves know right well and confess, that the Indians throughout all the Indies never wrought any displeasure unto the Spaniards: but rather that they reputed them as come from heaven, until such time as they, or their neighbours had received the first, sundry wrongs, being robbed, killed, forced, and tormented by them....

Now after sundry other forces, violences, and torments, which they wrought against them: the Indians began to perceive, that those were not men descended from heaven. Some of them therefore hid their **victuals**: others hid their wives and children: some others fled into the mountains, to separate themselves a far off from a nation of so hard natured and ghastly conversation. The Spaniards buffeted them with their fists and **bastouades**: pressing also to lay hands upon the Lords of the Towns.... The Spaniards with their Horses, their spears and lances, began to commit murders, and strange cruelties: they entered into Towns, Boroughs, and Villages, sparing neither children, nor old men, neither women with child, neither them that **lay In**, but that they ripped their bellies, and cut them in pieces, as if they had been opening of Lambs shut up in their fold. [De las Casas continues to describe the horrors.] They murdered commonly the Lords and nobility on this fashion: They made certain grates of perches laid on pitchforks, and made a little fire underneath, to the intent, that by little and little yelling and despairing in these torments, they might give up the ghost.

victuals: Food.

bastouades: Likely canes, used to whip a victim's bare soles.

lay In: Period of time for women prior to and after giving birth.

One time I saw four or five of the principal Lords roasted and broiled upon these gridirons.... I have seen all the aforesaid things and others infinite. And forasmuch, as all the people which could flee, hid themselves in the mountains, and mounted on the tops of them, fled from the men so without all manhood, empty of all pity, behaving them as savage beasts, the slaughterers and deadly enemies of mankind: they taught their hounds, fierce dogs, to tear them in pieces at the first view, and ... assailed and devoured an Indian as if it had been a swine. These dogs wrought great destructions and slaughters. And forasmuch as sometimes, although seldom, when the Indians put to death some Spaniards upon good right and law of due Justice: they made a Law between them, that for one Spaniard, they had to slay an hundred Indians....

DOCUMENT 114

Image: Jodocus Hondius, *Headless People of Guiana* (1599)[5]

Sir Walter Raleigh: Raleigh or Ralegh (1552–1618) was an English soldier and explorer favored by Queen Elizabeth I. He played a lead role in the English colonization of North America.

As seen in Document 47 above with the image of the "Blemmyes" of Africa, Europeans believed that there lived headless people in other parts of the world. The myth persisted, but now included in **Sir Walter Raleigh**'s account of his visit to Guiana, South America, printed in 1599. The engraver was Jodocus Hondius (1563–1612).

5 Map insert, p. 11, in the Levinus Hulsius edition of Sir Walter Raleigh, *Brevis & admiranda descriptio regni Guianae, avri abundantissimi, in America* (1599).

DOCUMENT 115

From Anonymous, *Description of the Samoyeden Land in Tartary* (1612)[6]

This is one of many travel accounts describing the activities of the merchant fleets of the Dutch Republic (Dutch East India Company) as they traversed the globe, setting up major trading colonies in the West and East Indies. In the process, the Dutch subordinated local populations to their economic dominance. They were also major figures in the global slave trade. Finding shorter routes to the Far East inspired some to explore the Arctic waters, and this whetted the appetite of Dutch readers for information on the peoples of that region. This pamphlet, printed in 1612 in Dutch, the writer claims came from a Russian original of 1609.

The appearance or glimmer of profit and benefits have always persuaded people to look at unknown countries and peoples. Also, the beautiful pelts (which were brought to us by the Russian merchants) were so greatly desired by our merchants that they became desirous of traveling through their lands, which were unknown to us. They have been helped in this somewhat by a journey which is described to us by a Russian who traveled from Moscow to … **Pechora**, where the people there received the Christian faith in 1518, and further to the **Oby**, and traveling further afield, where some fables were mixed in [with the account] of **Slatababa**, the golden old woman with her children and the monstrous people across the Oby.… [The English inspired the Dutch] to lust after the riches of China and Cathay out of which they had long been locked, so they hoped to find a way to these coasts.…

There lives a people in **Moscovia** who are named the children of Aniconij, and are of peasant origins, sprouting from a countryman named Anica … [who] being rich … was prickled with great desire, wanting to know what kind of land was possessed and populated by the people who brought the annual business in valuable pelts and many other wares, who were strange in speech, in clothing, religion, and manners, naming them Samoieden [Sámi], and also giving them many other names.… [The Sámi] saying that they did not live in cities, but that they lived together in tribes very peacefully and were ruled by some of the eldest among them, were also impure in their eating, and that they lived from the wild things they caught, knowing neither grain nor bread, and most are good shooters with bows which they

Pechora: A town in the Komi Republic, in northern Russia.

Oby: The Ob River in Western Siberia.

Slatababa: In the Ob River region a legend arose of a statue of the Golden Woman or Golden Hag that Europeans believed the Indigenous peoples of Siberia venerated.

Moscovia: The dominant princedom of Russia, originally the Grand Duchy of Moscow. By the sixteenth century its rulers had become the Tsars (emperors) of Russia.

6 Anonymous, *Beschryvinghe Vander Samoyeden Landt in Tartarien. Nieulijcks onder't ghebiedt der Moscoviten gebracht.… Met een verhael Vande opsoeckingh ende ontdeckinge vande nieuwe deurgang ofte straet int Noordwesten na de Rijcken van China ende Cathay* … (Amsterdam, 1612), fols. A2r–v, B1r–B4r. Translated by Gary Waite.

make from rough wood ... so these Aniconij became very powerful, and people wondered where they got these terrible riches, not knowing where they came from.

Boris Goddenoof: Boris Godunov, at the time informal Regent, then Tsar from 1598 to 1605.

... [At the court was the Tsar's brother-in-law **Boris Goddenoof**, who saw the potential wealth for Russia in the lands to the North and East] ... who showed great friendliness to them ... paying close attention to ... what riches the Empire could benefit from.... Boris began to burn with desire and commanded this investigation. Yes, he loved them as his own children, yes raised them [himself], giving them free letters in the Tsar's names, that they might possess their own lands without contradiction and use them eternally and inherently according to their will and pleasure, without having to provide any tributes....

[After his scheme was discovered by the Tsar,] Boris had some captains and some poor noblemen who were subservient to him, commanding them to go to the people of Aniconij ... so that they could be as ambassadors, providing them also with some soldiers, and also gifts of little worth to give to the peoples that they should come across ... to spy out good locations for fortifications or castles and that they should bring some of the people back to Moscow, were it possible to do so....

Having arrived, they did as they were commanded, showing great friendship to the people there, examining diligently everything that they saw, and showing the honor and giving over the many things of little worth which they pretended were very expensive and valuable, yes showing them great cheer and joy. The people, seeing these gifts, fell on their knees, seeing these men in their valuable clothes, not having seen this before, and believed that they were gods. The Moscovites spoke through translators who were Sámi, who ... told the [Sámi] about their Tsar, that he is a terrestrial god. Yes, they said so many similar things that these poor people were attracted to such wishful thinking, that they could not have wished for more, so they took it immediately. Yes, so much so that they agreed to allow some Moscovites to live with them for a long time, and that they would learn their language ... becoming subjects of the Moscovite Tsar, and to allow themselves to be appraised by the Moscovites for the annual tribute to the Moscovite Empire, yes, from adults to children. They began this with a pair of sable blankets which were accounted by them of little value, but regarded by the Moscovites as like jewels.... [The group travelled further north, observing the land], and also various Sámi, some of whom were riding on Elk, some sitting on sleds which were drawn by reindeer, some by dogs, which ran as fast as deer. In summary, they saw many wondrous things, and recorded everything in an orderly fashion, so that everything would be properly named when they returned. They took some willing Sámi with them, and they allowed some Moscovites into their land to learn the language. And so they returned to Moscow where they brought all this good news to the abovementioned Boris, and Boris to the Tsar, and looked with amazement upon the Sámi which they had brought, commanding them to shoot, which they were proud to do, that no one could believe it....

On the other side these wild people observed the life of the people in Moscow with great amazement, also the manner of the city, and more similar things. But they looked upon the Tsar with terror, being so expensively clothed, sitting on horse [surrounded by his uniformed guard] ... in sum, they believed that they found themselves before God's throne, and wished that they were instead with their fellow brothers to proclaim to them how blessed they were to obey such a head as the Tsar, whom they believed to be a god. They also tasted the food which they were given to eat in Moscow, asserting now that it tasted much better than the raw beasts in their land, or dried fish.

In summary they promised to accept the Tsar as their lord, and promised also to move their fellow brothers from afar to him as well. And further they requested the Tsar to be gracious to send them governors to rule over them, and that these representatives would receive their treasures from them. Concerning their idolatry, they would not abolish it and remain still in their customary ways, but they also believed that the Christian faith could be planted there if they received some qualified teachers....

DOCUMENT 116

King Charles I's Decree against Irish Beggars (1629)[7]

This two-page proclamation by the government of King Charles I was first published in 1629 and reprinted several times until 1634. It reflects the growing anxiety on the part of English elites over vagabonds and Travelers, as seen in Part 5 (Documents 94–96) above on the Roma.

Rogue: A person who flouts social norms.

under the colour: In the guise of.

Constable: Policing in England at this time was rudimentary, with sheriffs responsible for applying royal law in a county, assisted by constables.

Whereas this Realm has of late been pestered with a great number of Irish Beggars, who live here idly and dangerously, and are of ill example to the Natives of this Kingdom; And whereas the multitude of English **Rogues** & Vagabonds do much more abound than in former times, some wandering and begging **under the colour** of Soldiers and Mariners, others under the pretext of impotent persons, whereby they become a burden to the good people of the Land: All which happens by the neglect of the due execution of the Laws formerly with great providence made, for relief of the true poor and indigent, and for the punishment of the sturdy Rogues and Vagabonds:[8] For the reforming therefore of so great a mischief, and to prevent the many dangers which will ensue by the neglect thereof, The King's most excellent Majesty, by the advice of his Privy Council, and of his Judges, do straightly charge and command ... that all Irish Beggars which now are in any parts of this Kingdom wandering or begging, under what pretence soever, shall forthwith depart this Realm, and return into their own Country, and there abide: And if any Irish man or woman, shall after the end of six weeks, to be accounted from the date hereof, be found wandering or begging, that then he or she shall be apprehended, used, ordered, and punished as Rogues and Vagabonds, by the Laws of this Realm, and then shall be conveyed from **Constable** to Constable unto one of these Ports. [A list of ports follows.]

And his Majesty does further charge and command, that at the said Ports they be shipped at the charge of that County and Port respectively, those Ports having been the cause of this disorder, by permitting them to be there landed, contrary to the Laws, and that from thence, with the next wind and convenient means, they be transported and set on land on some

---

7 *By the King (Charles I). A Proclamation for the speedy sending away of the Irish Beggers out of this Kingdome, into their owne Countrey, and for the suppressing and ordering of the English Rogues and Vagabonds, according to the Lawes* (London: Bonham Morton and John Bill, 1629), fols. A1r–A1v.

8 These refer to the Poor Laws established in the sixteenth century transforming poor relief from a religious charity to a community-based form of support and distinguishing sharply between the deserving poor—widows, children, and the disabled—and the undeserving, those who could work but would not.

part of that Kingdom of Ireland, there to be disposed of according to the Laws of that Kingdom: And that from henceforth no man be so hardy, as to convey or bring into this Realm, any Irish person from that Kingdom, who is likely to be a Beggar here, nor that any such be suffered to Land in any Port of this Realm, upon pain of such forfeitures and penalties, as by the Laws of this Kingdom, or that Kingdom may be inflicted upon them for the same, and upon such further pains and punishments, as his Majesty by his Prerogative Royal may inflict or impose upon them....

DOCUMENT 117

From Edmund Campion, *Two Histories of Ireland* (1633)[9]

Jesuit: Member of the Society of Jesus, the anti-Protestant religious Order founded by St. Ignatius Loyola in 1540 to spread Catholicism.

Edmund Campion (1540–81) was an English **Jesuit** who in 1581 was arrested for high treason, as being a Catholic priest was then illegal in Anglican (Protestant) England. He was executed and in 1970 named a saint of the Catholic Church. According to his dedicatory foreword, Campion wrote his description from Dublin in 1571.

alms-givers: Providing money to the poor as a form of religious devotion.

Clerks: Clerics or clergy.

uplandish: Those from the "uplands," i.e., rural, Gaelic Irish.

Mere Irish: Archaic for Gaelic-speaking Irish people.

kyne: Archaic for cows.

THE [Irish] People are thus inclined; religiously frank, amorous, ireful, sufferable, of pains infinite, very glorious, many sorcerers, excellent horsemen, delighted with Wars, great **alms-givers**, passing in hospitality: the lewder sort both **Clerks** and Lay-men, are sensual and loose to lechery above measure. The same being virtuously bred up or reformed, are such mirrors of holiness and austerity, that other Nations retain but a show or shadow of devotion in comparison of them. As for abstinence and fasting which these days make so dangerous, this is to them a familiar kind of chastisement: In which virtue and diverse other, how far the best excel, so far in gluttony and other hateful crimes the vitious they are worse than too bad. They follow the dead corpses to the grave with howlings and barbarous out-cries, pitiful in appearance, whereof grew (as I suppose) the Proverb, to weep Irish. The **uplandish** are lightly abused to believe and avouch idle miracles and revelations vain and childish, greedy of praise they be, and fearful of dishonour. And to this end they esteem their Poets who write Irish learnedly, and pen their sonnets heroical, for the which they are bountifully rewarded. But if they send out libels in dispraise, thereof the Gentlemen, especially the **Mere Irish**, stand in great awe. They love tenderly their foster children, and bequeath to them a child's portion, whereby they nourish sure friendship, so beneficial every way, that commonly five hundred **kyne** and better are given in reward to win a noble man's child to foster. They are sharp-witted, lovers of learning, capable of any study whereunto they bend themselves, constant in travel, adventurous, intractable, kind-hearted, secret in displeasure.

9 Edmund Campion, *Two Histories of Ireland. The one written by Edmund Campion, the other by Meredith Hanmer Dr of Divinity* (Dublin, 1633), 13–20.

Of the Mere Irish

In some corners of the land they used a damnable superstition, leaving the right arms of their Infants males **unchristened** (as they termed it) to the intent it might give a more ungracious and deadly blow....

Solinus writes that they wanted (because they would seem Terrible and Martial) to imbrue their faces in the blood of their Enemies slain. ***Strabo*** the famous Geographer ... tells (without asseveration) that the Irish were great Gluttons, eaters of man's flesh: and counted it Honourable for Parents deceased, to be eaten up of their Children, and that in open sight they meddled with their Wives, Mothers, and Daughters [Campion says this was not incredible, given ancient stories of the Scots and Sythians]....

The Honourable state of Marriage they much abused, either in contracts, unlawful meetings, **the Levitical and Canonical degrees of prohibition**, or in divorce at pleasure, or in omitting Sacramental solemnities, or in retaining either Concubines or Harlots for Wives. Yea even at this day, where the Clergy is faint, they can be content to Marry for a year and a day of probation, and at the year's end, to return her home upon any light quarrels, if the Gentlewoman's friends be weak and unable to avenge the injurie. Never heard I of so many dispensations for Marriage, as those men shew, I pray God grant they be all authentic and built upon sufficient warrant....

Clear men they are of Skin and hue, but of themselves careless and bestial. Their Women are well favoured, clear coloured, fair handed, big and large, suffered from their infancy to grow at will, nothing curious of their feature and proportion of body.

... Shamrocks, Water-cresses, Roots, and other herbs they feed upon: Oatmeal and Butter they cram together. They drink Whey, Milk, and Beef broth, Flesh they devour without bread, **corn** such as they have they keep for their horses. In haste and hunger they squeeze out the blood of raw flesh, and ask no more dressing thereto, the rest boils in their stomachs with **Aquavitae**, which they swill in after such a surfeit, by quarts & **pottles**. Their kyne they let bleed which grow to a jelly they bake and over-spread with Butter, and so eat it in lumps....

unchristened: That is, unbaptized, although how this was done during the pouring of holy water over the head of the infant during baptism is unclear.

***Solinus*:** Gaius Julius Solinus (3rd century CE), a Roman geographer whose *De mirabilibus mundi* or "the wonders of the world," was based on Pliny.

***Strabo*:** Greek geographer and historian who died c. 24 CE.

the Levitical and Canonical degrees of prohibition: The degrees of consanguinity (blood relation); the Catholic Church maintained seven degrees, but allowed marriage of cousins.

corn: Generic term for grain, including wheat.

Aquavitae: Literally "water of life"; distilled spirits.

pottles: A liquid measure of about two liters.

DOCUMENT 118

Henry More on Indigenous Peoples of the Americas, from *An Explanation of the Grand Mystery of Godliness* (1660)[10]

In this work Henry More, a prominent Anglican philosopher of the **Cambridge Platonist school**, associates Native American religious practice with devil worship, and compares this to English witches, as well as to Jews, Muslims, and religious nonconformists. While some of the peoples described here did perform human sacrifice, the practice was hardly as universal as More suggests; one might also recall that the judicial treatment of criminals, heretics, and witches in Europe was also bloodthirsty.

Cambridge Platonist school: A loosely affiliated group of philosophers who used the ancient Greek thinker Plato to defend Christian beliefs against skepticism.

For Mankind being so much sunk and fallen from God by the temptation of the Devil....

Of which the whole *New-found World* seems to be an ample Testimony; there being very few places in America, but such as were discovered to be palpably and visibly under the power of the **old Serpent**, their religious Rites and Ceremonies being as uncouth and antic and more bloody and cruel than those that Witches are known to be tied to here. For the mind of these Apostate Spirits is, that the *Remnant* of the *Law of Nature* and *Light of Reason* in man should be quite obliterated, and that mankind should be wholly their Vassals, and that they should forget the Nobleness of their own condition, and stoop to whatsoever they require of them, which are commonly such things as become none but Mad-men and Beasts....

old Serpent: The serpent of the Garden of Eden story of the Fall, Genesis 2. Christian interpreters believed the serpent to be the devil in disguise.

5. In New-Spain they sought pardon of their Idols by whipping themselves on the naked shoulders, and taking up earth and eating it. In *Peru* they lay prostrate on the ground before their Idols, the more Zealous not sparing to pluck out their own eyes in a blind devotion. In *Hispaniola*, when they sacrificed, they were wont to thrust a consecrated hook down their throats to fetch all out of their stomachs; which done they sat round their Idol in an antic posture, wry-necked and cross-legged, praying for the acceptance of their Sacrifice.

6. The Priests and religious at *Mexico* were wont to rise at Midnight, having cast incense before their Idol, to retire into a large place where many lights were burning, and there with lancets and bodkins to pierce the calves of their legs near to the bones, anointing their Temples with the blood. They would also slit their **members** in the midst in a frantic pursuance of a

members: Genitalia.

10 Henry More, *An explanation of the grand mystery of godliness, or, A true and faithfull representation of the everlasting Gospel of our Lord and Saviour Jesus Christ* (London, 1660), 76–87.

thankless Chastity. They whipped themselves also with cords full of knots, besides their tedious and destructive fastings. These sad Ceremonies they also used in *Peru,* where they **swinged** themselves with stinging Nettles, and struck themselves over the shoulders with hard stones.

swinged: Whipped or scourged.

These and the like abuses ... which Satan has put upon Mankind, are a demonstration of his great contempt and hatred of us. But we shall come nearer now to make good that charge, which our Blessed Saviour, who came to destroy his dominion, most justly has laid upon this Usurper, *That he was a Murderer from the beginning*:[11] which is most evident from that execrable custom of *Sacrificing of men to him* ... which was an abomination practiced of old in most parts of the World, as the Testimony of Historians will make good.

Chap. XIV ... 1. The knowledge of this is fresh concerning the *Americans,* as that they in Virginia sacrificed Children to the Devil, as also in *Peru* for the health and prosperity of the ***Ingua***, and for success in war. The same they do in *Brazil.* The People of *Guiana*, of ***Paria*** and other adjacent parts do not only sacrifice men, but some of them after feed upon the sacrifice. ...

***Ingua*:** Presumably the Sapa Inca, the semi-divine emperor of the Incan Empire.

***Paria*:** Peru.

***Acosta*:** The Jesuit missionary and naturalist José de Acosta (c. 1539–1600), whose *Natural and Moral History of the Indies* was published in Spanish in 1590 and translated into several languages.

2. In *Florida* the Devil appears to them and complains that he is thirsty: But nothing quenches his thirst but the blood of men. ***Acosta*** relates of the *Mexicans*, that their Priests would tell their Kings that their Gods died for hunger: the meaning whereof was, that they must forthwith go out to war to get Captives for Sacrifices to their Gods.

3. In *Peru*, at the Inauguration of their new *Ingua*, they sacrificed two hundred children; they either cut off their necks, anointing themselves on the face with their blood, or drowned them and so buried them with certain Ceremonies....

4. The *Mexicans* indeed ... sacrificed only Captives to their Idols. But they were unmercifully lavish of the blood of their conquered enemy, their Sacrifices being often repeated, and they sacrificing at least forty or fifty at a time, making them to ascend to the top of an high Terrace in the Court of the Temple, where the chief Priest (as also his assistants) being clad in most ugly and diabolical dresses to astonish the people, opened the Breast of the Captive with a wonderous dexterity, pulled out the *Heart* with his hands, and showed it smoking to the *Sun*, to whom he did offer this heat and fume of the Heart, and then cast it at the Idols face, and with a spurn of his foot tumbled the Body of the Sacrifice down the stairs of the Temple.

5. ... There is one nasty piece of Cruelty that he says was used in *Mexico*, which was the **flaying** of a Slave, and appareling another man with his skin, who was to go dancing and leaping through all the houses and market-places

flaying: Skinning alive, a horrific form of execution reserved in Europe for convicted traitors.

11 Cf. John 8:44 (RSV), see Document 1 above.

of the City to beg money for the Idols; and they that refused to give, he was to give them a slap on the face with the bloody corner of the skin.

6. This is ill enough; but that something worse in *New-Spain*, where they flayed a woman, and covered a man with her skin, who was to dance about the streets two days together. So *despitefully Cruel and Tyrannical* has the *Rule of the Devil* been in the New-found Pagan world; and yet we shall not find him much better in the Old. For there we shall also find him a blood-thirsty murderer in most of the parts thereof.

DOCUMENT 119

From Georgius Hornius and Balthasar Bekker, *Church History, from the Creation of the World until the Year of the Lord* (1666, 1685)[12]

Composed originally by Georgius Hornius (1620–70), a German Reformed Protestant professor at the University of Leiden, this history of world religions was brought up to date in 1685 by Balthasar Bekker, a Reformed minister at Amsterdam who became famous for his *The Bewitched World* (*De Betooverde Weerelde*) of 1690–94 in which he denied demons a place in the natural world.

The new World, which is also named West Indies and America, was in the year 1492 discovered by Christopher Columbus under the reign of Ferdinand and Isabella Queen of Castile. The Spaniards have so exhausted the same with murder, that today the provinces are for the most part deserted. The abovementioned kingdoms were these two:

First, Mexico, which was established in 1327, whose last king was **Montezuma**, from whom the leader of the Spaniards seized the city of Mexico in 1502. Montezuma himself was stoned to death by the Mexicans, or perhaps, as in another account, strangled by the Spaniards in 1521.

Second, Peru or Cuscu, which **Franciscus Pizarba** discovered in 1525, and defeated the king **Atarus lipa**, imprisoning him, and contrary to his promise, strangled him, bringing the same region under the control of the Spaniards.

The Chileans and most of the **Arancanen** for the most part successfully defended themselves against the Spaniards to maintain their freedom. Among these was **Valdivia**, leader of the Spaniards, captured around the year 1551, and to whom they poured molten gold into his mouth as a reproach.

The other parts of America are wildernesses without law, without king, and especially without religion, apart from that in Florida, Virginia, New Netherlands, New France, where some people are subject to their kings.

Montezuma: Moctezuma Xocoyotzin (c. 1466–29 June 1520), Aztec ruler during the Spanish conquest.

Franciscus Pizarba: Francisco Pizarro (1478–1541), Spanish Conquistador who led the conquest of Peru.

Atarus lipa: Atahualpa, the last Inca Emperor whose realm was conquered by Pizarro.

Arancanen: Spanish term for the Mapuche people living in South-central Chile and Southwestern Argentina.

Valdivia: Pedro de Valdivia (1497–1553), Spanish conquistador and first royal governor of Chile, captured and killed in 1553 by the Mapuche. The stories of his death are varied, and all related by captured Mapuche, as no Spaniards survived the defeat.

12 Georgius Hornius and Balthasar Bekker, *Kerkelycke Historie, Van de Scheppinge des Werelts, tot 't Jaer des Heeren 1666 …*, 2nd ed. (Amsterdam, 1685), 72–77. These sections come from a separately titled section, *Short and Clear Introduction to a General World History (Korte en Klare Inleydinge Tot een Algemeyne Wereltlycke Historie; Van't Begin des Werelts).* Translated by Gary Waite.

DOCUMENT 120

From Cristobal Acuna, *Voyages and Discoveries in South-America* (1698)[13]

Cristóbal Diatristán de Acuña (1597–c. 1676) was a Spanish Jesuit missionary and rector of the Jesuit college of Cuenca, Peru. In 1639 he accompanied the Spanish naturalist Pedro Teixeira on an exploration of the Amazon, based on which he wrote his *Nuevo Descubrimiento del Gran Rio de las Amazonas* (*New Discovery of the Great Amazon River*), published in Spanish in 1641, followed by a French translation in 1682 and this English version in 1698.

THE Town of St. *Francis* in the Province of *Quito* is one of the finest in *America*; it is built upon one of those stupendous Mountains, which the Spaniards call *Cordeliers*, and *Tierras*, half a degree South of the **Equinoctial Line**; yet is it of the most agreeable Temperature, and the most plentiful and healthful Place in all *Peru*, and is never incommoded by excessive Heat. In 1635, 1636, and 1637, Captain *John de Palacios* having undertaken to attempt the Discovery of this River, to that end made a small Provision of Arms, desiring rather to acquaint himself with the Country, and to people it, than to subdue the Inhabitants of those Provinces by force of Arms. Several Monks of the **Order of St. *Francis*** were desirous to accompany him to **essay** the Conversion of these Barbarians....

Equinoctial Line: The Equator, dividing the world in half north and south.

Order of St. *Francis*: A mendicant religious order established in the early thirteenth century by St. Francis to teach and missionize.

essay: Archaic word meaning to attempt something.

These ... arrived at the Province of the long-haired Indians: This Country they found well peopled, but not being able to make any Establishment here by reason of the rough Treatment they met with from the Inhabitants, some of them gave over the Attempt, and returned to ***Quito***, but others were more resolute, and continued with Captain *de Palacios*, together with some few Soldiers that were always faithful to him: But these being almost all destroyed in several Battles, in one of which at last the Captain himself was killed, the Monks made their Escape as well as they could, and the two Lay-Friars we have spoken of, one of whom was *Dominic de Britto*, and the other *Andrew de Tolede*, dexterously saved themselves from the hands of the Indians; and having got to their **Bark**, with six Soldiers that remained, abandoned themselves to Providence, and suffered their Bark to be driven at the Pleasure of the Winds and Streams.

***Quito*:** Capital of Ecuador.

Bark: Barque, a small, sailed ship.

It pleased God so to favour their Voyage, that after they had been carried from Province to Province upon this great River, they happily landed at

13 Cristobal Acuna, *Voyages and discoveries in South-America the first up the river of Amazons to Quito in Peru, and back again to Brazil, perform'd at the command of the King of Spain by Christopher D'Acugna* ... (London, 1698), 32–35.

Para, a City in *Brazil*, forty Leagues distant from the Mouth of the *Amazon* Southward. The *Portuguese* possess it, and have made it a good Garrison, belonging to the Government of ***Maragnon***. The two Lay-Friars and the Soldiers were inquired of about their long and strange Voyage, but they were all eight of 'em so stupid, that they had made no particular Remark on any thing; only they said they had passed through divers Provinces of different Barbarians, who eat the Men which they take in War. ... [The friars then conversed with the governor of Maragnon.] They told him they went from *Peru*, that their Monastery was in the City of *Quito*; that they came out with many of their Brethren to labour to convert the wild People, but that the Indians had a greater mind to eat 'em, than to hear 'em preach; that their Captain being dead, and their Brethren put to flight, they with six Soldiers had put themselves into a Bark which miraculously came ashore at *Para*; and that they were ready to return to *Peru*, if they could meet with a convenient Passage. The Governor having deliberated on this Report, believed God had offered him a fair occasion to serve his Religion and his Country, and that he ought to attempt that Design in which so many others had failed.

Maragnon: Brazilian state of Maranhão. Saint Louis (Lewis) is the capital city.

DOCUMENT 121

From Denis Diderot, *Supplement to Bougainville's Voyage* (1772)[14]

Denis Diderot (1713–84) was one of the leading intellectuals of eighteenth-century France, and a proponent of Enlightenment philosophy. His most famous work was the multi-volume *Encyclopédie*, a compendium of knowledge that included articles by himself and other philosophers. This excerpt is from one of Diderot's controversial works, *Le supplément au voyage de Bougainville*, published in 1771, which contains various fictional stories intended to critique modern French society. In this story set in Tahiti, a Tahitian elder speaks to some French visitors, led by Bougainville.

An old man is speaking, the father of a large family. When the Europeans first arrived, he did not appear in any way frightened, curious, or surprised, but looked on them with disdain. When they approached him, he turned his back on them and retreated to his hut. But his troubled silence betrayed his thoughts only too well, and inwardly he mourned his native land and the passing of its golden years. Upon Bougainville's departure, as the Tahitians thronged the shore, clinging to his garments and clasping his comrades in their arms, weeping, the old man solemnly stepped forward and said:

"Weep, unhappy Tahitians! Weep! Not, though, at the leaving of these cruel, ambitious men, but at their coming. For one day you will see them for who they are. One day they will return, brandishing in one hand that **stick of wood** which you see attached to this man's belt and, in the other, the blade which hangs from that man's side. They will come to put you in chains and to cut your throats; they will subject you to their every excess and vice. And one day you will serve under them, and you will be as base, corrupted, and as wretched as they. Yet—as my time draws near, I take comfort in the knowledge that I will not live to see the calamity I foretell. Oh Tahitians! Oh my friends! There is a way by which you might spare yourselves this grievous fate. But I would rather die than offer you this counsel. May they depart, and may they live."

stick of wood: A crucifix.

Then, turning to Bougainville, he continued: "And you, leader of these brigands who obey your every command, quickly remove your vessel from our shores. We are innocent and contented; our happiness you can but

14 From Caroline Warman, ed., *Tolerance: The Beacon of the Enlightenment* (Cambridge: Open Book, 2017), 114–15. Denis Diderot, "Le supplément au voyage de Bougainville," in *Correspondance Littéraire*, ed. Friedrich-Melchior Grimm, issues of September 1773, October 1773, March 1774, April 1774; first published in Denis Diderot, *Œuvres*, vol. III, ed. Naigeon (Paris: Chez Desray et Déterville, 1798), 382–84. Used under CC BY 4.0.

disturb. We are guided by nature's purest instinct, and you have sought to erase its imprint from our souls. Here, all things are everyone's, yet you have preached some or other distinction between 'yours' and 'mine.' Our wives and daughters belong to us all equally, and you have shared this privilege with us; but in doing so you have roused in them an unknown fury. In your arms, they have become deranged, and you have become enraged in theirs. They have formed a hatred for one another, and you have butchered each other over them; they have returned to us stained with your blood. We are free, yet in our earth you have buried the title deeds to our future enslavement. You are neither god nor demon; who, then, are you to make us your slaves? Orou! Since you understand the language of these men, tell us all, as you have told me, what they have written on that strip of metal: 'This land is ours.' Yours, you say? How so? Because you have set foot here? If one day a Tahitian were to arrive on your shores and carve into one of your stones or the bark of one of your trees: 'This land belongs to the people of Tahiti,' what would you say then? So you are the stronger! What of it? When one of those worthless trinkets which are strewn about your vessel was taken, you cried out and wrought vengeance; and immediately you conceived a plan to plunder an entire Country. You are no slave, and would sooner die than become one; yet you wish to enslave us. You think then that Tahitians are incapable of dying in defence of their freedom? Well may you look to seize hold of him as you would a dumb beast—the Tahitian is your brother. You are both children of nature. What right do you have over him that he does not have over you? When you came, did we set upon you? Did we pillage your vessel? Did we make you our captive and leave you to the arrows of our enemies? Did we yoke you to our ploughs and put you to work in the fields like animals? No, we treated you in our own image. Let us alone with our ways; they are wiser and more honest than yours. We have no desire to trade what you call our ignorance for your useless enlightenment."

DOCUMENT 122

Image: Laplanders and Rein Deer as Exhibited at the Egyptian Hall, Piccadilly (1822)[15]

The previous parts have illustrated examples of the European practice of organizing ethnological shows (or human zoos) as pseudo-education and entertainment. This image shows an exhibition of Sámi peoples, derogatorily referred to as "Laplanders" (see p. 272). The British Museum describes this image, in part, as: "Karrina, a woman from Lapland, sitting in front of a dwelling constructed on poles and covered with furs, taking a token from a gentleman in a top-hat, the foremost of a crowd of Europeans visiting the exhibition, several of whom crowd around a pen full of reindeer to left and clothes and weapons displayed on the wall behind; Jennes, Karrina's husband, stands beside her to right with their five-year old son playing with a toy mounted soldier on wheels, watched by a soldier who stands with a lady on each arm."

15 Laplanders, Rein Deer & c. as Exhibited at the Egyptian Hall, Piccadilly, 1822, and Just arrived from Bullock's Museum, the greatest novelty in Hull: to be seen, at no. 13 Queen-Street, the only two esquimaux indians, ever brought to this kingdom: male and female, from the frozen regions of the North ..., Wellcome Collection.

DOCUMENT 123

Charles Dickens on "The Noble Savage" (1853)[16]

In 1853 British author Charles Dickens wrote the following article for his weekly magazine *Household Words*, in response to a London art exhibit showcasing paintings of Indigenous peoples in the American West. Dickens takes issue with what he sees as the romanticized use of the term "noble savage" to denote non-European peoples who represent the innately good side of human nature because they have not been corrupted by civilization. In the decades following Dickens's piece, the term took on a more critical tone, and was used more frequently to critique, rather than praise, Indigenous peoples.

To come to the point at once, I beg to say that I have not the least belief in the Noble Savage. I consider him a prodigious nuisance, and an enormous superstition. His calling rum fire-water, and me a pale face, wholly fail to reconcile me to him. I don't care what he calls me. I call him a savage, and I call a savage a something highly desirable to be civilised off the face of the earth. I think a mere gent (which I take to be the lowest form of civilisation) better than a howling, whistling, clucking, stamping, jumping, tearing savage. It is all one to me, whether he sticks a fish-bone through his visage, or bits of trees through the lobes of his ears, or bird's feathers in his head; whether he flattens his hair between two boards, or spreads his nose over the breadth of his face, or drags his lower lip down by great weights, or blackens his teeth, or knocks them out, or paints one cheek red and the other blue, or tattoos himself, or oils himself, or rubs his body with fat, or crimps it with knives. Yielding to whichsoever of these agreeable eccentricities, he is a savage—cruel, false, thievish, murderous; addicted more or less to grease, entrails, and beastly customs; a wild animal with the questionable gift of boasting; a conceited, tiresome, bloodthirsty, monotonous humbug.

Yet it is extraordinary to observe how some people will talk about him, as they talk about the good old times; how they will regret his disappearance, in the course of this world's development, from such and such lands where his absence is a blessed relief and an indispensable preparation for the sowing of the very first seeds of any influence that can exalt humanity; how, even with the evidence of himself before them, they will either be determined

16 Charles Dickens, "The Noble Savage," in *Household Words: A Weekly Journal* 1, no. 40 (New York: McElrath and Barker, 1853): 337–39.

to believe, or will suffer themselves to be persuaded into believing, that he is something which their five senses tell them he is not....

It is not the miserable nature of the noble savage that is the new thing; it is the whimpering over him with maudlin admiration, and the affecting to regret him, and the drawing of any comparison of advantage between the blemishes of civilisation and the tenor of his swinish life. There may have been a change now and then in those diseased absurdities, but there is none in him.

[Dickens next uses examples of Black peoples being exhibited in England as evidence of other "Noble Savages."]

To conclude as I began. My position is, that if we have anything to learn from the Noble Savage, it is what to avoid. His virtues are a fable; his happiness is a delusion; his nobility, nonsense.

DOCUMENT 124

From *The Diary of Abraham Ulrikab* (1880)[17]

Abraham Ulrikab (1845–81) was 35 years old when he wrote a diary about his experiences of being one of eight Inuit who traveled to Europe in 1880 to take part in a human zoo. Persuaded by an agent for German zoo owner Carl Hagenbeck, the Inuit from Labrador and Greenland were promised financial compensation, the chance to travel, and an opportunity to educate Europeans. Educated himself by **Moravian missionaries** in Labrador, Abraham was literate in **Inuktitut**, English, and German. His diary entries explain that the experience was far from what Abraham expected. The families were often put on display next to animals and made to demonstrate their seal hunting and kayaking skills for audiences. While on exhibition in Paris, all members of both families died from smallpox, against which they were unvaccinated. Their skeletons were exhumed and added to the anthropological collection of a French museum, where, as of 2024, they remain, despite repatriation appeals from the community of Hebron, Labrador. Of the estimated 35,000 people who were exhibited in human zoos from the mid-1870s to the late 1950s, Abraham Ulrikab is one the few participants for whom we have original writings available to a broader readership.

Moravian missionaries: Sent by the Moravian Church, founded originally in fifteenth-century Bohemia and which eventually joined the Protestant movement; they became the first Europeans to settle in Labrador, where they established eight missions, until they left Labrador in 2005.

Inuktitut: One of the principal Inuit languages; it is spoken primarily in the central and eastern Arctic.

My dear teacher Elsner!

I write to you, because I'd like to tell you the following. We are greatly sad. When they brought me to Europe, I probably totally ignored it at first, but then I prayed to God continuously that He might teach me, if it really was a mistake, because I believe in all His words. But because I was in deep misery, I often prayed to God to help me to free myself from this and to hear my sighs, because I even wasn't able anymore to take care of my relatives, which I was usually able to do, even when I did not believe in my Lord and Saviour yet who died for me. In different kind of ways we have been lured, but even all this I didn't recognize. But as I was in doubt to pay all my and my late father's debts from kayaking, I thought (at this chance) to collect some money for discharging them. I also believed that I might see you. Then I thought: Our way is destined by the Lord. We all cried a lot, my wife, I and our relatives; but none of them wanted to hold us back. This way

17 "The Diary of Abraham Ulrikab," in *The Diary of Abraham Ulrikab: Text and Context*, ed. and trans. Hartmut Lutz (Ottawa: University of Ottawa Press, 2005), 3–5. Reproduced with permission from the University of Ottawa Press.

we took our decision before the Lord. Not that we would have been tired of our teachers, but due to the weight of my debts, of which I still have 100 Shilling. I didn't want to act like a fool, but I remember to have wished to see Europe and some of the communities over there for a long time. But here I wait in vain for someone to talk about Jesus. Until now we only saw reckless people in our house. We pray that the Lord may help us here and everywhere we will travel with our show....

DOCUMENT 125

From Dr. Rudolf Virchow, "Eskimos at the Berlin Zoo," *Zeitschrift für Ethnologie* (1880)[18]

Physician and racial scientist, Dr. Rudolf Virchow (1821–1902) visited Abraham Ulrikab and his family as part of his "scientific" examinations of the Eskimo race. His 1880 ***Journal of Ethnology*** article illustrates continued efforts to catalog the appearance of global populations, and to equate physical characteristics with moral qualities and levels of intelligence. In the second part of this excerpt, Virchow answers his critics, who disputed his use of human beings as objects of study and the concept of human zoos more generally.

***Journal of Ethnology*:** Founded in 1869 as the primary academic journal for German ethnologists.

Although coming from the same area in Labrador, which is situated on almost the same latitude as the southern tip of Greenland, the Eskimos we are dealing with can be said to be comprised of two groups or families. They belong to coherent groups who differ not only in their religion but show several differences in their outer appearance as well. One group, the family of Abraham, consisting of the man, the woman Ulrike and two small children—along with the unmarried Tobias, come from the **mission of Hebron**.... [T]he missionaries were successful in supporting the education of these people to such an extent that they developed their intelligence to quite a degree and are capable of writing easily, of drawing, and of practicing several skills of a civilized life.... The other family, consisting of the man Tiggianiak, his wife Paieng, and his daughter Noggasak, however, are completely heathenish and, indeed, possess features that are eminently fit for learning about the primitive state of this people. Mr. Jacobson hired this family in Nakkwak, a station of the **Hudson Bay Company** at a fjord north of Hebron. The hair of our people from Labrador matches that of the people from Greenland in every respect. The color of the hair is black without exception. Already the small children have very dark hair, only the eyebrows are rather brownish. The adult men's hair is relatively long so that it covers the neck and even the shoulders of the heathens. It is very thick, shiny black, like ebony, similar to the manes of horses, by no means curly or wavy but very straight. The women's hair has the same quality, only they have it comparatively short and thus it rather gives the impression of a certain

mission of Hebron: Moravian mission, in operation from 1831 to 1959. In 1918, missionaries brought an outbreak of the Spanish Flu to the settlement, which killed approximately 86 of Hebron's 100 residents. Today it is the Hebron Mission National Historic Site of Canada.

Hudson Bay Company: This controlled vast land territories, and much of the fur trade, in what is now Canada. It then transitioned into a series of mercantile shops, and then to department stores. This "quintessentially Canadian" business was sold to an American businessman in 2006.

18 Rudolf Virchow, "Außerordentliche Zusammenkunft im Zoologischen Garten am 7. November 1880. Eskimos von Labrador," *Zeitschrift für Ethnologie* 12 (1880): 253–74. Reprinted in *The Diary of Abraham Ulrikab*, 57–62.

sparseness. Mrs. Ulrike has hers simply parted and braided. In contrast, the pagan woman and her daughter have a knot at the neck and at every temple, the knots at the temples are trimmed with long pendants which are plaited of reindeer hair and richly decorated with colourful (European) pearls. The eyebrows of most of them are thick, only Mrs. Ulrike's are thinner. Even the men hardly ever have sideburns, whereas moustache and goatee are thicker, only that the latter is restricted to the chin. A bit of a moustache can also be found on Mrs. Ulrike. The rest of the body, as far as I had a look at it, chest, forearm, lower leg, are almost completely hairless.

***Magdeburger Zeitung*:** A German daily newspaper.

zoological garden: Another term for a zoo (from zoology, or the study of animals), which has been frequently used in Germany.

I beg your indulgence to briefly reject a strong attack that was published in the ***Magdeburger Zeitung*** recently.... In an article entitled "The Eskimos in the **zoological garden** in Berlin" the author does not only oppose the exhibition of human beings, but he also declares explicitly that at second thought it can be expected that one would move away from showing human beings in zoological gardens. I will quote the ending briefly: "We are totally prepared to have our opinion smiled at and ridiculed as sentimental by some. Nevertheless, we have wanted to express it here. If these 'interesting' human specimens need to be exhibited at all, a sense of 'racial ethics' should prevent us from displaying our equals in zoos. It should be easy to identify appropriate localities elsewhere." The argumentation, which is based mainly on this consideration, starts with the fact—and this is what I actually want to consider—that there is no scientific interest, and that for the majority of the people there exists nothing but sheer curiosity.... Some things are only interesting as curiosities, however, those things we are exploring on behalf of science, like the progressing exploration of nature and human beings, are mainly brought home to us because they are interesting. Indeed, these theories about human beings are interesting for everybody who wants to be informed about our position within nature and our evolution. Those who cannot understand that the most important and magnificent questions that mankind can ask are driven by our curiosity about ourselves seem least qualified to write features. An editorial staff should at least think twice before including such comments in its papers. That is what I wanted to ensure. Furthermore, I testify that a positive scientific interest of the highest rank is connected with this attitude. Therefore, I do not want to miss the chance to thank Mr. Hagenbeck in public and to advise him that he should not let himself be kept from continuing the exhibitions in the manner he has done before—as he has done it up until now with the greatest benefit for anthropological science.

DOCUMENT 126

Images: Advertisements for The Black Prince: Best Tobacco London (c. 1700s), Warpath Tobacco (c. 1885), and a "Cigar Store Indian" (2006)[19]

Advertisers often used North American Indigenous people in advertisements for tobacco. They did this to make their products seem more authentic and exciting. The Black Prince: Best Tobacco London ad features a Black man, dressed in Indigenous clothing, at work on an American plantation. Many tobacco stores still decorate their entrances with "cigar store Indians." This represents another form of consumer racism, where stereotypes are used to sell products.

19 Advertisement for The Black Prince: Best Tobacco London, c. 1700s, woodcut by Francis Bedford; advertisement for Warpath Tobacco, c. 1885, Library of Congress Prints and Photographs Division, https://www.loc.gov/item/92509231/; "Cigar Store Indian," October 2006, photograph by WyrdLight/Antony McCallum. Used under Attribution-ShareAlike 2.5 Generic (CC BY-SA 2.5), https://creativecommons.org/licenses/by-sa/2.5/deed.en.

WARPATH
WESTERN BRANCH

HAVANA HOUSE

DOCUMENT 127

From Benjamin Douglas Howard, *Life with Trans-Siberian Savages* (1893)[20]

Ainu communities live on the island of **Hokkaido** in Japan and on **Sakhalin Island** in Russia. Both national governments subjected them to interventionist policies throughout the modern period, including an eradication of land rights. Benjamin Douglas Howard (1836–1900) attended medical school in America and served as a military doctor in that country's Civil War. Later in life he returned to England before embarking on a series of trips around the world. In this book, Howard claimed to be the first person in nearly three hundred years to write about the Ainu people of Sakhalin Island. He called them the "inaccessible remnant of a savage and secluded race."

Hokkaido: The second-largest island of Japan, and its northernmost prefecture. Long inhabited by the Ainu peoples; Japanese explorers and settlers began to arrive by the seventeenth century, and it was formally annexed in 1869. The Ainu people suffered assimilationist policies and a dispossession of their lands.

Sakhalin Island: The largest island in Russia, and situated in the Pacific Ocean, north of Japan. Long inhabited by the Ainu, Orok, and Nivkh peoples, the territory was colonized and then disputed by Russia and Japan in the nineteenth and twentieth centuries. Soviet Union solidified control after World War II, and today the island has a population of approximately 490,000 people.

... Although the Sakhalin Ainus are said to have once spread far southward in the Japanese empire, the weakness of their character seems to have disqualified them either for permanent conquest, for colonization, or even for amalgamation. With this integral weakness of the Ainus their backward movement northward was the inevitable, and rather the mechanical result of the resistance of a people physically weaker, but morally and numerically, superior to the invaders.

... These women were certainly as uninviting-looking females as I ever beheld ... these women, in their unadulterated and strictly natural state, had also the same stupid, stolid, vacant expression, were also all over the body nearly as hairy as the men, had the same blue-blackened lips, the same tattooed, fierce moustache, and had the same tattooed arms, tattooed finger-rings, and sea-shell earrings. But if you add to this, that they had never in their lives been washed, that the hair of their heads, which came below their waists, had never seen a comb, and that a double-teamed horse-rake could not have got through it, I need hardly say they were about as repulsive-looking creatures as it is possible to imagine.

Like the dogs however, they are not only useful but indispensable, as they do all the work; their lords and masters thinking it a degradation to touch any sort of work under any circumstances, except such as pertains strictly to their hunting and fishing.

20 Benjamin Douglas Howard, *Life with Trans-Siberian Savages* (London: Longmans, Green, and Co., 1893). For more information, see Minority Rights Group International: World Directory of Minorities and Indigenous Peoples, https://minorityrights.org/programmes/library/directory/.

This multifarious and endless work of the women is a subtle and adroit concession by the men to the superior capacity and rights of their women. This recognition is so full and complete that it never occurs to Ainu women, I think, to emulate their whiter sisters in demanding additional rights.

Notwithstanding their repulsiveness, these Ainu women have very great merits. One of their rules of life seems to be, "Speak only when you are spoken to." In all my experiences amongst other savage peoples, the perpetual scream and cackle of the ever-quarreling women, by day and by night, has been irrepressible and almost maddening. During all my stay in this village however, I never once overheard what could be supposed to be a quarrel or dispute ... I never for an instant saw in any one of their faces an expression of a wish to please, or a sign of being pleased. Nor did I ever see in any one of them what could be suspected of being a smile.... I came to feel, strange as it may seem, that some of these poor creatures thought themselves to be pretty.

DOCUMENT 128

From Strickland Constable, *Ireland from One or Two Neglected Points of View* (1899)[21]

This illustration draws alleged similarities between **Irish Iberian** and Negro features in contrast to the supposedly higher **Anglo-Teutonic**. The accompanying caption reads "The Iberians are believed to have been originally an African race, who thousands of years ago spread themselves through Spain over Western Europe. Their remains are found in the barrows, or burying places, in sundry parts of these countries. The skulls are of low **prognathous** type. They came to Ireland and mixed with the natives of the South and West, who themselves are supposed to have been of low type and descendants of savages of the Stone Age, who, in consequence of isolation from the rest of the world, had never been out-competed in the healthy struggle of life, and thus made way, according to the laws of nature, for superior races."

Irish Iberian: Also known as "Black Irish"; refers to a myth that some people in Ireland have dark hair and eyes because their ancestors mixed with another group; in this caption, Northern Africans, but there are also theories that they were shipwrecked soldiers from the Spanish Armada.

Anglo-Teutonic: A false nineteenth-century white supremacist belief that the British, Americans, and Germans all shared common ancestry.

prognathous: Refers to a person with a projecting chin or lower jaw.

IRISH IBERIAN. ANGLO-TEUTONIC. NEGRO.

The Iberians are believed to have been originally an African race, who thousands of years ago spread themselves through Spain over Western Europe. Their remains are found in the barrows, or burying places, in sundry parts of these countries. The skulls are of low, prognathous type. They came to Ireland, and mixed with the natives of the South and West, who themselves are supposed to have been of low type and descendants of savages of the Stone Age, who, in consequence of isolation from the rest of the world, had never been out-competed in the healthy struggle of life, and thus made way, according to the laws of nature, for superior races.

21 Strickland Constable, *Ireland from One or Two Neglected Points of View* (1899).

DOCUMENT 129

From Paul Gauguin, *Noa Noa. The Tahitian Journal* (1901) and Image: *Three Tahitian Women* (1896)[22]

post-Impressionist: French art movement, c. 1886–1905 that rejected what was seen as the trivial choice of subjects by Impressionists but continued to use many of their artistic techniques.

Paul Gauguin was a French **post-Impressionist** painter who inspired artists such as Pablo Picasso and Henri Matisse. In 1891, he left his wife and family to travel to Tahiti, as he wished to "escape European civilization and everything that is artificial and conventional." The following excerpt from his 1901 travel memoir, *Noa Noa*, describes how he married his second "wife," a 13-year-old girl. Two years later, Gauguin returned to Paris, where he had a very public affair with another teenager of Indian and Malayan ancestry, to whom he gave the nickname, "Annah the Javanese." European audiences lauded his paintings and sculptures for their supposedly authentic and primitive depictions of the peoples of the South Pacific. In 1895, Gauguin traveled to Tahiti again, and never returned to Europe. His paintings, such as *Spirit of the Dead Watching* (1892), *When Will You Marry Me* (1892), and *Where Do We Come From? What Are We? Where Are We Going?* (1897), remain very popular today. You may wish to look at these paintings online as you read this piece, and we've included a copy of Gauguin's *Three Tahitian Women* (1896) at the end of the document.

... Then I saw the queen, Maraü—such was her name—decorating the royal hall with flowers and materials. When the director of public works asked my advice about the *artistic* arrangements of the funeral, I pointed out the queen to him. With the beautiful instinct of her race she dispersed grace everywhere about her, and made everything she touched a work of art.

I understood her only imperfectly at this first meeting. Both the human beings and the objects were so different from those I had desired, that I was disappointed. I was disgusted by all this European triviality. I had disembarked too recently yet to distinguish how much of nationality, fundamental realness, and primitive beauty still remained in this conquered race beneath the artificial and meretricious veneer of our importations. I was still in a manner blind. I saw in this queen, already mature in years, only a commonplace stout woman with traces of noble beauty. When I saw her again later, I revised my first judgment. I fell under the spell of her "**Maori** charm." Notwithstanding all the intermixture, the Tahitian type was still

Maori: Māori are the Indigenous Polynesian people of mainland New Zealand (Aotearoa).

22 Paul Gauguin. *Noa Noa. The Tahitian Journal*, trans. O.F. Theis (New York: N.L. Brown, 1919; orig. 1901), 8–9, 12, 62–63; Paul Gauguin, *Three Tahitian Women* (1896), The Metropolitan Museum of Art, New York, The Walter H. and Leonore Annenberg Collection, Gift of Walter H. and Leonore Annenberg, 1997, Bequest of Walter H. Annenberg, 2002.

very pure in her. And then the memory of her ancestor, the great chief Tati, gave her as well as her brother and all her family an appearance of truly imposing grandeur. She had the majestic sculptural form of her race, ample and at the same time gracious....

Close to the river Fatü, there was a general scattering. Concealed among the stones the women crouched here and there in the water with their skirts raised to waist, cooling their haunches and legs tired from the march and the heat. Thus cleansed with the bosom erect and with the two shells covering the breasts rising in points under the muslin of the corsage, they again took up the way to Papeete. They had the grace and elasticity of healthy young animals. A mingled perfume, half animal, half vegetable emanated from them; the perfume of their blood and of the gardenias—*tiaré* which all wore in their hair....

At Taravao, the district farthest from Mataïea at the other extremity of the island, a gendarme lends me his horse, and I range along the east coast, which is little frequented by Europeans. At Faone, a tiny district which precedes the more important one of Itia, I hear a native calling out to me, "Halloa! Man who makes human beings!"—He knows that I am a painter.—"*Haëre maï tai maha* (come and eat with us)." This is the Tahitian formula of hospitality.

No persuasion is required, for the smile accompanying the invitation is engaging and gentle. I dismount from the horse. My host he takes the animal by the bridle and ties it to a branch, simply and skillfully, without a trace of servility. Together we enter a hut where men and women, and children are sitting together on the ground talking and smoking. Around them children play and prattle.

"Where are you going?" asks a beautiful Maori woman of about forty. "I'm going to Itia," "What for?" I do not know what idea flitted across my mind. Perhaps I was only giving expression to the real purpose of my journey, which had hitherto been hidden even to myself.

"To find a wife," I replied.

"There are many pretty women at Faone. Do you want one?"

"Yes."

"Very well! If she pleases you, I will give her to you. She is my daughter."

"Is she young?" "Yes."

"Is she pretty?" "Yes."

"Is she in good health?" "Yes."

"It is well. Go and bring her to me."

The woman went out. A quarter of an hour later, as they were bringing on the meal. A truly Maori one of wild bananas and shellfish, she returned, followed by a young girl who held a small bundle in her hand. Through her dress of almost transparent rose-colored muslin one could see the golden skin of her shoulders and arms. Two swelling buds rose on the breasts. She was a large child, slender, strong, of wonderful proportions. But in her beautiful face I failed to find the characteristics which hitherto I had found dominant on the island. Even her hair was exceptional, thick like a bush and a little crispy. In the sunlight it was all an orgy of chrome. They told me she was of Tonga origin.

I greeted her; she smiled and sat down beside me.

"Aren't you afraid of me?" "*Aïta* (no)."

"Do you wish to live in my hut for always?" "*Eha* (yes)."

"You have never been ill?" "*Aïta*!"

That was all. My heart beat, while the young girl on the ground before me was tranquilly arranging the food on a large banana-leaf, and offering it to me. I ate with good appetite, but I was preoccupied, profoundly troubled. This child of about thirteen years (the equivalent of eighteen or twenty in Europe) charmed me, made me timid, almost frightened me. What might be passing in her soul? And it was I, so old in contrast to her, who hesitated to sign a contract in which all the advantages were on my side, but which was entered into and concluded so hastily.

Perhaps, I thought, it is in obedience to her mother's command. Perhaps, it is an arrangement upon which they have agreed among themselves....

I was reassured when I saw in the face of the young girl, in her gestures and attitude the distinct signs of independence and pride which are so characteristic of her race. And my faith was complete and unshakable, when after a deep study of her, I saw unmistakably the serene expression which in young beings always accompanies an honorable and laudable act.—But the mocking line about her otherwise pretty, sensual, and tender mouth warned me that the real dangers of the adventure would be for me, not for her....

DOCUMENT 130

From James Bryce, "The Relations of the Advanced and the Backward Races of Mankind" (1902)[23]

James Bryce (1838–1922) was a British academic, lawyer, and prominent politician. His days at the University of Heidelberg in Germany influenced his belief in Teutonic freedom, the idea that the United States, Great Britain, and Germany were natural friends and allies. Bryce gave the following lecture as part of the prestigious Romanes series at Oxford University in 1902. Among other topics, he discussed contemporary fears that interactions between global communities of people would result in sexual race-mixing.

With this incomparably fuller and more exact knowledge of the families of Man there has come a far closer and more widespread contact of those various families with one another, and in particular of the more advanced and civilized races with the more backward, a contact so much closer and more widespread than ever in the past that it may be deemed to mark a crisis in the history of the world, which will profoundly affect the destiny of all mankind. It is of the phenomena of that contact and the problems which it raises that I propose to speak to you to-day....

The completion of this world-process is a specially great and fateful event, because it closes a page for ever. The conditions that are now vanishing can never recur. The **uncivilized and semi-civilized races** cannot relapse into their former isolation. In passing under the influences of civilized powers they have indeed given to the world a new kind of unity....

uncivilized and semi-civilized races: False reference to the different evolutionary states of humans and the outdated assumption that some "races" of the world are advanced.

When two races differing in strength, that is to say, either in numbers, or in physical capacity, or in mental capacity, or in material advancement, or in military resources, come into political or social contact some one of four possible results follows. Either the weaker race dies out before the stronger, or it is absorbed into the stronger, the latter remaining practically unaffected, or the two become commingled into something different from what either was before, or, finally, the two continue to dwell together unmixed, each preserving a character of its own.

Let us consider each of these possible cases. Where the backward race is either small in numbers or of weak physical stamina, and is still in the savage stage, it vanishes quickly. This need not be the fault of the stronger race. Sometimes, no doubt, the invader or immigrant kills off the natives,

23 James Bryce, *The Relations of the Advanced and the Backward Races of Mankind. The Romanes Lecture, delivered in the Sheridan Theatre* (Oxford: Clarendon Press, 1902), 8.

who resent the seizure of their hunting-grounds or prove themselves thievish neighbours. Sometimes the conqueror reduces the natives to a slavery under which the latter perish, as in the awful instance of the extermination of the Indians of the Greater Antilles under Spanish rule, an extermination practically complete within half a century after Columbus discovered them. Sometimes the introduction of new diseases, which the bodies of the natives cannot resist, sweeps them off in vast numbers, as nearly the whole **Hottentot nation** died of small-pox, and a considerable part of the **Fijian islanders** of measles.

Hottentot nation: False term used by Europeans to refer to peoples in Southern Africa.

Fijian islanders: Indigenous people of the Fiji Islands.

Alcoholic drinks are specially pernicious to an aboriginal race, because it is usually wanting in self-control, and is supplied with liquor more fiery and poisonous than Europeans consume. Sometimes the mere change of habits of life induces physical decline, as when the pursuit of wild creatures ceases to be possible, or when pasture lands have been enclosed for cultivation by the stronger immigrant. Even a change in housing or clothing may prove deadly. I was told in Hawaii that the reduction of the native population from about 300,000 in **Captain Cook**'s time to about 30,000 in 1883 was largely due to the substitution of wooden houses for the old wigwams, whose sides, woven of long grass, had secured natural ventilation, and to the use of clothes, which the native, accustomed to nothing more than a loincloth, did not think of changing or drying when drenched with rain. Moreover, many primitive races are always on the verge of want; and when a famine occurs, they may be brought so low that the survivors scatter and disappear. ... It is through one or more of these causes—for they often act simultaneously—that the Red Indians have almost vanished from North America east of the Rocky Mountains (a few tribes having, however, been, peaceably transported to new seats); that the aborigines of Tasmania died out thirty years ago; that those of Australia have gone from the civilized south-eastern corner of that continent, and may soon be confined to its northern coasts; that the **Ainos** are diminishing in Northern Japan, as the **Ostiaks** and **Tunguses** are in Siberia; that the **Bushmen** are practically extinct in South Africa, and that the **Veddas** of Ceylon had, long before Europeans reached that isle, been driven into the recesses of the forests, where now only a handful are left.

Captain Cook: Captain in the British Royal Navy, famous for his voyages between 1768 and 1779 to what is now New Zealand and Australia.

Ainos: Ainu people of Northern Japan.

Ostiaks: Ostyak, an archaic term used for several Indigenous peoples of Siberia.

Tunguses: Tungusic peoples of Siberia.

Bushmen: The San People of Southern Africa.

Veddas: A minority Indigenous people in Sri Lanka.

From cases of destruction, I pass to cases of absorption. When the aborigines among whom a stronger immigrant race comes are neither low savages nor physically feeble, it may befall them to be imperceptibly blent with and lost among the stronger and more numerous or more prolific race. This is of course most likely to happen when the interval between the peoples is not a wide one. Probably it was thus that the **Celts of Britain** absorbed, being perhaps modified by, their so-called Iberian predecessors, as the Russian settlers are to-day absorbing some of the tribes they have

Celts of Britain: The Celts lived in what is now Great Britain from approximately 1000 BCE, through the Iron Age, the Roman Age, and into the post-Roman era.

found in Siberia. The **Yakut** learns to speak Russian and becomes a sort of Christian, while the Russian, though he adopts the Yakut dress and way of life, does not sink into a savage; and the population ends by being Russian.... So, in the **Caucasus** tiny peoples that had for ages dwelt apart in upland valleys, with mighty glaciers above them and forest gorges beneath, have now been brought under the yoke of Russia, and are losing their ancient faiths and modes of speech to become, if not Russians, yet Georgians or Imeritians of the low country....

The race that accepts an alien type may be the stronger race in everything but intelligence and culture. Sometimes strength, if it takes the form of a dogged persistence in its ancient ways, is the undoing of a people. Many of the **Red Indian tribes** have perished off the earth because they could not or would not adjust themselves to the conditions which the advent of the whites imposed. The black man submits and survives....

For **intermarriage** to take place, it is not necessary that the races should stand on the same or nearly the same level of civilization, still less be equal in mental gifts or physical force. Two colliding races are seldom equal, as indeed conquerors are presumably superior in force, colonizers presumably more active and enterprising. Neither does language form a serious bar.... Nothing really arrests intermarriage except physical repulsion, and physical repulsion exists only where there is a marked difference in physical aspect, and especially in colour....

Yakut: A Turkic ethnic group who mainly live on territories that are now the Republic of Sakha, along the Arctic Ocean. Tsarist repression of the Yakut began in the early seventeenth century and continued into the twentieth century, including under the collectivization programs of the Stalinist regime.

Caucasus: A region between the Black Sea and the Caspian Sea, which includes Armenia, Azerbaijan, Georgia, and parts of Southern Russia.

Red Indian tribes: Derogatory reference to the Indigenous peoples of North America.

intermarriage: In this context, refers to marriage between people of different "races."

DOCUMENT 131

1925 Russian Commentary on the Giliak Peoples, from Bruce Grant, *In the Soviet House of Culture: A Century of Perestroikas* (1995)[24]

Giliak, or Nivkh: See p. 272.

Mongols: East Asian peoples who controlled the largest land empire in history, led by rulers such as Genghis Khan (r. 1206–27) and Kublai Khan (r. 1260–94); see Document 74.

collectivization: Under Joseph Stalin, the rapid and forced shift from private farms to collectivized agriculture. The process caused several famines, including the Holodomor in Ukraine and led to the deaths of millions of people.

Socialist revolution: A process that began with the 1917 Russian Revolution, to turn Russia from a monarchy to a communist state and encompassed widespread political, economic, social, and cultural measures.

Rybnovsk district: A region on northern Sakhalin Island

The **Giliak, or Nivkh**, peoples live on the northern half of Sakhalin Island and have long maintained diplomatic and social ties with the Russian, Chinese, and Japanese peoples. Many scholars assert they were allied to the **Mongols** as early as the thirteenth century. By the seventeenth century, they were serving as intermediaries between the Russians, Manchu, Japanese, and Ainu peoples. The Russian Empire annexed the region in 1860 and in the following decades, the Nivkh peoples lost much of their autonomy and cultural traditions. This process was exacerbated when Russian authorities built a penal colony on Sakhalin where prisoners introduced epidemics of smallpox and influenza to the Indigenous peoples. The Soviet process of **collectivization**, and its insistence on agriculturalism, further damaged the traditional Nivkh hunter-gatherer way of life, and communities were frequently targeted as enemies of the **Socialist revolution**, as illustrated in this document.

In the villages of **Rybnovsk district**, located alongside Russian settlements, Giliaks lived somewhat more cleanly. Here, along with the art of card playing, drinking, and cursing, the Giliaks have absorbed a number of aspects of Russian life. Many Giliak yurtas [tents] are fashioned after Russian houses. In many, soap can be found. However, the presence of dirt should in no way be looked upon as a consequence of their cultural heritage. It is the direct consequence of the continual economic oppression of the native and absolute absence of political rights. From the arrival of Russians, the natives have been hounded from the favorable fishing grounds where they have lived for centuries. From the de facto master of the land, he has quickly been transformed into the object of shameless exploitation. With the loss of the fishing grounds, the haul has diminished but the demand has remained the same.... Hungry years have become more frequent, and the native has been confronted with the pressing dilemma: What to buy now? Buy a net and forget about a hunting rifle? Or buy a rifle and forget about a net? And how do you get the fish in order to trade for one or the other? Do you feed less fish to your family and dogs in order to sell more? What then do you eat?

---

24 Bruce Grant, *In the Soviet House of Culture: A Century of Perestroikas* (Princeton: Princeton University Press, 1995), 80.

Under such economic conditions it is no surprise that Giliaks have been reduced to the dirt and sloth of which it has become so popular to speak, dirt and sloth which indicate the absence of any purpose in life excepting the purpose of a full stomach and the most immediate of needs. "Soon our Giliak will die out altogether"—is how the surrounding population looks to the future. At the start this might have been posed as a question. However, after years of oppression, darkness, illness, and work of cabals, it is looked upon as fact with the greatest of certainty.

The Sakhalin climate and the surrounding environment do not especially incline one to either laziness or the contemplative mood. On the contrary, they incline one to energy and the urge to struggle. To suggest that dirt and laziness are characteristic of the Giliak people is nonsense. The Sakhalin Giliaks long ago began to make strides to improve their living conditions and continue to do so today. They began to build "Russian-style houses" already thirty-five years ago, and if you visit the village of Viskovo, you will see that they wash their floors too.

DOCUMENT 132

From Reginald Ruggles Gates, "The Australian Aborigines in a New Setting" (1960)[25]

The Canadian-born eugenicist Reginald Ruggles Gates (1882–1962) began his career as a plant geneticist, but following the publication of his book, *Heredity and Eugenics*, in 1932, became better known for his racial science research. In 1938 he used blood samples from children at a residential school in Nova Scotia to investigate whether any "pure blood Micmac Indians" survived in that area. Near the end of his career, Ruggles Gates traveled to Lapland, South Africa, India, Australia, New Zealand, Japan, Canada, and Mexico to study the effects of sexual miscegenation among different peoples. This article on Indigenous peoples in Australia appeared in the journal *Man*, which was published by the **Royal Anthropological Institute of Great Britain and Ireland**.

Royal Anthropological Institute of Great Britain and Ireland: Founded in 1871, the RAI is the world's oldest scholarly organization dedicated to the study of anthropology.

Arunta tribe: Aboriginal Australian peoples who today call themselves the Arrernte.

Spencer and Gillen: Francis James Gillen and Walter Baldwin Spencer were anthropologists and ethnologists who wrote *The Native Tribes of Central Australia* (1899).

half-castes: Derogatory term used for people of mixed heritage and commonly used by Europeans to describe those descended of white settlers and Indigenous peoples in Australia.

Reserves: Or reservations; government-mandated housing areas that sought to keep Aboriginal peoples separate from white settlers.

first cross: Crude term referring to the first pregnancy to result from intercourse between different "races" in a family genealogy.

A visit to Australia in 1958 to study the aborigines produced unexpectedly fruitful results. First contacts were made with them in Perth and its vicinity, then in Adelaide. More were seen when travelling north by train to Alice Springs in the heart of the Australian continent. This desert area ringed round by hills was the home of the **Arunta tribe**, now called Áranda, made famous by the works of **Spencer and Gillen**.

In this town of over 10,000 inhabitants many pure aborigines and **half-castes** throng the streets, being occupied as streetcleaners, truckers, gardeners, and servants by day and retiring to nearby **Reserves** at night. In the elementary school over half the children are of mixed racial descent, mostly aborigines x White. A genetic study was made ... of many of these families. Contact with Europeans only began about 1870, so most of the families studied could be traced back three generations to the **first cross**. …

There is still a traditional view that the Australian aborigines are not only the most primitive living race, which is in some respects substantially true, but that they are physically a surviving remnant of Neandertal man. Recent discoveries and views regarding Neandertaloids ... complicated rather than simplify their relation to *Homo sapiens*, and it will probably be some time before this relationship fully clears up. The question thus arose, was Neandertal man derived from the earlier Mid-Pleistocene *Pithecanthropus* type? This appears to be not unlikely on present evidence. First-hand contact

25 Reginald Ruggles Gates, "The Australian Aborigines in a New Setting," *Man* 60 (April 1960): 53–56.

with the aborigines, however, leaves no doubt that the bulk are essentially neanthropic, although some individuals have been described with marked Neandertaloid characters. [Gates then details previous research by scholars.]

Evidence of the aboriginal skin-colour genetics, presented elsewhere ... , shows how extraordinarily different it is from the African races. The same applies to the Papuans.... It has been shown ... that in the African races four genes, Q, R, S, T, will account for the full black of the Negro, R, S and T for the "mahogany" colour of the Pygmies, S and T for the yellow of the Bushmen and Hottentots, T by itself producing only the Caucasian or white-**brunet** skin colour. A skin-colour chart based only on the various colour segregates in Negro x White thus fits all the African races.

brunet: An earlier form of brunette, here used to refer to a darker complexion.

It was soon found that this colour does not at all fit the Australian skin colour, which may be described as generally brownish mahogany, though it may be darker, especially in Northern Australia. Studies of many families of aborigines x Whites reveals a single main gene for melanin in the skin, with a minor gene for melanin in the skin, with a minor gene producing only brunet skin colouration. When the natives wear clothes, as they do near the towns, the covered part of their skin is nearly white. They are thus more susceptible than Caucasians to tanning. Their skin colour is like a veneer which largely or entirely disappears either in shade or in crosses with Europeans.

Thus, in skin colour as well as in hair form, which is wavy or somewhat curly, the aborigines are relatively close to the Caucasian race. Although geographically so remote from Europeans, they are physically and genetically much nearer than are the races of Africa. Indeed, they are best classified as archaic Caucasians, as the further evidence will show. The tawny hair in many aboriginal children is apparently a gene mutation, corresponding roughly to the gene for fair hair in European children, but differing in some respects. It is therefore a parallel mutation, and it probably arose in Australia within recent centuries or millennia.

A number of significant features in the aboriginal skull have a very definite bearing on racial relationships. The marked brow ridges which, as we have seen, very much in their degree of development, are especially characteristic of the male. Combined with a retreating **glabella**, depressed root of the nose and sunken orbits they give a look of ferocity to the native which really quite belies his mild friendly nature....

glabella: The smooth part of the forehead above and between the eyebrows.

There is another aspect of the aboriginal facial features. Many anthropologists accept a relationship between the Australian aborigines and the Ainu of Japan.... In this way we may regard the Caucasoids with the Ainu and Australians as one network of descent, while the Mongoloids, derived partly from *Sinanthropus*, form another nexus of descent, involving also the American Indians with various ingredients of Mongoloid and Ainoid elements. In Africa south of the Sahara the wooly-haired races have evolved more independently. The relation of these Africans to the Melanesians and Negritos is still obscure.

DOCUMENT 133

United Nations, Declaration on the Rights of Indigenous Peoples (2007)[26]

The General Assembly of the United Nations adopted this Declaration on 13 September 2007, by a majority of 144 states in favor, 4 votes against (Australia, Canada, New Zealand, and the United States) and 11 abstentions (Azerbaijan, Bangladesh, Bhutan, Burundi, Colombia, Georgia, Kenya, Nigeria, Russian Federation, Samoa, and Ukraine). By 2011, the four countries who voted against the declaration had reversed their votes. As you read the following preamble (see the full text in the link), consider how the global history of settler-Indigenous interactions led to the writing of this document.

The General Assembly,

Guided by the purposes and principles of the Charter of the United Nations, and good faith in the fulfilment of the obligations assumed by States in accordance with the Charter,

Affirming that indigenous peoples are equal to all other peoples, while recognizing the right of all peoples to be different, to consider themselves different, and to be respected as such,

Affirming also that all peoples contribute to the diversity and richness of civilizations and cultures, which constitute the common heritage of humankind,

Affirming further that all doctrines, policies and practices based on or advocating superiority of peoples or individuals on the basis of national origin or racial, religious, ethnic or cultural differences are racist, scientifically false, legally invalid, morally condemnable and socially unjust,

Reaffirming that indigenous peoples, in the exercise of their rights, should be free from discrimination of any kind,

Concerned that indigenous peoples have suffered from historic injustices as a result of, inter alia, their colonization and dispossession of their lands, territories and resources, thus preventing them from exercising, in particular, their right to development in accordance with their own needs and interests,

Recognizing the urgent need to respect and promote the inherent rights of indigenous peoples which derive from their political, economic and

26 United Nations Declaration on the Rights of Indigenous Peoples, https://www.un.org/development/desa/indigenouspeoples/wp-content/uploads/sites/19/2018/11/UNDRIP_E_web.pdf.

social structures and from their cultures, spiritual traditions, histories and philosophies, especially their rights to their lands, territories and resources,

Recognizing also the urgent need to respect and promote the rights of indigenous peoples affirmed in treaties, agreements and other constructive arrangements with States,

Welcoming the fact that indigenous peoples are organizing themselves for political, economic, social and cultural enhancement and in order to bring to an end all forms of discrimination and oppression wherever they occur,

Convinced that control by indigenous peoples over developments affecting them and their lands, territories and resources will enable them to maintain and strengthen their institutions, cultures and traditions, and to promote their development in accordance with their aspirations and needs,

Recognizing that respect for indigenous knowledge, cultures and traditional practices contributes to sustainable and equitable development and proper management of the environment,

Emphasizing the contribution of the demilitarization of the lands and territories of indigenous peoples to peace, economic and social progress and development, understanding and friendly relations among nations and peoples of the world,

Recognizing in particular the right of indigenous families and communities to retain shared responsibility for the upbringing, training, education and well-being of their children, consistent with the rights of the child,

Considering that the rights affirmed in treaties, agreements and other constructive arrangements between States and indigenous peoples are, in some situations, matters of international concern, interest, responsibility and character,

Considering also that treaties, agreements and other constructive arrangements, and the relationship they represent, are the basis for a strengthened partnership between indigenous peoples and States....

Recognizing and reaffirming that indigenous individuals are entitled without discrimination to all human rights recognized in international law, and that indigenous peoples possess collective rights which are indispensable for their existence, well-being and integral development as peoples,

Recognizing that the situation of indigenous peoples varies from region to region and from country to country and that the significance of national and regional particularities and various historical and cultural backgrounds should be taken into consideration,

Solemnly proclaims the following United Nations Declaration on the Rights of Indigenous Peoples as a standard of achievement to be pursued in a spirit of partnership and mutual respect.

[Forty-six specific Articles follow this text.]

DOCUMENT 134

Nina Berglund, "Sámi Still Battling Discrimination" (2016)[27]

The Sámi, as one of the Indigenous populations of the Scandinavia region, have long faced discriminatory policies by European governments, as detailed in this 2016 article. Since then, however, the Sámi have prevailed in human-rights court challenges over large-scale projects they feared would damage the environment, and Norwegian schools now fly the Sámi flag alongside the Norwegian. These are significant signs of changing attitudes in at least this region for Indigenous peoples.[28]

The Easter holidays were typically festive for Norway's indigenous Sámi people, marking a high season for weddings and other traditional celebrations as the days grow longer and lighter. This year some ominous clouds had been gathering, however, following a string of disturbing incidents and claims of discrimination by Sámi leaders.

"We've been seeing an alarming negative development under this government (the conservative minority coalition formed by the Conservative and Progress parties)," Aili Keskitalo, president of the Sámi's own parliament (**Sametinget**), told newspaper Dagsavisen earlier this year. "This applies especially to budget priorities. We believe the managed reduction of Sámi priorities amounts to systematic discrimination."

Sámi people and events have also been subjected to several other disturbing incidents in recent months that can be viewed as even more alarming. On February 6, when the Sámi were celebrating their own **national day** that was established in 1993, a leading member of the **Progress Party, Ulf Leirstein**, sent out a message on Twitter that Sámi and many others considered highly offensive. Leirstein claimed he hadn't realized the Sámi had "their own country" and should thus "pay for their own parliament, support for Sámi culture, etc."

Just a few weeks later, Sámi taking part in the **Youth Olympics** in Lillehammer were subjected to harassment during a display of reindeer racing known as **reinkappkjøring**. "Cut the heads off these reindeer, we don't want to see any Sámi," yelled some young passersby who then disappeared

Sametinget: Since 1993, the Sámi Parliament of Sweden has been a democratically elected and autonomous authority that represents people who speak the Sámi language, identify culturally or ethnically as Sámi, or have a parent or grandparent that speaks or spoke a Sámi language. There are also national Sámi parliaments in Finland, Norway, and Russia.

national day: The Sámi National Day is February 6, which is celebrated in memory of the first Sámi congress in Trondheim in 1917.

Progress Party, Ulf Leirstein: Leirstein represented the Progress Party in the Swedish Parliament (Storting) from 2005 to 2019, until a sex scandal involving minors forced him to become an independent. The party is on the far-right of the political spectrum and supports a socially conservative, anti-immigrant, anti-EU, and a law-and-order platform.

Youth Olympics: International sport competition for athletes between 15 and 18 years old, hosted by the International Olympic Committee and held every four years. Lillehammer, Norway hosted the Winter event in 2016.

reinkappkjøring: Sport where a driver races with reindeer using either a wagon or skis. Several international competitions, including a World Championship, are held annually.

27 Nina Berglund, "Sámi Still Battling Discrimination," News in English: Views and News from Norway, 24 March 2016, https://www.newsinenglish.no/2016/03/24/sami-still-battling-discrimination/.

28 Email correspondence with Nina Berglund, 16 November 2022. We are grateful to her for providing links to more recent news items: https://www.newsinenglish.no/2022/02/08/some-progress-amid-sami-celebrations/ and https://www.newsinenglish.no/?s=Sami.

into the crowd. "I was speechless," reindeer owner Anders Nils Eira from Karasjok told Norwegian Broadcasting (NRK). He said he'd never experienced such blatant harassment as a Sámi in Norway. Organizers of the Youth Olympics said they were "shocked and disappointed," and condemned the verbal abuse.

Trøndelag: A county in central Norway; the largest city is Trondheim.

Not long after that, Sámi reindeer herders in **Trøndelag** were told their grazing lands would become the site of a huge windmill project on the Fosen peninsula. The project under development by energy firms including state-owned Statkraft, Trønderenergi and Nordic Wind Power DA has been characterized as a "tragedy" for the southern Sámi reindeer herders in the area. The Sámi Parliament has appealed the decision on the grounds that the reindeer operations are an important part of the local Sámi culture, while state officials including the government support the project as an important part of promoting renewable energy and cutting carbon emissions.

Keskitalo: Aili Keskitalo has served as president of the Sami parliament for three terms, from 2005 to 2007, 2013 to 2016, and 2017 to 2021.

Sámi leader **Keskitalo** is left battling what she sees as discrimination on several fronts. The allegedly waning state support in the form of effective budget cuts has, she says, serious consequences for a culture under constant threat.

"One example is the shutdown of the southern Sámi school in central Norway, which was eliminated with a stroke of the pen," Keskitalo said. That has sparked concern from the United Nations' committee on racial discrimination, which has asked for a clarification from the Norwegian government after Sámi officials reported the school's closure to the UN. The **sørsamisk language** taught at the school has been "red-listed" by **UNESCO** as in danger of disappearing.

sørsamisk language: Or Southern Sámi; an endangered language. It is now being taught at several language schools and at three universities in Norway.

UNESCO: United Nations Educational, Scientific and Cultural Organization, founded after World War II.

fornorsking period: Forced assimilation of the Sámi people, begun by the Norwegian government in the eighteenth century and continuing until the establishment of the Sametinget in 1993.

Riddu Riddu music festival: Riddu Riđđu Festivàla is an international Indigenous festival, which takes place annually in Manndalen, Norway.

Keskitalo claimed that this year's state budget was the weakest in terms of support for the Sámi since what's called the **fornorsking period**, when Sámi were subjected to efforts to make them more Norwegian. "This leaves us with an uncomfortable feeling that there's an agenda here that no one wants to talk about," Keskitalo told Dagsavisen. "It's difficult to interpret it other than that the government doesn't want the Sámi culture to develop."

Helga Pedersen, a former government minister and veteran politician for the opposition Labour Party from Northern Norway, agrees that the Sámi "have been shoved out into the cold" lately. She cited funding cuts for legal help for Sámi in Norway's northernmost county of Finnmark, the loss of the Sámi school and even a cut in critical funding status for the annual **Riddu Riddu music festival**. It all led to Sámis protesting in front of the Norwegian Parliament in Oslo late last year for the first time since the still-controversial destruction of wild waterways outside Alta 30 years ago, to create new sources of electricity.

Pedersen claims there's been major backsliding on Sámi issues in recent years. "After the creation of the Sámi parliament and a consultation agreement between the government and Sametinget, conflicts have been taken up in formal settings where the Sámi have a place around the table," Pedersen told Dagsavisen. "Now the Sámi are outside demonstrating. This is a serious setback."

Keskitalo went further, claiming in her own New Year's address to the Sámi Parliament that "the same authorities who did what they could to destroy Sámi culture now think the culture should be rebuilt on Norwegian terms." She contends the government is consciously fornorsking again, resulting in "uncomfortable reminders of a time we thought we had put behind us." If that's not the case, she said, the government must change its course....

There are around 55,000 Sámi in Norway, the largest of the indigenous population that traditionally moved around Arctic areas of Norway, Sweden (20,000), Finland (8,000), and Russia (2,000). Despite the offensive remarks made by the politician from the Progress Party on their national day, celebrations were festive also in Oslo, where Keskitalo herself took part in a variety of events that included breakfast at City Hall, Sámi-Norwegian church services at the **Akershus Fortress and Castle**, special food displays and concerts, with the four-coloured Sámi flag flying.

Akershus Fortress and Castle: A medieval castle in Oslo, Norway.

"We Sámi are unfortunately accustomed to harassment, and mostly ignore it," Keskitalo said....

SELECT BIBLIOGRAPHY

Agai, Bekim, Umar Ryad, and Mehdi Sajid, eds. *Muslims in Interwar Europe: A Transcultural Historical Perspective.* Edinburgh: Edinburgh University Press, 2017.

Aitken, Robbie, and Eve Rosenhaft. *Africa in Europe: Studies in Transnational Practice in the Long Twentieth Century.* Liverpool: Liverpool University Press, 2013.

—. *Black Germany: The Making and Unmaking of a Diaspora Community, 1884–1960.* Cambridge: Cambridge University Press, 2013.

Aly, Gotz. *Why the Germans? Why the Jews? Envy, Race Hatred, and the Prehistory of the Holocaust.* Translated by Jefferson Chase. New York: Metropolitan Books, 2011.

Andreassen, Rikke. *Human Exhibitions: Race, Gender and Sexuality in Ethnic Displays.* London: Routledge, 2016.

Bankier, David. *Probing the Depths of German Antisemitism: German Society and the Persecution of the Jews.* New York: Berghahn Books, 2000.

Bethencourt, Francisco. *Racisms: From the Crusades to the Twentieth Century.* Princeton, NJ: Princeton University Press, 2014.

Bland, Lucy. "White Women and Men of Colour: Miscegenation Fears in Britain after the Great War." *Gender and History* 17, no. 1 (2005): 29–61.

Brattain, Michelle. "Race, Racism, and Antiracism: UNESCO and the Politics of Presenting Science to the Postwar Public." *American Historical Review* 112, no. 5 (2007): 1386–413.

Bryan, Beverley, Stella Dadzie, and Suzanne Scafe. *The Heart of the Race: Black Women's Lives in Britain.* Brooklyn, NY: Verso, 1985.

Bush, Barbara. *Imperialism, Race and Resistance: Africa and Britain.* London: Routledge, 1999.

Buxton, Hilary. "Imperial Amnesia: Race, Trauma and Indian Troops in the First World War." *Past & Present* 241, no. 1 (2018): 221–58.

Cagliotti, Angelo Matteo. "Race, Statistics, and Italian Eugenics: Alfredo Niceforo's Trajectory from Lombroso to Fascism (1876–1960)." *European History Quarterly* 47, no. 3 (2017): 461–89.

Camiscoli, Elisa. "Reproducing Citizens, Reproducing the 'French Race': Immigration, Demography, and Pronatalism in Early Twentieth-Century France." *Gender and History* 13, no. 3 (2001): 593–621.

Campt, Tina M. *Other Germans: Black Germans and the Politics of Race, Gender, and Memory in the Third Reich.* Ann Arbor: University of Michigan Press, 2005.

Citro, Constance F., Marilyn Dabady, and Rebecca M. Blank. *Measuring Racial Discrimination.* Washington, DC: National Academies Press, 2004.

Conklin, Alice L. *In the Museum of Man: Race, Anthropology, and Empire in France, 1850–1950.* Ithaca, NY: Cornell University Press, 2013.

Das, Santanu. *Race, Empire and First World War Writing.* Cambridge: Cambridge University Press, 2011.

Dimmock, Matthew. *Mythologies of the Prophet Muhammad in Early Modern English Culture*. Cambridge: Cambridge University Press, 2013.

El-Tayeb, Fatima. "Blood Is a Very Special Juice: Racialized Bodies and Citizenship in Twentieth-Century Germany." *International Review of Social History* 44 (1999): 149–69.

Evans, Andrew. *Anthropology at War: World War I and the Science of Race in Germany*. Chicago: University of Chicago Press, 2010.

Fanon, Frantz. *Black Skin, White Masks*. New York: Grove Press, 1952.

Fehrenbach, Heide. *Race after Hitler: Black Occupation Children in Postwar Germany and America*. Princeton, NJ: Princeton University Press, 2005.

Florvil, Tiffany M. *Mobilizing Black Germany: Afro-German Women and the Making of a Transnational Movement*. Champaign, IL: University of Illinois Press, 2020.

Friedman, Jerome. "Jewish Conversion, the Spanish Pure Blood Laws and Reformation: A Revisionist View of Racial and Religious Antisemitism." *Sixteenth Century Journal* 18 (1987): 3–30.

Gilroy, Paul. *There Ain't No Black in the Union Jack: The Cultural Politics of Race and Nation*. London: Routledge, 1987.

Gross, Jan. *Fear: Anti-Semitism in Poland after Auschwitz*. Princeton, NJ: Princeton University Press, 2007.

Hall, Catherine. "Gendering Property, Racing Capital." *History Workshop Journal* 78 (2014): 22–38.

Harris, Ruth. *Dreyfus: Politics, Emotion, and the Scandal of a Century*. New York: Picador, 2010.

Hellyer, H.A. *Muslims of Europe: The 'Other' Europeans*. Edinburgh: Edinburgh University Press, 2009.

Heng, Geraldine. *The Invention of Race in the European Middle Ages*. Cambridge: Cambridge University Press, 2018.

Honeck, Mischa, Martin Klimke, and Anne Kuhlmann, eds. *Germany and the Black Diaspora: Points of Contact, 1250–1914*. New York: Berghahn, 2013.

Hsia, R. Po-chia. *The Myth of Ritual Murder: Jews and Magic in Reformation Germany*. New Haven: Yale University Press, 1988.

Kendi, Ibram X. *Stamped from the Beginning: The Definitive History of Racist Ideas in America*. New York: Nation Books, 2016.

Kenrick, Donald. *The Gypsies of the Second World War: The Final Chapter*. Hatfield, UK: University of Hertfordshire Press, 2006.

Kuehl, Stefan. *For the Betterment of the Race: The Rise and Fall of the International Movement for Eugenics and Racial Hygiene*. Basingstoke, UK: Palgrave Macmillan, 2013.

Kushner, Tony. "'Without intending any of the most undesirable features of a colour bar': Race Science, Europeanness and the British Armed Forces during the Twentieth Century." *Patterns of Prejudice* 46, nos. 3–4 (2012): 339–74.

Langmuir, Gavin I. *Toward a Definition of Antisemitism*. Berkeley, CA: University of California Press, 1990.

Lewy, Gunter. *The Nazi Persecution of the Gypsies*. Oxford: Oxford University Press, 2000.

MacMaster, Neil. *Racism in Europe, 1870–2000*. Basingstoke, UK: Palgrave Macmillan, 2001.

Majid, Anouar. *We Are All Moors: Ending Centuries of Crusades against Muslims and Other Minorities.* Minneapolis, MN: University of Minnesota Press, 2012.

Mandel, Maud S. *Muslims and Jews in France: History of a Conflict*. Princeton, NJ: Princeton University Press, 2014.

Martone, Eric, et al., eds. *Encyclopedia of Blacks in European History and Culture*. Westport, CT: Greenwood Press, 2009.

Massaquoi, Hans. *Destined to Witness: Growing Up Black in Nazi Germany*. New York: HarperCollins, 2014.

Matar, Nabil I. *Turks, Moors, and Englishmen in the Age of Discovery*. New York: Columbia University Press, 1999.

Matera, Marc. *Black London: The Imperial Metropolis and Decolonization in the Twentieth Century*. Oakland, CA: University of California Press, 2015.

Mazon, Patricia, and Reinhild Steingrover, eds. *Not So Plain as Black and White: Afro-German Culture and History*. Rochester, NY: University of Rochester Press, 2009.

Mitchell, Robin. *Vénus Noire: Black Women and Colonial Fantasies in Nineteenth Century France: The Black Female Body as a Site of Cultural Meaning*. Athens, GA: University of Georgia Press, 2020.

Olusoga, David. *The World's War: Forgotten Soldiers of Empire*. London: Head of Zeus, 2014.

Opitz, May, Katharina Oguntoye, and Dagmar Schultz, eds. *Showing Our Colors: Afro-German Women Speak Out*. Amherst, MA: Amherst University Press, 1992.

Otele, Olivette. *African Europeans: An Untold History*. New York: Basic Books, 2021.

Pagels, Elaine. *The Origin of Satan: How Christians Demonized Jews, Pagans, and Heretics*. New York: Penguin, 1995.

Perry, Kennetta Hammond. *London Is the Place for Me: Black Britons, Citizenship and the Politics of Race*. Oxford: Oxford University Press, 2015.

Pitts, Johny. *Afropean: Notes from Black Europe.* London: Penguin, 2020.

Pollard, John. "Skinhead Culture: The Ideologies, Mythologies, Religions and Conspiracy Theories of Racist Skinheads." *Patterns of Prejudice* 50, nos. 4–5 (2016): 398–419.

Rattansi, Ali. *Racism: A Very Short Introduction*. Oxford: Oxford University Press, 2007.

Renshaw, Daniel. "Prejudice and Paranoia: A Comparative Study of Antisemitism and Sinophobia in Turn-of-the-Century Britain." *Patterns of Prejudice* 50, no. 1 (2016): 38–60.

Rizzo, Tracey, and Steven Gerontakis. *Intimate Empires: Body, Race, and Gender in the Modern World*. Oxford: Oxford University Press, 2017.

Rubin, Miri. *Gentile Tales: The Narrative Assault on Late Medieval Jews*. Philadelphia: University of Pennsylvania Press, 2004.

Said, Edward. *Orientalism*. New York: Vintage, 1978.

Saini, Angela. *Superior: The Return of Race Science*. Boston: Beacon Press, 2019.

Schaefer, Richard T., ed. *Encyclopedia of Race, Ethnicity, and Society*. Vol. 1. Thousand Oaks, CA: SAGE, 2008.

Schwartz, Stuart B. *All Can Be Saved: Religious Tolerance and Salvation in the Iberian Atlantic World.* New Haven, CT: Yale University Press, 2009.

Smith, Helmut. *The Butcher's Tale: Murder and Anti-Semitism in a German Town*. New York: W.W. Norton, 2002.

Stoler, Ann Laura. *Carnal Knowledge and Imperial Power: Race and the Intimate in Colonial Rule*. Berkeley, CA: University of California Press, 2010.

Stovall, Tyler. "The Color Line behind the Lines: Racial Violence in France during the Great War." *American Historical Review* 103, no. 3 (1998): 737–69.

—. *Paris Noir: African Americans in the City of Light*. New York: Houghton Mifflin, 1996.

Teter, Magda. *Blood Libel: On the Trail of an Antisemitic Myth*. Cambridge, MA: Harvard University Press, 2020.

Todd, Lisa M. "Studying Sexual and Racial 'Mixture': Eugen Fischer and the Rehoboth Basters of German Southwest Africa, 1908–1913." In *After the Imperialist Imagination: Two Decades of Research on Global Germany and Its Legacies*, edited by Sara Pugach, David Pizzo, and Adam Blackler, 79–92. Oxford: Peter Lang, 2020.

Torres, Max S., Maria Elena Martinez, and David Nirenberg, eds. *Race and Blood in the Iberian World*. Münster: LIT Verlag, 2012.

Turda, Marius, and Maria Sophia Quine. *Historicizing Race*. London: Bloomsbury, 2020.

Van der Pijl, Yvon, and Karina Goulordava. "Black Pete, 'Smug Ignorance,' and the Value of the Black Body in Postcolonial Netherlands." *NWIG: New West Indian Guide/ Nieuwe West-Indische Gids* 88, no. 3/4 (2014): 262–91.

Varsa, Eszter. "The (Final) Solution of the Gypsy-Question: Continuities in Discourses about Roma in Hungary, 1940s–1950s." *Nationalities Papers* 45, no. 1 (2017): 114–30.

Vince, Natalya. "Transgressing Boundaries: Gender, Race, Religion, and 'Françaises Musulmanes' during the Algerian War of Independence." *French Historical Studies* 33, no. 3 (2010): 445–74.

Waite, Gary K. *Jews and Muslims in Seventeenth-Century Discourse: From Religious Enemies to Allies and Friends*. London: Routledge, 2019.

Webster, Wendy. *Mixing It: Diversity in Second World War Britain*. Oxford: Oxford University Press, 2018.

Weitz, Eric. *A Century of Genocide: Utopias of Race and Nation*. Princeton, NJ: Princeton University Press, 2015.

Wells, Andrew. "Race and Racism in the Global European World before 1800." *History Compass* 13, no. 9 (2015): 435–44.

Wiesen, S. Jonathan. "American Lynching in the Nazi Imagination: Race and Extra-Legal Violence in 1930s Germany." *German History* 36, no. 1 (2017): 38–59.

ONLINE RESOURCES

Black Central Europe: https://blackcentraleurope.com

United States Holocaust Memorial Museum: https://www.ushmm.org

European Roma Rights Centre: http://www.errc.org

Documentation and Cultural Center for the German Roma and Sinti: https://dokuzentrum.sintiundroma.de/en/

PERMISSIONS ACKNOWLEDGEMENTS

"A.2 Road, Dartford (Gypsies)," columns 1163–72, from *Orders of the Day, Volume 658: debated on 2 May 1962*, Great Britain House of Commons Debates. Copyright © UK Parliament. Used under Open Parliament License v3.0.

Ahmad bin Qasim (Al-Hajarī). From Chapter 1: "France and Holland," *In the Lands of the Christians: Arabic Travel Writing in the Seventeenth Century*, First English Translations, ed. and trans. Nabil Matar, pp. 17–18, 24. Routledge, 2003. Copyright © 2003 by Taylor & Francis Books, Inc. Reprinted by permission of Routledge through PLSclear.

Berglund, Nina. From "Sámi Still Battling Discrimination," NewsInEnglish.no Views and News from Norway, 24 March 2016. https://www.newsinenglish.no/2016/03/24/sami-still-battling-discrimination/. Reprinted courtesy of the author.

Bergsten, Susanné. "Abused and Shunned—Being of Asian Descent in Sweden during COVID-19," Human Rights Watch, 6 April 2020. Copyright © 2020 by Human Rights Watch. https://www.hrw.org/news/2020/04/06/abused-and-shunned-being-asian-descent-sweden-during-covid-19. Reprinted with permission.

Berk, Eta Fuchs. Chapter 2: "In the Eye of the Holocaust: Auschwitz 1944," from *Chosen: A Holocaust Memoir*, Goose Lane Publishers, 1992.

"The Courage of a Mother: Kadefa Rizvanović," Survivor Stories, Remembering Srebrenica. Copyright © 2021 Remembering Srebrenica. https://srebrenica.org.uk/survivor-stories/kadefa-rizvanovic. Reprinted with permission.

Diderot, Denis. "Supplement to Bougainville's Voyage, 1772," from *Tolerance: The Beacon of the Enlightenment*, ed. and trans. Caroline Warman, et al. Open Book Publishers, 2016. http://dx.doi.org/10.11647/OBP.0088. Used under Creative Commons Attribution 4.0 International License (CC BY 4.0), https://creativecommons.org/licenses/by/4.0/.

Erasmus, Desiderius. From "On War against the Turks [De bello turcico]," *The Erasmus Reader*, ed. Erika Rummel, pp. 315–33. University of Toronto Press, 1990. Copyright © University of Toronto Press 1990. Reprinted with permission.

European Roma Rights Centre. From "Mob Violence against Roma in Poland," 15 July 1997. Copyright © 1997 European Roma Rights Centre. http://www.errc.org/roma-rights-journal/mob-violence-against-roma-in-poland. Reprinted with permission.

Fanon, Frantz. From *Black Skin, White Masks* [*Peau noire, masques blancs*], trans. Charles Lam Markmann. Pluto Press, 1986. Copyright © 1952 Editions du Seuil, Paris. Translation copyright © 1967 Grove Press, Inc.

Frederick Wilhelm III. From "Edict Concerning the Civil Status of the Jews in the Prussian State," 11 March 1812, originally published by Gesetz-Sammlung für die Königlichen Preußischen Staaten, 1812 [Collection of Laws for the Royal Prussian States 1812]. Georg Decker [1812]. In "From Absolutism to Napoleon (1648–1815)," trans. Richard Levy, *German History in Documents and Images*, German Historical Institute, Washington, DC (www.germanhistorydocs.ghi-dc.org). Reprinted with permission.

Gates, Reginald Ruggles. From "The Australian Aborigines in a New Setting."

Man 60 (April 1960): 53–56. https://doi.org/10.2307/2796246. Copyright © 1960 Royal Anthropological Institute of Great Britain and Ireland. Reprinted by permission of the publisher, conveyed through Copyright Clearance Center, Inc.

Grant, Bruce. From "Russian Commentary on the Giliak Peoples," 1925, from *In the Soviet House of Culture: A Century of Perestroikas*, p. 80. Copyright © 1995 Princeton University Press. Reprinted by permission of Princeton University Press, conveyed through Copyright Clearance Center, Inc.

Hawqal, Ibn. From *Kitāb ṣūrat al-arḍ* [*Book of the Picture of the Earth*], trans. Theresa Jäckh, in "973: Ibn Ḥawqal on Christian-Muslim Marriages in Sicily," *Transmediterranean History* 2, vol. 1 (2020), https://doi.org/10.18148/tmh/2020.2.1.28. Reprinted courtesy of the translator.

From "Heidelberger Manifest [Heidelberg Manifesto]," *Frankfurter Rundschau*, 4 March 1982. In "Two Germanies (1961–1989)," trans. Allison Brown, *German History in Documents and Images*, German Historical Institute, Washington, DC (www.germanhistorydocs.ghi-dc.org). Reprinted with permission.

Himmler, Heinrich. "'Fighting the Gypsy Plague,' Circular of the Reichsführer SS (8 December 1938)," from *The Racial State: Germany 1933–1945*, trans. Michael Burleigh and Wolfgang Wippermann, pp. 120–21. Copyright © 1991 Cambridge University Press. Reprinted by permission of Cambridge University Press through PLSclear.

From "How the Hereros Were Exterminated," *Words Cannot be Found: German Colonial Rule in Namibia—An Annotated Reprint of the 1918 Blue Book*, Sources for African History, Vol. 1, ed. Jeremy Silvester and Jan-Bart Gewald, pp. 115–16. Brill, 2003. Reprinted by permission of Brill, conveyed through Copyright Clearance Center, Inc.

Jewish Telegraphic Agency. Abridged from "Anti-Semitism Continues to Mar Presidential Politics in Poland," 4 December 1990. Copyright © 1990 Jewish Telegraphic Agency. Reprinted with permission.

Ladany, Shaul. From "The Olympian Who Survived Munich and the Holocaust," *Sports History Weekly*, 12 July 2020. www.SportsHistoryWeekly.com. Reprinted courtesy of Gilbert Sports Publishing, Inc.

Luther, Martin. Excerpted from *On the Jews and Their Lies*, from *Luther's Works: The Christian in Society IV*, Vol. 47, ed. Franklin Sherman, trans. Martin H. Bertram, pp. 268–78. Fortress Press, 1971. Reprinted with permission. (The views expressed by Luther in this work do not reflect the views of either the Evangelical Lutheran Church in America or the Lutheran Church Missouri Synod.) From *On War against the Turk* (1529), in *Luther's Works*, Vol. 46, *Christian in Society III*, ed. Helmut T. Lehmann and Robert C. Schultz. Fortress Press, 1967. Reprinted by permission of Fortress Press.

Margolis, Hillary. "Denmark's Face Veil Ban Latest in Harmful Trend," Human Rights Watch—Dispatches, 1 June 2018. Copyright © 2018 Human Rights Watch. https://www.hrw.org/news/2018/06/01/denmarks-face-veil-ban-latest-harmful-trend. Reprinted with permission.

Open letter by Elizabeth I to the mayors of England, 11 July 1596 (PC 2/21 f.304), The National Archives, www.nationalarchives.gov.uk. Used under Open Government License v.3.0.

From "Oral History Interview with Maria Sava Moise," 9 September 1991, and "Oral History Interview with Stefan Moise," 14

April 1991, interviews by Linda Kuzmack. The Jeff and Toby Herr Oral History Archive, United States Holocaust Museum: RG-50.030.0165, RG-50.030.0164. Reprinted courtesy of the United States Holocaust Museum.

Orwell, George. From *Burmese Days*, Harper and Brothers, 1934. Copyright © 1934 by George Orwell. Copyright renewed 1962 by Sonia Pitt-Rivers. Used by permission of HarperCollins Publishers.

Powell, Enoch. From "Rivers of Blood" Speech (20 April 1968), Immigration speeches, 1968-02–1976-10, GBR/0014/POLL 3/2/1/20. Churchill Archives Centre. Copyright © The J. Enoch Powell Literary Trust. Reprinted with permission.

Rezigat, Mahfoud (Rahim). "It Was a Horrible Night," from *Stories of an Unspeakable Night: October 17, 1961: A Massacre of Algerians in the Heart of Paris*, report by Assiya Hamza, translation by Tom Wheeldon, France 24, https://www.france24.com/en/. Reprinted with permission.

Rorke, Bernard. From "A Spectre Is Haunting Europe—Spike in Anti-Roma Pogroms as EU Election Campaigns Kick Off," 15 April 2019, ERRC News. Copyright © 2019 European Roma Rights Centre. http://www.errc.org/news/a-spectre-is-haunting-europe---spike-in-anti-roma-pogroms-as-eu-election-campaigns-kick-off. Reprinted with permission.

"Six Years a Slave: Indian Farm Workers Exploited in Italy," 11 July 2021, France 24. Copyright © 2021 AFP. Reprinted by permission of Agence France-Presse (AFP).

United Nations. "UN Rights Chief 'Appalled' at Recent Treatment of Refugees, Migrants by Hungarian Authorities," 17 September 2015, UN News: Global Perspective Human Stories. Copyright © 2015 United Nations. https://news.un.org/en/story/2015/09/509072.

United Nations Secretary-General. From the "United Nations Secretary-General's Video Message on the International Day to Combat Islamophobia," 17 March 2021. Copyright © United Nations.

Virchow, Rudolf, Dr. From "The Diary of Abraham Ulrikab" (1880); "Eskimos at the Berlin Zoo"; as translated and reprinted in *The Diary of Abraham Ulrikab: Text and Context*, ed. and trans. Hartmut Lutz, pp. 3–5, 57–62. University of Ottawa Press, 2005. Text copyright © 2005 Hartmut Lutz. Reproduced with permission from the University of Ottawa Press.

Wolf, Kenneth Baxter. From "Sentencia-Estatuto de Toledo, 1449." Medieval Texts in Translation, 22 May 2009. canilup.googlepages.com. Reprinted by permission of the translator.

IMAGES

Anthropologist Eva Justin creating a plaster cast on a Romani man (1938), Racial Biological Research Center of the Reich Health Office, Germany. The Federal Archives, Koblenz, Germany, Image R 165 Bild-244-66. Used under Attribution-ShareAlike 3.0 Germany (CC BY-SA 3.0 DE Deed) https://creativecommons.org/licenses/by-sa/3.0/de/deed.en.

The Board Game: Juden Raus! Jews Out! (c. 1938). Courtesy of The Wiener Holocaust Library Collections.

...But We've Got to Beat the Jap First, poster, 1945; *Women Working in Industry in Britain during the Second World War*, photograph by London News Agency; Imperial War Museum Collections, objects 205020944 and 29035. Copyright © Imperial War Museum

(Art.IWM PST 8101, HU 36288). Used with permission.

"Cigar Store Indian," Windsor, UK, October 2006. Photograph by WyrdLight/Antony McCallum, Wikimedia Commons. Used under Attribution-ShareAlike 2.5 Generic (CC BY-SA 2.5) https://creativecommons.org/licenses/by-sa/2.5/deed.en.

Courtet, Emile. *Jewish Virtues According to Gall's Method* [*Les qualites du Juif d'apres la methode de Gall*], "La Libre Parole Illustre," Paris, 23 December 1893. The Jewish Museum, no. 1990-189. Photo © The Jewish Museum, New York. Photo by John Parnell. Courtesy of The Jewish Museum, New York/Art Resource, NY.

Entartete Musik (Degenerate Music) poster (1938), designed by Ludwig Tersch. Courtesy of Alamy Stock Photo.

"First Arrival of the Romanies outside Bern" (1484), from the manuscript *Diebold Schilling, Spiezer Chronik*, Bern, Burgerbibliothek, Mss.h.h.I.16 (http://www.e-codices.unifr.ch/en/list/one/bbb/Mss-hh-I0016). Reprinted by permission of The Burgerbibliothek of Bern.

Hiemer, Ernst. Illustrations from *Der Giftpilz* [*The Poisonous Mushroom*], Der Sturmer, 1938. United States Holocaust Memorial Museum Photo Archives # 40000, 40001, 40002, 40008, 40014. Copyright © of United States Holocaust Memorial Museum.

Painting of the crucifixion of William of Norwich, 15th century, from a church in Loddon, United Kingdom. Photograph courtesy of Nick Stone.

The Solingen Arson Attack, 30 May 1993, photograph by Jochen Eckel. Courtesy of Sueddeutsche Zeitung Photo/Alamy Stock Photo.

About the Publisher

The word "broadview" expresses a good deal of the philosophy behind our company. Our focus is very much on the humanities and social sciences—especially literature, writing, and philosophy—but within these fields we are open to a broad range of academic approaches and political viewpoints. We strive in particular to produce high-quality, pedagogically useful books for higher education classrooms—anthologies, editions, sourcebooks, surveys of particular academic fields and sub-fields, and also course texts for subjects such as composition, business communication, and critical thinking. We welcome the perspectives of authors from marginalized and underrepresented groups, and we have a strong commitment to the environment. We publish English-language works and translations from many parts of the world, and our books are available world-wide; we also publish a select list of titles with a specifically Canadian emphasis.

broadview press

This book is made of paper from well-managed FSC® - certified forests, recycled materials, and other controlled sources.